AF606894

Fragments of Epic Memory

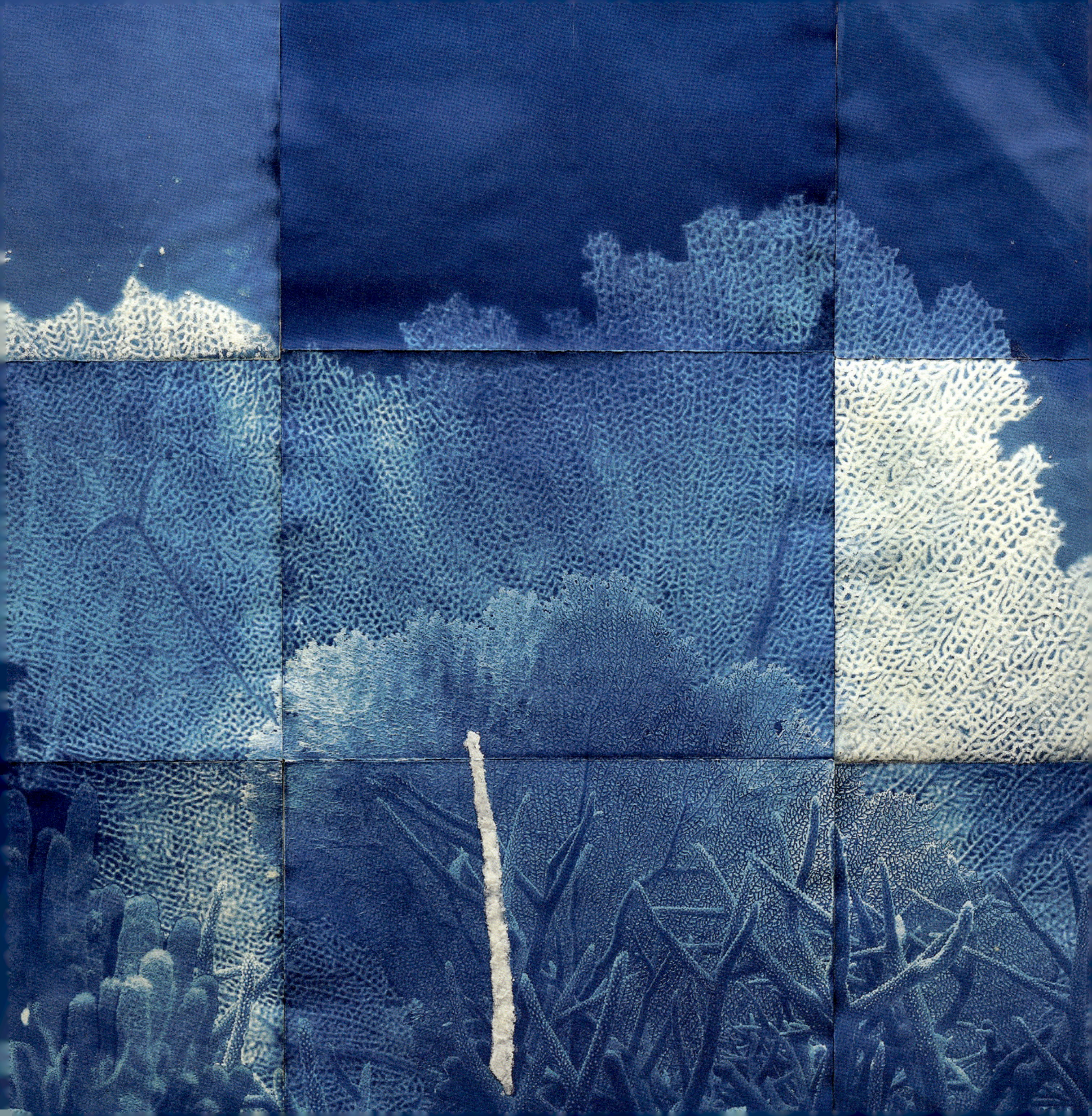

Fragments of Epic Memory

Edited by
Julie Crooks

ART GALLERY
OF ONTARIO

DELMONICO BOOKS • D.A.P.
New York

Director's Foreword 7
Curator's Acknowledgements 10
Moko Jumbie: An Introduction 12

14 Derek Walcott
The Antilles: Fragments of Epic Memory

Seeing the Unseizable: Confronting the Past and Considering the Future 30
Julie Crooks

46 Edward Kamau Brathwaite
Calypso

64 Harclyde Walcott
Photography in the City of Bridgetown: The Nineteenth Century

72 Mahadai Das
They Came in Ships

Indentureship and the Art of Speculation 74
Andil Gosine

88 Erna Brodber
The World the Freedman/Woman Made

The Epic Creativity of Frank Walter 100
Barbara Paca

118 Michel-Rolph Trouillot
Epilogue from Silencing the Past: Power and the Production of History

My Mother, Dorothy Henriques Wells 126
Mary Wells, with a preface by Emily Cluett

The Afflicted Gaze of Peter Dean Rickards 134
Annie Paul

148 Kei Miller
The Cartographer Tries to Map a Way to Zion

178 C.L.R. James
The San Domingo Masses Begin

242 Claude McKay
If We Must Die

244 Josefina Báez
A 1 2 3 Portrait of a Legend

250 Kaie Kellough
The Unity of Worlds

Reimagining History as Narrative in Contemporary Art 158
Marsha Pearce

"The Quintessential Caribbean People": The Garifuna of St. Vincent and the Grenadines... and the World 186
Melanie J. Newton

Blacklight 202
Christian Campbell

Poetic Images and Political Places: The Work of Caribbean-Canadian Artists Sandra Brewster and Manuel Mathieu 212
Dominique Fontaine

How to Kill a Soundboy: A Conversation with Leasho Johnson 228
O'Neil Lawrence

Further Reading 254
List of Works 256
Credits 264

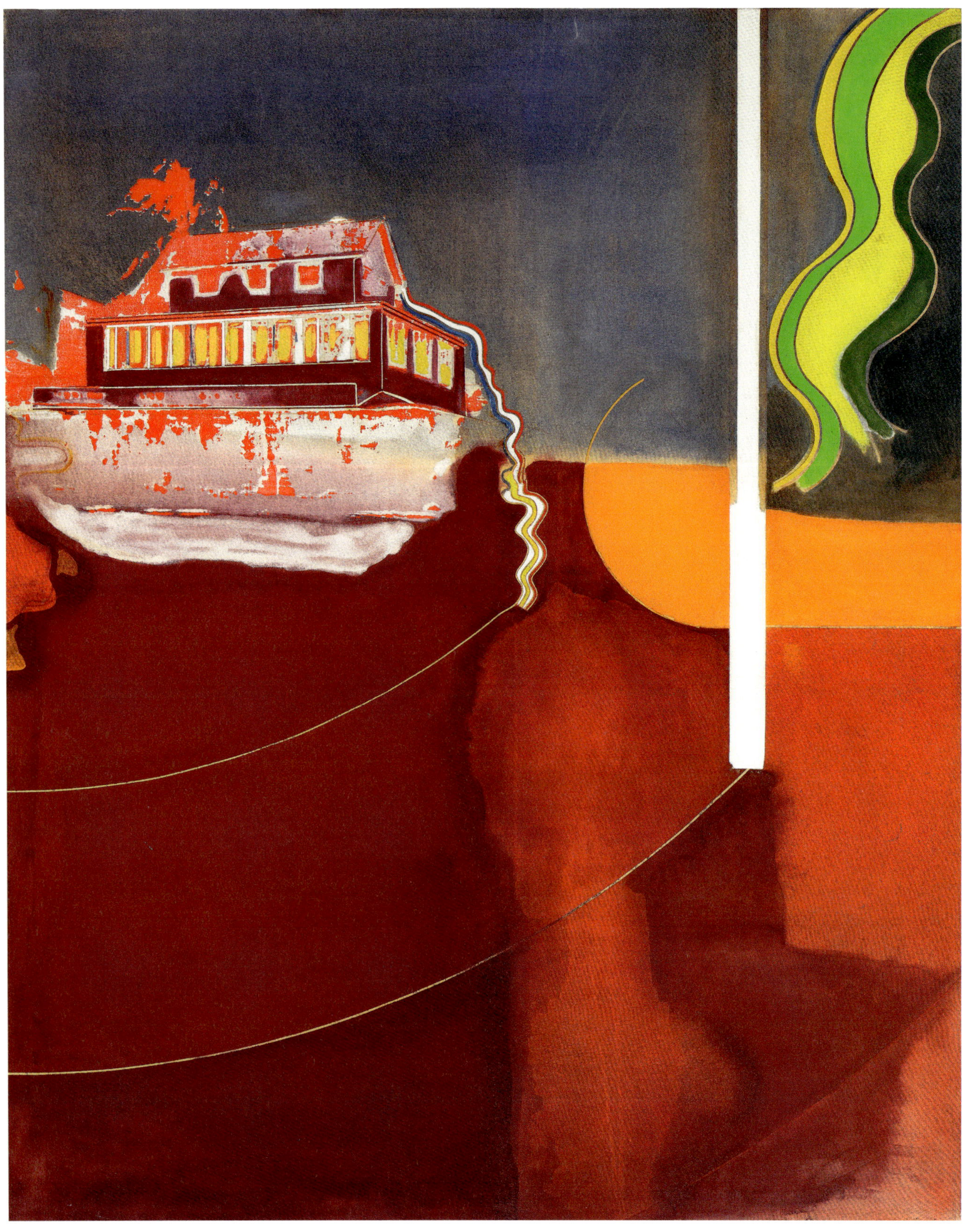

Sir Frank Bowling, *Mother's House and Night Storm*, 1967

Director's Foreword

Stephan Jost

Michael and Sonja Koerner Director, and
CEO, Art Gallery of Ontario

Toronto, where the Art Gallery of Ontario is located, and its surrounding area, is home to some of Canada's largest Caribbean communities. These communities were front of mind when we acquired the Montgomery Collection of Caribbean Photographs (1840–1940), a monumental addition to our permanent collection. A rare visual record of more than 3,500 historical images from a range of countries, including Jamaica, Barbados, and Trinidad, this trove has positioned the AGO as a global leader in Caribbean photographic research.

That acquisition was also the spark that ignited the idea for *Fragments of Epic Memory*, which showcases more than 200 works from the Montgomery Collection. Presented alongside paintings, sculpture, and video works by modern and contemporary artists of Caribbean descent, the photographs offer an illuminating and nuanced exploration of the history of the region and its residents—one that is an unfiltered view into the conditions of Caribbean life within the colonial environment following emancipation. *Fragments of Epic Memory* is the inaugural exhibition from our new Department of Arts of Global Africa and the Diaspora, established in 2020 to build on our existing foundations and acknowledge the multiple histories and influences that intersect, deepen, and complicate in so many ways our understanding of Western and contemporary art.

We are grateful to our valued supporters, who have shown tremendous generosity and enthusiasm for the exhibition. Thanks to our Lead Sponsor, TD Bank Group, through the TD Ready Commitment, our Supporting Sponsor, Panasonic, and our Contributing Sponsor, KPMG. We also deeply appreciate the generous support of Phil Lind & Ellen Roland, the Volunteers of the AGO, and Women's Art Initiative, and for the generous assistance of Cindy & Shon Barnett, David W. Binet, Dr. Carlyle Farrell, Friends of Global Africa & the Diaspora, and The Michael Young Family Foundation. We also appreciate the Canada Council for the Arts, which provides support for contemporary programming at the AGO.

For their generosity in bringing the Montgomery Collection of Caribbean Photographs to the AGO, we would especially like to thank Patrick Montgomery, as well as Dr. Liza & Dr. Frederick Murrell, Bruce Croxon & Debra Thier, Wes Hall & Kingsdale Advisors, Cindy & Shon Barnett, Donette Chin-Loy Chang, Kamala-Jean Gopie, Phil Lind & Ellen Roland, Martin Doc McKinney, Francilla Charles, Ray & Georgina Williams, Thaine & Bianca Carter, Charmaine Crooks, Nathaniel Crooks, Andrew Garrett & Dr. Belinda Longe, Neil L. Le Grand, Michael Lewis, Dr. Kenneth Montague & Sarah Aranha, Lenny & Julia Mortimore, and The Ferrotype Collective.

As part of this exhibition, the AGO was privileged to commission a new work by the British-Trinidadian artist Zak Ové, whose *Moko Jumbie*, a twenty-first-century reimagining of a guardian figure rooted in African diasporic mythologies, stands tall in Walker Court, watching over guests as they enter the main gallery. We are grateful to David W. Binet and Ray & Georgina Williams for their generosity in helping us acquire this remarkable artwork.

An exhibition of this scope would not have been possible without the inspired vision and expertise of numerous staff. I wish to acknowledge the monumental efforts of curator Dr. Julie Crooks and her team for realizing this landmark project from the Department of Arts of Global Africa and the Diaspora. Massive thanks to Julian Cox, Deputy Director & Chief Curator; Jessica Bright, Chief, Exhibitions, Collections & Conservation; and Design Studio Manager, Malene Hjørngaard, and her production team. I would also like to acknowledge the work of the AGO's Manager of Publishing, Jim Shedden, and his department for their dedication in producing this publication. Many thanks as well to the contributing authors who have shared their critical insights in this volume, which offers further pathways to engage with this expansive body of work. On a personal note, I would like to thank and acknowledge the importance of artist Arthur Sims and educator Andre Farquharson for shaping my understanding of the people and cultures of the Caribbean.

We thank the institutions, gallerists, and individual collectors who loaned works to the show: Helen and Keith Atteck; BAND Toronto; Barbados Museum and Historical Society; Sandra Brewster; Vanley Burke; Robert Charlotte; Centre International de Documentation et d'Information Haïtienne, Caribéenne et Afro-canadienne (CIDIHCA), Montreal; Daniel Faria Gallery; Kirk Davis; Jeannette Ehlers; Dr. Carlyle Farrell; Aaron Francis; Gomo George; Abigail Hadeed; Nadia Huggins; Hydro Quebec; Sheldon Inwentash and Lynn Factor; Jack Shainman, New York; James Cohan Gallery; Roshini Kempadoo; The Komal Shah & Gaurav Garg Collection; Suchitra Mattai; Dr. Kenneth Montague / The Wedge Collection; Patrick Montgomery; Montreal Museum of Fine Arts; Wendy Nanan; National Gallery of Canada; Zak Ové; Newton Paul; Rachel-Lea Rickards / Estate of Peter Dean Rickards; Peter Ross; Tyler Park Presents; Vancouver Art Gallery; Rodell Warner; Mary Wells; Alberta Whittle; and several private collectors who wish to remain anonymous.

This ambitious show comes at a time when we are acutely aware of how critical it is for members of Black communities to see themselves and their experiences reflected—and celebrated—within cultural institutions across Canada. We are honoured to showcase these historical photographs alongside the illuminating work of a generation of artists from the Caribbean and its diaspora as part of our ongoing commitment to champion diverse voices within all areas of our programming.

Curator's Acknowledgements

For Evelyn Germaine Gaye (1932–2013)

I began planning this exhibition in October 2019. By March 2020, the COVID-19 pandemic brought about the first of many subsequent lockdowns. A few months later, in May 2020, George Floyd was murdered by a Minneapolis police officer—the catalyst for a necessary reckoning and the global acknowledgement of the Black Lives Matter movement. The confluence of these events and the seismic changes they brought about deeply affected my curatorial approach: the past 18 months have involved a lot of reflection, collaboration, soul-searching, and commiseration.

I am profoundly grateful to the artists, scholars, galleries, AGO staff, and other individuals who contributed in some way to *Fragments of Epic Memory*. Planning an exhibition during a global pandemic was, unsurprisingly, a challenging feat. I would like to extend a special thank you to Stephan Jost, Michael and Sonja Koerner Director, and CEO; and Julian Cox, Deputy Director & Chief Curator, for their guidance and their support of this expansive exhibition. My sincere gratitude goes to the exhibition team led by our unflappable Project Manager, Melissa Ramage: Design Studio Manager Malene Hjørngaard, Production Assistant Evelyn Quinn, 2D Designer Evelina Petrauskas, 3D Designer Theodora Doulamis, Design Consultant Tara Keens-Douglas, Executive Coordinator Jill Offenbeck, Consulting Writer and Researcher Carlie Manners, and last but certainly not least, Curatorial Assistant Alexandra Gooding, who juggled the fast pace and impossible demands of exhibition-making with strength, patience, and uncanny attention to detail. It is due to this team's dedication, steely fortitude, and spirit of collaboration that my curatorial vision was fully realized. I am also indebted to my fellow AGO curators, with whom I've had many long conversations about the scope, substance, and vision for *Fragments of Epic Memory*. Thank you for your sage counsel and unwavering support.

Many thanks are also due to members of the logistics team who installed the exhibition—including the site-specific installation of *Moko Jumbie* in Walker Court—and to Roland Hardy, who constructed the custom-made table cases that house the Montgomery Collection photographs. They are a work of art unto themselves!

The creation of this catalogue was deftly managed by our in-house team: Publishing Manager Jim Shedden, Publishing Coordinator Kathryn Yuen, Senior Editor Sarah Liss, and Assistant Editor Nives Hajdin. In addition, many thanks to the following contributors for their enriching scholarship and expertise: Christian Campbell, Emily Cluett, Dominique Fontaine, Andil Gosine, O'Neil Lawrence, Melanie Newton, Barbara Paca, Annie Paul, Marsha Pearce, and Mary Wells.

I must, of course, express a heartfelt thank you to all of the incredible artists represented in this exhibition: Hurvin Anderson, Sybil Atteck, Belkis Ayón, Firelei Báez, Sir

Frank Bowling, Sandra Brewster, Vanley Burke, Charles Campbell, Robert Charlotte, Andrea Chung, June Clark, Christopher Cozier, Jeannette Ehlers, Roy Francis, Gomo George, Abigail Hadeed, Nadia Huggins, Leasho Johnson, Roshini Kempadoo, Wifredo Lam, Diane Liverpool, Kelly Sinnapah Mary, Manuel Mathieu, Suchitra Mattai, Dennis Morris, Wendy Nanan, Zak Ové, Ebony G. Patterson, Peter Dean Rickards, Paul Anthony Smith, Frank Walter, Rodell Warner, Dorothy Henriques Wells, Alberta Whittle, Aubrey Williams, and Natalie Wood.

In addition, I am indebted to the following individuals and institutions who very generously agreed to lend their most treasured objects and artworks in the furtherance of this exhibition: Helen and Keith Atteck; BAND Toronto; Barbados Museum and Historical Society; Sandra Brewster; Vanley Burke; Robert Charlotte; CIDIHCA, Montreal; Daniel Faria Gallery; Kirk Davis; Jeannette Ehlers; Dr. Carlyle Farrell; Aaron Francis; Gomo George; Abigail Hadeed; Nadia Huggins; Hydro Quebec; Sheldon Inwentash and Lynn Factor; Jack Shainman, New York; James Cohan Gallery; Roshini Kempadoo; The Komal Shah & Gaurav Garg Collection; Suchitra Mattai; Dr. Kenneth Montague / The Wedge Collection; Patrick Montgomery; Montreal Museum of Fine Arts; Wendy Nanan; National Gallery of Canada; Zak Ové; Newton Paul; Rachel-Lea Rickards / Estate of Peter Dean Rickards; Peter Ross; Tyler Park Presents; Vancouver Art Gallery; Rodell Warner; Mary Wells; Alberta Whittle; and several private collectors who wish to remain anonymous.

I would also like to extend a very special thank you to my quiet but formidable research assistant, Camila Collins Araiza, who assisted in innumerable ways with the research and preparation of the Montgomery Collection for the exhibition. In addition, she organized two study days in July 2020, during which invited scholars, historians, and artists participated in a webinar to share their respective research and expertise in the context of the Montgomery Collection. In that short time, we created a space for the discussion of themes related to the history of Caribbean photography, including emancipation, historical silences, decolonization, violence (and its many forms), freedom, and the overall visual culture of the region. These conversations played a key role in my curation of *Fragments of Epic Memory* and the accompanying catalogue, and I must extend my sincere thanks to the extraordinary session participants: Emilie Boone, Steeve Buckridge, Shenelle Charles, Adrienne Duperly, Kevin Farmer, Andil Gosine, O'Neil Lawrence, Melanie Newton, Mark Sealy, Mimi Sheller, Krista Thompson, and Harclyde Walcott.

I extend special thanks to Beverly Braithwaite for kindly allowing the use of Edward Kamau Braithwaite's poem *Calypso* as an audio recording in the exhibition. I am also profoundly grateful to Elizabeth Walcott-Hackshaw and Anna Walcott-Hardy from the Derek Walcott Estate, who very generously granted us permission to use the title *Fragments of Epic Memory*. This exhibition is indebted and dedicated to these giants of Caribbean literature, whose expressive writing influenced me—and this presentation of work—in no small measure. Finally, I am immensely thankful for my husband, Nathaniel, and our sons, Zachary, Thaddeus, and Harrison, who inspire me every day.

Dr. Julie Crooks
Curator, Arts of Global Africa and the Diaspora, Art Gallery of Ontario

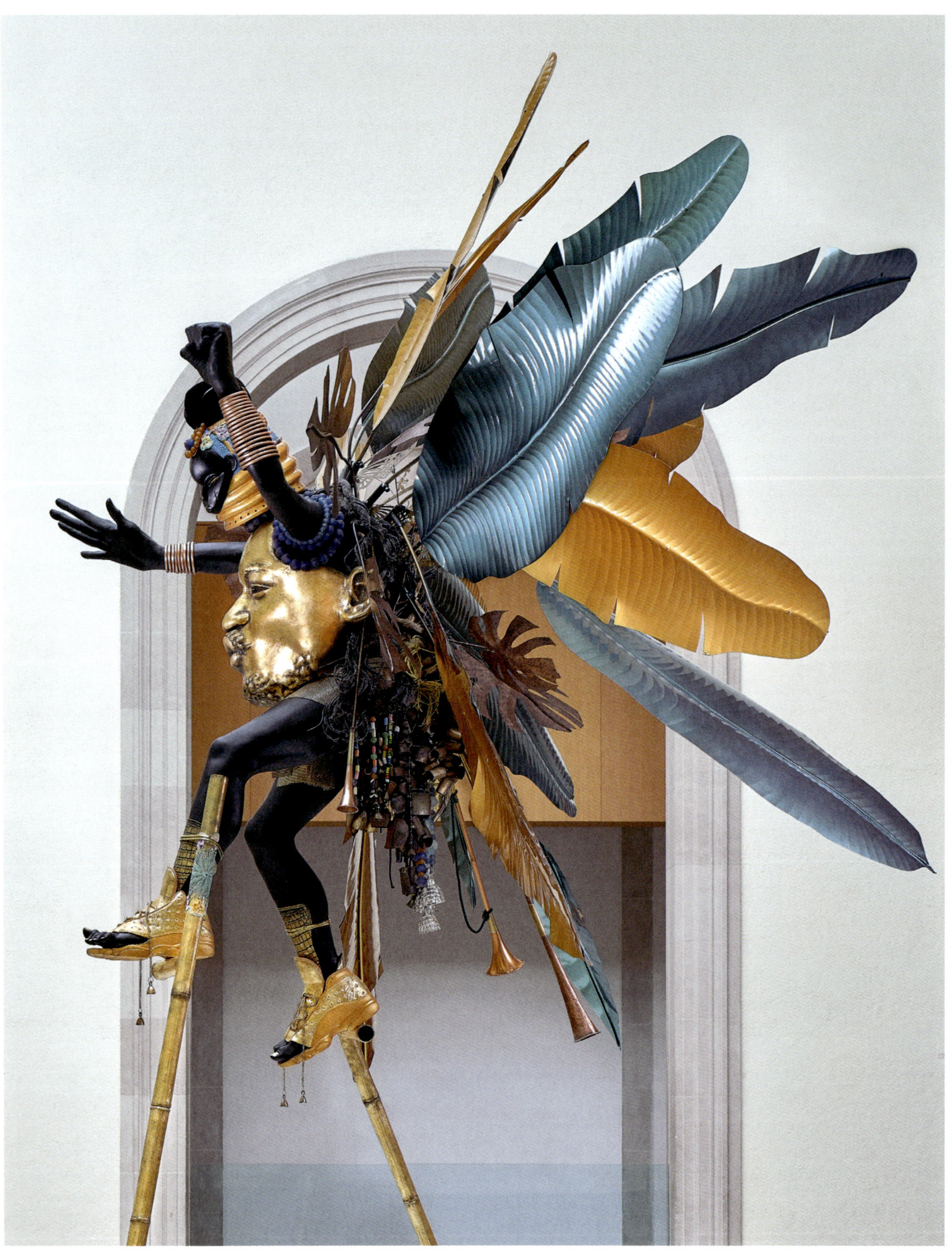

Zak Ové, *Moko Jumbie*, 2021

*Mo*ko Ju*m*bi*e*: *An* I*nt*r*o*duc*t*io*n*

Julie Crooks

When visitors arrive at the AGO to see *Fragments of Epic Memory*, they are greeted by an epic eighteen-foot *Moko Jumbie* sculpture that stands tall in Walker Court, a central space in the Gallery. Commissioned from artist Zak Ové for this exhibition, the majestic sculpture depicts a stilt-walking figure central to carnival celebrations in Trinidad and other Caribbean islands. A guardian who travelled to the region to protect enslaved peoples from evil, the Moko Jumbie character blends African diasporic mythologies: in Central Africa, "Moko" refers to a healer, while "Jumbie" is a Caribbean term for spirits. Here, the sculpture acts as a beacon, inviting viewers to take in its myriad adornments, such as antique glass beads, cowbells, and gold Air Jordan sneakers, each of which symbolizes a different incarnation of the figure. The serene countenance on *Moko Jumbie*'s stylized Mende helmet mask provides a contrast to the figure's dynamism: it is caught in mid-stride on long, elegant golden stilts. For Ové, *Moko Jumbie* represents "a joyous freedom, hope for a better life, and the physical representation of walking tall toward a brighter future."

So, take a breath.
Stand still. Get your bearings.
Then walk, slowly at first, into it.[1]

1 Kevin Adonis Browne, *High Mas: Carnival and the Poetics of Caribbean Culture,* (Jackson: University Press of Mississippi, 2018), 198.

The Antilles: Fragments of Epic Memory

Derek Walcott

Felicity is a village in Trinidad on the edge of the Caroni plain, the wide central plain that still grows sugar and to which indentured cane cutters were brought after emancipation, so the small population of Felicity is East Indian, and on the afternoon that I visited it with friends from America, all the faces along its road were Indian, which, as I hope to show, was a moving, beautiful thing, because this Saturday afternoon *Ramleela,* the epic dramatization of the Hindu epic the *Ramayana,* was going to be performed, and the costumed actors from the village were assembling on a field strung with different-coloured flags, like a new gas station, and beautiful Indian boys in red and black were aiming arrows haphazardly into the afternoon light. Low blue mountains on the horizon, bright grass, clouds that would gather colour before the light went. Felicity! What a gentle Anglo-Saxon name for an epical memory.

Under an open shed on the edge of the field, there were two huge armatures of bamboo that looked like immense cages. They were parts of the body of a god, his calves or thighs, which, fitted and reared, would make a gigantic effigy. This effigy would be burnt as a conclusion to the epic. The cane structures flashed a predictable parallel: Shelley's sonnet on the fallen statue of Ozymandias and his empire, that "colossal wreck" in its empty desert.

Drummers had lit a fire in the shed and they eased the skins of their tables nearer the flames to tighten them. The saffron flames, the bright grass, and the hand-woven armatures of the fragmented god who would be burnt were not in any desert where imperial power had finally toppled but were part of a ritual, evergreen season that, like the cane-burning harvest, is annually repeated, the point of such sacrifice being its repetition, the point of the destruction being renewal through fire.

Deities were entering the field. What we generally call "Indian music" was blaring from the open platformed shed from which the epic would be narrated. Costumed actors were arriving. Princes and gods, I supposed. What an unfortunate confession! "Gods, I suppose" is the shrug that embodies our African and Asian diasporas. I had often thought of but never seen *Ramleela*, and had never seen this theatre, an open field, with village children as warriors, princes, and gods. I had no idea what the epic story was, who its hero was, what enemies he fought, yet I had recently adapted the *Odyssey* for a theatre in England, presuming that the audience knew the trials of Odysseus, hero of another Asia Minor epic, while nobody in Trinidad knew any more than I did about Rama, Kali, Shiva, Vishnu, apart from the Indians, a phrase I use pervertedly because that is the kind of remark you can still hear in Trinidad: "apart from the Indians."

It was as if, on the edge of the Central Plain, there was another plateau, a raft on which the *Ramayana* would be poorly performed in this ocean of cane, but that was my writer's view of things, and it is wrong. I was seeing the *Ramleela* at Felicity as theatre when it was faith.

Multiply that moment of self-conviction when an actor, made-up and costumed, nods to his mirror before stopping on stage in the belief that he is a reality entering an illusion and you would have what I presumed was happening to the actors of this epic. But they were not actors. They had been chosen; or they themselves had chosen their roles in this sacred story that would go on for nine afternoons over a two-hour period till the sun set. They were not amateurs but believers. There was no theatrical term to define them. They did not have to psych themselves up to play their roles. Their acting would probably be as buoyant and as natural as those bamboo arrows crisscrossing the afternoon pasture. They believed in what they were playing, in the sacredness of the text, the validity of India, while I, out of the writer's habit, searched for some sense of elegy, of loss, even of degenerative mimicry in the happy faces of the boy-warriors or the heraldic profiles of the village princes.

I was polluting the afternoon with doubt and with the patronage of admiration. I misread the event through a visual echo of History—the cane fields, indenture, the evocation of vanished armies, temples, and trumpeting elephants—when all around me there was quite the opposite: elation, delight in the boys' screams, in the sweets-stalls, in more and more costumed characters appearing; a delight of conviction, not loss. The name Felicity made sense.

Consider the scale of Asia reduced to these fragments: the small white exclamations of minarets or the stone balls of temples in the cane fields, and one can understand the self-mockery and embarrassment of those who see these rites as parodic, even degenerate. These purists look on such ceremonies as grammarians look at a dialect, as cities look on provinces and empires on their colonies. Memory that yearns to join the centre, a limb remembering the body from which it has been severed, like those bamboo thighs of the god. In other words, the way that the Caribbean is still looked at, illegitimate, rootless, mongrelized. "No people there," to quote Froude, "in the true sense of the word." No people. Fragments and echoes of real people, unoriginal and broken.

The performance was like a dialect, a branch of its original language, an abridgement of it, but not a distortion or even a reduction of its epic scale. Here in Trinidad, I had discovered that one of the greatest epics of the world was seasonally performed, not with that desperate resignation of preserving a culture, but with an openness of belief that was as steady as the wind bending the cane lances of the Caroni plain. We had to leave before the play began to go through the creeks of the Caroni Swamp, to catch the scarlet ibises coming home at dusk. In a performance as natural as those of the actors of the *Ramleela*, we watched the flocks come in as bright as the scarlet of the boy archers, as the red flags, and cover an islet until it turned into a flowering tree, an anchored immortelle. The sigh of History meant nothing here. These two visions, the *Ramleela* and the arrowing flocks of scarlet ibises, blent into a single gasp of gratitude. Visual surprise is natural in the Caribbean; it comes with the landscape, and faced with its beauty, the sigh of History dissolves.

We make too much of that long groan which underlines the past. I felt privileged to discover the ibises as well as the scarlet archers of Felicity.

The sigh of History rises over ruins, not over landscapes, and in the Antilles, there are few ruins to sigh over, apart from the ruins of sugar estates and abandoned forts. Looking around slowly, as a camera would, taking in the low blue hills over Port of Spain, the village road and houses, the warrior-archers, the god-actors and their handlers, and music already on the soundtrack, I wanted to make a film that would be a long-drawn sigh over Felicity. I was filtering the afternoon with evocations of a lost India, but why "evocations"? Why not "celebrations of a real presence"? Why should India be "lost" when none of these villagers ever really knew it, and why not "continuing," why not the perpetuation of joy in Felicity and in all the other nouns of the Central Plain: Couva, Chaguanas, Charley Village? Why was I not letting my pleasure open its windows wide? I was enticed like any Trinidadian to the ecstasies of their claim, because ecstasy was the pitch of the sinuous drumming in the loudspeakers. I was entitled to the feast of Husein, to the mirrors and crepe-paper temples of the Muslim epic, to the Chinese Dragon Dance, to the rites of that Sephardic Jewish synagogue that was once on Something Street. I am only one-eighth the writer I might have been had I contained all the fragmented languages of Trinidad.

Break a vase, and the love that reassembles the fragments is stronger than that love which took its symmetry for granted when it was whole. The glue that fits the pieces is the sealing of its original shape. It is such a love that reassembles our African and Asiatic fragments, the cracked heirlooms whose restoration shows its white scars. This gathering of broken pieces is the care and pain of the Antilles, and if the pieces are disparate, ill-fitting, they contain more pain than their original sculpture, those icons and sacred vessels taken for granted in their ancestral places. Antillean art is this restoration of our shattered histories, our shards of vocabulary, our archipelago becoming a synonym for pieces broken off from the original continent.

And this is the exact process of the making of poetry, or what should be called not its "making" but its remaking, the fragmented memory, the armature that frames the god, even the rite that surrenders it to a final pyre; the god assembled cane by cane, reed by weaving reed, line by plaited line, as the artisans of Felicity would erect his holy echo.

Poetry, which is perfection's sweat but which must seem as fresh as the raindrops on a statue's brow, combines the natural and the marmoreal; it conjugates both tenses simultaneously–the past and the present, if the past is the sculpture and the present the beads of dew or rain on the forehead of the past. There is the buried language and there is the individual vocabulary, and the process of poetry is one of excavation and of self-discovery. Tonally the individual voice is a dialect; it shapes its own accent, its own vocabulary and melody in defiance of an imperial concept of language, the language of Ozymandias, libraries and dictionaries, law courts and critics, and churches, universities, political dogma, the diction of institutions. Poetry is an island that breaks away from the main. The dialects of my archipelago seem as fresh to me as those raindrops on the statue's forehead, not the sweat made from the classic exertion of frowning marble, but the condensations of a refreshing element, rain and salt.

Deprived of their original language, the captured and indentured tribes create their own, accreting and secreting fragments of an old, an epic vocabulary, from Asia and from Africa, but to an ancestral, an ecstatic rhythm in the blood that cannot be subdued by slavery or indenture, while nouns are renamed and the given names of places accepted like Felicity village or Choiseul. The original language dissolves from the exhaustion of distance like fog trying to cross an ocean, but this process of renaming, of finding new metaphors, is the same process that the poet faces every morning of his working day, making his own tools like Crusoe, assembling nouns from necessity, from Felicity, even renaming himself. The stripped man is driven back to that self-astonishing, elemental force: his mind. That is the basis of the Antillean experience, this shipwreck of fragments, these echoes, these shards of a huge tribal vocabulary, these partially remembered customs, and they are not decayed but strong. They survived the Middle Passage and the *Fatel Rozack*, the ship that carried the first indentured Indians from the port of Madras to the cane fields of Felicity, that carried the chained Cromwellian convict and the Sephardic Jew, the Chinese grocer and the Lebanese merchant selling cloth samples on his bicycle.

And here they are, all in a single Caribbean city, Port of Spain, the sum of history, Trollope's "non-people." A downtown babel of shop signs and streets, mongrelized, polyglot, a ferment without a history, like heaven. Because that is what such a city is, in the New World: a writer's heaven.

A culture, we all know, is made by its cities.

Another first morning home, impatient for the sunrise–a broken sleep. Darkness at five, and the drapes not worth opening; then, in the sudden light, a cream-walled, brown-roofed police station bordered with short royal palms, in the colonial style, back of it frothing trees and taller palms, a pigeon fluttering into the cover of a cave, a rain-stained block of once-modern apartments, the morning sideroad into the station without traffic. All part of a surprising peace. This quiet happens with every visit to a city that has deepened itself in me. The flowers and the hills are easy, affection for them predictable; it is the architecture that, for the first morning, disorients. A return from American seductions used to make the traveller feel that something was missing, something was trying to complete itself, like the stained concrete apartments. Pan left along the window and the excrescences rear–a city trying to soar, trying to be brutal, like an American city in silhouette, stamped from the same mould as Columbus or Des Moines. An assertion of power, its decor bland, its air conditioning pitched to the point where its secretarial and executive staff sport competing cardigans; the colder the offices, the more important, an imitation of another climate. A longing, even an envy of feeling cold.

In serious cities, in grey, militant winter with its short afternoons, the days seem to pass by in buttoned overcoats, every building appears as a barracks with lights on in its windows, and when snow comes, one has the illusion of living in a Russian novel, in the nineteenth century, because of the literature of winter. So, visitors to the Caribbean must feel that they are inhabiting a succession of postcards. Both climates are shaped by what we have read of them. For tourists, the sunshine cannot be serious. Winter adds depth and darkness to life as well as to literature, and in the unending summer of the tropics not even poverty or poetry (in the Antilles, "poverty" is "poetry" with a V, *une vie*, a condition of life as well as of imagination) seems capable of being profound because the nature around it is so exultant, so resolutely ecstatic, like its music. A culture based on joy is bound to be shallow. Sadly, to sell itself, the Caribbean encourages the delights of mindlessness, of brilliant vacuity, as a place to flee not only winter but the seriousness that comes only out of culture with four seasons. So how can there be a people there, in the true sense of the word?

They know nothing about seasons in which leaves let go of the year, in which spires fade in blizzards and streets whiten, of the erasures of whole cities by fog, of reflection in fireplaces; instead, they inhabit a geography whose rhythm, like their music, is limited to two stresses: hot and wet, sun and rain, light and shadow, day and night, the limitations of an incomplete metre, and are therefore a people incapable of the subtleties of contradiction, of imaginative complexity. So be it. We cannot change contempt.

Ours are not cities in the accepted sense, but no one wants them to be. They dictate their own proportions, their own definitions in particular places and in a prose equal to that of their detractors, so that now it is not just St. James but the streets and yards that Naipaul commemorates, its lanes as short and brilliant as his sentences; not just the noise and jostle of Tunapuna but the origins of C.L.R. *James's Beyond a Boundary*, not just Felicity village on the Caroni plain, but Selvon Country, and that is the way it goes up the islands now: the old Dominica of Jean Rhys still very much the way she wrote of it; the Martinique of the early Cesaire; Perse's Guadeloupe, even without the pith helmets and the mules; and what delight and privilege there was in watching a literature–one literature in several imperial languages, French, English, Spanish–bud and open island after island in the early morning of a culture, not timid, not derivative, any more than the hard white petals of the frangipani are derivative and timid. This is not a belligerent boast but a simple celebration of inevitability: that this flowering had to come.

On a heat-stoned afternoon in Port of Spain, some alley white with glare, with love vine spilling over a fence, palms and a hazed mountain appear around a corner to the evocation of Vaughn or Herbert's "that shady city of palm-trees," or to the memory of a Hammond organ from a wooden chapel in Castries, where the congregation sang "Jerusalem, the Golden." It is hard for me to see such emptiness as desolation. It is that patience that is the width of Antillean life, and the secret is not to ask the wrong thing of it, not to demand of it an ambition it has no interest in. The traveller reads this as lethargy, as torpor.

Here there are not enough books, one says, no theatres, no museums, simply not enough to do. Yet, deprived of books, a man must fall back on thought, and out of thought, if he can learn to order it, will come the urge to record, and in extremity, if he has no means of recording, recitation, the ordering of memory which leads to metre, to commemoration. There can be virtues in deprivation, and certainly one virtue is salvation from a cascade of high mediocrity, since books are now not so much created as remade. Cities create a culture, and all we have are these magnified market towns, so what are the proportions of the ideal Caribbean city? A surrounding, accessible countryside with leafy suburbs, and if the city is lucky, behind it, spacious plains. Behind it, fine mountains; before it, an indigo sea. Spires would pin its centre and around them would be leafy, shadowy parks. Pigeons would cross its sky in alphabetic patterns, carrying with them memories of a belief in augury, and at the heart of the city there would be horses, yes, horses, those animals last seen at the end of the nineteenth century drawing broughams and carriages with top-hatted citizens, horses that live in the present tense without elegiac echoes from their hooves, emerging from paddocks at the Queen's Park Savannah at sunrise, when mist is unthreading from the cool mountains above the roofs, and at the centre of the city seasonally there would be races, so that citizens could roar at the speed and grace of these nineteenth-century animals. Its docks, not obscured by smoke or deafened by too much machinery, and above all, it would be so racially various that the cultures of the world—the Asiatic, the Mediterranean, the European, the African—would be represented in it, its humane variety more exciting than Joyce's Dublin. Its citizens would intermarry as they chose, from instinct, not tradition, until their children find it increasingly futile to trace their genealogy. It would not have too many avenues difficult or dangerous for pedestrians, its mercantile area would be a cacophony of accents, fragments of the old language that would be silenced immediately at five o'clock, its docks resolutely vacant on Sundays.

This is Port of Spain to me, a city ideal in its commercial and human proportions, where a citizen is a walker and not a pedestrian, and this is how Athens may have been before it became a cultural echo.

The finest silhouettes of Port of Spain are idealizations of the craftsman's handiwork, not of concrete and glass, but of baroque woodwork, each fantasy looking more like an involved drawing of itself than the actual building. Behind the city is the Caroni plain, with its villages,

Indian prayer flags, and fruit vendors' stalls along the highway over which ibises come like floating flags. Photogenic poverty! Postcard sadnesses! I am not re-creating Eden; I mean, by "the Antilles," the reality of light, of work, of survival. I mean a house on the side of a country road, I mean the Caribbean Sea, whose smell is the smell of refreshing possibility as well as survival. Survival is the triumph of stubbornness, and spiritual stubbornness, a sublime stupidity, is what makes the occupation of poetry endure, when there are so many things that should make it futile. Those things added together can go under one collective noun: "the world."

This is the visible poetry of the Antilles, then. Survival.

If you wish to understand that consoling pity with which the islands were regarded, look at the tinted engravings of Antillean forests, with their proper palm trees, ferns, and waterfalls. They have a civilizing decency, like botanical gardens, as if the sky were a glass ceiling under which a colonized vegetation is arranged for quiet walks and carriage rides. Those views are incised with a pathos that guides the engraver's tool and the topographer's pencil, and it is this pathos which, tenderly ironic, gave villages names like Felicity.
A century looked at a landscape furious with vegetation in the wrong light and with the wrong eye. It is such pictures that are saddening rather than the tropics itself. These delicate engravings of sugar mills and harbours, of native women in costume, are seen as a part of History, that History which looked over the shoulder of the engraver and, later, the photographer. History can alter the eye and the moving hand to conform a v iew of itself; it can rename places for the nostalgia in an echo; it can temper the glare of tropical light to elegiac monotony in prose, the tone of judgement in Conrad, in the travel journals of Trollope.

These travellers carried with them the infection of their own malaise, and their prose reduced even the landscape to melancholia and self-contempt. Every endeavour is belittled as imitation, from architecture to music. There was this conviction in Froude that since History is based on achievement, and since the history of the Antilles was so genetically corrupt, so depressing in its cycles of massacres, slavery, and indenture, a culture was inconceivable and nothing could ever be created in those ramshackle ports, those monotonously feudal sugar estates. Not only the light and salt of Antillean mountains defied this but the demotic vigour and variety of their inhabitants. Stand close to a waterfall and you will stop hearing its roar. To be still in the nineteenth century, like horses, as Brodsky has written, may not be such a bad deal, and much of our life in the Antilles still seems to be in the rhythm of the last century, like the West Indian novel.

By writers even as refreshing as Graham Greene, the Caribbean is looked at with elegiac pathos, a prolonged sadness to which Levi-Strauss has supplied an epigraph:

Tristes Tropiques. Their *tristesse* derives from an attitude to the Caribbean dusk, to rain, to uncontrollable vegetation, to the provincial ambition of Caribbean cities where brutal replicas of modern architecture dwarf the small houses and streets. The mood is understandable, the melancholy as contagious as the fever of a sunset, like the gold fronds of diseased coconut palms, but there is something alien and ultimately wrong in the way such a sadness, even a morbidity, is described by English, French, or some of our exiled writers. It relates to a misunderstanding of the light and the people on whom the light falls.

These writers describe the ambitions of our unfinished cities, their unrealized, homiletic conclusion, but the Caribbean city may conclude just at that point where it is satisfied with its own scale, just as Caribbean culture is not evolving but already shaped. Its proportions are not to be measured by the traveller or the exile but by its own citizenry and architecture. To be told you are not yet a city or a culture requires this response. I am not your city or your culture. There might be less of *Tristes Tropiques* after that.

Here, on the raft of this dais, there is the sound of the applauding surf: our landscape, our history recognized, "at last." *At Last* is one of the first Caribbean books. It was written by the Victorian traveller Charles Kingsley. It is one of the early books to admit the Antillean landscape and its figures into English literature. I have never read it but gather that its tone is benign. The Antillean archipelago was there to be written about, not to write itself, by Trollope, by Patrick Leigh-Fermor, in the very tone in which I almost wrote about the village spectacle at Felicity, as a compassionate and beguiled outsider, distancing myself from Felicity village even while I was enjoying it. What is hidden cannot be loved. The traveller cannot love, since love is stasis and travel is motion. If he returns to what he loved in a landscape and stays there, he is no longer a traveller but in stasis and concentration, the lover of that particular part of earth, a native. So many people say they "love the Caribbean," meaning that someday they plan to return for a visit but could never live there, the usual benign insult of the traveller, the tourist. These travellers, at their kindest, were devoted to the same patronage, the islands passing in profile, their vegetal luxury, their backwardness and poverty. Victorian prose dignified them. They passed by in beautiful profiles and were forgotten, like a vacation.

Alexis Saint-Leger Leger, whose writer's name is Saint-John Perse, was the first Antillean to win this prize for poetry. He was born in Guadeloupe and wrote in French, but before him, there was nothing as fresh and clear in feeling as those poems of his childhood (*Pour fêter une enfance*, *Éloges*, and later *Images à Crusoé*), that of a privileged white child on an Antillean plantation. At last, the first breeze on the page, salt-edged and self-renewing as the trade winds, the sound of pages and palm trees turning as "the odour of coffee ascents the stairs."

Caribbean genius is condemned to contradict itself. To celebrate Perse, we might be told, is to celebrate the old plantation system, to celebrate the *beque* or plantation rider, verandahs and "mulatto" servants, a white French language in a white pith helmet, to celebrate a rhetoric of patronage and hauteur; and even if Perse denied his origins, great writers often have this folly of trying to smother their source, we cannot deny him any more than we can the African Aime Cesaire. This is not accommodation; this is the ironic republic that is poetry, since, when I see cabbage palms moving their fronds at sunrise, I think they are reciting Perse.

The fragrant and privileged poetry that Perse composed to celebrate his white childhood and the recorded Indian music behind the brown young archers of Felicity, with the same cabbage palms against the same Antillean sky, pierce me equally. I feel the same poignancy of pride in the poems as in the faces. Why, given the history of the Antilles, should this be remarkable? The history of the world, by which of course we mean Europe, is a record of intertribal lacerations, of ethnic cleansings. At last, islands not written about but writing themselves! The palms and the Muslim minarets are Antillean exclamations. At last! The royal palms of Guadeloupe recite *Éloges* by heart.

Later, in *Anabase*, Perse assembled fragments of an imaginary epic, with the clicking teeth of frontier gates, barren wadis with the froth of poisonous lakes, horsemen burnoosed in sandstorms, the opposite of cool Caribbean mornings, yet not necessarily a contrast any more than some young brown archer at Felicity, hearing the sacred text blared across the flagged field, with its battles and elephants and monkey-gods, in a contrast to the white child in Guadeloupe assembling fragments of his own epic from the lances of the cane fields, the estate carts and oxens, and the calligraphy of bamboo leaves from the ancient languages, Hindi, Chinese, and Arabic, on the Antillean sky. From the *Ramayana* to Anabasis, from Guadeloupe to Trinidad, all that archaeology of fragments lying around, from the broken African kingdoms, from the crevasses of Canton, from Syria and Lebanon, vibrating not under the earth but in our raucous, demotic streets.

A boy with weak eyes skims a flat stone across the flat water of an Aegean inlet, and that ordinary action with the scything elbow contains the skipping lines of the *Iliad* and the *Odyssey*, and another child aims a bamboo arrow at a village festival, another hears the rustling march of cabbage palms in a Caribbean sunrise, and from that sound, with its fragments of tribal myth, the compact expedition of Perse's epic is launched, centuries and archipelagoes apart. For every poet it is always morning in the world. History a forgotten, insomniac night; History and elemental awe are always our early beginning, because the fate of poetry is to fall in love with the world, in spite of History.

There is a force of exultation, a celebration of luck, when a writer finds himself a witness to the early morning of a culture that is defining itself, branch by branch, leaf by leaf, in that self-defining dawn, which is why, especially at the edge of the sea, it is good to make a ritual of the sunrise. Then the noun, the "Antilles" ripples like brightening water, and the sounds of leaves, palm fronds, and birds are the sounds of a fresh dialect, the native tongue. The personal vocabulary, the individual melody whose metre is one's biography, joins in that sound, with any luck, and the body moves like a walking, a waking island.

This is the benediction that is celebrated, a fresh language and a fresh people, and this is the frightening duty owed.

I stand here in their name, if not their image, but also in the name of the dialect they exchange like the leaves of the trees whose names are suppler, greener, more morning-stirred than English–*laurier canelles, bois-flot, bois-canot*–or the valleys the trees mention–*Fond St. Jacques, Matoonya, Forestier, Roseau, Mahaut*–or the empty beaches–*L'Anse Ivrogne, Case en Bas, Paradis*–all songs and histories in themselves, pronounced not in French but in patois.

One rose hearing two languages, one of the trees, one of school children reciting in English:

I am monarch of all I survey,
My right there is none to dispute;
From the centre all round to the sea
I am lord of the fowl and the brute.
Oh, solitude! where are the charms
That sages have seen in thy face?
Better dwell in the midst of alarms,
Than reign in this horrible place…

While in the country to the same metre, but to organic instruments, handmade violin, chac-chac, and goatskin drum, a girl named Sensenne singing:

Si mwen di 'ous ça fait mwen la peine
'Ous kai dire ça vrai.
(If I told you that caused me pain
You'll say, "It's true.")
Si mwen di 'ous ça pentetrait mwen
'Ous peut dire ça vrai
(If I told you you pierced my heart
You'd say, "It's true.")
Ces mamailles actuellement
Pas ka faire l'amour z'autres pour un rien.
(Children nowadays
Don't make love for nothing.)

It is not that History is obliterated by this sunrise. It is there in Antillean geography, in the vegetation itself. The sea sighs with the drowned from the Middle Passage, the butchery of its aborigines, Carib and Aruac and Taino, bleeds in the scarlet of the immortelle, and even the actions of surf on sand cannot erase the African memory, or the lances of cane as a green prison where indentured Asians, the ancestors of Felicity, are still serving time.

That is what I have read around me from boyhood, from the beginnings of poetry, the grace of effort. In the hard mahogany of woodcutters: faces, resinous men, charcoal burners; in a man with a cutlass cradled across his forearm, who stands on the verge with the usual anonymous khaki dog; in the extra clothes he put on this morning, when it was cold when he rose in the thinning dark to go and make his garden in the heights–the heights, the garden, being miles away from his house, but that is where he has his land–not to mention the fishermen, the footmen on trucks, groaning up mornes, all fragments of Africa originally but shaped and hardened and rooted now in the island's life, illiterate in the way leaves are illiterate; they do not read, they are there to be read, and if they are properly read, they create their own literature.

But in our tourist brochures the Caribbean is a blue pool into which the republic dangles the extended foot of Florida as inflated rubber islands bob and drinks with umbrellas float towards her on a raft. This is how the islands from the shame of necessity sell themselves; this is the seasonal erosion of their identity, that high-pitched repetition of the same images of service that cannot distinguish one island from the other, with a future of polluted marinas, land deals negotiated by ministers, and all of this conducted to the music of Happy Hour and the rictus of a smile. What is the earthly paradise for our visitors? Two weeks without rain and a mahogany tan, and, at sunset, local troubadours in straw hats and floral shirts beating "Yellow Bird" and "Banana Boat Song" to death. There is a territory wider than this–wider than the limits made by the map of an island–which is the illimitable sea and what it remembers.

All of the Antilles, every island, is an effort of memory; every mind, every racial biography culminating in amnesia and fog. Pieces of sunlight through the fog and sudden rainbows, *arcs-en-ciel.* That is the effort, the labour of the Antillean imagination, rebuilding its gods from bamboo frames, phrase by phrase.

Decimation from the Aruac downwards is the blasted root of Antillean history, and the benign blight that is tourism can infect all of those island nations, not gradually, but with imperceptible speed, until each rock is whitened by the guano of white-winged hotels, the arc and descent of progress.

Before it is all gone, before only a few valleys are left, pockets of an older life, before development turns every artist into an anthropologist or folklorist, there are still cherishable places, little valleys that do not echo with ideas, a simplicity of rebeginnings, not yet corrupted by the dangers of change. Not nostalgic sites but occluded sanctities as common and simple as their sunlight. Places as threatened by this prose as a headland is by the bulldozer or a sea almond grove by the surveyor's string, or from blight, the mountain laurel.

One last epiphany: A basic stone church in a thick valley outside Soufrière, the hills almost shoving the houses around into a brown river, a sunlight that looks oily on the leaves, a backward place, unimportant, and one now being corrupted into significance by this prose. The idea is not to hallow or invest the place with anything, not even memory. African children in Sunday frocks come down the ordinary concrete steps into the church, banana leaves hang and glisten, a truck is parked in a yard, and old women totter towards the entrance. Here is where a real fresco should be painted, one without importance, but one with real faith, mapless, Historyless.

How quickly it could all disappear! And how it is beginning to drive us further into where we hope are impenetrable places, green secrets at the end of bad roads, headlands where the next view is not of a hotel but of some long beach without a figure and the hanging question of some fisherman's smoke at its far end. The Caribbean is not an idyll, not to its natives. They draw their working strength from it organically, like trees, like the sea almond or the spice laurel of the heights. Its peasantry and its fishermen are not there to be loved or even photographed; they are trees who sweat, and whose bark is filmed with salt, but every day on some island, rootless trees in suits are signing favourable tax breaks with entrepreneurs, poisoning the sea almond and the spice laurel of the mountains to their roots. A morning could come in which governments might ask what happened not merely to the forests and the bays but to a whole people.

They are here again, they recur, the faces, corruptible angels, smooth black skins and white eyes huge with an alarming joy, like those of the Asian children of Felicity at *Ramleela;* two different religions, two different continents, both filling the heart with the pain that is joy.

But what is joy without fear? The fear of selfishness that, here on this podium with the world paying attention not to them but to me, I should like to keep these simple joys inviolate, not because they are innocent, but because they are true. They are as true as when, in the grace of this gift, Perse heard the fragments of his own epic of Asia Minor in the rustling of cabbage palms, that inner Asia of the soul through which imagination wanders, if there is such a thing as imagination as opposed to the collective memory of our entire race, as true as the delight of that warrior-child who flew a bamboo arrow over the flags in the field at Felicity; and now as grateful a joy and a blessed fear as when a boy opened an exercise book and, within the discipline of its margins, framed stanzas that might contain the light of the hills on an island blest by obscurity, cherishing our insignificance.

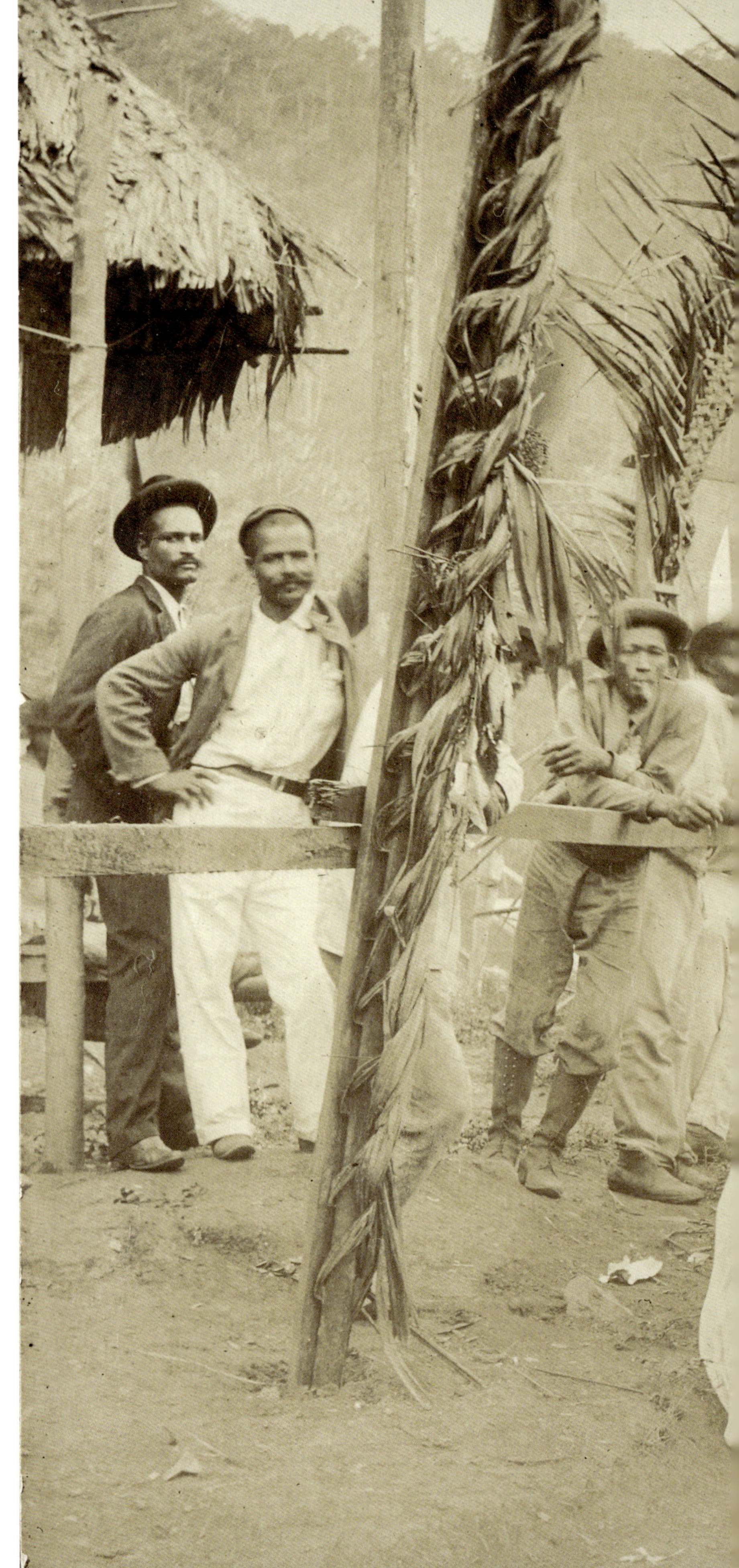

Unknown photographer, *Emancipation Day, Jamaica*, August 1, c. 1895

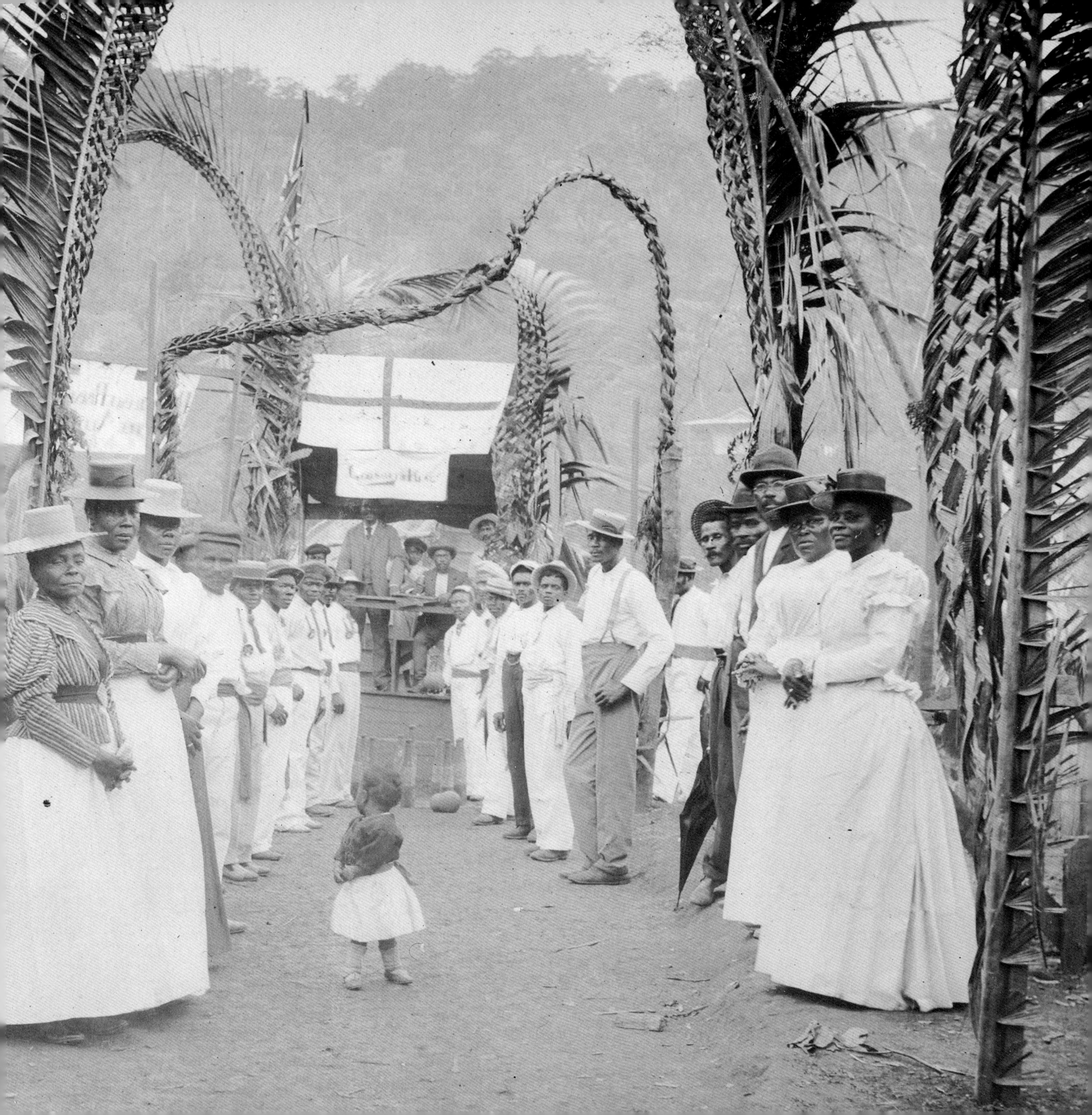

Seeing the Unseizable:

Confronting the Past and Considering the Future

Julie Crooks

I don't think there has been anything in human history quite like the meeting of Africa, Asia, and Europe in this American archipelago we call the Caribbean. But is so recent since we assumed responsibility for our own destiny, that the antagonistic weight of the past is felt as an inhibiting menace ... how to control the burden of this history and incorporate it into our collective sense of the future.[1]

— **George Lamming**
Coming, Coming Home: Conversations II (2000)

Only our own painful, strenuous looking, the learning of looking, could find meaning in the life around us.[2]

— **Derek Walcott**
What the Twilight Says (1998)

Acquired by the Art Gallery of Ontario in 2019, the Montgomery Caribbean Photography Collection comprises almost 4,000 photographs, lithographs, and ephemera. The collection, which spans the period of emancipation to the first half of the twentieth century, documents specific Caribbean countries and the Circum-Caribbean region between 1838 and the 1940s. In preparation for *Fragments of Epic Memory*, I regularly revisited this trove of photographs. Over time, the collection revealed a range of subjects, themes, and genres framed predominately by European photographers—some identified, others unknown. Yet out of the thousands of photographs I encountered, one in particular continues to resonate. This image, unassumingly located in a small, nondescript album, in many ways encapsulates the sentiment of Derek Walcott's words in the epigram above.

The Learning of Looking

On first glance, the photograph (c. 1915, fig. 1) does not seem particularly provocative—there are many similar photographs in the collection, ones that record generic scenes of crowded streets and chaos—in particular the frenzied Caribbean marketplace of the late nineteenth century. The unknown photographer seems to have captured an image that informs and constructs a typical view of the Caribbean: exotic; in need of colonial surveillance, control, and documentation. But then: a figure in the foreground, a young boy, stands beside an older woman (perhaps his mother), barely noticeable within the overall composition. Affixed to his left eye is an oddly shaped object (perhaps an optical device), through which he returns the camera's gaze. This ostensibly simple, discreet gesture is rendered more remarkable by what appears in the background of the photograph. Here, clusters of women vendors and customers move with vitality and purpose, unaware that there is an encounter unfolding in the foreground. For the photographer, the boy would be incidental, irrelevant to the overall scene. For me, however, the power of the boy's enigmatic gesture of recognition (or refusal) is undeniable. For me, this "punctum"[3] forms the focal point that transfixes. The boy concentrates on making himself *visible* by returning the photographer's cold, all-encompassing gaze. As he shifts from subject to spectator, his gaze fixes on the man wielding the camera. This captured act disrupts the power imbalance inherent in colonial regimes of vision, thus limiting full access to and "possession" of the boy's likeness.

This young child's small but mighty act is vital because such recalcitrant "looking" or "seeing" occludes instrumentalization: it resists being captured by the colonial archive. Instead, as Mary Lou Emery suggests, "the art of seeing brings forth a new body, no longer imprisoned in a single identity... its wholeness newly and dynamically diversified and thus "unseizable."[4]

The framing analytic of Caribbean *vision scape*[5] constructs enduring images of the region and its subjects as commodified, dispossessed, and picturesque. In its place, both Walcott's "strenuous looking" and Emory's "unseizable" inform and shape the overarching logic of *Fragments of Epic Memory*. Although these two notions may seem contradictory, each provides a generative foundation to examine historical photographs produced in the aftermath of enslavement while reflecting on emancipation and how this concept is envisioned in various ways through the practices of modern and contemporary artists. The challenge, perhaps, is to think through the ways in which fragmentation and disruption can provide a sort of refuge for those surveying images of imperial hegemony within the heterogeneity of Caribbean transnational artistic practices.

Fragments of Epic Memory is organized around more than 200 photographs selected from the

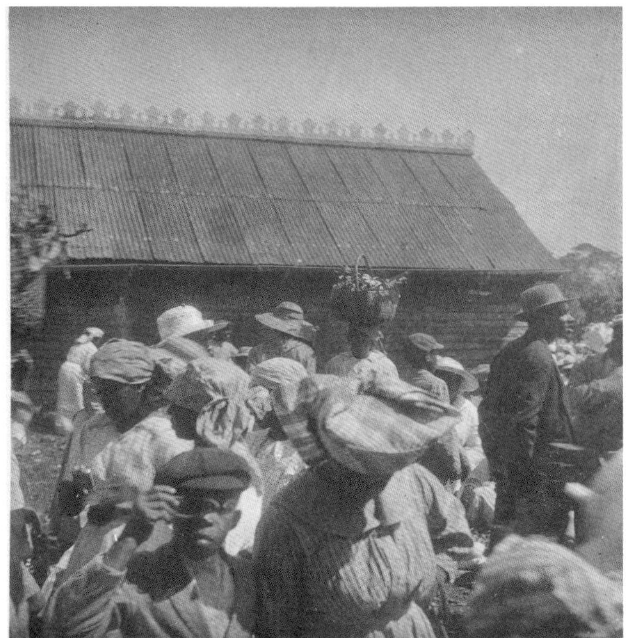

1

Fig. 1
Unknown photographer,
***Boy with optical device at market, location unknown*, c. 1915.**
Gelatin silver print, 27.9 × 20.3 cm.
Album: 29 pages with gelatin silver prints. In *West Indies (Cuba, Puerto Rico, Jamaica, Panama)*. Art Gallery of Ontario, Montgomery Collection of Caribbean Photographs, purchase, with funds from Dr. Liza & Dr. Frederick Murrell, Bruce Croxon & Debra Thier, Wes Hall & Kingsdale Advisors, Cindy & Shon Barnett, Donette Chin-Loy Chang, Kamala-Jean Gopie, Phil Lind & Ellen Roland, Martin Doc McKinney, Francilla Charles, Ray & Georgina Williams, Thaine & Bianca Carter, Charmaine Crooks, Nathaniel Crooks, Andrew Garrett & Dr. Belinda Longe, Neil L. Le Grand, Michael Lewis, Dr. Kenneth Montague & Sarah Aranha, Lenny & Julia Mortimore, and The Ferrotype Collective, 2019. 2019/2188.
Photo: Art Gallery of Ontario.

Montgomery Collection. These photographs, set in dialogue with works by twenty-seven modern and contemporary artists, are loosely organized around three themes: "Ghosting/Post Emancipation," "See.We.Here,"[6] and "Freedom/Futures." I am again indebted to Walcott, as the exhibition's name is borrowed from the title of his Nobel Prize speech, *The Antilles: Fragments of Epic Memory*,[7] in which he describes the fragmentary nature of memory as a defining feature of the Caribbean archipelago. Inspired by Walcott, *Fragments* adopts a non-linear approach across time periods, bringing together Montgomery photographs with Caribbean and diasporic art-making to re-vision and reflect on the region and its histories through the lens of an ongoing struggle for liberation.

Cumulatively, the photographs chosen from the Montgomery Collection broadly address the aftermath of enslavement, with a focus on the period that immediately followed emancipation in 1838. In the exhibition space, custom-made table cases that resemble the curved hulls of slave ships display photographs that illustrate the visual economy of the region chiefly from the 1840s onward. The photographs allow us to bear witness to the ways in which de facto plantation systems facilitated ongoing colonial profiteering in extractive economies. While sugar continued to be produced after emancipation, the industry no longer held a monopoly over labour and resources in the region. Between the 1870s and the 1890s, new crops such as cacao, coffee, tobacco, and bananas were actively cultivated or reintroduced. Myriad images document sugar cane estates, banana fields, bustling ports, and workers—the majority of whom were of African descent and were forced to remain close to the land and the conditions of enslaved labour despite the abolishment of slavery. Euro-American photographers on a quest to brand the "tropics" for Western markets captured the Caribbean as commodifiable and consumable.

Such hypervisibility, as evinced in photographs, meant "not only that everything can be seen," as Avery Gordon notes, "but also everything is available and accessible for consumption."[8] Yet as the example of the young boy attests, not every subject is captured with this intention. That boy is the ghostly presence who haunts collections featuring colonial subjects throughout history; ultimately, he casts a spectral aura over *this* exhibition. Indeed, as Gordon adroitly acknowledges, "visibility and invisibility involve constant negotiation between what can be seen and what is in the shadows."[9]

Ghosting/Post-Emancipation

The artists showcased in *Fragments* confront the ghosts of Caribbean colonial regimes, even as their works reflect a range of media and methods that span different time periods. The spectral presence (in the Caribbean, this is known as duppy or jumbie[10]) that haunts their works evokes themes related to the transatlantic slave trade, with its attendant experiences of loss, trauma, and suffering. While acknowledging such hauntings, these creators harness that energy through these encounters to produce art that suggests emancipatory potential.

In her large-scale work *A Litany for Survival* (2019, fig. 2), Andrea Chung deftly mobilizes photography's past to navigate colonial histories of extraction and ongoing harm to Caribbean ecosystems. Her medium is the cyanotype, a photographic process developed in 1841. Chung is interested in the collision between narratives of scientific interest and those of post-emancipated Caribbean society, as seen in the mobilization of photography to document botanical specimens, and their exotic colonial locales (and the residents of those locales). In *A Litany for Survival,* sugar crystals are applied to specific areas of the surface of a print depicting different coral species. The texture creates delicate patterns that symbolize the extractive sugar industry in the Caribbean and its dependence on exploitative labour. Chung expertly comingles the indexical, the expressive, and the poetic, producing a work that powerfully summons both the elemental past and the enduring legacies that shape the future.

Roshini Kempadoo's series *Ghosting* (2004, fig. 3) uses photography and "critical fabulation"[11] to create images that trace and reconstruct the lived experiences of plantation workers in Trinidad who were formerly enslaved or indentured labourers. Kempadoo's evocative works identify the physical site of the plantation and the buildings and fields that surround it. She manipulates and overlays maps, census documents, and archival photographs, creating narratives that fill in the colonial archive's

2

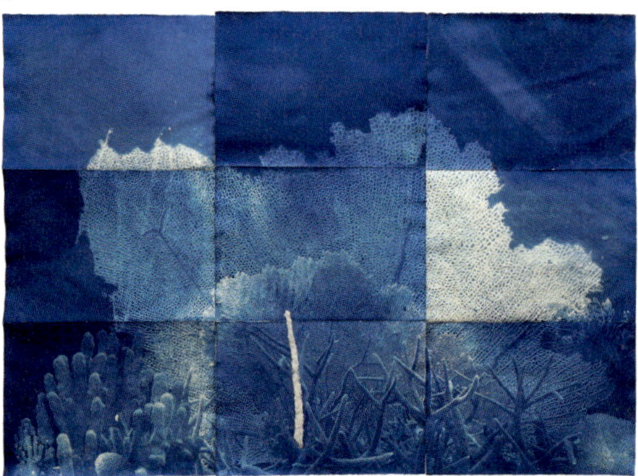

3

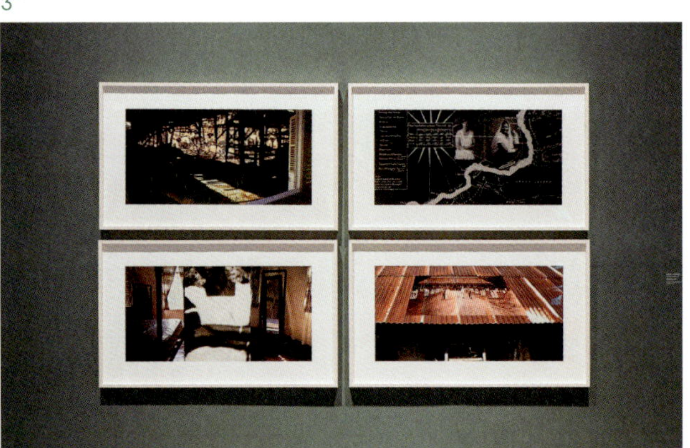

Fig. 2
Andrea Chung
A Litany for Survival, 2019. Cyanotype and sugar, 170.2 × 228.6 cm.
Courtesy of the artist and Tyler Park Presents, Los Angeles. © Andrea Chung. Image courtesy of courtesy of the artist, Klowden Mann, and Tyler Park Presents, Los Angeles; photo: Michael Underwood.

Fig. 3
Roshini Kempadoo
Ghosting, 2004.
Set of four archival pigment prints; printed 2021, 77.47 × 127 cm. Courtesy of the artist. © Roshini Kempadoo.

4

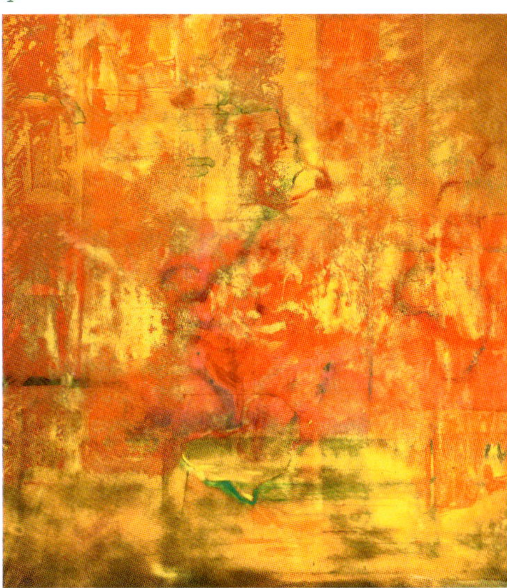

5

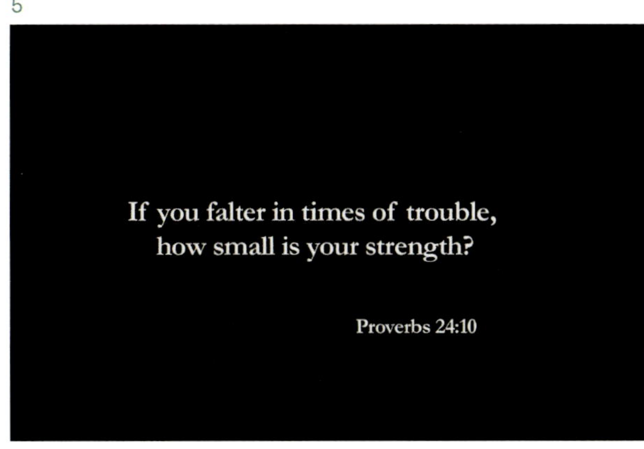

Fig. 4
Sir Frank Bowling
***Middle Passage*, 1970.**
Acrylic paint and oil-based ink on canvas, 319.9 x 280.3 cm. National Gallery of Canada, Ottawa, promised gift of Michael Nesbitt, Winnipeg. SLB-2021.0008.1.

Fig. 5
Peter Dean Rickards / The Afflicted Yard
***Proverbs 24:10*, 2008.**
Video (black-and-white, sound, 2 min. 35 sec.). Courtesy of The Estate of Peter Dean Rickards – Diana and Peter Rickards Trustees.

loud silences. As Michel-Rolph Trouillot argues, this sort of intentional silencing is caused by "an uneven power in the production of sources, archives and narratives."[12] In response, Kempadoo's *Ghosting* haunts works in the Montgomery Collection by rupturing the silence created by previously constructed narratives of the Caribbean.

Another central work in this section, Sir Frank Bowling's groundbreaking *Middle Passage* (1970, fig. 4), also explores the theme of ghosting. The title of the painting refers to the brutal oceanic trafficking of Africans to the "New World." A riot of form and colour vibrates on the canvas,[13] illuminating the faint outline of the African continent. Ghostly black portraits—silkscreened photographs of bodies and faces—skim the surface of the canvas, evoking those lost during the transatlantic journey. These images hover alongside familial memories related to "home." *Middle Passage*, like *Mother's House and Night Storm* (1967), another spectacular painting by Bowling exhibited as part of *Fragments*, is haunted by the ghosts of Bowling's childhood in Guyana. Reflecting on the vibrant luminous light that can be seen in this painting (and others in his "Map" series), Bowling said, "I understood the light in my pictures.... I saw a crystalline haze, maybe an East wind and water rising up into the sky... the light is about Guyana."[14] *Middle Passage* functions as both focal point and historical anchor. Its beauty and virtuosity combine with the pain evoked by its searing title, resulting in a palimpsest of history and memory which, according to Bowling, "can hardly ever be erased."[15]

Within the exhibition, a range of time-based works that similarly conjoin aesthetic engagement with pain's affective charge serve to bridge thematic clusters. Nadia Huggins's *Circa No Future* (2016–2019), Peter Dean Rickards's *Proverbs 24:10* (2008, fig.5), and Ebony Patterson's *...Three Kings Weep...* (2019) all explore the performance of gender identity and masculinities in the Caribbean. Each of these durational works evokes moments of poetic transformation, whether staged or organic. The contours and fissures of how pain shapes lives can be parsed in Charles Campbell's sculptural piece *Maroonscape I: Cockpit Archipelago* (2019) and Alberta Whittle's film *business as usual: hostile environment* (2020), both of which explore histories of trauma inflicted on

Black life through state-sanctioned racism and violence. In *business as usual,* Whittle highlights the legacy of the Windrush scandal in the United Kingdom as well as the disproportionate numbers of COVID deaths within Black and brown communities. *Maroonscape I*, meanwhile, renders in 3D a topographical map of Jamaica's rugged and hilly Cockpit country where escaped slaves sought refuge and which ultimately became home to a sovereign community called the Maroons. These two works and their accompanying soundscapes radiate prescience in their explorations of the incompleteness of the project of emancipation and the ongoing structures of domination in the Caribbean and the West. But as Campbell suggests, "We are survivors of, and party to, the schemes that dominate us, and this enables us to participate in a different imaginary."[16]

See.We.Here.[17]

In Jamaican vernacular or patois, the expression "Si me 'ere" is, according to authors Melanie Archer and Mariel Brown, "an instruction used to call attention to the speaker—whether for his or her physical appearance, or to note the occurrence of a significant moment in that person's life—an arrival, so to speak."[18] This section explores the ways in which self-representation, modes of self-fashioning, self-possession, resistance, and ideas around citizenship operate as emancipatory counterpoints to visual regimes of control and power. The act of strenuous looking and the notion of the "unseizable" are useful strategies for engaging with the works that fall under this rubric.

Groupings of studio portraits (comprising selections from the Montgomery Collection as well as private collections) reflect the desire of Caribbean subjects to represent themselves in the ways in which they wished to be seen. These portraits evoke a range of subjectivities and conditions and represent countless collaborations between the subjects and innumerable photographers. While we are not privy to the nuances of such negotiations, one can surmise that even with increased democratization of the medium by the turn of the nineteenth century, only a very few elite individuals could afford to patronize a photographer. While studio portraits may have served as markers of "self-representation," one must also consider the formidable power imbalances related to race, class, and social status in

6

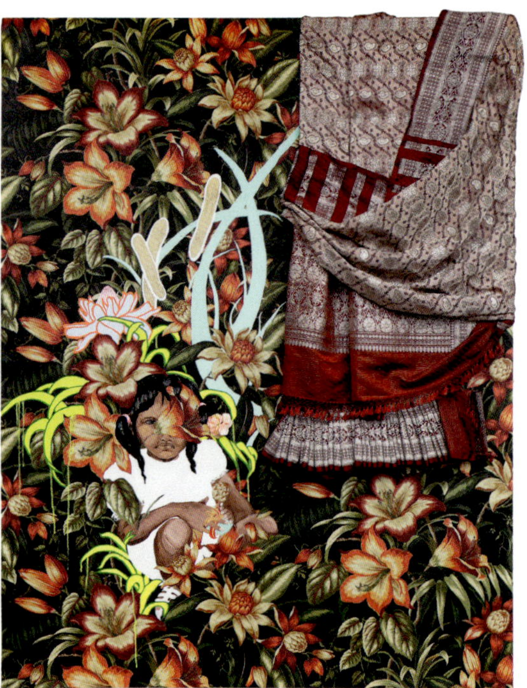

Fig. 6
Suchitra Mattai
Demerara Dreams, 2019.
Artist's mother's sari, gouache, acrylic, faux flower, and oil on printed fabric, 167.64 × 132.08 cm.
Courtesy of Paul and Heather Wilkinson.
© Suchitra Mattai.

7

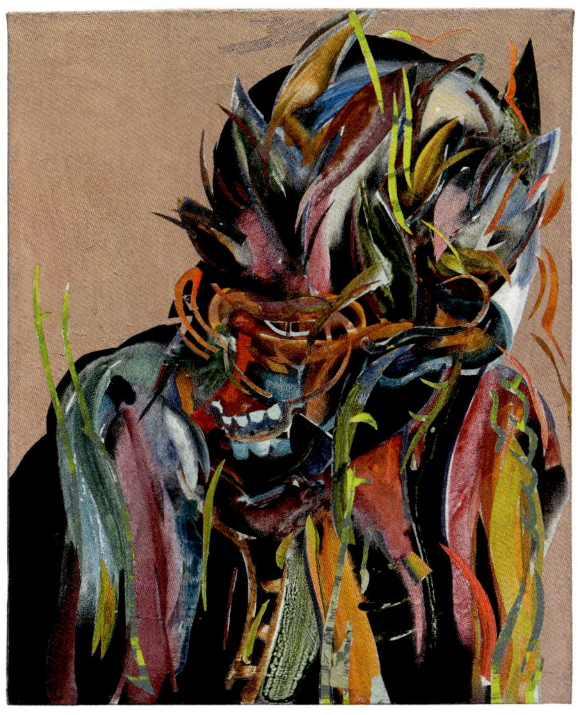

Fig. 7
Leasho Johnson
Jaw bone (man looking back at the cane fields), 2019.
Charcoal, watercolour, distemper, acrylic, oil stick, and oil paint on canvas, 76.2 x 60.96 × 2.54 cm. Art Gallery of Ontario, purchase, with funds from Friends of Global Africa and the Diaspora, 2021. 2021/30. © Leasho Johnson. Photo: Art Gallery of Ontario.

post-emancipation Caribbean societies. Displayed alongside the portraits are photographs related to Caribbean vernacular culture that illustrate histories of resistance, carnival, and masquerade performance within the region and its diaspora.

The groupings in "See.We.Here." attend to the ongoing practices by artists of Caribbean descent who have a shared desire to "call attention" to self, agency, and belonging while pushing beyond colonial boundaries and constraints. The modern and contemporary artists throughout *Fragments of Epic Memory* are, by and large, transnational in scope. Their works reflect the Caribbean both inside and outside its borders. Movement, migration, and exile are some of the key themes at the heart of the creative production featured in this section. *Black Bullets* (2012), a time-based media work by Jeanette Ehlers, a Danish Trinidadian living in Denmark, is a haunting and visceral homage to the Haitian revolution. In *Demerara Dreams* (2019, fig. 6), a large-scale mixed-media work, Suchitra Mattai uses a mixture of paint, photographs, and fabric from her mother's vintage sari. Mattai, who was born in Georgetown, Guyana, and lives in Boulder, Colorado, mines her family's legacy of indentured labour while drawing on craft-based practices and notions of home. Born in London and of Dominican descent, Gomo George has been part of the art scene in Winnipeg and Toronto since the 1980s. His work *Women's Carnival Group* (2002) captures a carnival scene in Dominica. George used an original photograph taken in 1958 by Dominican photographer K.A. Richards for this photorealist work, which is painted in intricate detail with a vibrant colour palette.

Freedom/Futures

The final section presents works that are concerned with disrupting the hypervisibility[19] and violence of the archive by using subversive conceptual approaches as a way of imagining an alternative. The artists here embrace "fragmentation" as a methodological foil. They deploy a variety of inventive strategies related to the illegible and the obscure while rethinking notions of looking and seeing in the context of the embodiment of Black and racialized individuals. Leasho Johnson's *Jaw bone (man looking back at the cane fields)* (2019, fig. 7) enacts a recuperation of queerness within the larger narrative of the transatlantic slave trade. The figure

Jawbone[20] emerges out of the cane fields, a space of repression, labour, and terror. Eschewing portraiture, Johnson anchors the work in abstraction, defying expectations around figurative representation. This allows him to create space for the Black queer body free from societal scrutiny. Johnson enacts strenuous looking by situating the cane fields as an imaginative space for creating queer mythologies.[21]

In his *Augmented Archives* (2021, fig. 8), Rodell Warner pushes back against the violence involved in the assembling of colonial photographic archives. Warner mines the Internet for vernacular photographs from the Caribbean—he often uses selections from the Montgomery Collection as source material—which he embeds with a digital layer. Employing twenty-first-century technology to intervene in the archive "puts an asterisk on the human beings in the photos to prompt the viewer to imagine their internal lives—the parts of these people not acknowledged in these photographs, or by those taking them."[22]

Illegibility and opacity are at play in pieces by Paul Anthony Smith and Christopher Cozier, works that are engaged in a kind of conceptual conversation. In the large-scale colour photograph *Untitled, 7 Women* (2019), Smith depicts a contemporary carnival scene featuring young women in colourful costume. The artist uses picotage, a method in which a sharp tool is used to pick up the surface of the print, obscuring the subject; he creates patterns that reference Caribbean breeze block fences, architectural elements intended to conceal elements from public view. In *NOW SHOWING: 12:30* (2010–2012, fig. 9), Cozier presents a collection of seemingly random and banal drawings (what he describes as "note taking"[23]) of objects, symbols, and references triggered by memory. Here, among the images, is a fragment of a breeze block fence—which, as Nicolas Laughlin suggests, "is not so much to be seen as to be seen through ... it frames and fragments a view of what is on the other side."[24] For Cozier and the other artists featured in this section, acts of looking and seeing are not benign endeavours; they are always complicated by the weight of history.

The exhibition concludes with two paintings by Firelei Báez—*Adjusting the Moon (The right to non-imperative clarities): Waxing*, and *Adjusting the Moon (The right to non-imperative clarities): Waning*

8

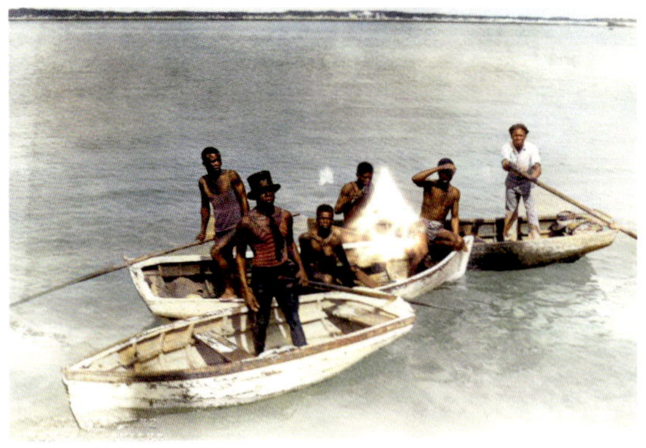

9

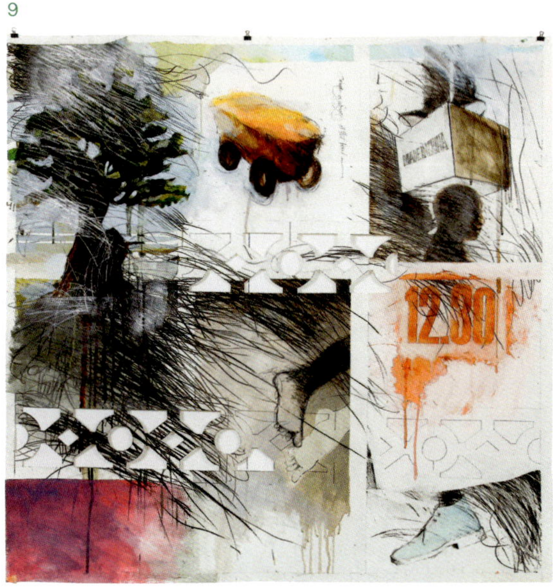

Fig. 8
Rodell Warner
***Augmented Archive 020 (colourized)*, 2021.**
Single-channel video with sound, dimensions variable.
Courtesy of the artist.
© Rodell Warner.

Fig. 9
Christopher Cozier
***NOW SHOWING 12:30*, 2010–2012.** Mixed media on paper, 149.9 × 152.4 cm.
Collection of Dr. Carlyle Farrell. © Christopher Cozier. Image courtesy of the artist.

(2019-2020, fig. 10)—which can perhaps be viewed as a beginning rather than the final stop on the journey. Cast within arch-shaped panels (a major design element in the exhibition, and an allusion to colonial architectural elements), the paintings feature shape-shifting Ciguapa figures[25] who have burst through their bodily boundaries. Obscured by radiant multicolour fragments, the beings step through their *trompe l'oeil* frame, creating the illusion of three-dimensionality—and, by extension, of "reality." Baez created an original backdrop for the paintings that depicts repeating arches—a *trompe l'oeil* effect. Once again, the flat surface creates the artifice of the "real." The installation is a reminder of the tactics employed by the little boy in the market, the person who engaged in strenuous looking so as not to be hampered by the vision of colonialism and its residues. Polyphonic in its curatorial vision. *Fragments of Epic Memory* challenges the totalizing perspectives about the Caribbean and its diasporas. Such perspectives are writ large in the Montgomery Collection and embodied by the racialized subjects depicted therein. But as Achille Mbembe notes in his observations about archives, it cannot be the "depository, the entire history of a society, of all that has happened in that society."[26] When those photographs are placed in dialogue with works by the artists in the exhibition, a space is created in which, following from Mbembe, "we are presented with pieces of time to be assembled, fragments of life to be placed in order... in an attempt to formulate a story that acquires its coherence through the ability to craft links between the beginning and the end." *Fragments* is a generative link in the ongoing project of Caribbean and transnational visuality and contemporary art-making practices.

10

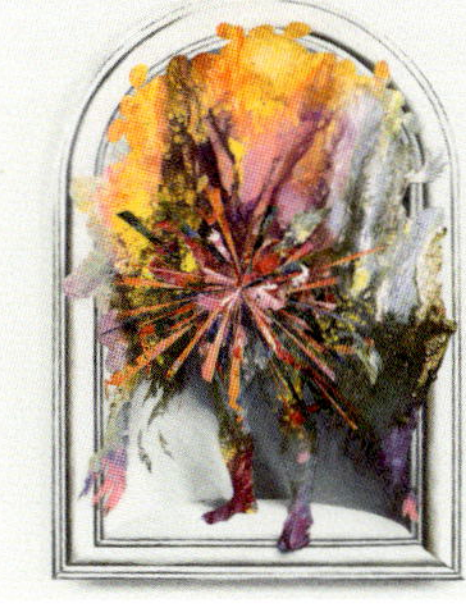

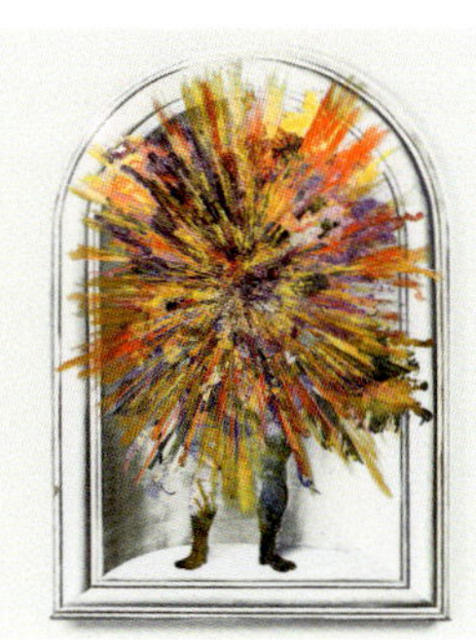

Fig. 10
Firelei Báez
Adjusting the Moon (The right to non-imperative clarities): Waxing [left] and Waning [right], 2019–2020. Oil and acrylic on panel, 289.6 × 198.1 × 3.8 cm. Private collection, Toronto, Canada [left], The Komal Shah & Gaurav Garg Collection [right]. © Firelei Báez. Image courtesy of the artist and James Cohan, New York.

1 George Lamming, *Coming, Coming Home: Conversations II* (Philipsburg, Saint Martin: House of Nehisi, 2000), 25.

2 Derek Walcott, "What the Twilight Says," in *What the Twilight Says, Essays from Derek Walcott* (New York: Farrar, Straus & Giroux, 1998), 967.

3 Roland Barthes describes the punctum of a photograph as "that accident which pricks me (but also bruises me, is poignant to me)." See *Camera Lucida: Reflections on Photography,* trans. R. Howard (New York: Hill and Wang, 2010).

4 Mary Lou Emery, *Modernism, The Visual and Caribbean Literature* (Cambridge, UK: Cambridge University Press, 2009), 241.

5 See Deborah Poole, *Vision, Race, and Modernity: A Visual Economy of the Andean Image World* (New Jersey: Princeton University Press, 1997).

6 See the chapter by the same name in Roshini Kempadoo's *Creole in the Archive: Imagery, Presence and the Location of the Caribbean Figure* (London: Rowman & Littlefield, 2016).

7 Derek Walcott, *The Antilles: Fragments of Epic Memory,* Nobel Prize lecture, December 7, 1992.

8 Avery Gordon, *Ghostly Matters: Haunting and the Sociological Imagination* (Minneapolis: University of Minnesota Press, 1997), 16.

9 Ibid.

10 Writing in 1961, MacEdward Leach noted that the word is "certainly African, for it is found today in West Coast African languages. In Sierra Leone, for example, the word 'duppy' has two meanings depending on the region and culture group. It means either a child or a ghost....The idea of a duppy or spirit floating around is very African, and is connected with the belief that the spirits of the dead ancestors are always hovering around the village, protecting and watching to see that the tribal laws are well-kept In the Caribbean." MacEdward Leach, "Jamaican Duppy Lore," *The Journal of American Folklore*, 1961:74, 207–215. See also, Vincent Brown, The Reaper's Garden: Death and Power in the World of Atlantic Slavery. (Cambridge, MA: Harvard University Press, 2008), 224–248.

11 "Critical fabulation" is a term coined by Saidiya Hartman, a professor of English and comparative literature at Columbia University, in her essay "Venus in Two Acts." Critical fabulation is the combining of historical and archival research with critical theory and fictional narrative to fill in the blanks left in the historical record. The term refers to a method of writing Hartmann has used as a way to contest the archive. In *small axe* 12, no. 2 (June 2008): 1–14.

12 Michel-Rolph Trouillot, *Silencing the Past: Power and the Production of History* (Boston: Beacon Press, 2015), 27.

13 Bowling's dedication to modernism and Abstract Expressionism was ignited by his time in New York in the late 1960s.

14 From Melissa Chemam, "Land of Many Waters: An Interview with Frank Bowling." https://artuk.org/discover/stories/land-of-many-waters-an-interview-with-frank-bowling. Accessed Dec. 20, 2021.

15 Ibid.

16 Monica Uszerowitz, "The Revolutionary Potential of a 'Caribbean Future,'" in *FRIEZE*, October 2019.

17 The title of this section, "See.We.Here.," is taken from Roshini Kempadoo's book chapter, "See We Here: Determining the Caribbean Self," in *Creole in the Archive: Imagery, Presence and the Location of the Caribbean Figure* (London: Rowman & Littlefield, 2016).

18 Melanie Archer and Mariel Brown, *See Me Here: A Survey of Contemporary Self-Portraits from the Caribbean* (Trinidad: Robert & Christopher Publishers, 2014).

19 Saidiya V. Hartman, *Scenes of Subjection* (London: Oxford University Press, 1997).

20 The character Jawbone is also loosely based on veteran Jamaican dancehall DJ "King Yellowman." Popular in the 1980s, he was born with albinism and had part of his jaw removed due to cancer.

21 For a more in-depth reading on Johnson's interest in dancehall, see "'Church Inna Session': Leasho Johnson, Mapping the Sacred through the Profane in Jamaican Popular Culture," *Smallaxe.net: Caribbean Queer Visualities*. smallaxe.net/cqv/issue-01/pdfs/CQV-086 patriciaJ-SAUNDERS.pdf.

22 Rodell Warner, "Artists Breathe New Life into Archives," *Hyperallergic*, https://hyperallergic.com/637431/artists-breathe-new-life-into-archives/.

23 Nicolas Laughlin, "Work in Progress," published in conjunction with the exhibition *Christopher Cozier: In Development* (New York: David Krut Projects, 2013).

24 Ibid.

25 The feminine-archetypal Ciguapa is a trickster from Dominican folklore who, for Báez, embodies the potential to defy oppressive conventions and break through generations of trauma.

26 Achille Mbembe, "The Power of the Archive and Its Limits," in *Refiguring the Archive*, ed. Carolyn Hamilton. (Springer, 2002), 19–27.

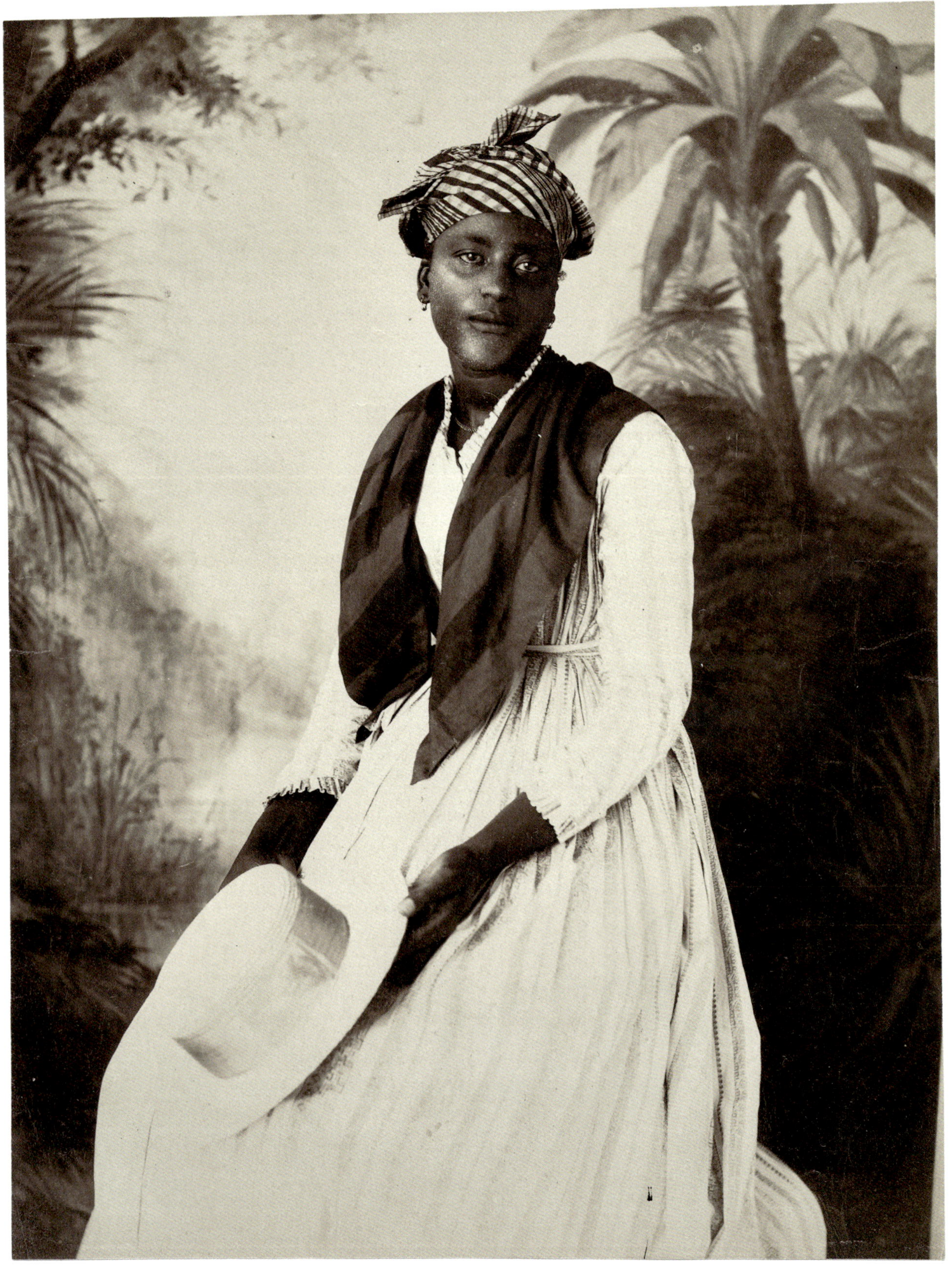

Gaston Fabre, *Woman, Martinique,* c. 1890s

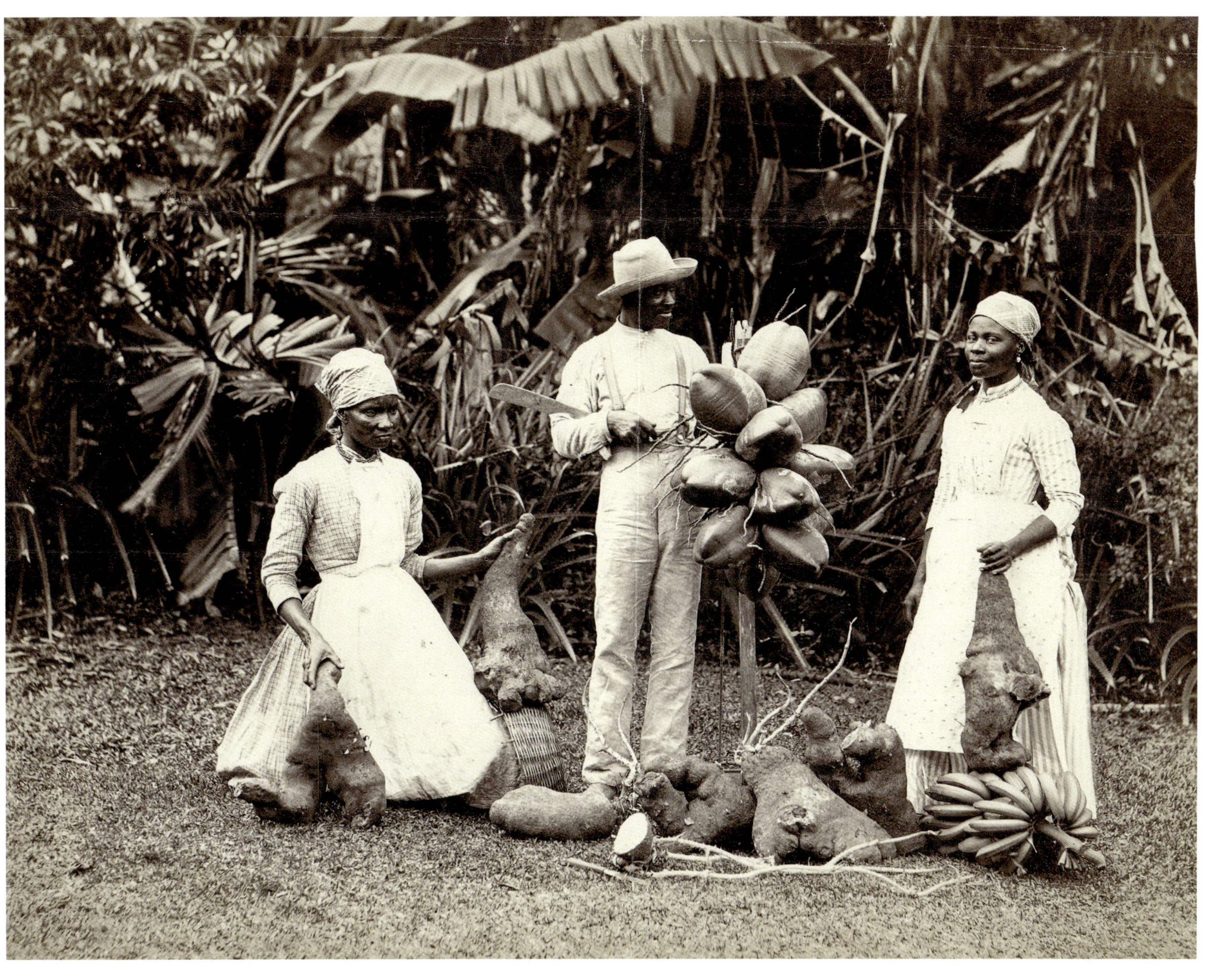

Reverend Dr. James Johnston, *Domestics with Yams and Cocoanuts,* c. 1895

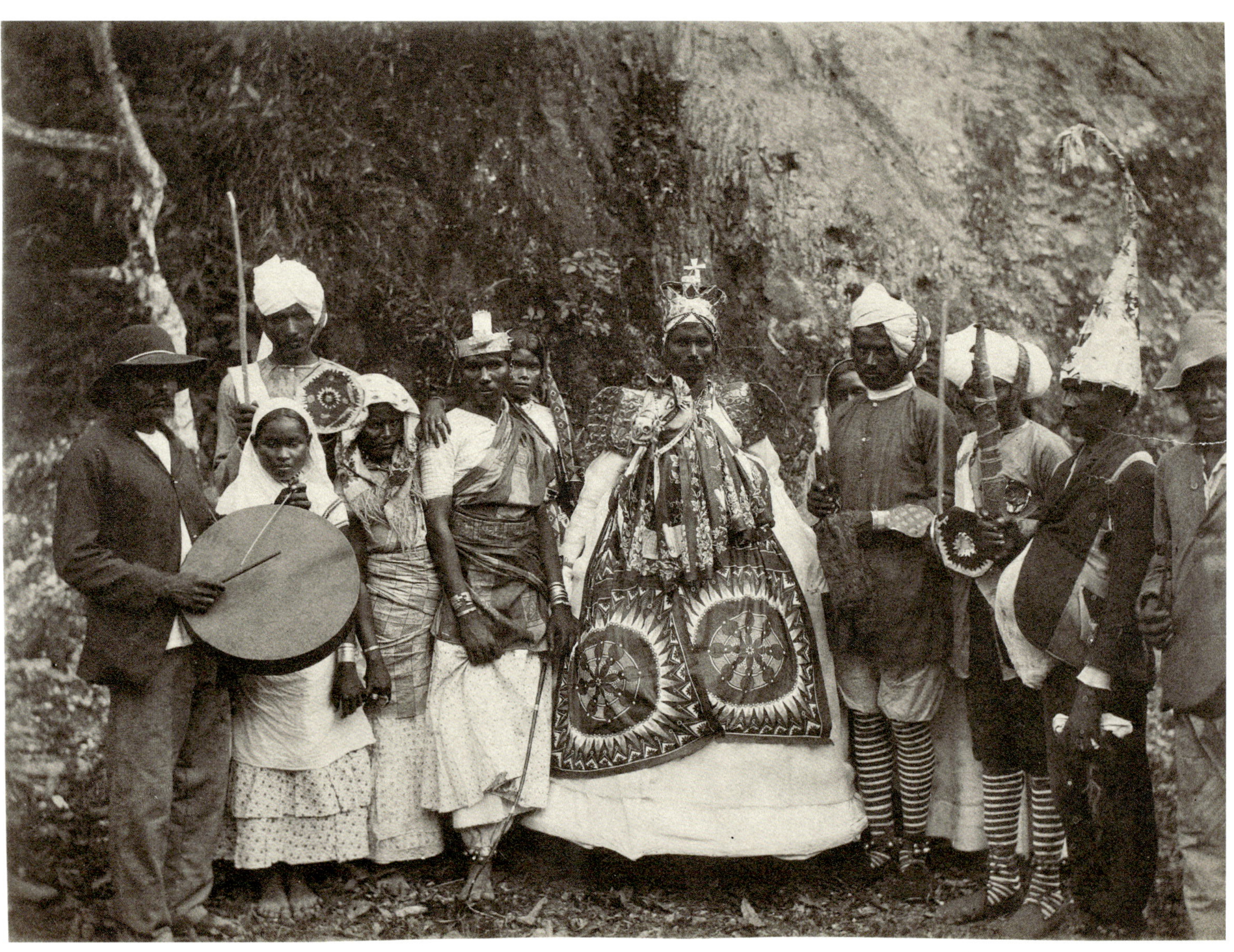

Unknown photographer, *Festival*, *Trinidad*, c. 1890

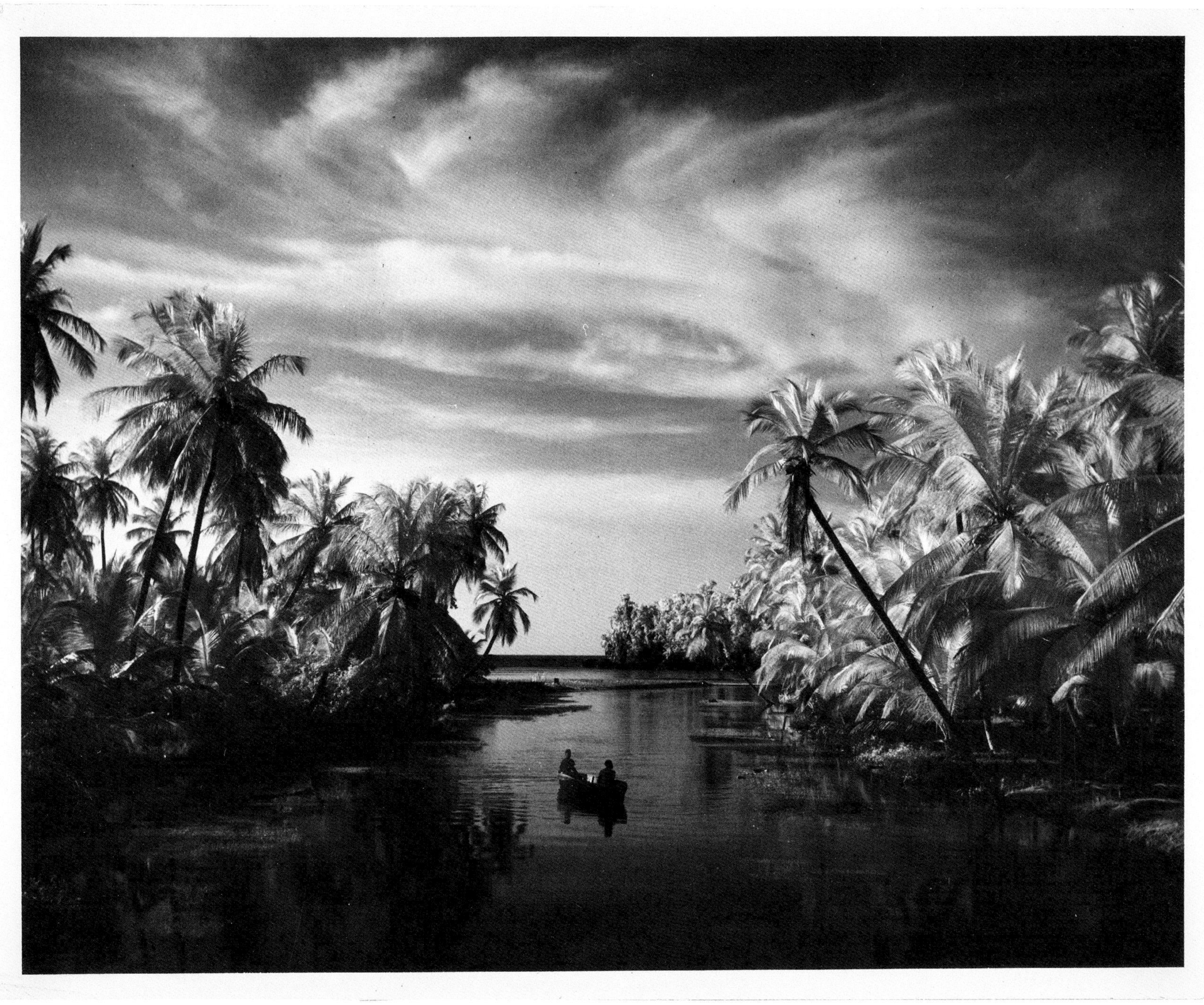

Unknown photographer, *White River, Jamaica,* c. 1915

Calypso

Edward Kamau Brathwaite

1
The stone had skidded arc'd and bloomed into islands:
Cuba and San Domingo
Jamaica and Puerto Rico
Grenada Guadeloupe Bonaire

curved stone hissed into reef
wave teeth fanged into clay
white splash flashed into spray
Bathsheba Montego Bay

bloom of the arcing summers…

2
The islands roared into green plantations
ruled by silver sugar cane
sweat and profit
cutlass profit
islands ruled by sugar cane

And of course it was a wonderful time
a profitable hospitable well-worth-your-time
when captains carried receipts for rices
letters spices wigs
opera glasses swaggering asses
debtors vices pigs

O it was a wonderful time
an elegant benevolent redolent time–
and young Mrs. P.'s quick irrelevant crime
at four o'clock in the morning…

3
But what of black Sam
with the big splayed toes
and the shoe black shiny skin?

He carries bucketfulls of water
'cause his Ma's just had another daughter.

And what of John with the European name
who went to school and dreamt of fame
his boss one day called him a fool
and the boss hadn't even been to school…

4
Steel drum steel drum
hit the hot calypso dancing
hot rum hot rum
who goin' stop this bacchanalling?

For we glance the banjo
dance the limbo
grow our crops by maljo

have loose morals
gather corals
father our neighbour's quarrels

perhaps when they come
with their cameras and straw
hats: sacred pink tourists from the frozen Nawth

we should get down to those
white beaches
where if we don't wear breeches

it becomes an island dance
Some people doin' well
while others are catchin' hell

o the boss gave our Johnny the sack
though we beg him please
please to take 'im back

so the boy now nigratin' overseas…

Excerpted from "Rights of Passage: III Islands and Exiles" in The Arrivants: A New World Trilogy *(Oxford: Oxford University Press, 1990).*

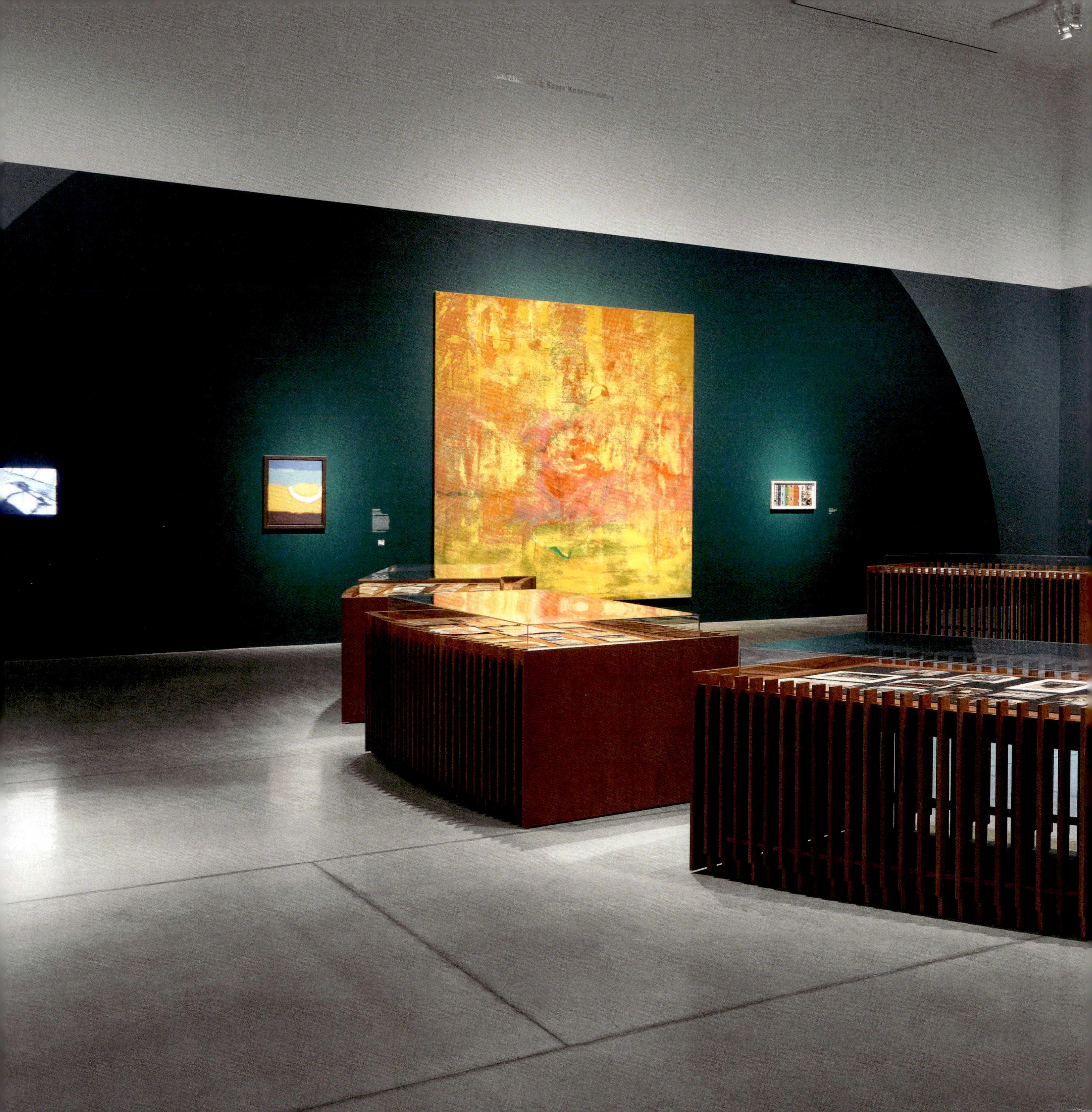

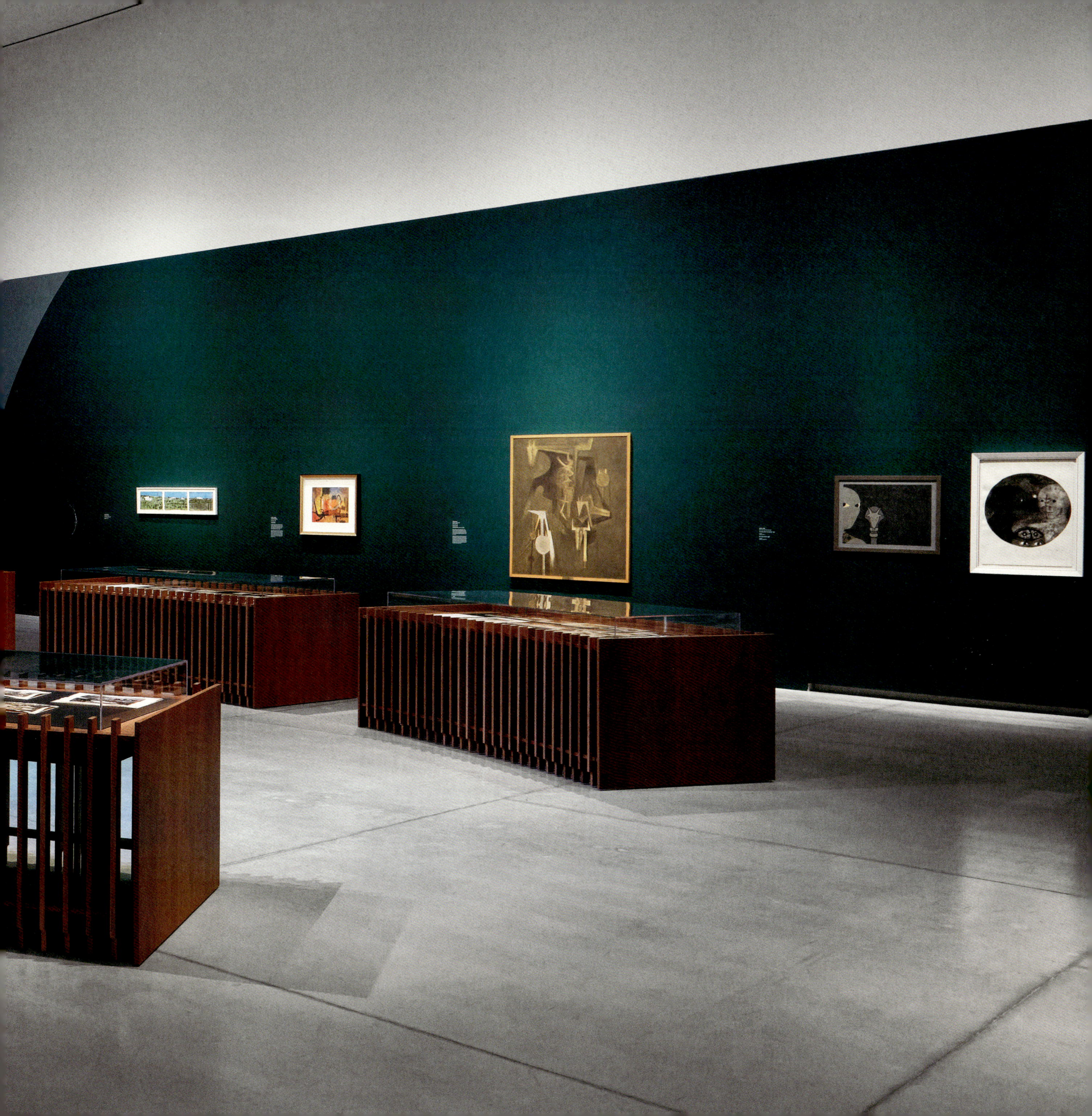

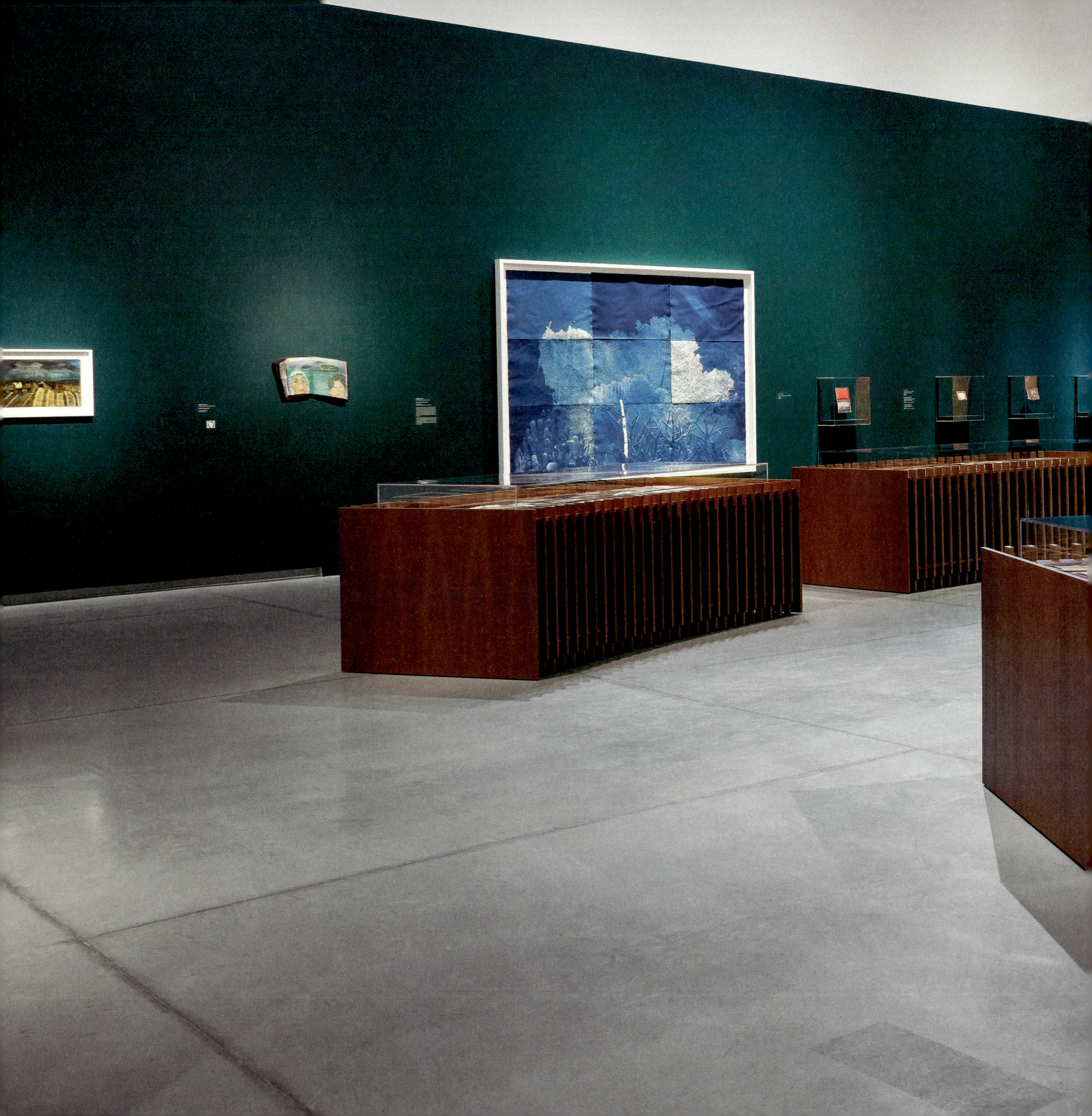

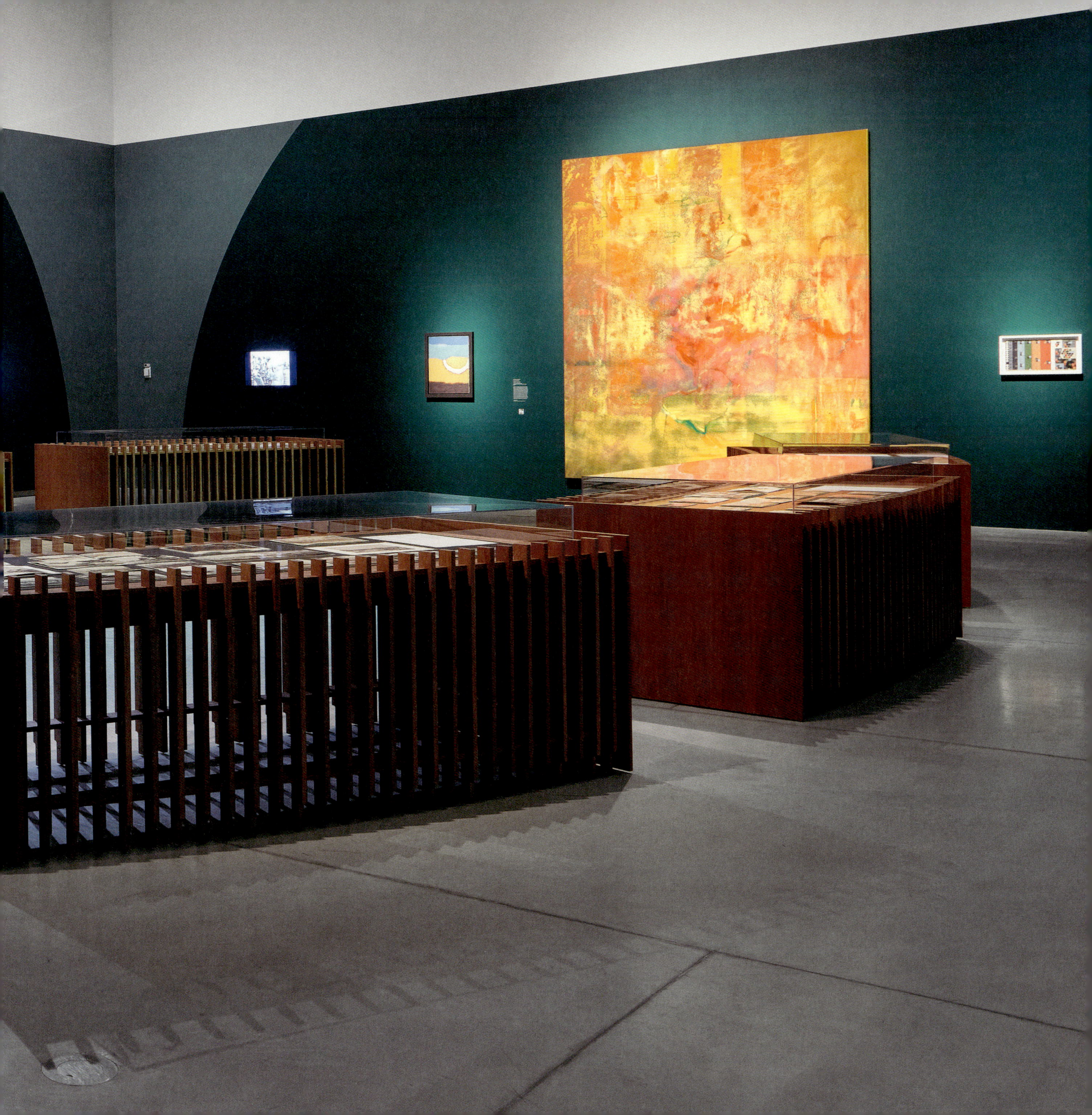

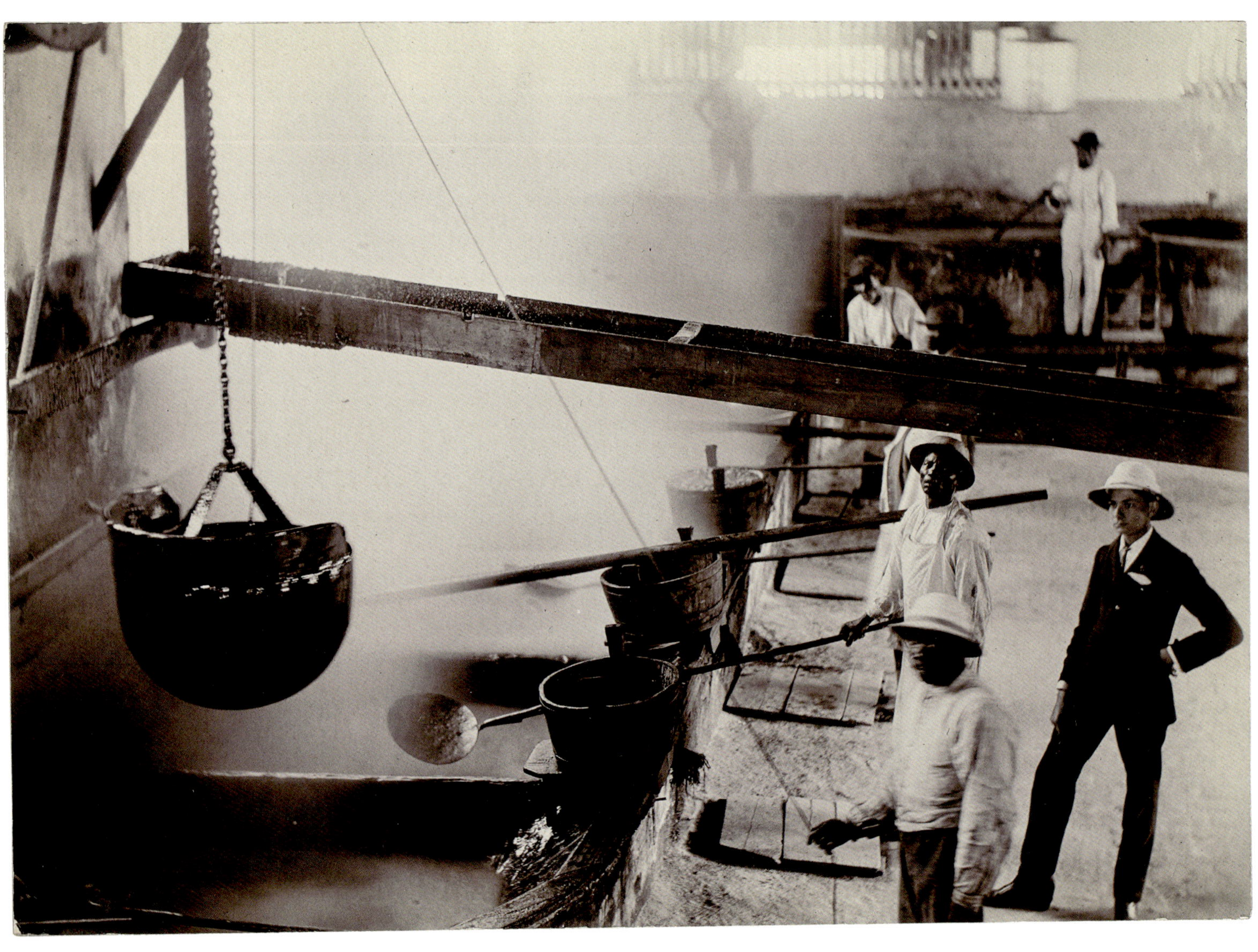

Unknown photographer, *Boiler House at Spring Hall, St. Lucy, Barbados*, c. 1900

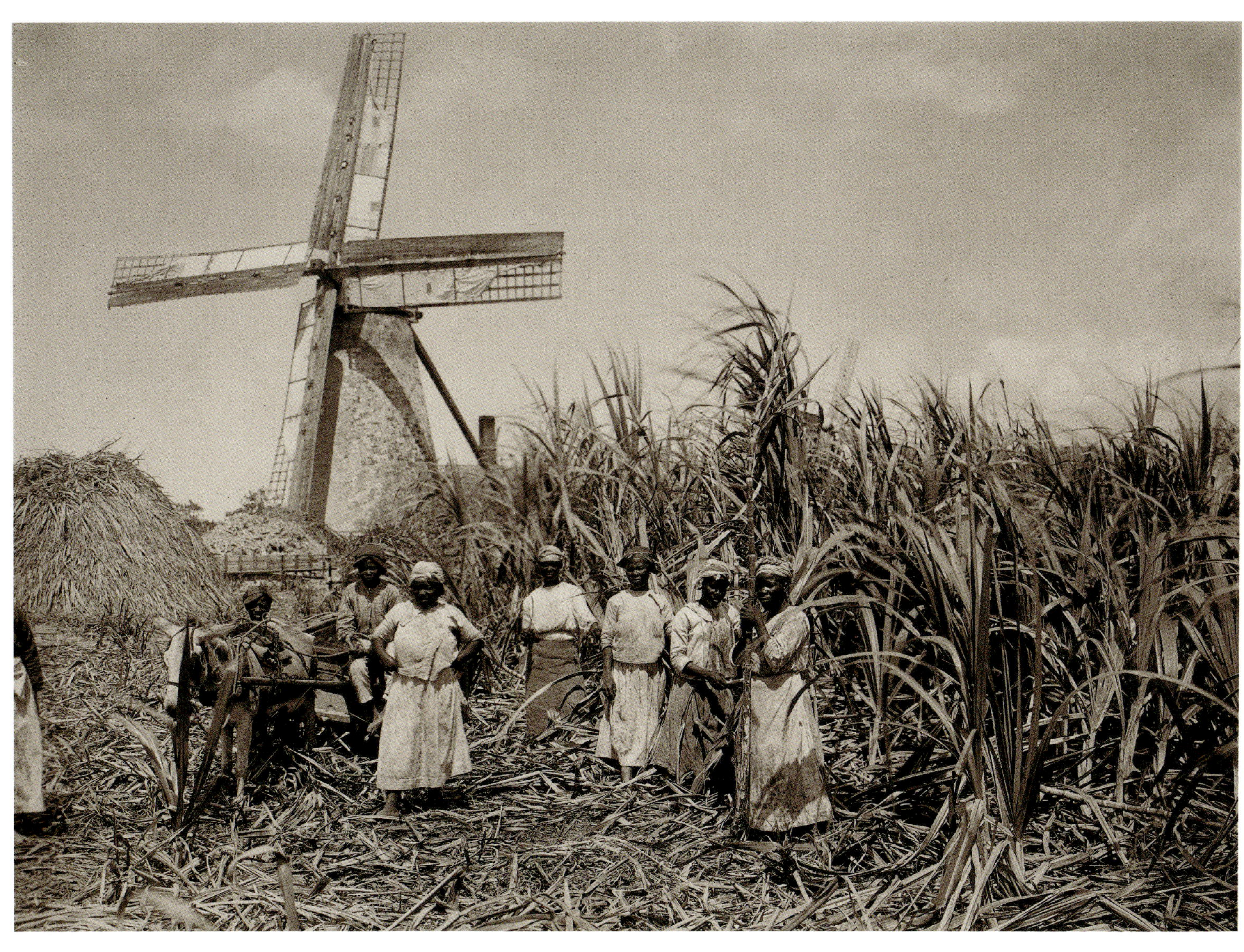

Unknown photographer, *Sugar Cane Workers, Barbados,* c. 1890

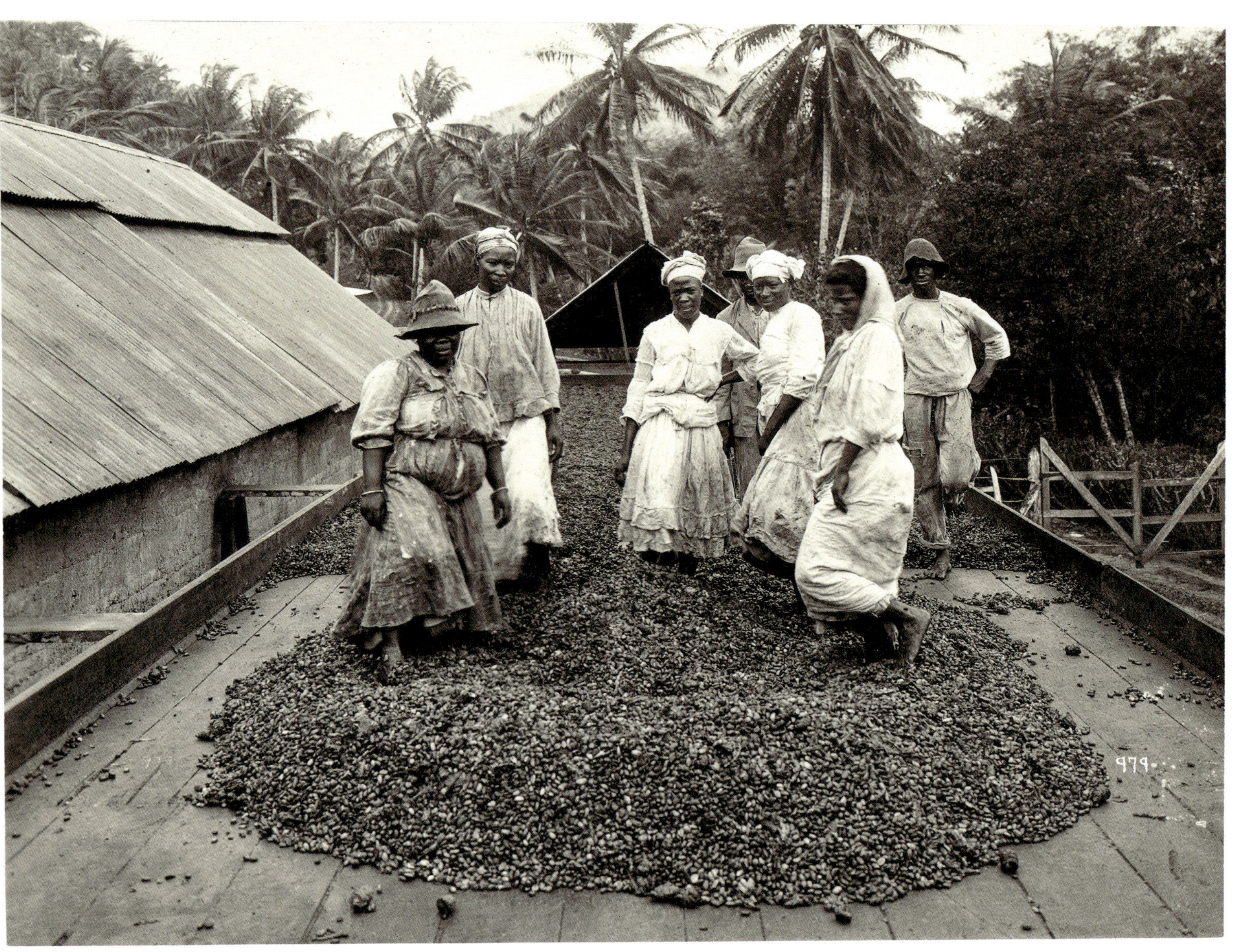

Unknown photographer, *Coffee Plantation*, *Port of Spain*, *Trinidad*, c. 1890

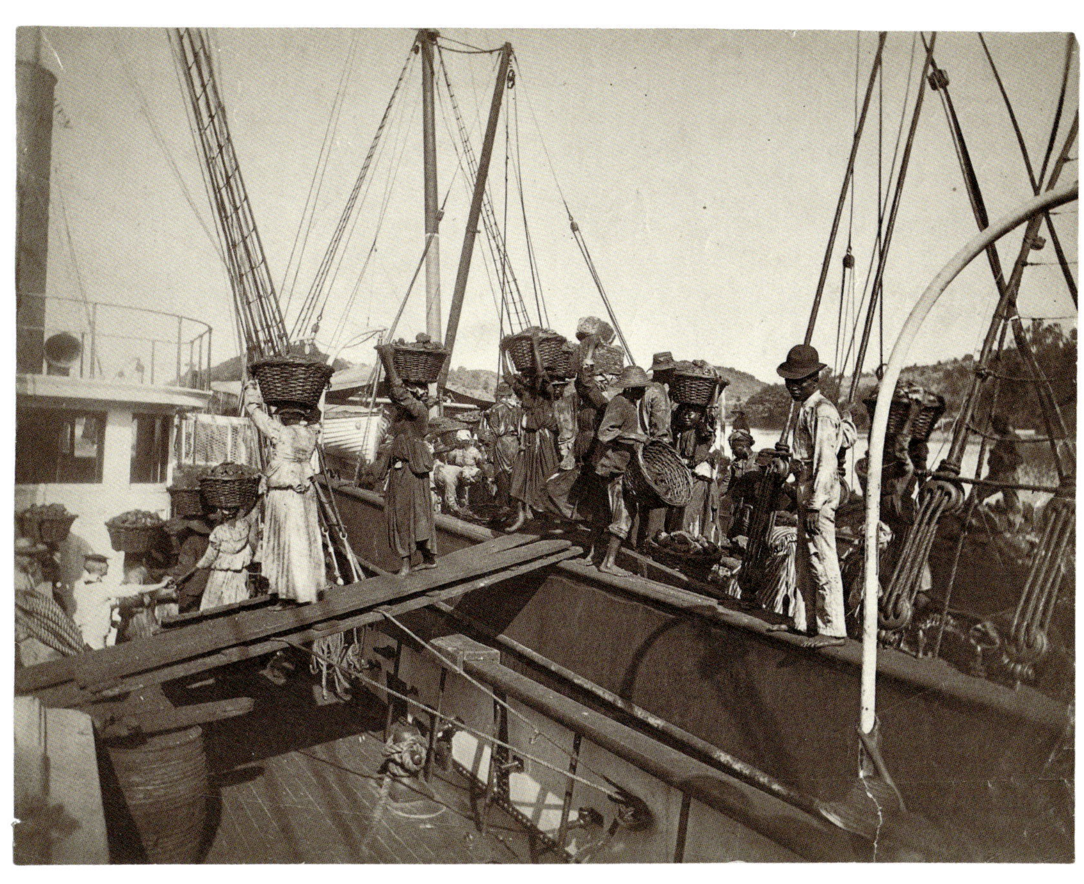

Unknown photographer, *Coaling The Albatross, St. Lucia,* after 1882

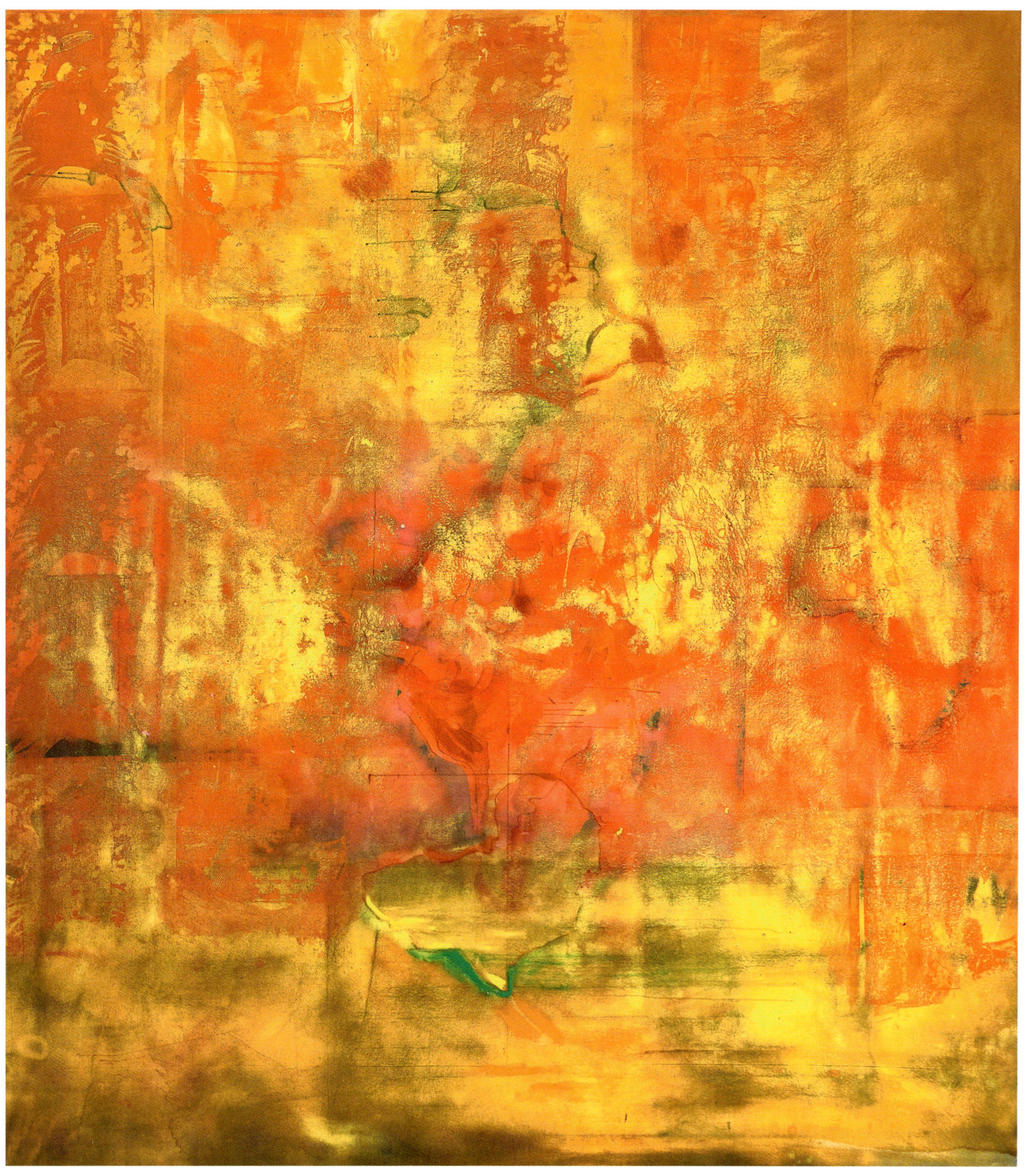

Sir Frank Bowling, *Middle Passage*, 1970

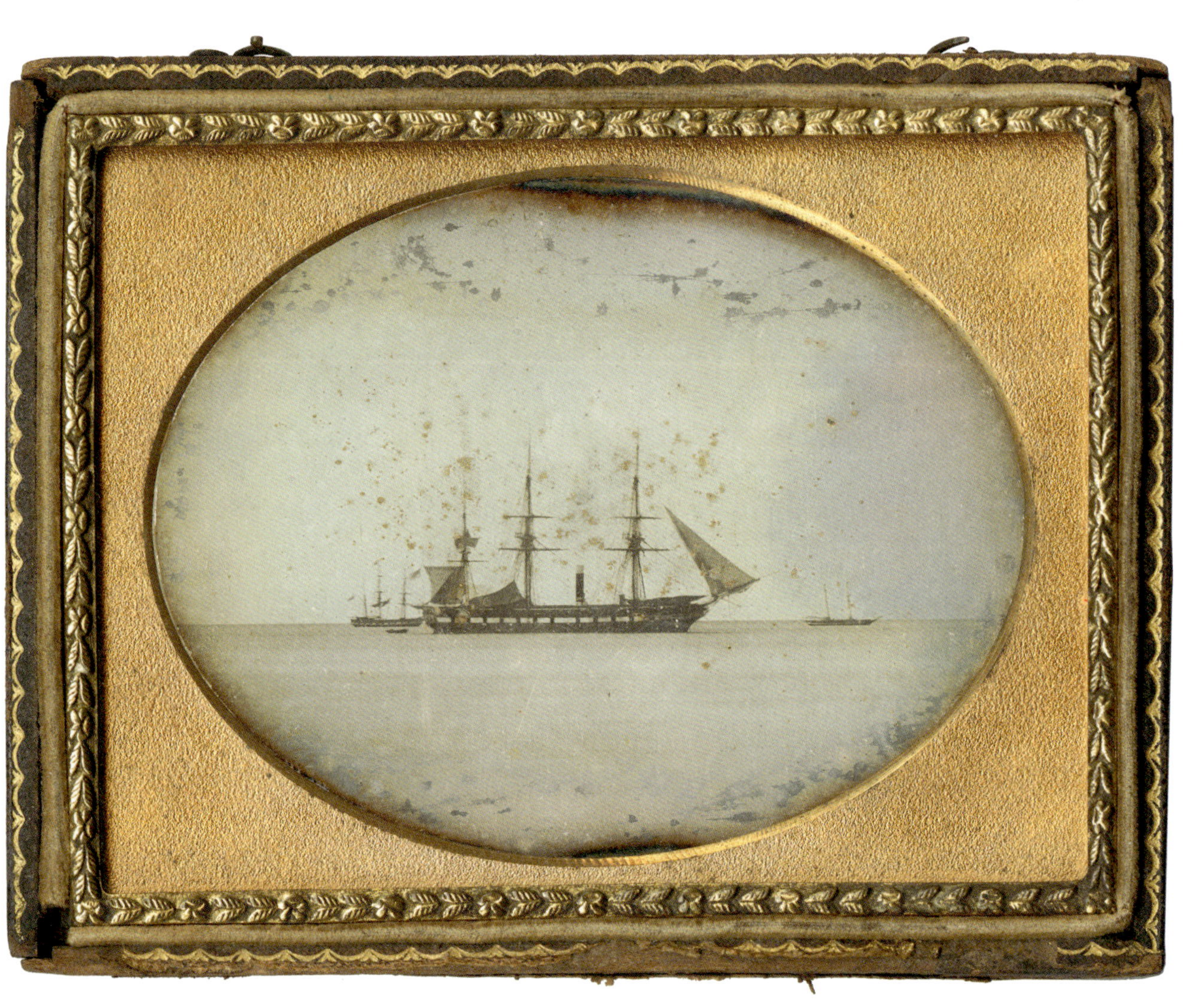

W.H. Freeman, *H.M.S. Dauntless in Quarantine for Yellow Fever Outbreak*, 1853

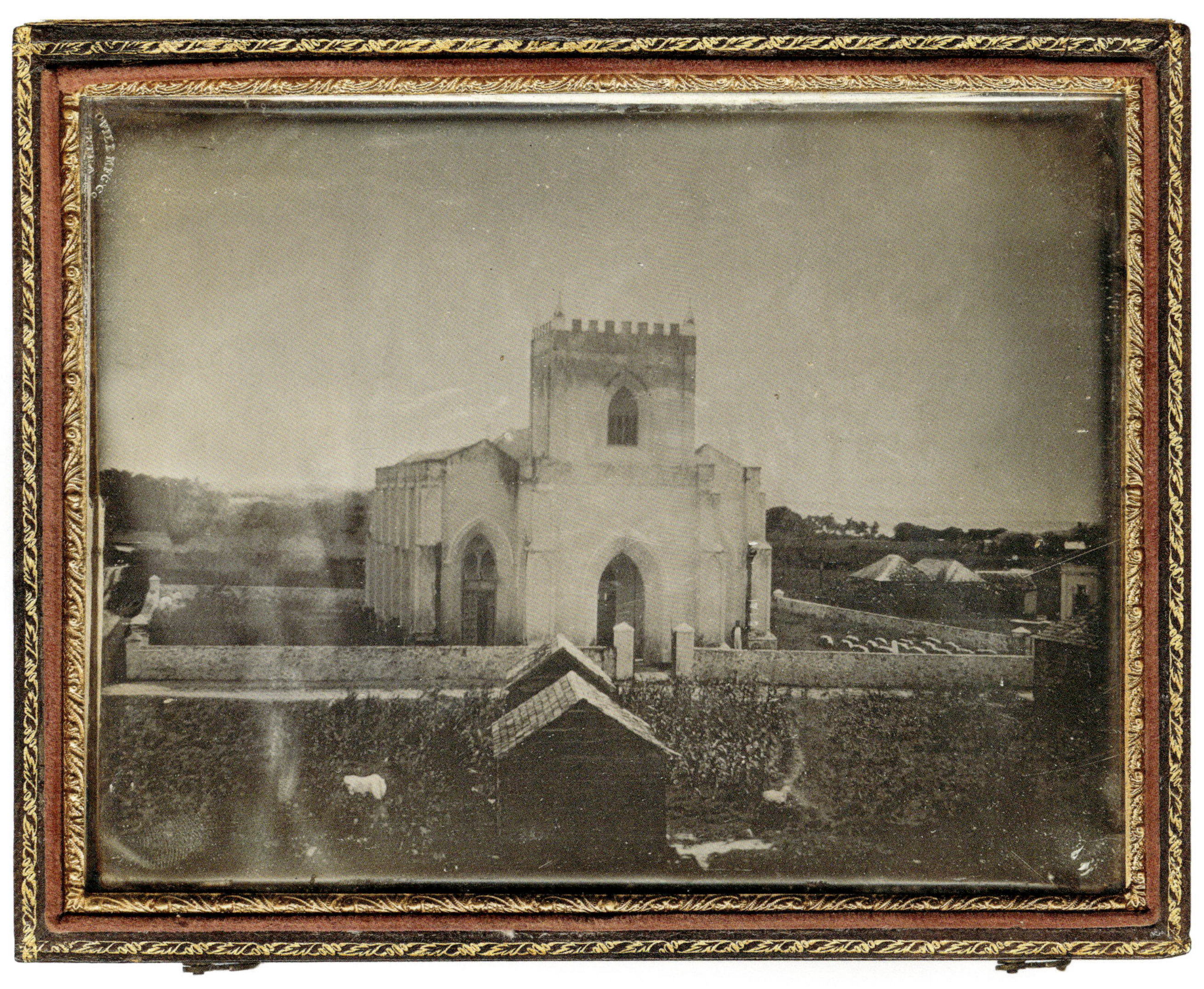

W.H. Freeman, *Church of St. Matthias, Barbados*, 1853

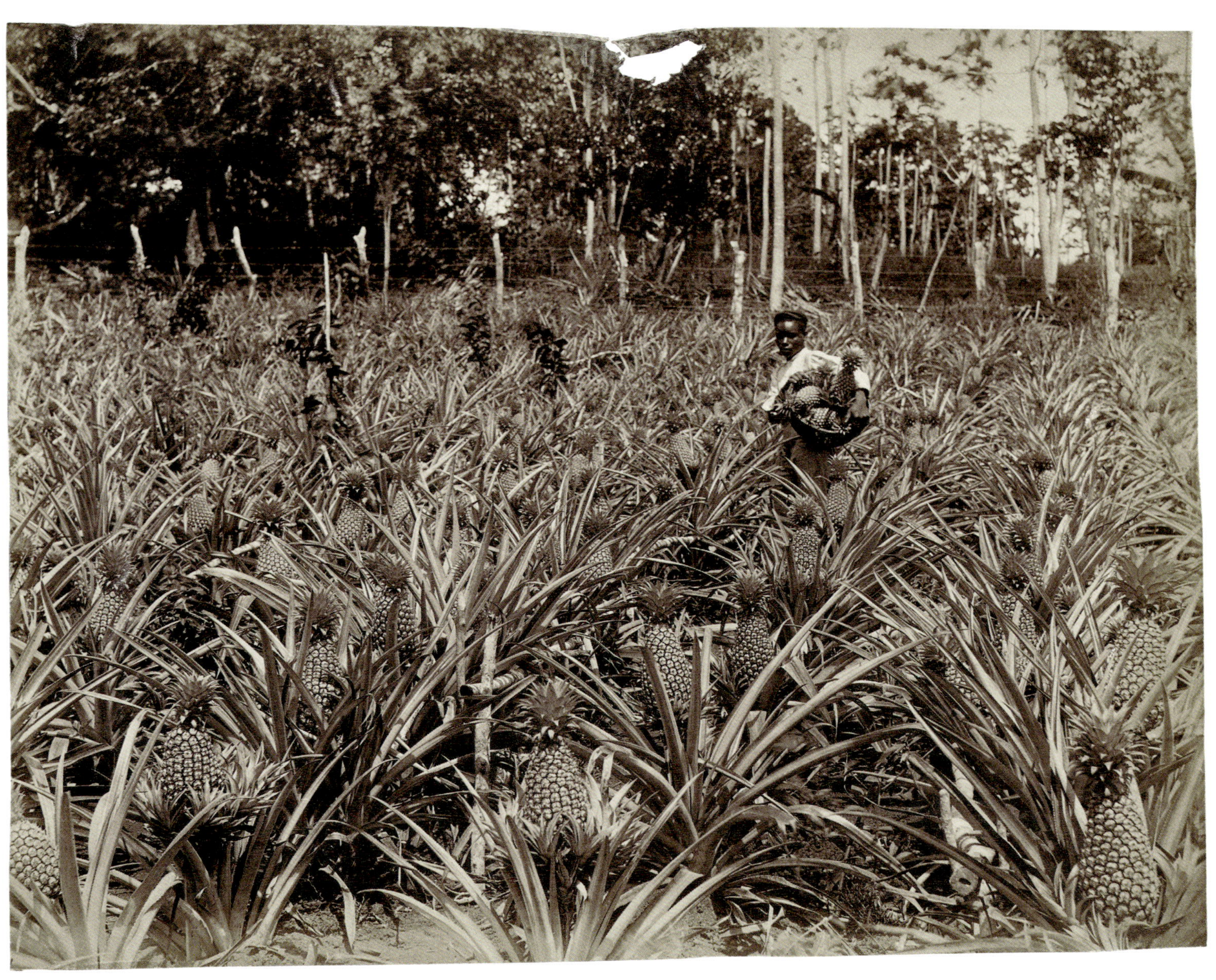

Reverend Dr. James Johnston, *Pineapple Field*, c. 1890

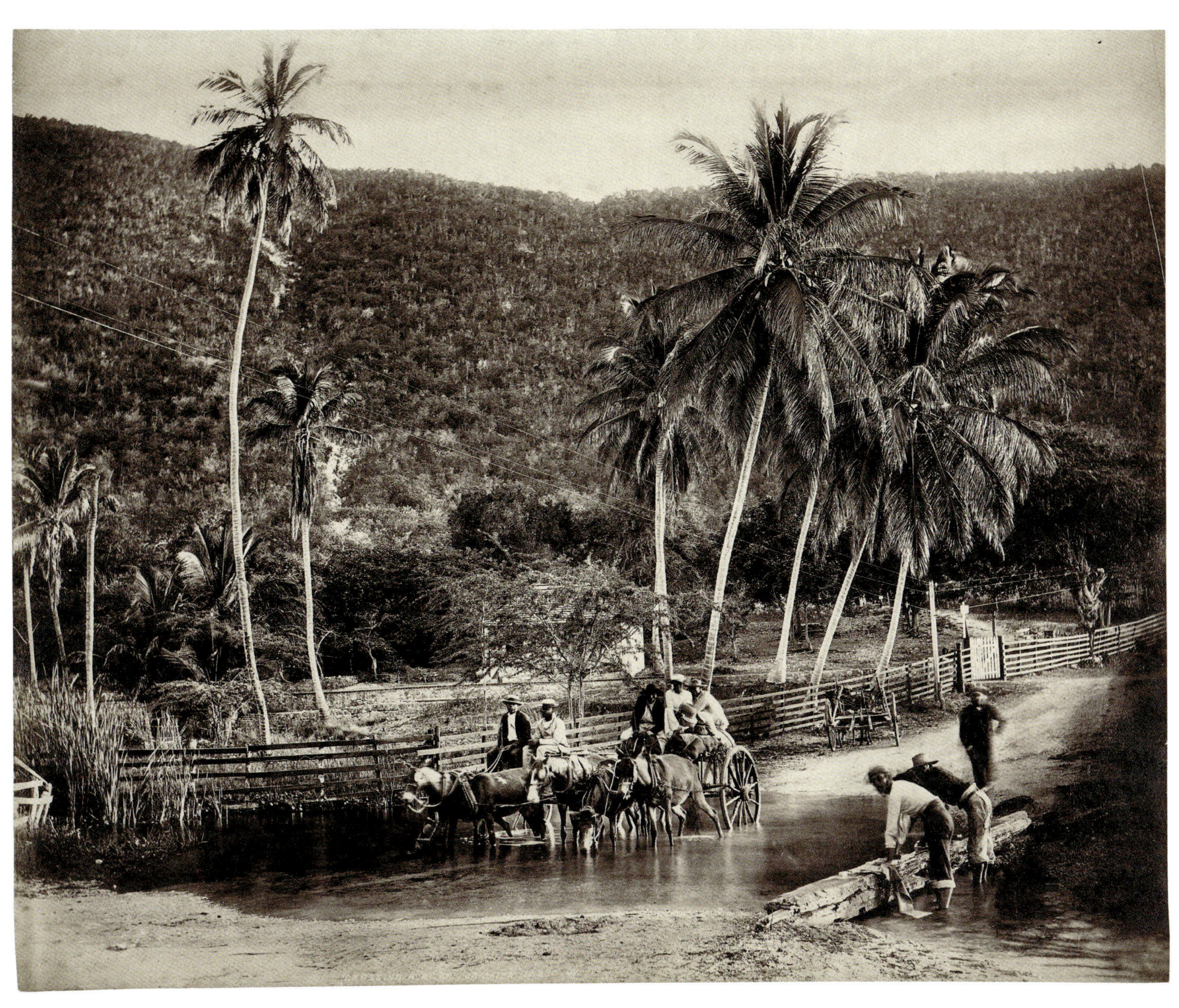

J. Valentine & Sons, *Crossing a River*, 1891

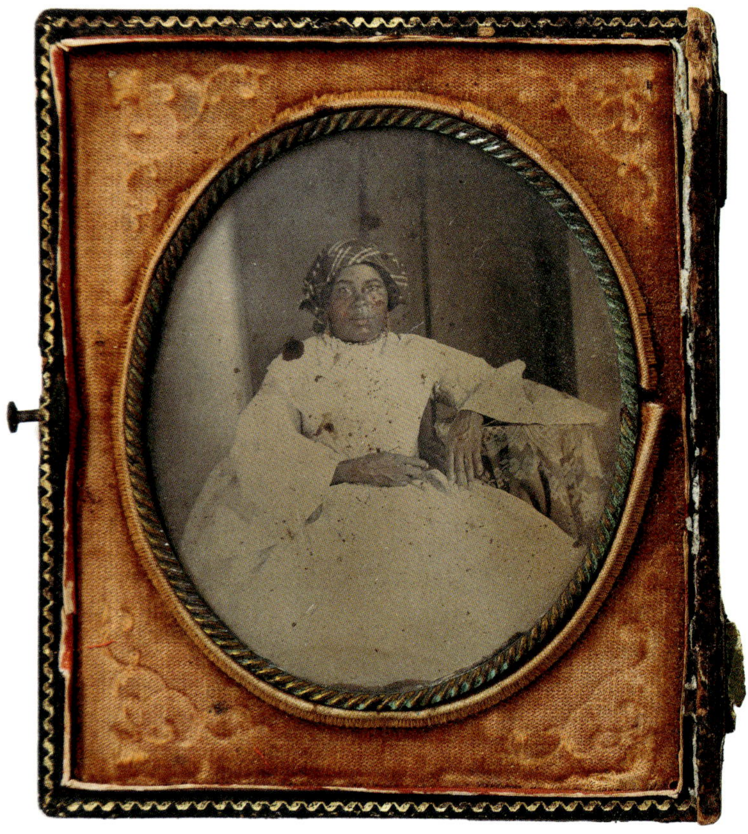

Unknown photographer, *Portrait of a Lady*, 1850s–1860s

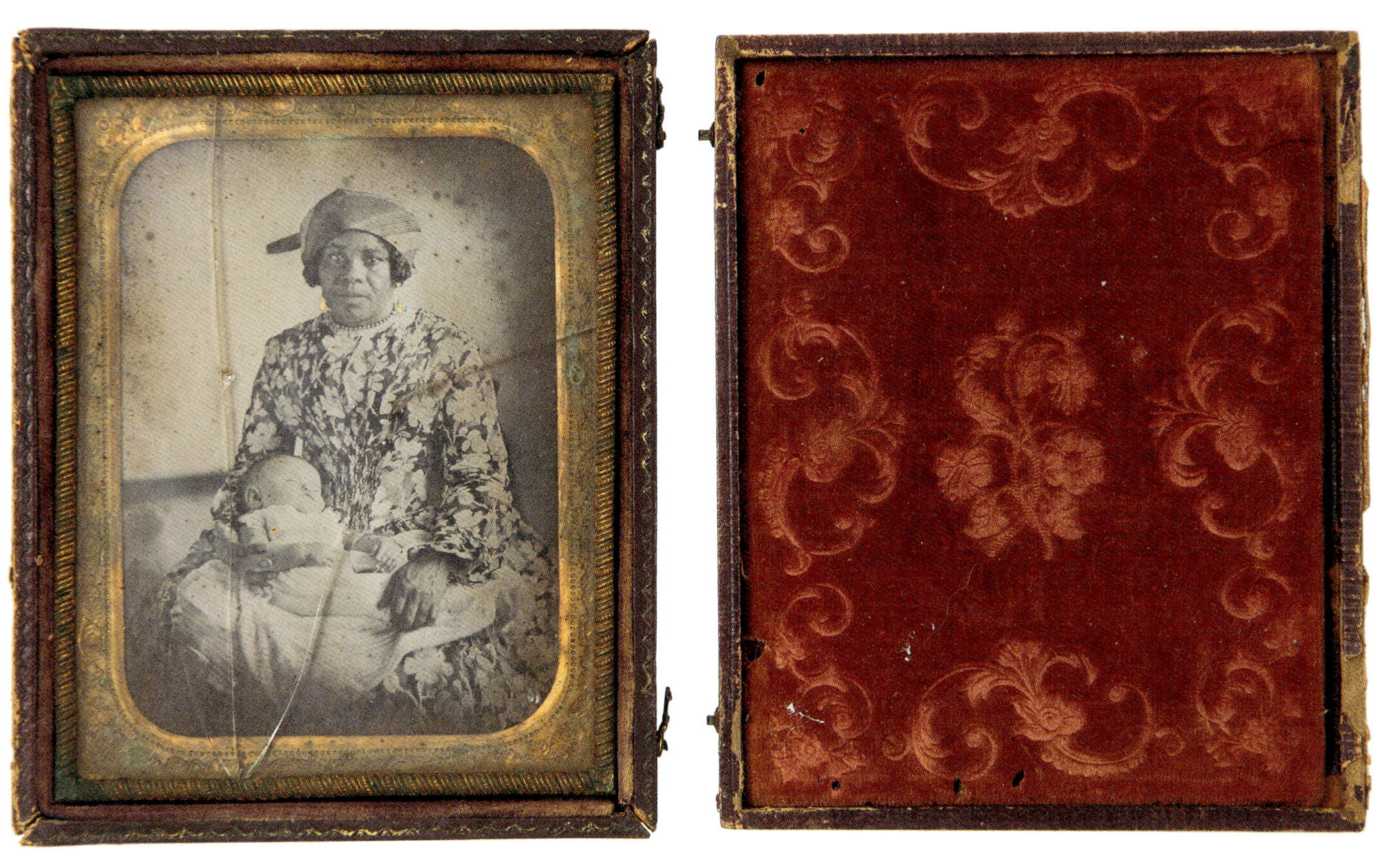

Unknown photographer, *Harriette Thomas Weekes, nurse with her infant charge,* c. 1858

Photography in the City of Bridgetown: The Nineteenth Century

Harclyde Walcott

In the Saturday November 20, 1841 issue of the "Barbadian Newspaper" the following advertisement appeared:

"Daguerreotype likenesses.
JAMES D. BILLINGE, M.D.
(of London, late of New York)
Respectfully announces to the Ladies and Gentlemen of Barbados, that he is now prepared to take Photographic Likenesses by the Daguerreotype process.

It would be impossible accurately to describe within the short limits of an advertisement, the truly ingenious and beautiful art of M. Daguerre, upon which all the literary journals of Europe and America for the last three years have abounded with notices of its rapid advancement; it may however be remarked that it has now arrived at such perfection as enables the operator to produce a perfect likeness in the extraordinary short period of thirty seconds, and at a very moderate experience.

Specimens will be exhibited to visitors at the Picture Gallery (late the residence of John Hayes, Esq. Deceased)

Hours of attendance from 10 am to 4 pm
November 20-3n."

This is the earliest advertisement of photography in Bridgetown and by extension, Barbados. For quite some time it has been thought that the starting point of the documented history of photography in Barbados was located in the "Barbados Globe" advertisement of February 5, 1852 in which Mr. J. W. H. Campion advertises his services at #19, James Street. In fact all the texts on photography in Barbados have used this date as their earliest referenced start point.

The Campion advertisement in full reads:

"J. W. H. Campion begs respectfully to
announce to his former friends
and patrons and the public generally
his return to the island and his intention
during his stay to take portraits and views at
the reduced price of one dollar and upwards.
He assures those who may be desirous
Of giving him their support
That every means will be taken
To ensure faithful and correct likenesses.

Rooms at #19 James Street, opposite Mr. R. W. Campion's Gold and Silver Smith establishment.

Terms cash.
Feb 3, 1852"

The evidence currently available suggests that the history of photography in Barbados does in fact begin with Dr. James D. Billinge, M.D. and this, his November 20, 1841, advertisement. This is not to suggest that there may not have been individuals who may have had their photographs, (and one uses photograph here in its generic sense), taken while abroad and may have in fact brought these photographs back with them to Barbados or that photographs may not have brought or sent to Barbados. But rather that the probability is very high that it was the goodly doctor who in fact began the actual practice of photography in Barbados, and took the first photographs in Barbados.

The advertisement in essence announces the arrival of a modern, advanced and refined technique and indeed technology to Barbados. The fact that the author of the advertisement, who we must assume to have been Dr. Billinge, although it could equally have been the then editor of the "Barbadian Newspaper," Abel Clinkett, indicates that "it would be impossible accurately to describe within the short limits of an advertisement," suggests that the author's perception is that there is only a limited familiarity with the process in the country. The advertisement certainly reads as if he is introducing a process that the population may have heard about, quite possibly some may have read about, but none would have in fact experienced in the island.

Additionally, one takes note of the fact the advertisement is addressed respectfully to the "ladies and gentlemen of Bridgetown," and infers from this mode of address, given the norms of the period, to whom the advertisement is targeted. The reference to lady and gentleman during the period is quite specific and refers essentially to those who are of the landed families, those who have social standing, status and wealth. The vast majority of the formerly enslaved, now very recently freed members of the population are not during this period generally allowed the implied dignity of this appellation.

However, the advertisement on its own, though useful, does not provide the "proof positive" for the claim. That proof one finds located in an editorial comment in the "Bridgetown section" of the "Barbadian Newspaper", of Wednesday November 17, 1841. Here one reads:

"The Daguerreotype

This extraordinary, highly interesting, and novel discovery in science, the taking of the most inevitably exact likenesses in the most speedy manner through the medium of rays of light, is about to be brought before the notice of the public by Dr. Billinge, a gentleman who has lately arrived from America. We have frequently read explanations of and allusions to this singular process of photographic likeness taking, and are extremely glad that an opportunity is now offered to the public of becoming practically acquainted with the Daguerreotype. Dr. Billinge promises much, and has already been led to expect considerable encouragement, especially as the expenses of it are so low, as to enable persons generally, to participate in the advantages he holds out to them. Notice of his intentions will in due time appear—meanwhile we recommend him to the notice of the public."

And so it is, that with this editorial common the art and science of the daguerreotype, as well as the Dr. Billinge, are introduced to the public. This editorial comment therefore represents the first mention in the Barbadian press of a practitioner in Barbados.

The practice of image making, called photography, was announced to the world on January 7, 1839, and is now widely accepted to have been in fact invented at least twice, in England by William Henry Fox Talbot (1800-1877) and in France by Louis Jacques Mande Daguerre, (1787-1851) separately, using different techniques. It is of some significance that shortly thereafter a studio opens in Bridgetown.

The daguerreotype is a "highly detailed image formed on a sheet of copper very thinly plated with silver," the result of the reaction of vapors from heated mercury with exposed silver iodide. Daguerreotypes are very vulnerable to chemical and physical damage and for this reason, carry a backing made of a metallic material and a covering of glass all sealed in an air tight fashion with tape and is usually presented in a case of some kind. The daguerreotype was a "unique image and if another copy was needed, the whole process had to be redone." It was a highly time-consuming process, with the individual who is sitting to be photographed having to remain still for extended periods of time, because the process required very long exposure times, in some cases thirty minutes or more.

These ambrotypes (plates 1 and 2) are in all, except one way, highly representative of the photography of the period, the exception having to do with the fact that the frequency of the in-studio portrait of the individual of color is low.

Ambrotypes are much like daguerreotypes, and are presented in a similar fashion, but are processed in a different way. In the second ambrotype (plate 2), the highlights are "soft and pearly" rather than crisp, and high levels of reflection are also absent. Principally because ambrotypes were easier and less expensive to produce, they quickly replaced the daguerreotype in popularity.

Both methods were used in Bridgetown, principally for in studio portraiture. One must be cognizant of the fact that the camera did not go outdoors until much later, largely because of the relatively unsophisticated nature of the technology of the time. For this reason the in studio posed portrait, usually of the individual, is the photographic representation that is characteristic of the period.

In these images one is immediately struck by the dignity of their sense of personhood, by the centredness and confidence evident in the way they look into the lens. The preciseness of dress is also another indicator, and even "the poser's" less than flattering work, which results in the awkwardness of the arms and hands has not been able to rob them of their inherent dignity.

In the pioneering days of the art, the whole business of fixing the individual in a specific pose was very important and in fact became thought of as an art in itself, and the practitioner responsible, usually the photographer's assistant, was designated "the poser." One should not underestimate the importance of this individual and the role he played in the early days of photography, for very often it was he who was responsible for the quality of the look of naturalness or lack there of, that we see in the photograph.

Excerpted from "Photography in the City of Bridgetown: The Nineteenth Century," Journal of the Barbados Museum and Historical Society 49 *(November 2003): 219–253.*

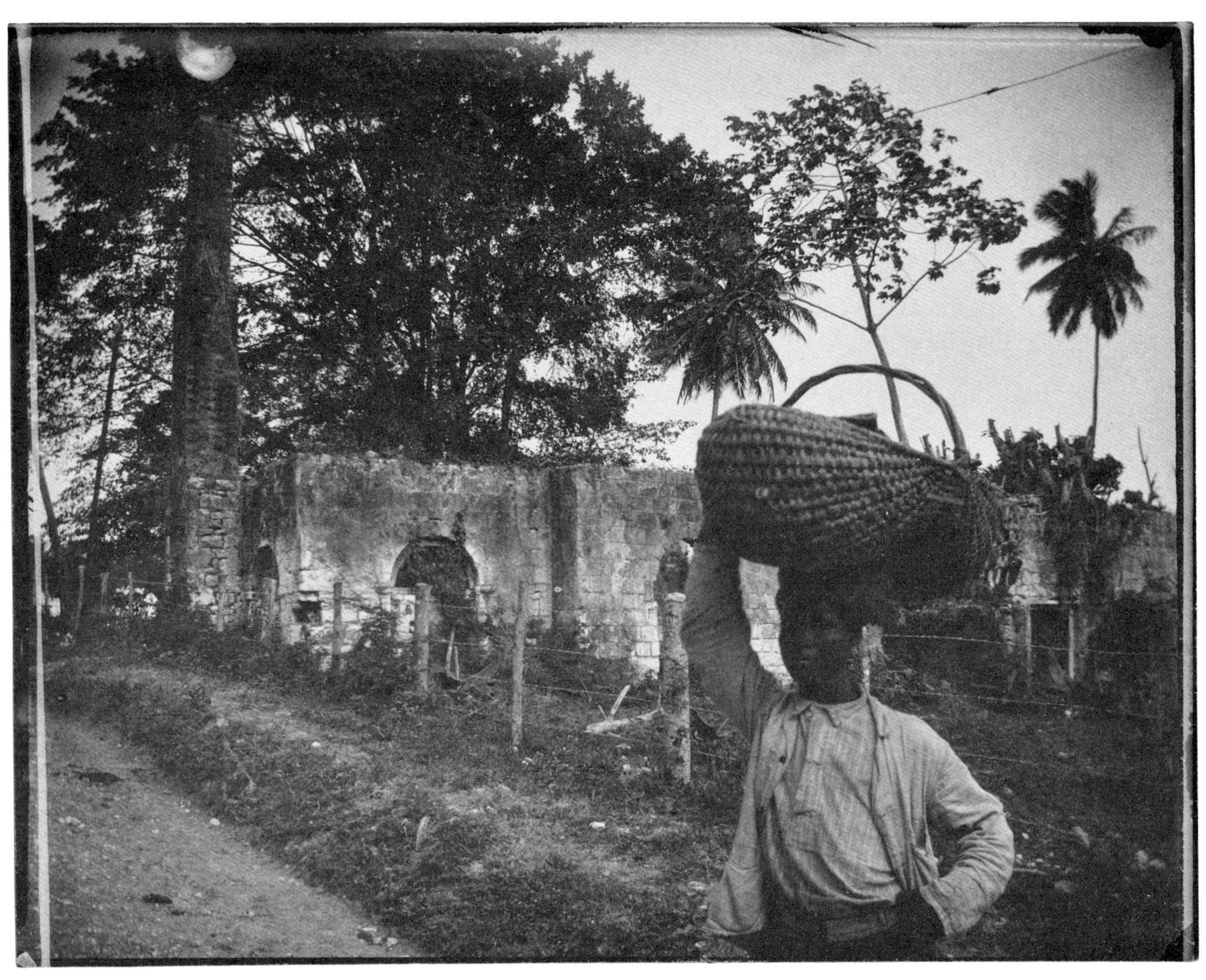

Unknown photographer, *Woman with Basket on Head,* c. 1895

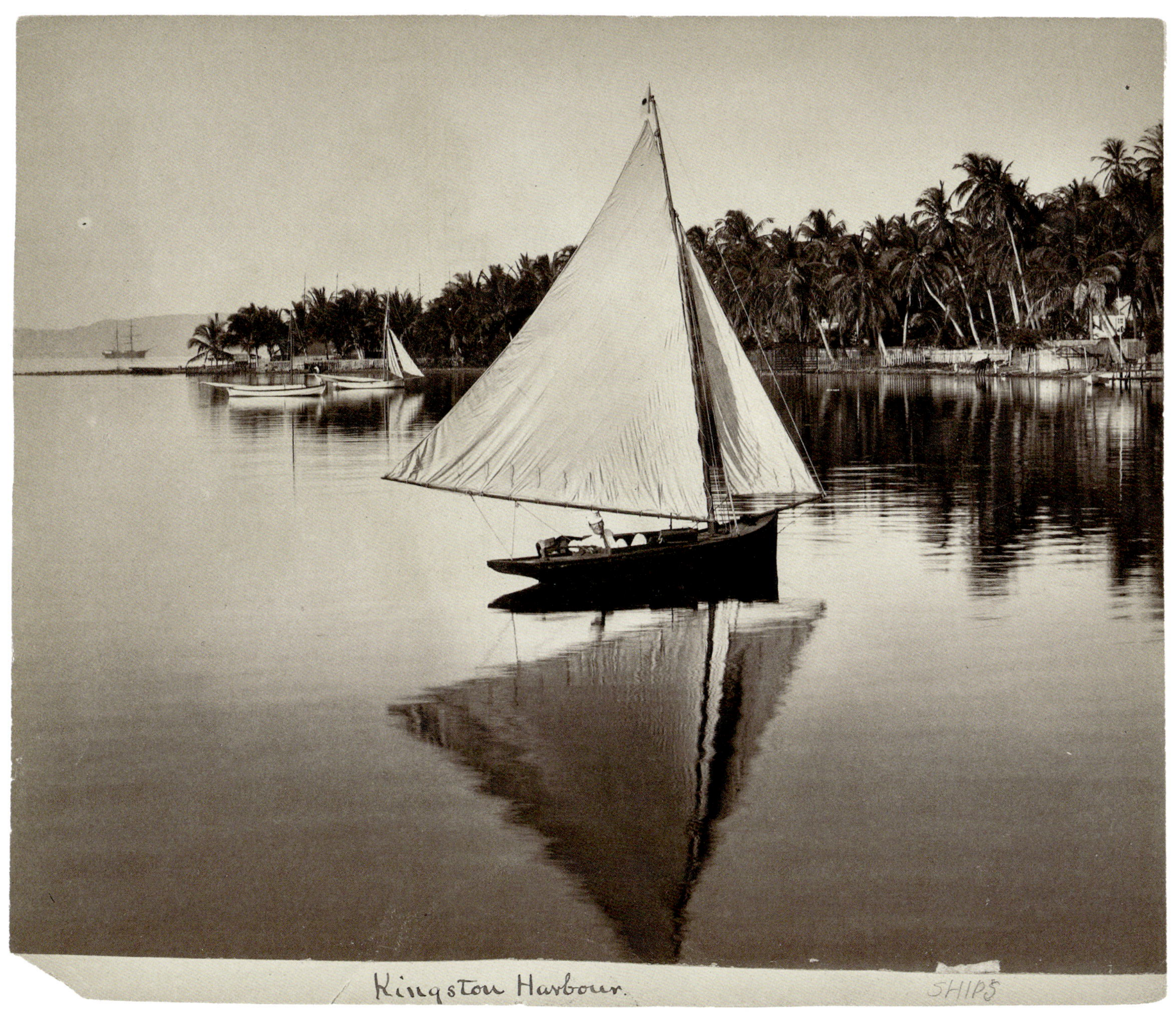

J. Valentine & Sons, *A Bit in Kingston Harbor*, 1891

Andrea Chung, *A Litany for Survival*, 2019

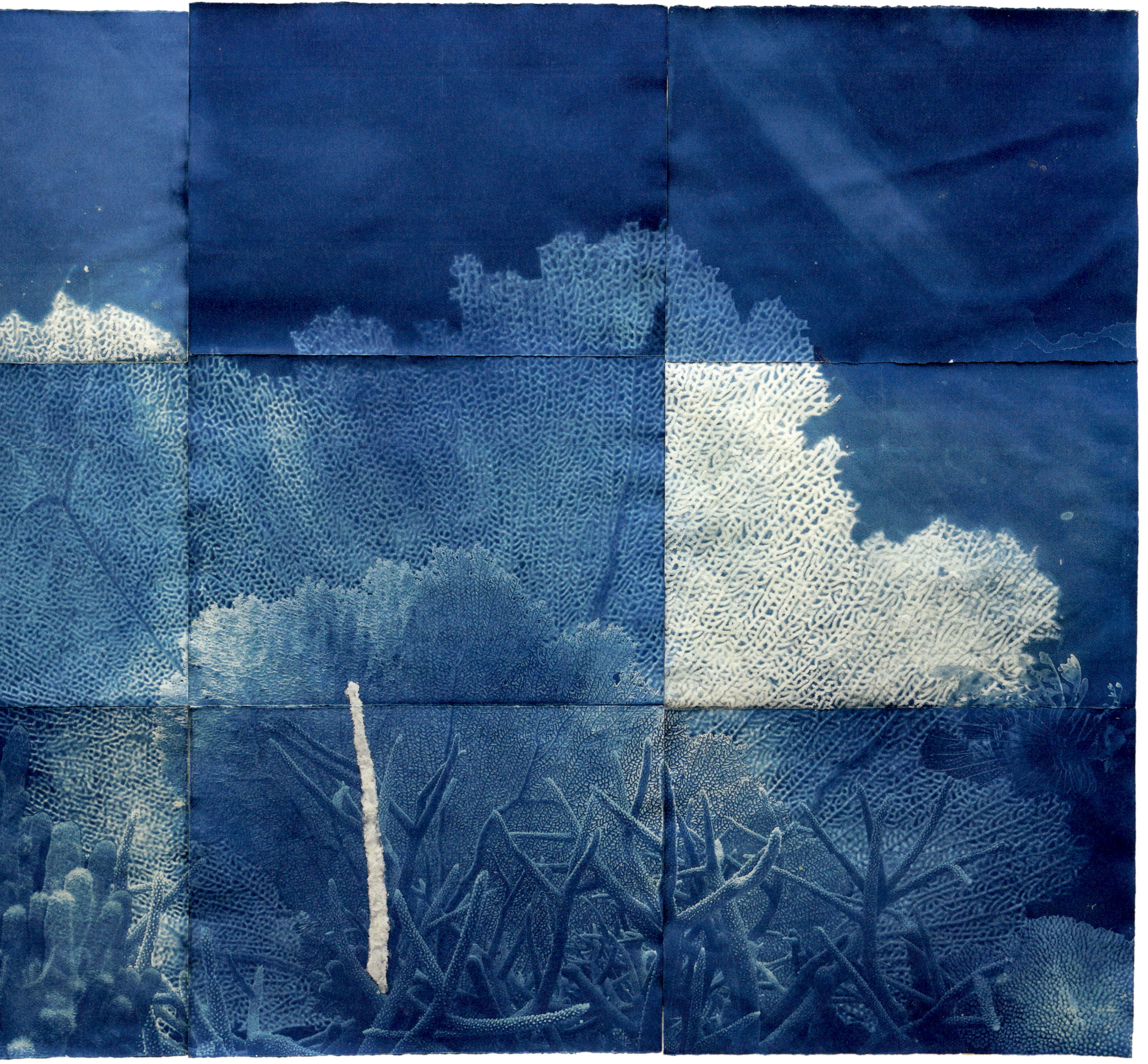

They Came in Ships

Mahadai Das

They came in ships.

From across the seas, they came.
Britain, colonising India, transporting her chains
from Chota Nagpur and the Ganges Plain.

Westwards came the Whitby,
The Hesperus,
the Island-bound Fatel Rozack.

Wooden missions of imperialist design.
Human victims of her Majesty's victory.

They came in fleets.
They came in droves
like cattle
brown like cattle,
eyes limpid, like cattle.

Some came with dreams of milk-and-honey riches,
fleeing famine and death:
dancing girls,
Rajput soldiers, determined, tall,
escaping penalty of pride.
Stolen wives, afraid and despondent,
crossing black waters,
Brahmin, Chammar, alike,
hearts brimful of hope.

I saw them dying at streetcorners, alone, hungry
for a crumb of British bread,
and a healing hand's mighty touch.
I recall my grandfather's haunting gaze;
my eye sweeps over history
to my children, unborn
I recall the piracy of innocence,
light snuffed like a candle in their eyes.

I alone today am alive.

I remember logies, barrackrooms, ranges,
nigga-yards. My grandmother worked in the field.
Honourable mention.

Creole gang, child labour.
Second prize.
I recall Lallabhagie, Leonora's strong children,
and Enmore, bitter, determined.

Remember one-third quota, coolie woman.
Was your blood spilled so I might reject my history –
forget tears among the paddy leaves.

At the horizon's edge, I hear
voices crying in the wind. Cuffy shouting:
'Remember 1763!' – John Smith – 'If I am
a man of God, let me join with suffering.'
Akkara – 'I too had a vision.'

Des Voeux cried,
'I wrote the queen a letter,
for the whimpering of the coolies in logies
would not let me rest.'
The cry of coolies echoed round the land.
They came, in droves, at his office door
beseeching him to ease their yoke.

Crosby struck in rage against planters,
in vain. Stripped of rights, he heard
the cry of coolies continue.

Commissioners came,
capital spectacles in British frames
consulting managers about costs of immigration.
The commissioners left, fifty-dollar bounty remained.
Dreams of a cow and endless calves,
and endless reality in chains.

Indent-ureship and the Art of Speculation

Andil Gosine

1

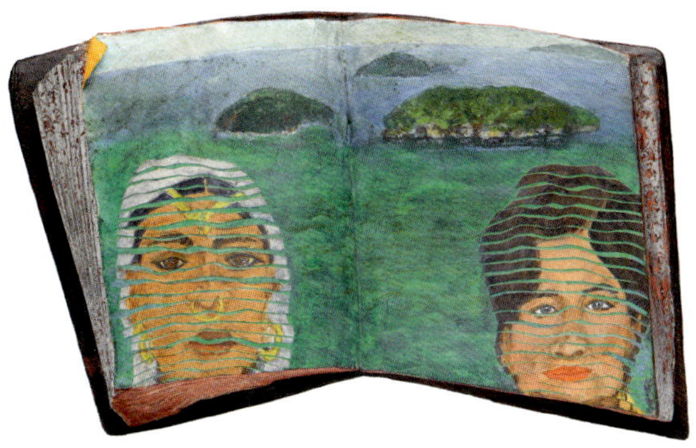

Fig. 1
Wendy Nanan
Nelson Island, 2012.
Papier-mâché and acrylic, 30.48 × 53.34 × 106.68 cm.
Courtesy of the artist.
© Wendy Nanan; Nelson Island, 2012. Photo: Art Gallery of Ontario.

Nelson Island (2012, fig. 1), Wendy Nanan's papier-mâché sculpture, is named for her ancestors' likely first point of disembarkation when they arrived in Trinidad, sometime between 1845 and 1917. They were brought to the Caribbean at a critical juncture in the region's history. As revolts by enslaved people and abolitionist efforts gained traction in the early nineteenth century, British colonial traders looked to a new system of exploitative labour that could maintain the same levels of production, profiteering, and power that slavery had permitted them. Under this new scheme called *indentureship*, "free" labourers would be contracted over several years for low wages and with restrictive conditions of movement. Workers were sourced from Portugal, Ireland, China, Sierra Leone, and other places touched by colonial expansion and trade. In 1826, Mauritius became the first British colony to indenture Indian migrants. On January 13, 1838, eight months before enslaved peoples would become recognized as free persons across the British empire, the *Whitby* set off from a port in Calcutta, and 112 days later, its surviving 244 passengers landed in then–British Guiana as the Caribbean's first Indian indentured workers. By 1917 hundreds of thousands more Indian workers were brought to the region, including to Trinidad, where, as in Guyana, their descendants now constitute the largest ethnic demographic. Indentured workers were also taken by deceit, force, or choice to Jamaica, Suriname, St. Kitts, St. Vincent, St. Lucia, and Grenada, as well as to the French colonies Martinique and Guadeloupe.

Indian migrants arriving to Trinidad usually first disembarked at Nelson Island, located at its northwestern tip. There, they would remain quarantined for a short period of time and inspected by the so-called Protector of Immigrants, in an effort to stop transmission of diseases that might have been brought from Asia, and to give them time to regain strength from the punishing ship journey. Their few possessions, usually wrapped in jahaji bundles, cloth sacks attached to walking sticks, were also subject to inspection and sterilization. Recovered migrants who were deemed healthy were then taken to plantations on the main island. "I have visited Nelson Island a few times," Nanan says, "you feel [this] history when you go there, even though it's quite a different place now."[1] In her sculpture, the figure on the left is presented as many indentured women were pictured, wearing an orhni headscarf and jewellery. On the right is the recognizable face of Kamla Persad-Bissessar, also a descendant of indentured workers, who was elected as Trinidad and Tobago's first woman prime minister in 2010. "I remember on the day after Kamla won the election, I shared a smile with a stranger in town," Nanan recalls. "It was from another Indian woman I had not seen before... we were acknowledging our past suffering and where we now reach. With Kamla's win, we had irrefutably claimed our space on this land. It was a moment of shared quiet pride and self-belief."

The book form of *Nelson Island* is about time. "We are like images rippling, from the past, present and future, in a constant sea. How could that weary immigrant woman [on the left], leaving her past behind, clutching her jahaji bundle, arriving in a strange land after a perilous voyage, how could she ever have imagined, stepping onto that island that one day one of her descendants would be the head of that country's government?" Nanan is a trailblazer herself, recognized as Trinidad's first professional Indo-Caribbean woman artist. Critically lauded for her papier-mâché sculptures and figure-drawing practice, in 2020 she also became the first Caribbean woman to have a solo retrospective exhibition at the Art Museum of the Americas, in Washington, DC.

The book is also a nod to the erasure of indentured workers' narratives, and Nanan's own attempt to fill in the missing pages of her history. Records of indentured workers' experiences are thin and poorly kept. Often the wrong details about age and origin were noted in logbooks, and names were misspelled—in some cases, changed by the migrants themselves for a variety of reasons including to resist the shackles of caste. Consequently, as is true for enslaved African peoples, many family histories are untraceable. The invisibilization of indentured workers' history and their and their descendants' contributions to the making of the modern Caribbean also did not end with colonial rule, and scholars and creatives continue to challenge the disregard of their stories and cultures from formal institutional renderings of the region. Poet-philosopher Khal Torabully, for example, through his conceptualization of *coolitude* (after Aimé Césaire's *négritude*), challenges the dominant theorization of the Caribbean as a hybrid creole space comprising European, African, and (sometimes) Indigenous cultures, and argues for recognition of the long and substantial engagement of Asians in producing the region.

"There is a big part of my history I know nothing about," confesses painter Kelly Sinnapah Mary from her home studio in Saint François, Guadeloupe. "Growing up, I don't remember anyone speaking about my ancestors, not at school, not even at home. That absence grew heavy, and at some point I had to confront it." Sinnapah Mary's ancestors were likely among the thousands of mostly Tamils who were brought to Guadeloupe in 1861, but she can't be sure. Because a great deal of shame was also attached to indentureship, as expressed by the use of the intentionally pejorative *coolie* moniker used to name labourers, family histories were often not passed down between parents and children. Language itself was lost. Sometimes, stories were embellished. It is not uncommon, for example, to hear Indo-Caribbean people exceptionalize themselves as not having indentured ancestors.

2

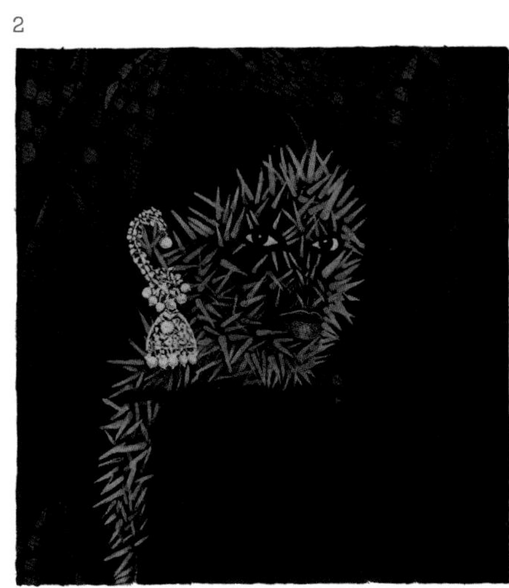

Fig. 2
Kelly Sinnapah Mary
***Notebook of No Return*,**
2017. Acrylic on paper, 50.8 × 43.2 cm. Private collection. © Kelly Sinnapah Mary. Photo: Art Gallery of Ontario.

To fill in the blanks of her history, Sinnapah Mary turned to images—some of them not unlike the ones that constitute the Montgomery Collection of Caribbean Photographs, which provided the basis for the exhibition *Fragments of Epic Memory* (2021). "I constituted an 'iconography bank' of old family photos, postcards, and other types of images representing Indian women [during the period of indentureship], women in families, in Indian costumes or with Indian objects, images of worship," she says, "they all fed my imagination." All of the paintings the artist produced from this series share the same title, *Notebook of No Return* (2017, fig. 2), a recasting of Aimé Césaire's landmark text that underlines the impossibility of successful fact finding. Explaining the portrait of an imagined Indian ancestor from the series that is included in the *Fragments* exhibition, Sinnapah Mary suggests that the heritage of indentureship is complex. "I wanted the characters in this series to be ghostly and monstrous," she says, "straight out of the depths of black waters, while borrowing their thorns from the white sea urchins. I also wanted them to be healers, but with a very human and gentle gaze at the same time."

Guyanese American visual artist Suchitra Mattai similarly turned to archival images to investigate her own history. Mattai was three years old when her family left Guyana in 1977, first for Nova Scotia and eventually going to the United States, where she now lives. "I realized I couldn't even go searching [in the archives]," she says, "because 'Mattai' is a made-up last name." Her foggy memories of Guyana as "green" and "lush" appear as the tropical fabric print in mixed media painting *Demerara Dreams* (2019, fig. 3), but its other elements, including her self-portrait and an attached piece of her mother's sari, are drawn from Polaroid portraits in her family album. Mattai describes how she sees the images of indentured women that appear in her work: "I have looked at a lot of those photographs and of course they are problematic. We see the way white photographers view the arriving migrants, not the way they see themselves." Her engagement with this archive was to usurp its original intentions, she says. "I wanted the figures in my portraits to have agency."

To create her 2004 interactive digital series *Ghosting* (2004, fig. 4), scholar-artist Roshini Kempadoo drew on remnants of oral accounts, published documents, photographs, and maps to inform her reimagination of nineteenth and early twentieth-century Trinidad and create complex characters and stories. Kempadoo calls the Caribbean her "mythological home," a place where she spent formative teen years and that she has frequently returned to throughout her life. Her parents were part of the Windrush generation that moved to Britain in the 1950s, where she was born and has lived for most of her life. Her acute awareness of the malleable representations of the Caribbean that are produced, especially, from outside it is evident in her scholarly and artistic practice. Kempadoo uses the term *contiguous* to characterize the visual archives of the Caribbean. The contiguous Caribbean archive, she says, is "heterogeneous and contradictory, and not just the preserve of a single individual, state institution or private company,"[2] and is better viewed as a launchpad for investigation than as an arbiter of fact. Archival images, Kempadoo points out, "can do a disservice" by conveying particular constructions of a moment or period as universal fact. "The way I started reading against the grain of historical record is to ask 'what if…?' I use this 'what if' scenario [to ask about] 'this person who might have been present at a historical moment; how might we imagine this person?'" Rather than turn to historical visual material like the Montgomery Collection for definitive answers,

3

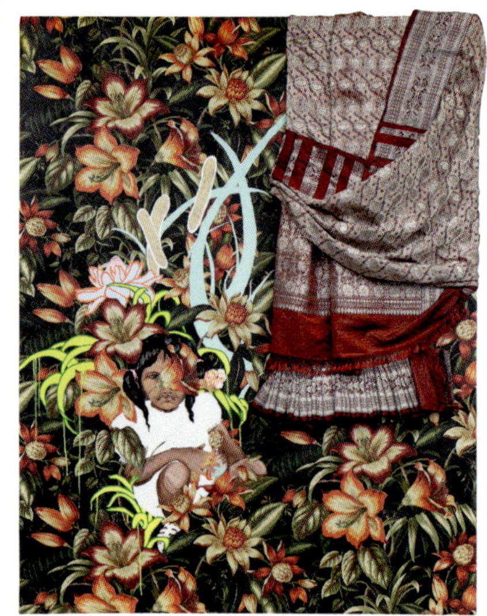

4

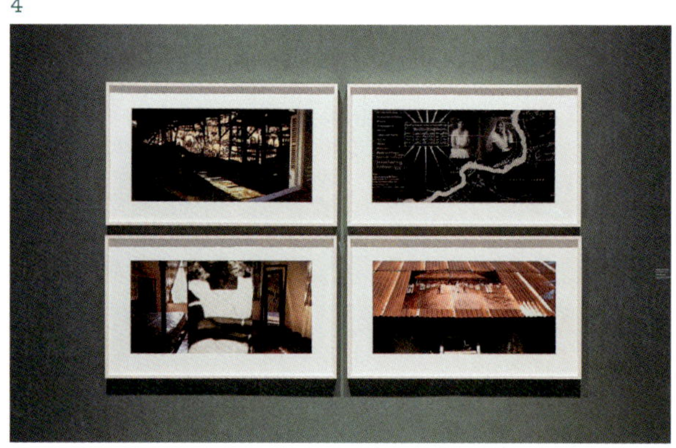

Fig. 3
Suchitra Mattai
Demerara Dreams, 2019.
Artist's mother's sari, gouache, acrylic, faux flower, and oil on printed fabric, 167.64 × 132.08 cm.
Courtesy of Paul and Heather Wilkinson.
© Suchitra Mattai.
Photo: Wes Magyar.

Fig. 4
Roshini Kempadoo
Ghosting, 2004. Set of four archival pigment prints; printed 2021, 77.47 × 127 cm.
Courtesy of the artist.
© Roshini Kempadoo.

Kempadoo says her approach is "to find characters that I can speculate from, and also read some interesting stories and interviews." The scenes shared in *Ghosting* are a result of "a speculative process that intercedes, interjects, and interferes with the archives," one which underlines the always-potential dynamism of the material. "The minute the archive is interpreted, it's a creative, imaginary act," she concludes.

1 Unless otherwise noted, all cited quotations are from interviews conducted with the artists by the author in 2020.

2 Roshini Kempadoo, *Creole in the Archive: Imagery, Presence and the Location of the Caribbean Figure* (Lanham, MD: Rowman & Littlefield, 2016), 5.

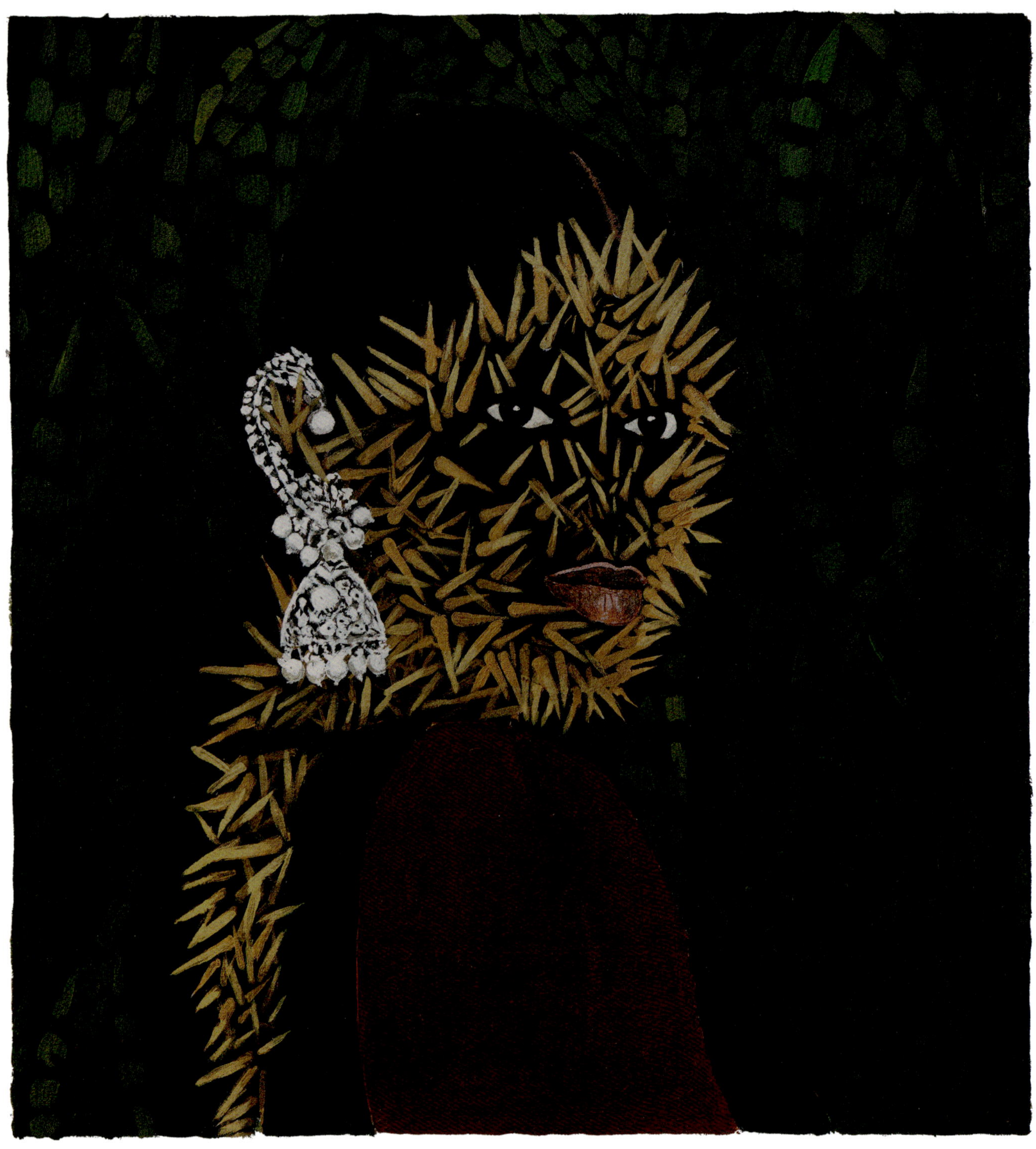

Kelly Sinnapah Mary, *Notebook of No Return*, 2017

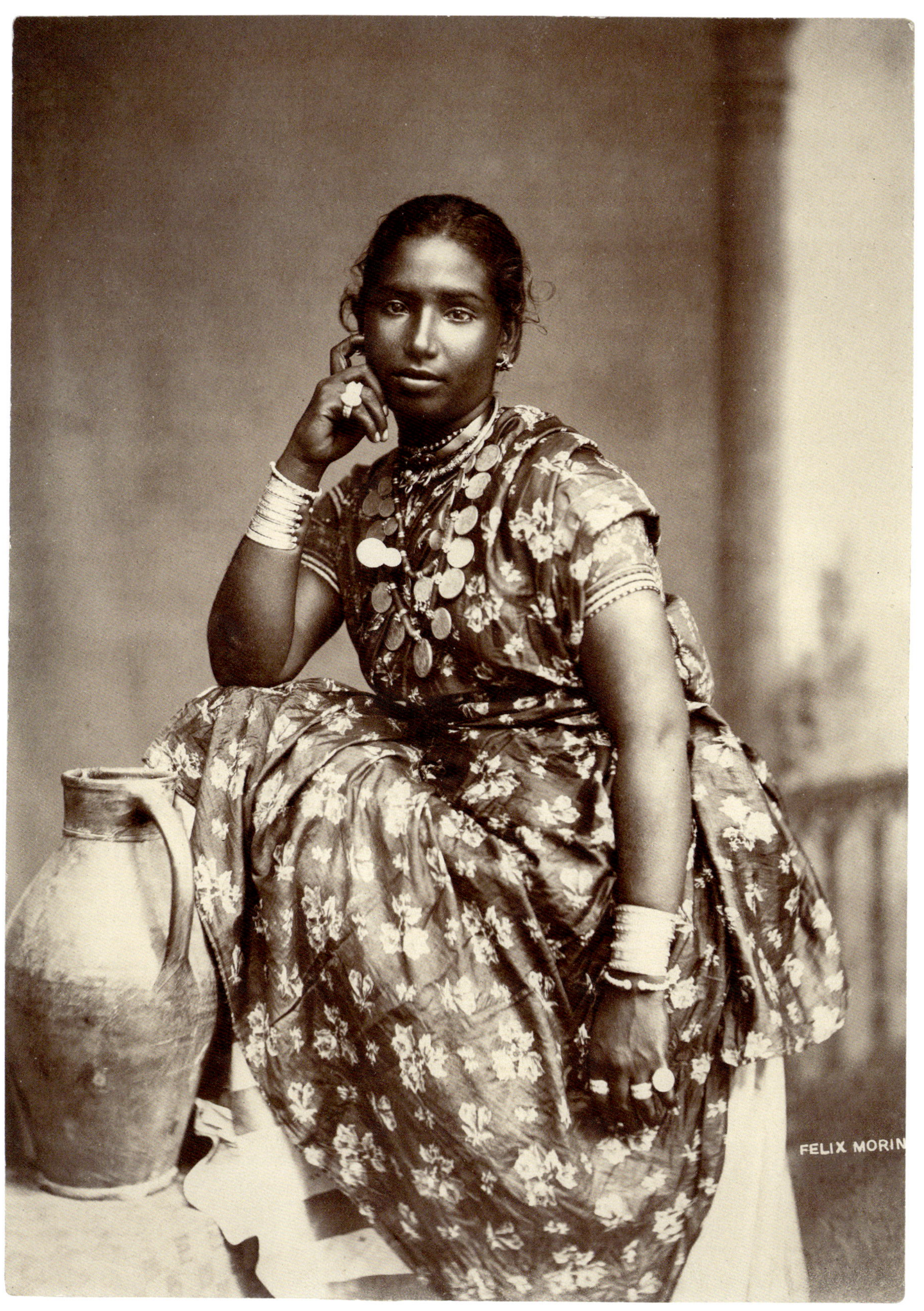

Felix Morin, *Woman, Trinidad,* c. 1890

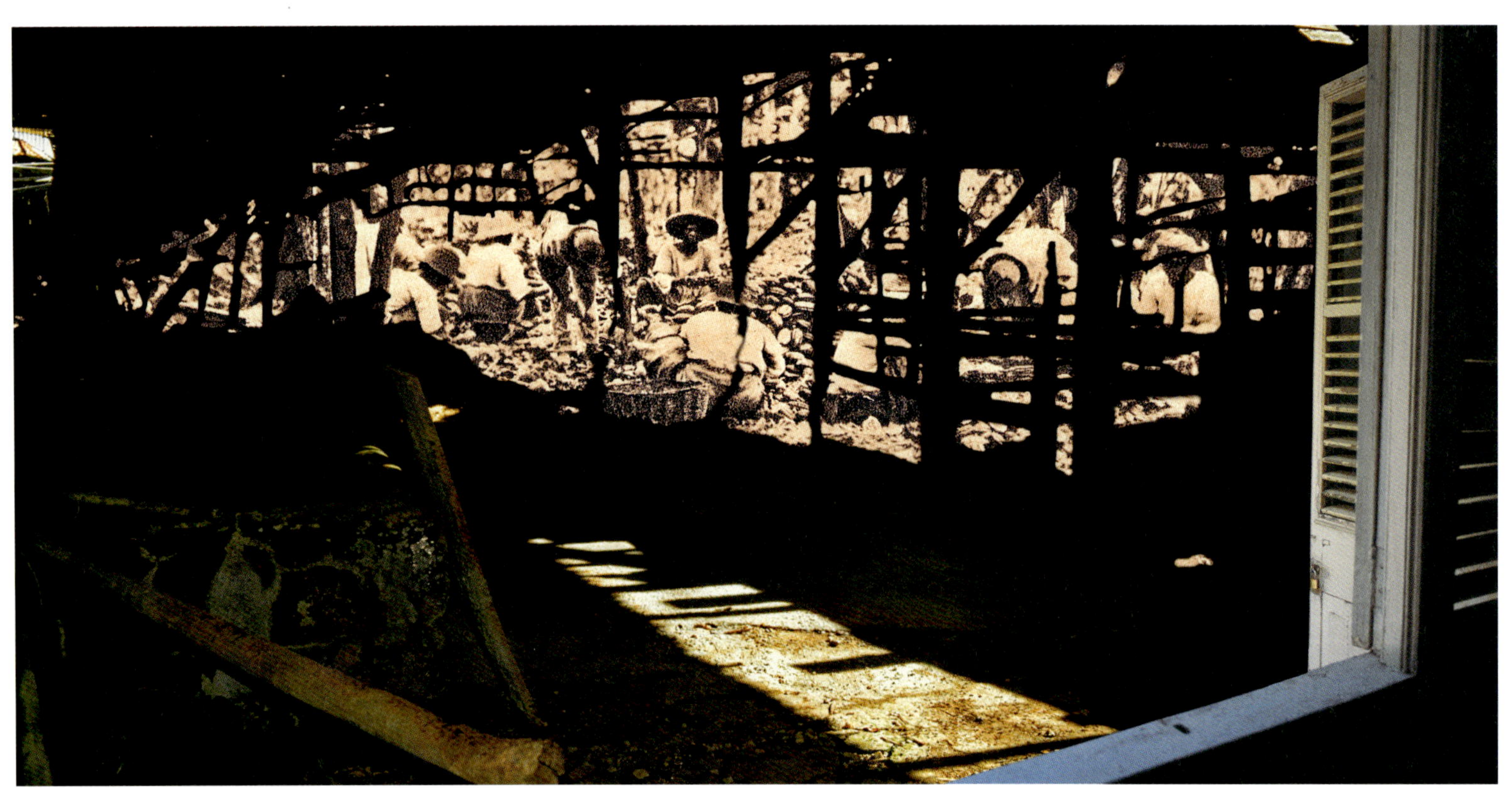

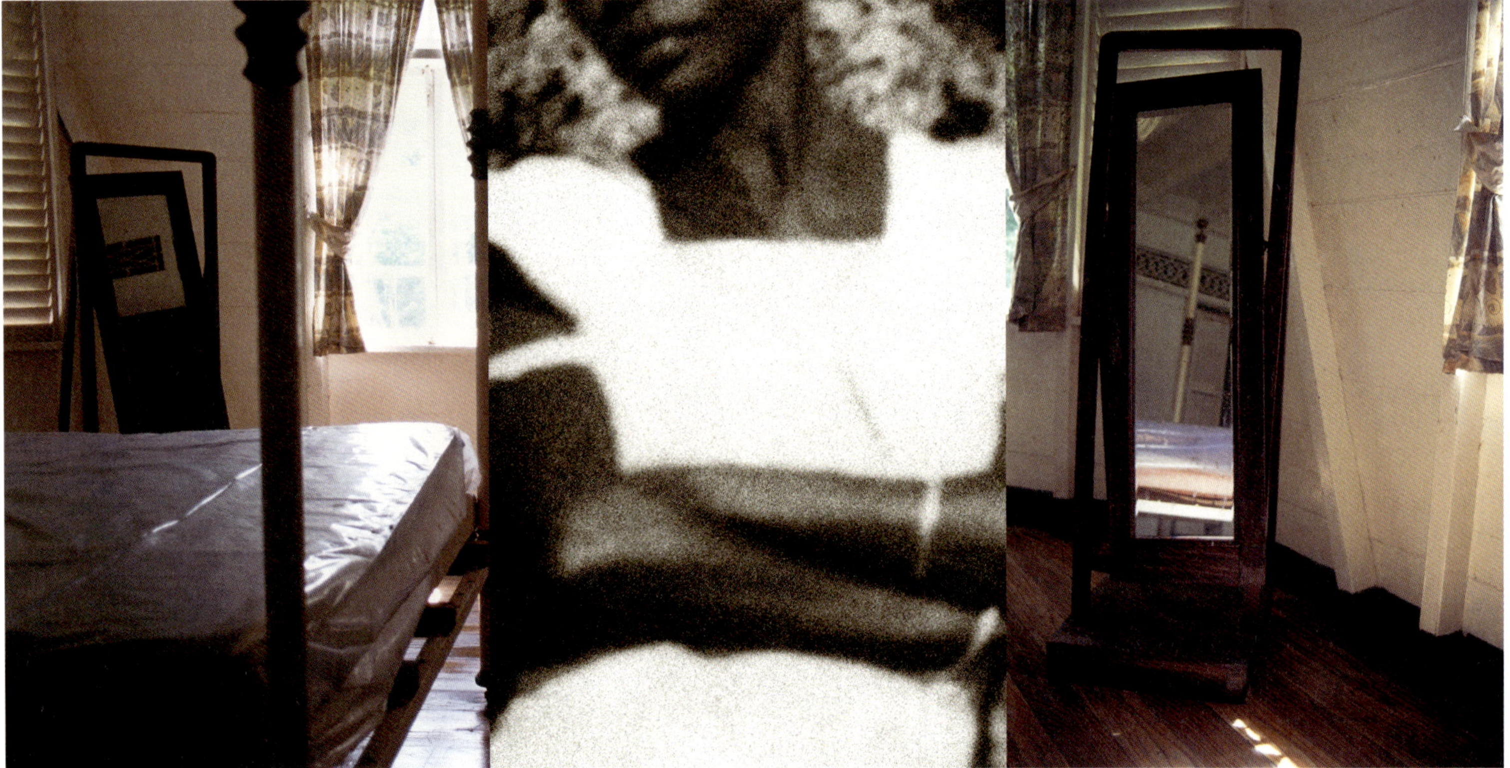

Roshini Kempadoo, *Ghosting*, 2004

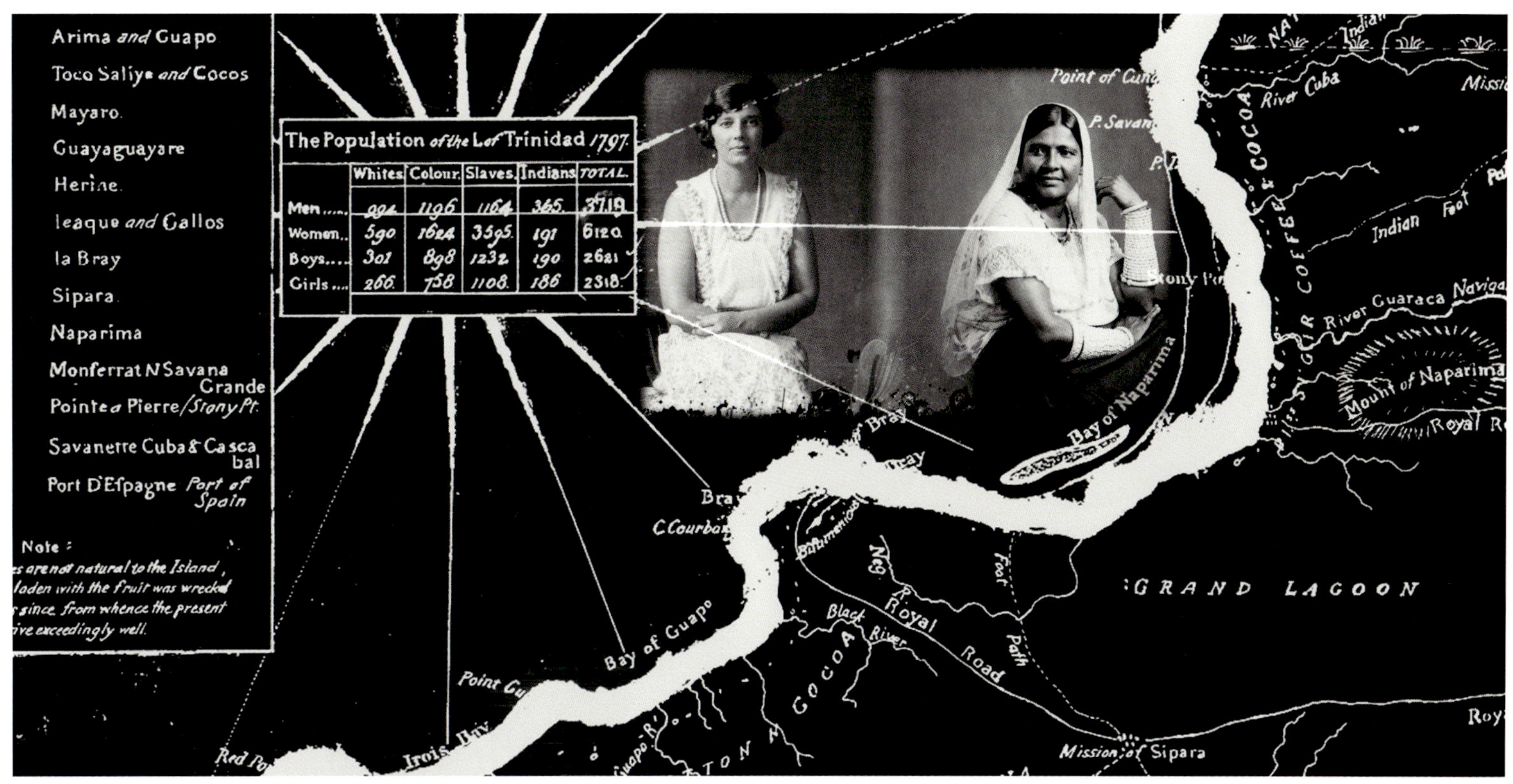

The Population of the I. of Trinidad 1797.	Whites.	Colour.	Slaves.	Indians.	TOTAL.
Men	994	1196	1164	365.	3719
Women..	590	1624	3595.	191	6120.
Boys....	301	898	1232	190	2621
Girls	266.	758	1108.	186	2318.

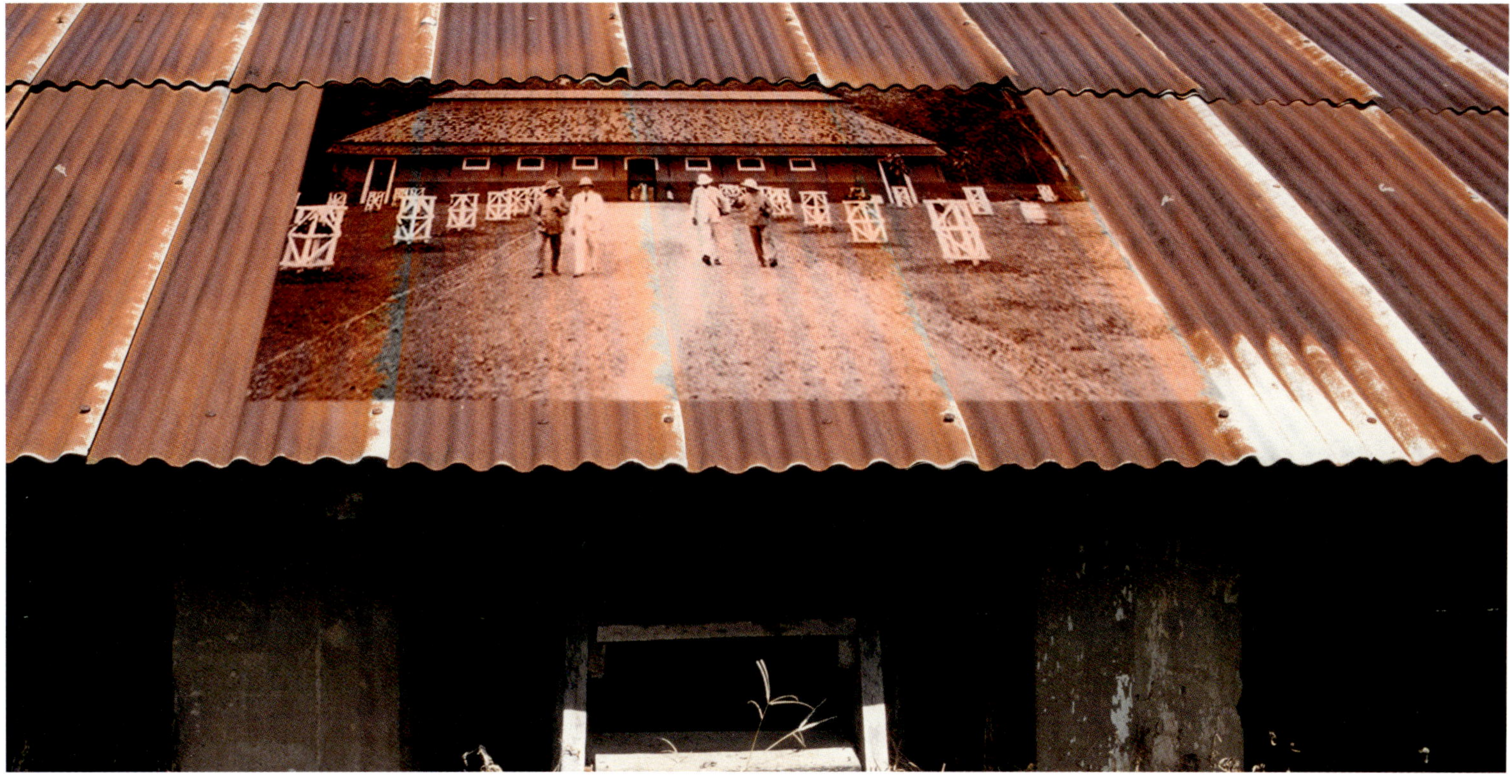

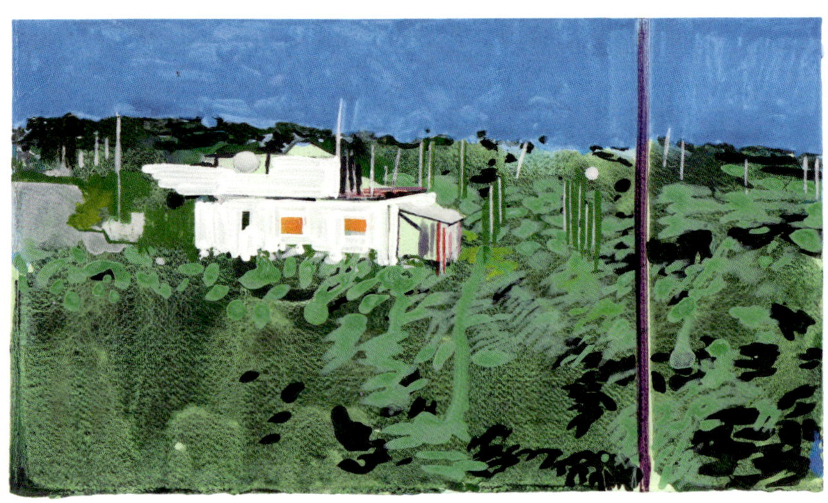

Hurvin Anderson, *Rose Avenue (Drawing)*, 2006

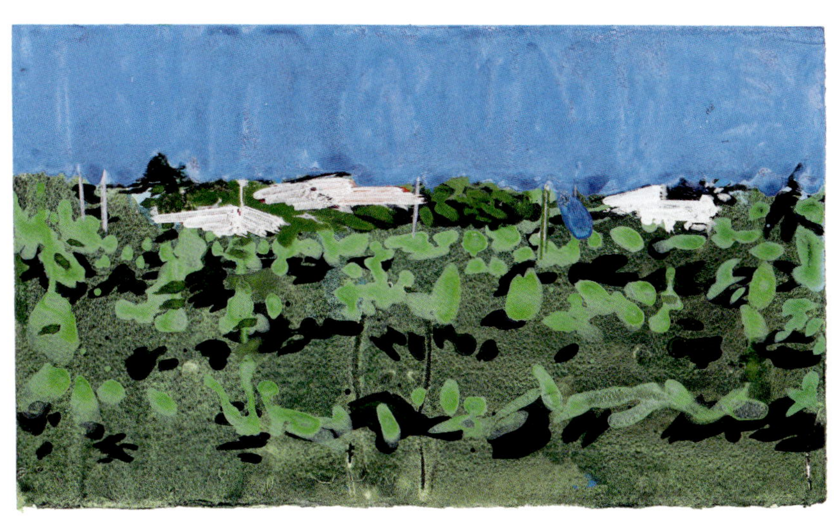

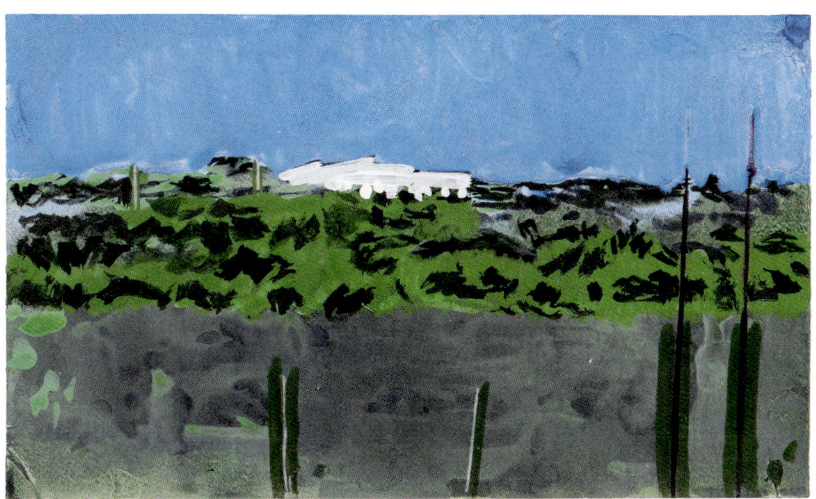

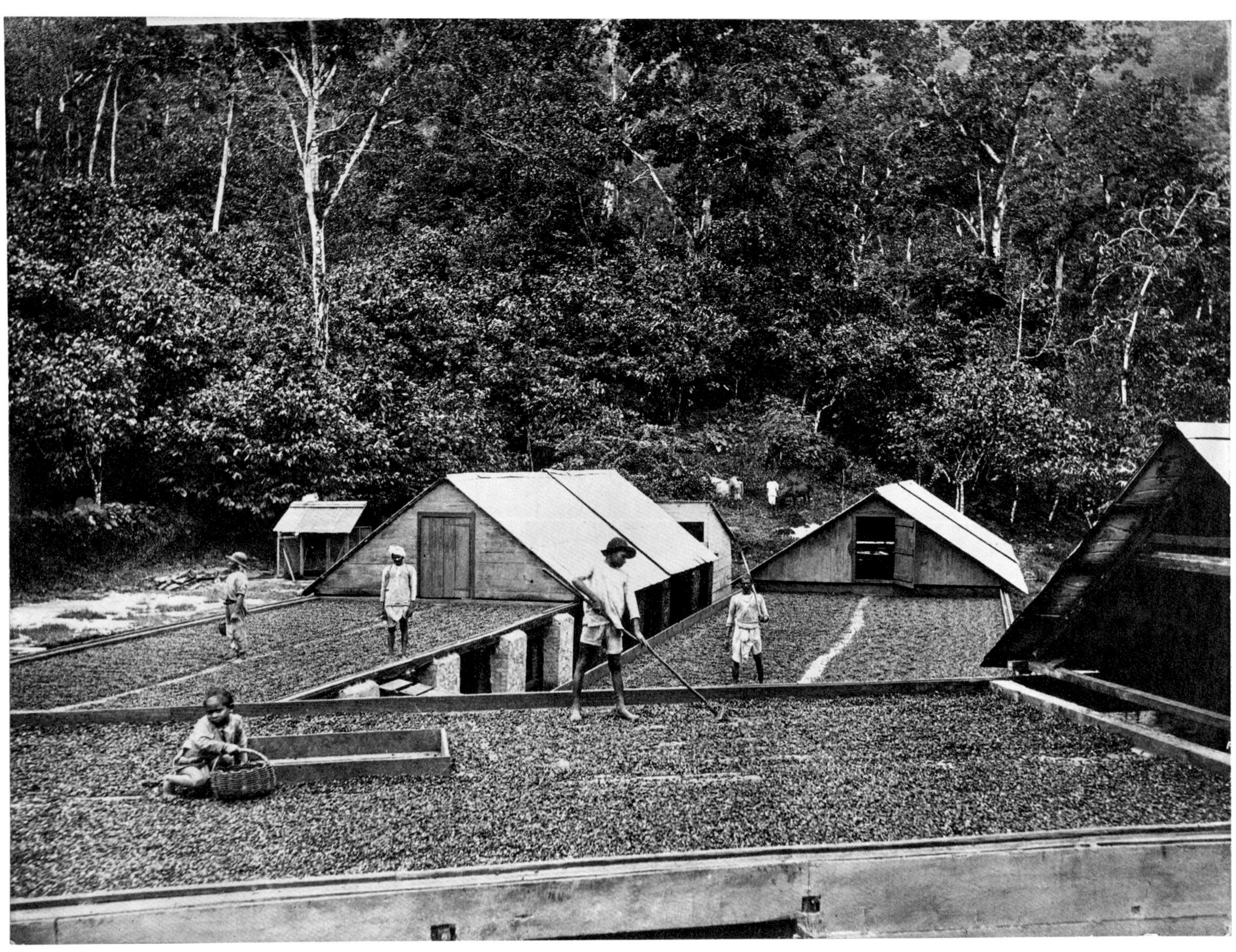

Unknown photographer, *Drying Cacao, Trinidad*, 1910

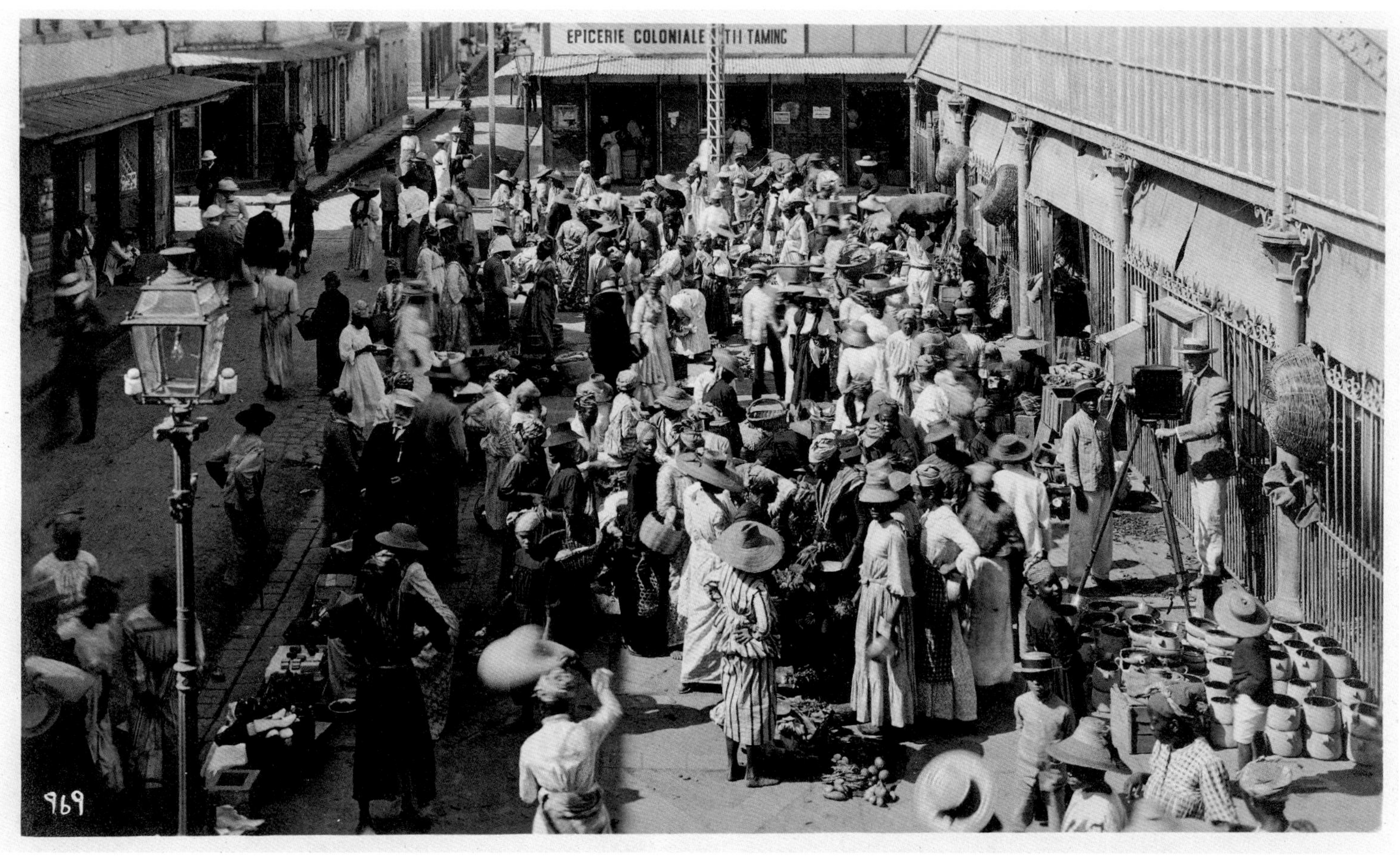

Unknown photographer, *Market, Fort de France, Martinique,* c. 1905

The World *the* F*re*edm*an*/ Wom*an* *Made*

Erna Brodber

Queen Victoria gi wi free
Gi wi free, gi wi free
This is the year
Of Jubilee[1]

the freed slaves had sung.

The process of "giving free" had been set in motion before the good queen ascended the throne. It was in the "3rd and 4th" year of the reign of William IV in 1834 that the "act for the abolition of slavery throughout the British Colonies" was passed. Please take note of the sub-titles. It was not just an act for the abolition of slavery, it was an act "for promoting the Industry of the manumitted slaves, and for compensating the Persons hitherto entitled to the services of such slaves."[2] These "persons" throughout the British West Indies, were to be compensated to the tune of £20,000. "Such slaves," on August 1, 1834, were to be made into apprentices rather than slaves. In this state, they served their former master in an "as slave" role for 40½ hours per week and for the rest of the time, practiced freedom. In this part-free state, African-Jamaicans were to have stayed for seven years. The hope that they would be rid of the interference of the British government in the running of their affairs made the Jamaica Assembly follow Nevis, St. Kitts, Montserrat, the Virgin Islands, and Barbados, and in June of 1838 decide to end apprenticeship from

August 1, 1838. After this date we were officially free.

To understand the environment in which the now free African-Jamaican had to build a life, it is wise to look some more into the process by which freedom came to him officially. Freedom was a gift from the British government which, true to Biblical terms, can be said to have redeemed us for £20,000. The British were the ultimate political power in Jamaica and could intervene in the running of the colony. Theoretically they could have intervened at any time and imposed "freedom." That they did so in 1834 is due to several factors, one of these being Sam Sharp's rebellion of 1831. Sharp's rebellion was widely discussed in Britain and brought the issue of British involvement in what some saw as an inhumane institution to a head. Sharp's rebellion, as we have seen, was not that of the new "nagar," who could be expected to be less rebellious with time. It was not that of the lower end of slaves, who with ameliorated conditions could be expected to be satisfied. This was a revolt of the upper reaches of the slave system, of people many of whom and certainly most of its leaders, had never had a lash on their backs.

Sharp was a driver on the Croyden estate and a respected Baptist leader whose master allowed him to travel freely. George Taylor was a saddler and a Baptist deacon who also was allowed to travel; Tharp was a driver, Charles Campbell a carpenter and Thomas Dove a literate headman.[3] The British working class, beginning to be seen and heard at that time, could identify with such men, who like them were artisans and Christians. British intellectuals were reformist and getting more so. Harsh reprisals and the dignity with which the rebels accepted hanging, projected them as upright men defending ideals, men in search of freedom and willing to help themselves to it. The intellectuals' anti-slavery fervour was increased. This sentiment percolated throughout Britain and several petitions were sent to the House of Commons, where there was already a strong anti-slavery faction. Had the sugar and coffee interests been of as much economic and military value to British, as they had been during the struggles with Napoleon in the 1790s to 1815, sentiment might have been set aside. But it was not.

Even the more pure capitalists, who had been pro-slavery before, were now changing their position. The feeling amongst them was that there were more men like Sharp and his fellow conspirators among the Jamaican slaves and that men like those no longer had the mentality of slaves, would not work well in a slave economy and would before long destroy it. They now felt that the foundations on which the Jamaican economy were built was in decay and the whole edifice in danger. A different approach to labour was indicated. The arguments and sentiments of the various British factions left the Jamaicans, with their old slave system, isolated. They, however, did not seem to appreciate that the tide of public opinion was against their way of life, that there was a new ideology in ascendancy, which required that individuals be freed from arbitrary power and that men like Sharp, Tharp, Taylor, Dove, and Campbell were no longer seen in intellectual quarters as Long's fleecy animals but as Christian artisans, who should be helped towards self-discipline and individual responsibility.[4]

Instead of reforming their system, the Jamaican plantocracy continued to maltreat a people who, contrary to their prophesies concerning reprisals, had killed no one on August 1, 1834, the day of abolition. This behaviour continued to isolate them and to force the British government to disregard their laws and to intervene directly to protect apprentices, the quasi-free, from abuse. Their current governor, Lionel Smith, had said of their local governing body:

> It is impossible for anyone to answer for the conduct of the House of Assembly. Many are there in the island who would be delighted to get up an insurrection for the pleasure of destroying the negroes and the missionaries. They are, in fact, mad.[5]

To prevent further interference from Britain in their internal affairs, the Jamaican assembly opted for total emancipation. In this social-psychological climate, with the ill-will of their former masters towards them for forcing them into a new kind of labour system, and with tensions between the local assembly and Britain about this, the newly freed people—the cause of dissension in the family—sat down to build an independent life among people, who for centuries had only seen them as extensions of themselves.

The freed African-Jamaicans had been given no compensation money. Their ex-masters who ruled the land were annoyed by the fact of their new status, were not sure how to handle relationships with them, and were not likely to stretch out a hand to them individually or politically. On the contrary, they could be expected to be positively hostile. They could expect no material help from Britain for was not self-discipline and responsibility the other side of the freedom which British public opinion had wished for them? And what notion of freedom for African-Jamaicans did those, who legislated this opinion into fact, have? A clue lies in the title of the Abolition Act…"for promoting the industry of the manumitted slave." Freedom meant freedom to work; the idea of a prescribed social space in which this freedom and freedom to work were to take place, persisted in the mind of the local elite as well as in the mind of their betters in Britain. Let us look at the Emancipation Proclamation read in public places of the eve of August 1, 1838.

It reads, *inter alia*

> By the Queen
> A Proclamation
>
> Whereas an act has been passed by the Legislature of this our Island of Jamaica for terminating the system of apprenticeship on the first day of August next, and thereby granting the Blessings and

Privileges of unrestricted freedom to all classes of the inhabitants and whereas it is incumbent on all the inhabitants of this our island to testify their grateful sense of the Divine favor [*sic*], we do therefore by and with the advice of our privy Council of this our said island, *direct and point* that Wednesday the said first day of August next be observed in all churches and chapels as a day of General Thanksgiving to the Almighty God for these His Mercies and of humble intercession for his continued blessing and protection on this most important occasion, and we do hereby call upon persons of all classes within this our said island to observe the said first day of August next *with the same reverence and respect which is observed and due on the sabbath.* [emphasis mine][6]

This was the Proclamation of 1838 declaring full freedom. It "direct[ed] and point[ed]" how the freedman should celebrate his freedom. African-Jamaican celebration of freedom was to be contained within the confines of a particular cultural system represented by the Christian church. Similar strictures were placed on his crafting of his free life as we see in the title of the Abolition Act.

Thomas C. Holt summarizes more succinctly, than I can, the context within which African-Jamaicans were to build their world as per the intentions of those who designed the legal parameters of his freedom.

They would be free, but only after being re-socialized to accept the internal discipline that ensured the survival of the existing order. They would be free to bargain in the marketplace but not free to ignore the market. They would be free to pursue their own self-interest but not free to reject the cultural conditioning that defined what that self-interest should be. They would have opportunities for social mobility, but only after they learnt their proper place.[7]

The "Industry" called for in the Abolition Act of 1834 presented no problem for the freedman. In the two years between full emancipation and mid-1840, 2074 freedmen had got themselves freeholds.[8] Five years later ten times as many, being 20,724, had done so too. This means that seven years after full emancipation about 21 per cent of freedmen had made themselves into peasants. Their lots were small as lots went in Jamaica: they were under 20 acres. Along with the growth in the number of freeholds went a growth in the number of towns. Lands had come into the freedman's hands through the decline of coffee and sugar estates. The area in which I live is a case in point. By 1848 plantations in the South St. Mary - North Catherine areas had ceased production.[9] The Palmetto Grove estate declared itself no longer able to grow sugar cane profitably and the coffee estates of Woodside, RockSpring, Smailfield, Louisiana, Richmond Hill, Stapleton, Waterton went out of agro industry. Windsor Castle had by 1843 cut up 252 acres to be sold to former slaves.[10] None of these lots was bigger than seven acres. Petersfield[11] which shares a border with Woodside had begun earlier and Palmetto Grove consistently sold out its periphery into little one- and three-acre plots after 1846.[12] Land transfers into the hands of freedmen continued into the 1850s, freedmen buying into sub-division, buying as individuals and as a corporate entity: "the negroes of William Kelly" "holed and patented" three pieces of canelands in Fort Stewart, St. Mary.[13]

During slavery planters had found it economical to have their enslaved workers plant foodstuff to feed themselves. Thus they had been given provision grounds. A law of 1792[14] stipulated that they be given a day off every fortnight, except in crop time, when other plans had to be made concerning their free time. This time they had used to attend to their gardens. They were also due every Sunday. This became the day on which they went to the markets to sell their surplus. These Sunday markets became a traditional meeting place, but more importantly, part of an economic institution created, and to the extent that one can speak of "control" in a slave society, controlled by the enslaved. Though everything a slave owned belonged by law to his master, it was rare that a master required of him/her the returns from his grounds and his sales. A law of 1826[15] gave the slave legal right to his property, although it was still possible for the master through the Supreme Court to seize whatever he had that was valued at more than £20. There were several things he should not possess, according to the law, but the only ones about which the Jamaican planters were consistently adamant was the owning of a horse and a gun.

As a slave then, the freedman had known money and had known how to conduct business, so much so that Diana Wilson and Jestina Sewell could in 1836-1837 have bought the unexpired term of their bondage for £35 each from the Woodside estate.[16] Obviously the freedman came out of slavery with enough money to buy land which was going at about £3 an acre in the 1840s.[17] One could even buy a cow: Mrs. Beatrice Williams' grandmother, a St. James freedwoman,[18] was the first woman to own a cow in that parish. You could obviously add dairy farming to your other skills as a farmer to answer the charge of the Abolition Act that you be industrious. The planters' needs facilitated this "industry," forcing some to make lands available to the freed people: some among them told themselves that selling lands to the potential workers would create a nucleus of labour available to them; there were others who simply needed the money. There were others who rented and leased for the same purposes as those who sold. The lands sold were usually the hilly backlands.

On these lands the freedmen planted ground provisions for home supplies and for the internal market. Free people living in the towns had been their customers. With the mass of their own people no longer supplied with essentials by the master there would now be a larger market and quite likely a wider range of goods—a market for fish and meat and clothes for instance. Speculating as well as higglering would now be in the freed person's menu. The speculating dealt with non-ground provisions, with goods that were likely to be imported and implied a relationship with merchants in the towns. The freedmen planted what they had planted for their masters; they planted coffee; they planted sugar cane and processed it. This peasant agriculture-cum-marketing system in time fed into the American fruit market with its interest in coffee and later in bananas and oranges. By the mid 1840s, less than ten years after full freedom, the establishment had to note that its grant of freedom had produced a distinct class of people. They found a new name for us. The literature now referred to us as the "small settler." The development of a black peasantry did not please local white planter interest; nor did it please the British government, which had initiated its freedom. An economic interest of your own did not allow you to be at the beck and call of another, and this was precisely what was felt to be needed, if the "promotion of the industry" of the ex-slave was to maintain the plantation system—as the British architects of freedom had intended. The freedman, on the other hand, was steadily moving outside of the confines of the system in which a class of people gave their labour to another in a total way, accompanied in this move by the anger of the planter class. It was the planters now who by the late 1840s were in danger of being isolated. The storm clouds had been there from the apprenticeship period.

Those people who had championed the abolition of slavery in 1834 had made all children six years of age and under free immediately. They had expected that these children, with their parents still in partial slavery, would have been around to continue in the "pickney" gang doing a little light weeding, tending to the mules, and helping to manure the fields, chores which took little energy but were important and which had traditionally been done by children. The parents of these freed children had a different view of their freedom. One estate in St. Thomas, which had had 50 children of work age in 1834, had only 16 left by 1836.[19] It is thought that the enslaved sent their freed children off to relatives in the towns. Some estates tried to get around this by offering the education parents saw as the route to social mobility for their children. On the Blue Mountain and Greenwall estates in the St. Andrew hills, parents did allow children under six to be formed into gangs in return for an hour and half of education per day. Lucky Valley estate in North St. Catherine was another one such: 14 of the 21 children residents went to school under such arrangements. These children at Lucky Valley, in return for their schooling, reared provisions at the back of the school. In some places to have one's children out of the clutches of the estate was better than education. A school in Kellits kept by the bookkeeper could only attract two of the 90 children. In 1835 apprentices in parts of St. David and St. Mary refused to allow their children to work in the fields even when free education and allowances were offered.

Women's labour was another issue. Women had borne the brunt of the labouring tasks on estates.

It was they, according to Holt, who were the most vociferous in their protection of their free time during the apprenticeship period. Children had, on estates during slavery, been taken care of by old women while their mothers went back to work. The apprentice and the freewoman now wanted to take on to herself the care of her children. It appears, from the evidence of African-Jamaicans born in the early 20th century,[20] that the freed and free-women were now, with full freedom, moving into a specialized part of the internal marketing system–the planting of women's crops, legumes and vegetables, into such agro-industries as the preparation of coconut oil, sugar head, and other sweet meats, and were concentrating on taking the produce, which men grew and which they turned into edibles, to the markets. It appears that they were in the process of building an alternative form of making a living. With women and children unexpectedly out of the labour market the planters were faced with a new creation–the blackman in his castle with his own small social system of wife and children, over whom he presided; a woman with a source of livelihood that had no association with them except possibly as landlord. Their ex-slaves' castles even had names just as theirs had. Here in my Woodside, St. Mary, by the 1870s there was Happy Content, Poorman's Corner, Primrose Cottage.

…

Obeah is about avenging. In the hands of tricksters it could wreak havoc. There were laws in the domain, controlled by the planters, against obeah, but given obeah's necessarily secretive character, these laws were ineffectual. A spiritually-based antidote had to be applied to it. Myal was that antidote. In contrast to obeah, myal was a group-based force and therefore more public. It was myal that the white society saw. Its anti-obeah activity, which involved marches to cotton trees to pull out obeah, and its drumming and the spirit possession, must have seemed like savage madness to those who didn't understand the need to clean a sub-section of the society in which the practice of obeye had got into the hands of the immoral.

Myal began to be observed in 1842 when groups of these cleaners, delivering themselves in Christian terminology, said they were sent by God to release souls bound by obeah men and buried under cotton trees.[21] How could people who had burnt their witches, who still held to the notion of a distinction between cleric and laity and the notion that God reached the laity through the clergy, take this? A people who had never heard of the Chinese cure based upon the energy field, whose Freud was not yet born? A black system of understanding and consequent behaviour confronted the white establishment. They saw the behaviour of the freedman and freemen as a sign that the black population had regressed into behaviour they did not understand, and behaviour that they did not understand, was wrong behaviour.

With their withdrawal from the estates, with hard times and no access to a socio-economic theory which better explained their situation, both obeah and myal thrived among the freedmen as central parts of their understanding of their reality. Creolised African rituals, such as these, had existed on estates during slavery but to a lesser extent. They had been witnessed by whites, some of whom mentioned them in their writings. They had obviously been seen as opera. With the end of slavery these same rites, no longer performed by "our" people, whose behaviour could amuse us because we could control it, became frightening signs of degradation. Says special magistrate Fyfe in 1854 of ancestor rites, which are likely to have been practiced in slavery

> whilst they will lavish pounds on a funeral, they grudge a shilling for the medicine that might avert it. Disease entails trouble, death is followed by merriment and feasting.[22]

Fyfe served in St. Mary, St. George, Metcalfe and possibly St. David. Others of his class agreed with him. The magistrate for Trelawny added that "Their march back to barbarism has been rapid and successful."[23] Some saw the hope for change in the education of the African-Jamaican from early in his infancy.

Obeah might have been a relatively pure African import. Myal was fashioned out of the mix of good African witchcraft and Christianity. The freedman had again taken what he needed from the master's culture and recreated it to suit his purposes.

Excerpted from "The World the Freedman/Woman Made," in The Continent of Black Consciousness: on the History of the African Diaspora from Slavery to the Present Day *(London: New Beacon Books Ltd, 2003), 48–74.*

1 Emancipation Songs collected in Woodside, St Mary, Jamaica 1996.

2 *Jamaica. Minutes of the Council. July 1832 to September 1839.* Jamaica Archives, 1b/5/3/24 March 1834.

3 For this and other data in this piece, I rely heavily on Thomas C. Holt's *The Problem of Freedom – race, labour and politics in Jamaica and Britain 1832–1838* (Baltimore: John Hopkins University Press, 1992): 16.

4 Edward Long, *The History of Jamaica,* Vol II (London: Frank Cass, 1774): 352.

5 Holt, *The Problem of Freedom*, 105.

6 As at note 2. May 1938.

7 Holt, *The Problem of Freedom,* 53.

8 Holt, *The Problem of Freedom,* see chapter 5.

9 *Great Britain Parliament, House of Commons select committee on sugar and coffee planting* (DETAILS, 1848): 229.

10 STM 51, Map Collection, National Library of Jamaica.

11 STM 1397, Map Collection, National Library of Jamaica.

12 STM 586, Map Collection, National Library of Jamaica.

13 STM 614, Map Collection, National Library of Jamaica. Map undated. Reference says it is about 1857.

14 Orlando Patterson, *The Sociology of Slavery* (Kingston: Sangster's Bookstore, 1967): 84.

15 Patterson, *The Sociology of Slavery*, 80.

16 Wills: Liber 109.112 and 110.103. Island Record Office, Jamaica.

17 Holt, *The Problem of Freedom*, 145.

18 Erna Brodber, "Oral Historian" (tape 60 StjFa) in *Life in Jamaica in the Early Twentieth Century: a presentation of ninety oral accounts*, ISER Documentation Centre, Mona, Jamaica, 1980.

19 Holt, *The Problem of Freedom*, 151–152.

20 Erna Brodber, *The Second Generation of Freemen in Jamaica 1907–1944*, PhD thesis, University of the West Indies, 1985.

21 Patterson, *The Sociology of Slavery*, 181–188.

22 Holt, *The Problem of Freedom*, 167.

23 Holt, *The Problem of Freedom*, 167.

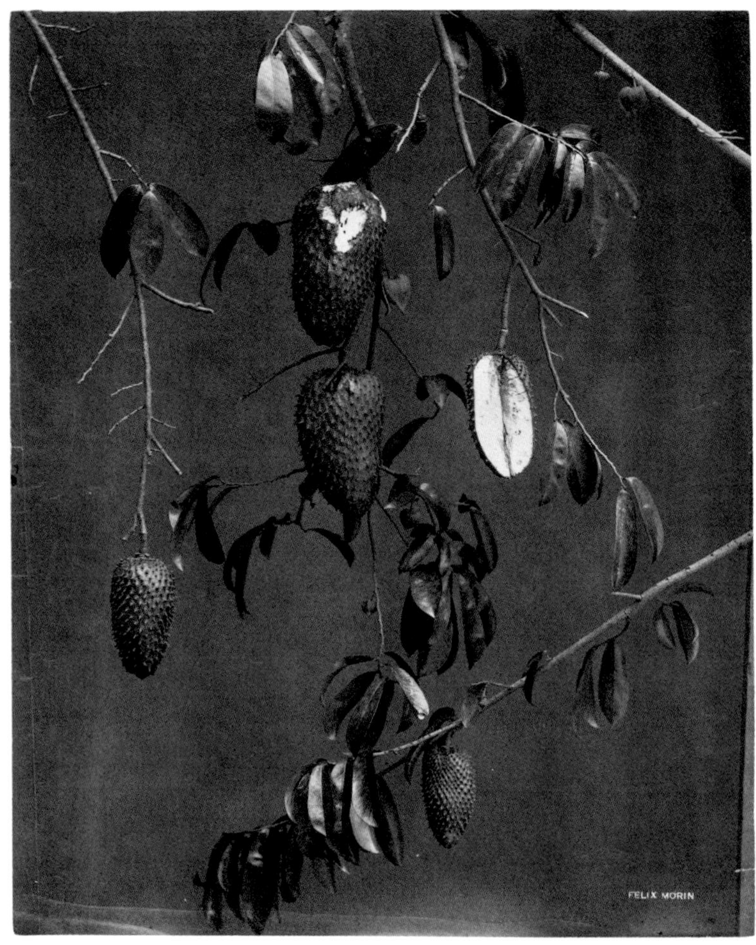

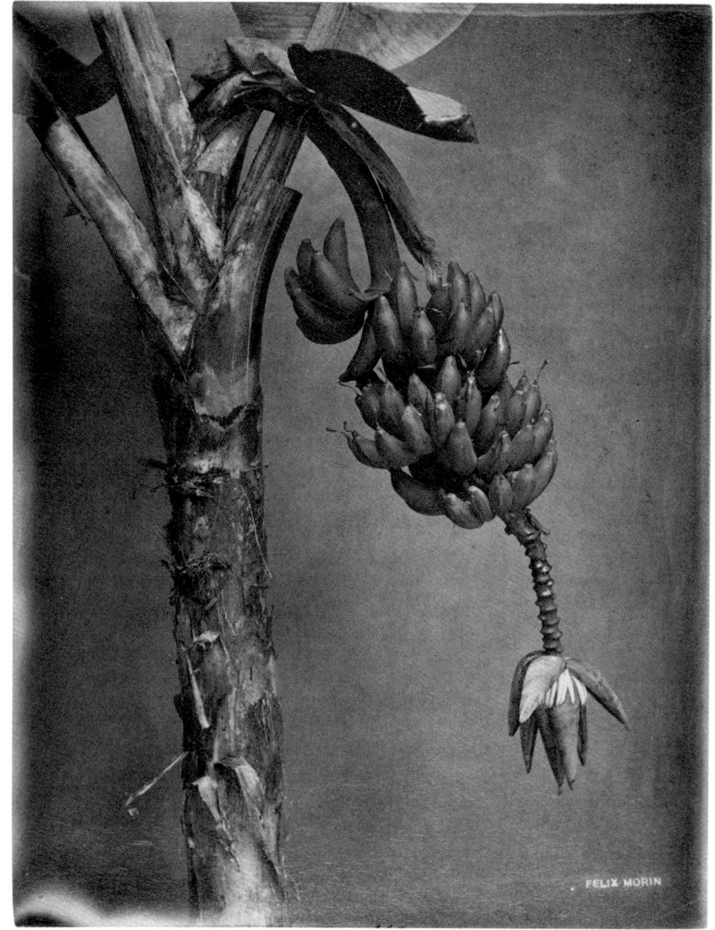

Left
Felix Morin, *Soursop Fruit (Anonna Muricata or Corossol)*, c. 1890

Right
Felix Morin, *Bananas, Trinidad*, c. 1890

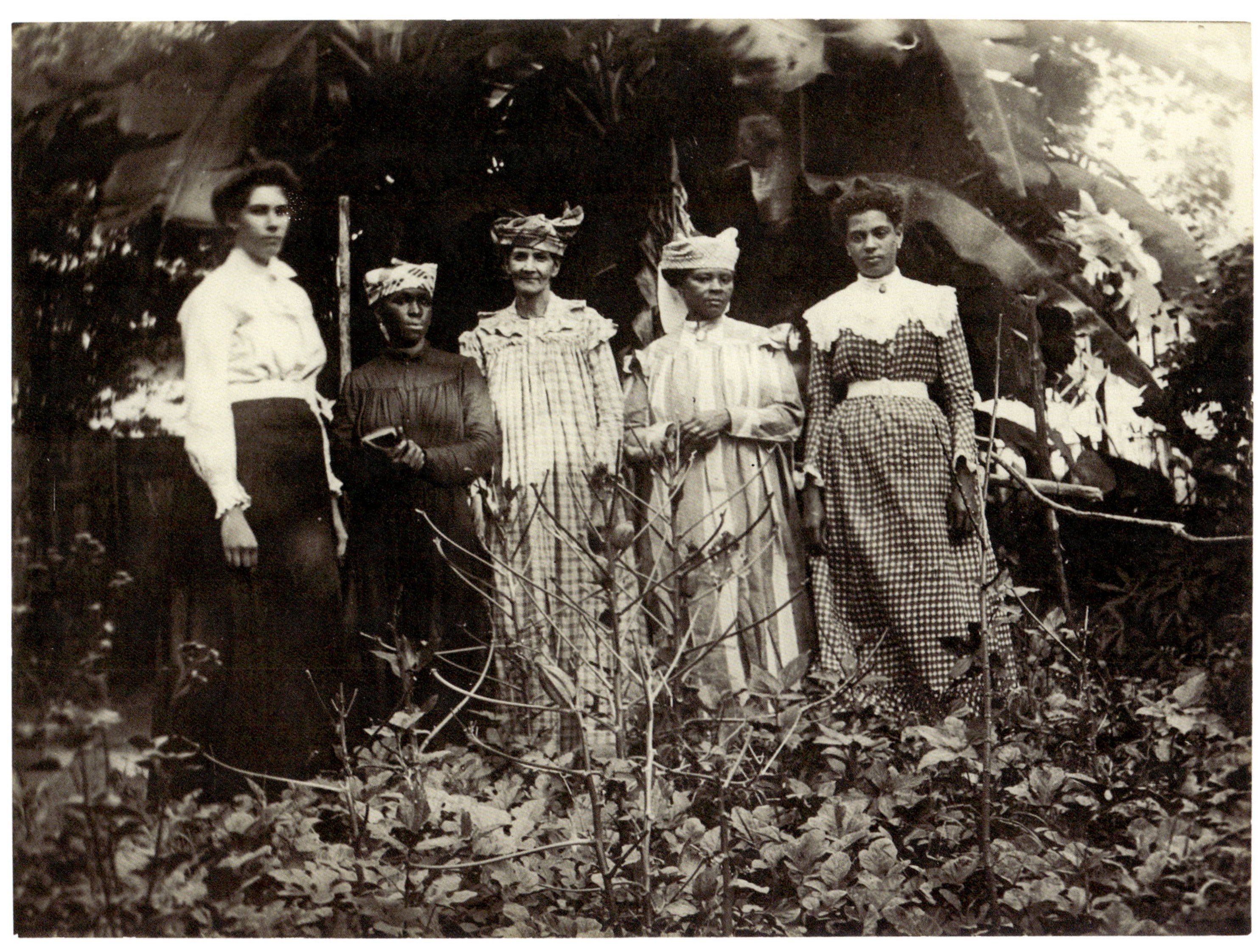

Unknown photographer, *Jamaican Women*, c. 1900

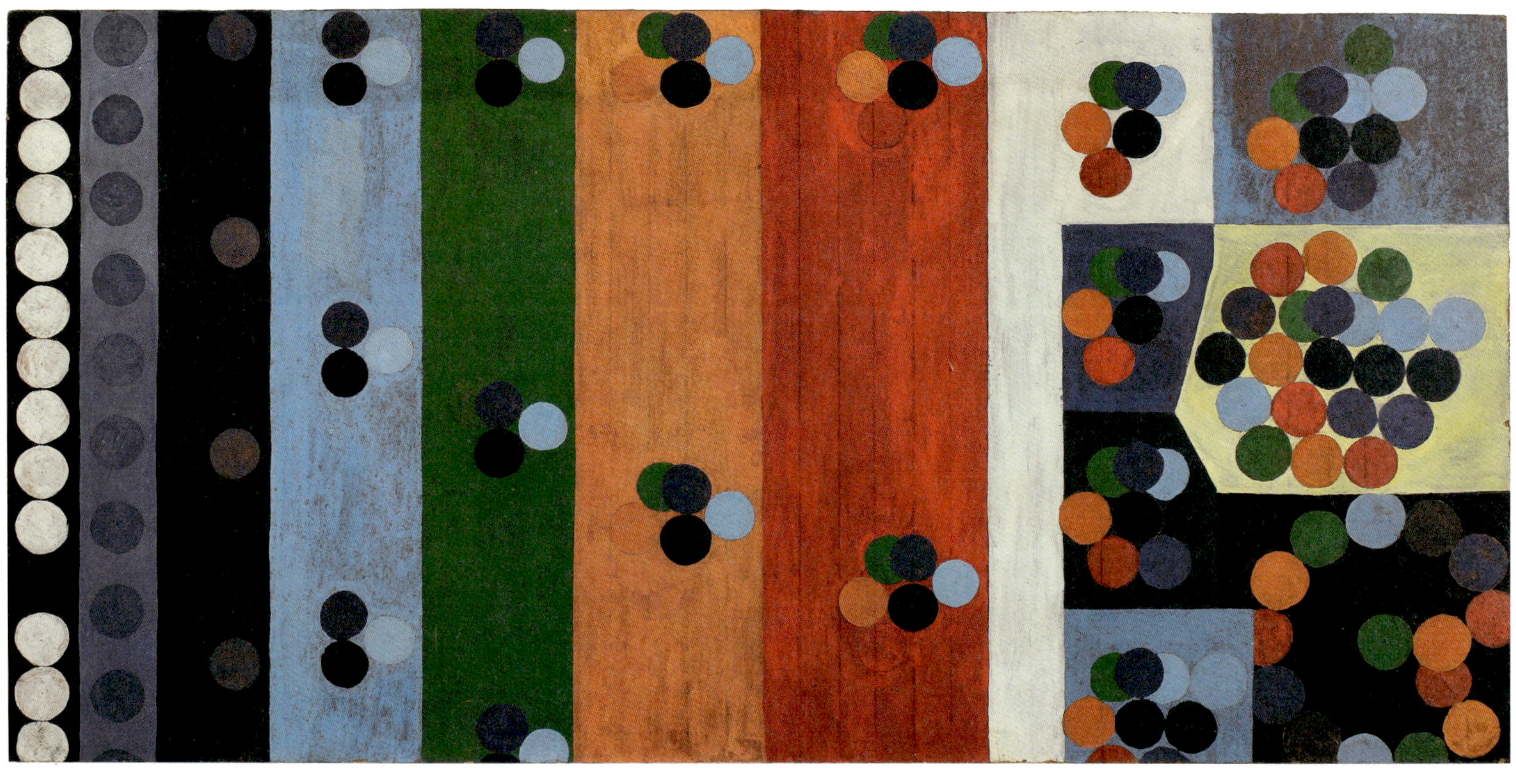

Frank Walter, *Complex of Life*, 1960

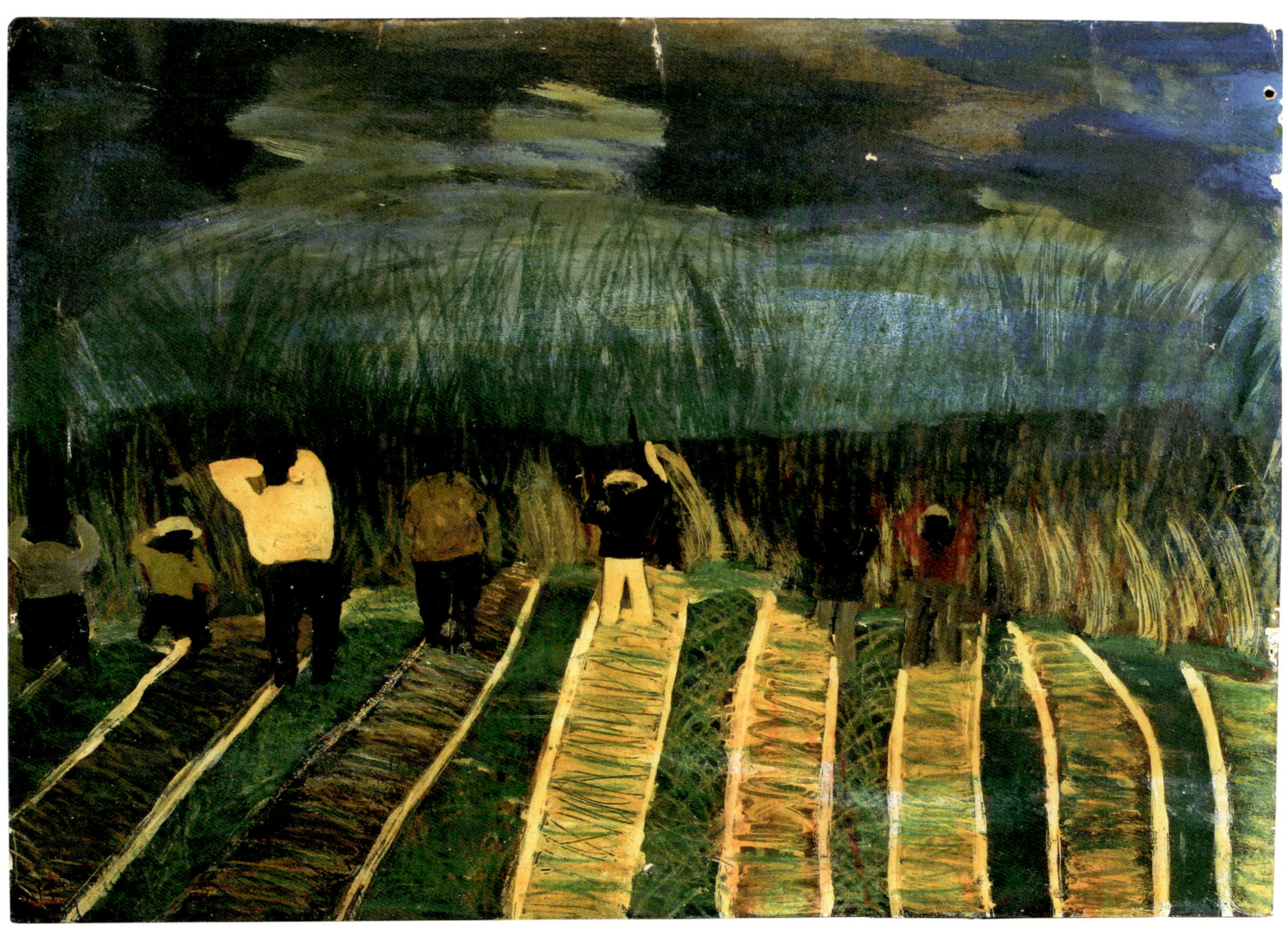

Frank Walter, *Plantation Fields and Workers*, c. 1968–1974

The *Epic* *Creativity* *of* *Frank* *Walter*

Barbara Paca[1]

2

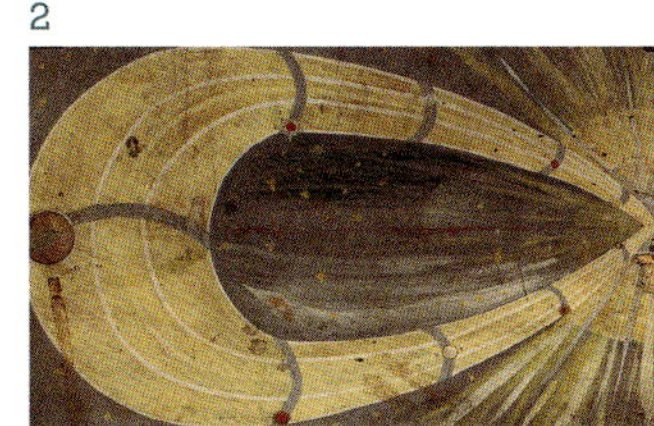

1

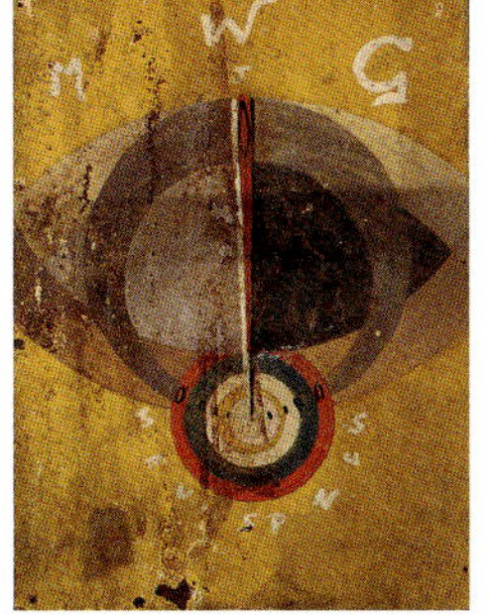

4

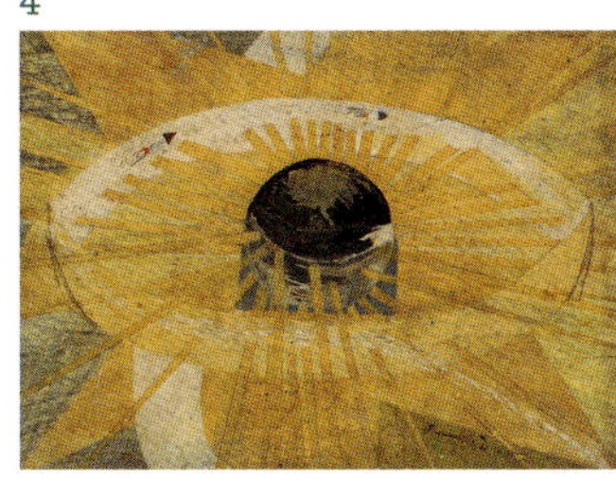

3

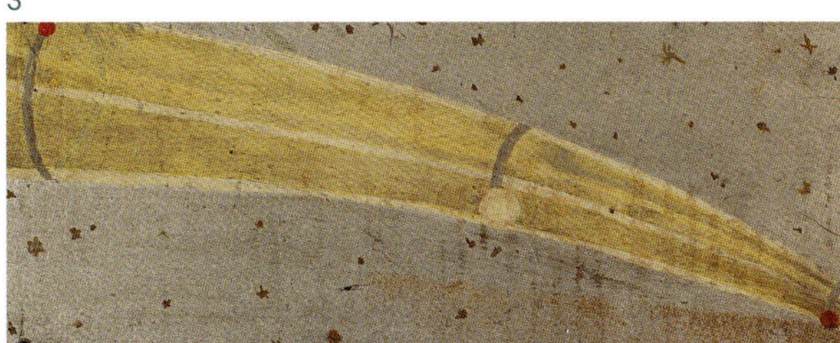

Fig. 1
Frank Walter
MWG Milky Way Galaxy, [n.d.] (from *Milky Way Galaxy* series). Oil on Masonite, 31.5 × 21.4 x 0.4 cm. © Courtesy Sir Selvyn and Kathleen, Lady Walter. Photo: Kenneth M. Milton Fine Arts.

Fig. 2
Frank Walter
Right Side of the Milky Way Galaxy, [n.d.] (from *Milky Way Galaxy* series). Oil on wood, 29.5 × 47.5 x 1.5 cm. © Courtesy Sir Selvyn and Kathleen, Lady Walter. Photo: Kenneth M. Milton Fine Arts.

Fig. 3
Frank Walter
Left Side of the Milky Way Galaxy, [n.d.] (from *Milky Way Galaxy* series). Oil on wood, 13.9 × 37 × 1.3 cm. © Courtesy Sir Selvyn and Kathleen, Lady Walter. Photo: Kenneth M. Milton Fine Arts.

Fig. 4
Frank Walter
Centrifugal Sun Rockets, [n.d.] (from *Milky Way Galaxy* series). Oil on plywood, 30.1 × 37.3 × 0.8 cm. © Courtesy Sir Selvyn and Kathleen, Lady Walter. Photo: Kenneth M. Milton Fine Arts.

Poetry is an island that breaks away from the main.

— Derek Walcott
The Antilles: Fragments of Epic Memory

If poetry is an island that breaks away from the main, then Frank Walter's art is a luminous slow-moving comet in the constellation of artistic creativity.

Frank Walter is the father of modern painting in the Caribbean. The story of his life reads like Odysseus, and his recording of that life, through painting, sculpture, photography, writing, and music, has forever changed the canon of art. His astonishing body of work reflects an ability to simultaneously travel to disparate regions, real and imagined, and recall experiences with a level of detail that seduces the viewer into some of the most wonderful, albeit unlikely, settings.

Frank Walter's relations loved to share stories about Walter's space capsule. With trademark infectious joy he would describe the contraption, made from oil drums. He was going to the moon. And beyond. His music, writing, and the intriguing paintings that make up the *Milky Way Galaxy Series* (n.d., figs. 1-6), convince me that his trip was a success. As a time-traveller, Walter opened doors to many kinds of histories and futures, on earth and in other universal dimensions.

Even when working in his tiny studio in St. John's, he was able to conduct a discourse on elevated topics in philosophy and history, establishing eye-contact with young Antiguan students or friends while dabbing paint onto a tiny piece of card meticulously cut from a Polaroid film box. As a child, he could write a Latin poem while whistling a tune and dangling his feet in the sea. As a planter, he could transport himself to another world while both feet were firmly on the ground in a sugar cane field. What allowed him extreme compartmentalization? Probably the same thing that propelled him to work day and night to create such a collection of works. His extreme genius carried with it both a recognition that he and his countrymen were the unknown thread of epic histories and a desire to engage with others in the knowledge of those truths.

This is the story of an artist who went away (and in Walter's case, really went away) and returned. He was born the same year as Aubrey Williams, and their early lives ran parallel: both were well-educated, regarded as bright young stars, plantation managers, had a keen interest in the histories of Indigenous cultures, travelled to England at the same time, and ended up working as artists. Unlike Aubrey Williams, Walter's time in England was difficult. Furthermore, it was clear that his time in the UK was a means to another end—and that was of homecoming.

As the first person of colour to hold a managerial post on a sugar plantation in Antigua, he was regarded as one of Antigua's rising talents, and was encouraged to study overseas and presumably stay for a so-called better life. He traded that opportunity for a grander plan: Walter would travel abroad for ten years to gain an understanding of cutting-edge technology in agriculture and industry, and bring that knowledge back to improve the lives of his fellow countrymen. Little did he know that this plan would unravel, and that he would ultimately alter the canon of art history for the Caribbean and Latin America forever.

In looking closely at the photograph taken on his day of departure for England on August 17, 1953 (fig. 7), one can see that it was uncomfortably hot. He leans stiffly against a car in a summer suit with arms crossed and a stunning beauty at his side. Walter was entrusted with the responsibility of chaperoning his relation, Eileen Galway, to the UK, as she was destined for central London's prestigious Gray's Inn. She would become the first female Antiguan to receive a law degree. It is clear from the picture that she had a keen intellect and possessed a healthy dose of self-confidence. She had no idea at the time, nor did she ever know, that she would be the love of Frank Walter's life until his dying day.

The exhibition *Fragments of Epic Memory* (2021) includes Walter's paintings *Plantation Fields and Workers* (c. 1968-1974, fig. 8) and *Complex of Life* (1960, fig. 9), representing the bookends of Walter's life. Figurative and Abstract. The real and the imagined. Or was it?

The speech Derek Walcott delivered upon his acceptance of the 1992 Nobel Prize in Literature, "The Antilles: Fragments of Epic Memory," articulates the ways in which European authors looked upon the Caribbean with "elegiac pathos."[2] Like Walcott, Walter rejected the European interpretation of his homeland as a *triste tropique*. Living in nature, he had full access to the stars. His seaside world carried with it fresh sea breezes, the pungent scent of blossoming trusses of silver agave plants intertwined with

5

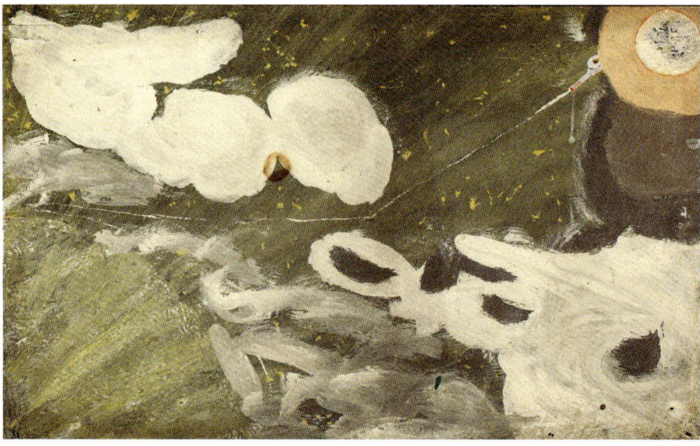

6

7

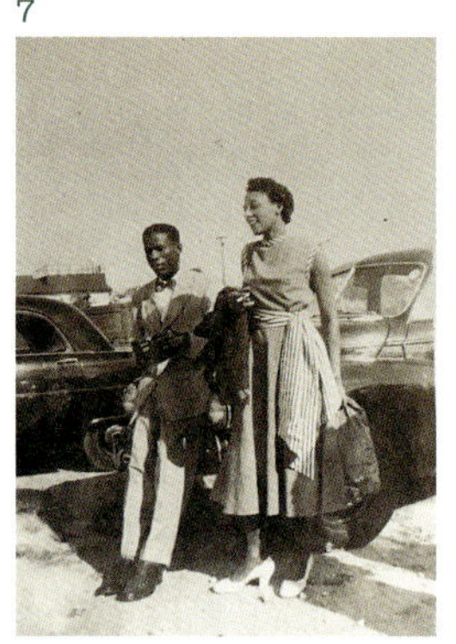

Fig. 5
Frank Walter
Moon Voyage, [n.d.] (from *Milky Way Galaxy* series).
Oil on wood, 20.5 × 47 × 1.3 cm.
© Courtesy Sir Selvyn and Kathleen, Lady Walter. Photo: Kenneth M. Milton Fine Arts.

Fig. 6
Frank Walter
Moon Crater. c. 1994 (from *Milky Way Galaxy* series).
Oil on wood, 6.8 × 21.5 x 0.8 cm.
© Courtesy Sir Selvyn and Kathleen, Lady Walter. Photo: Kenneth M. Milton Fine Arts.

Fig. 7
Departure, August 17, 1953. Photograph.

8

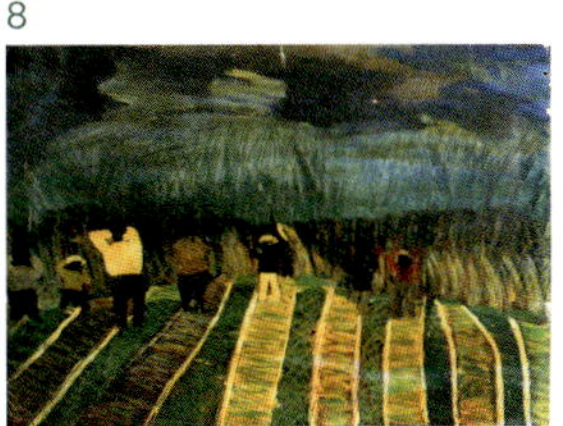

9

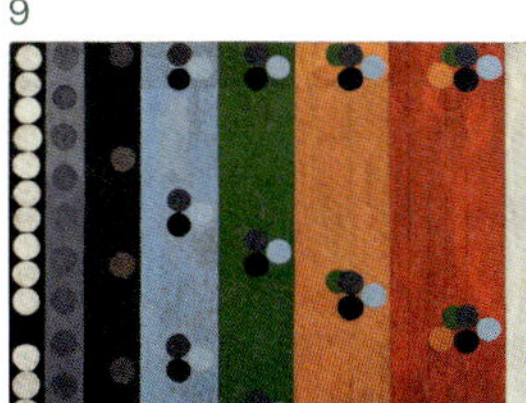
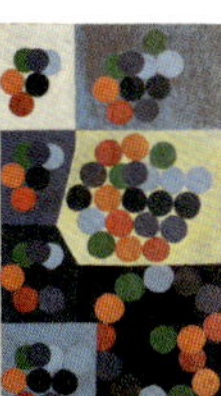

10

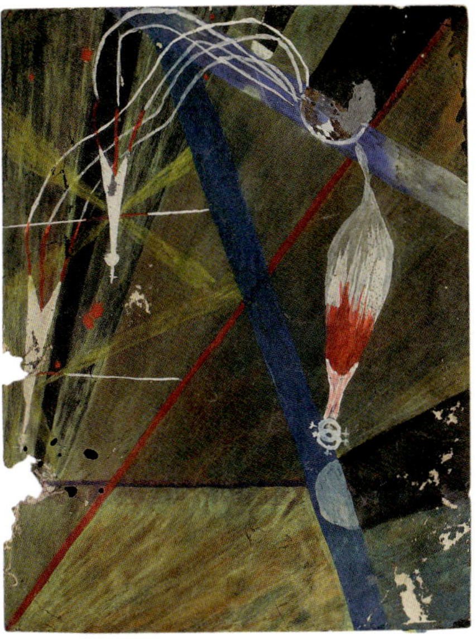

`Fig. 8`
Frank Walter
Plantation Fields and Workers, c. 1968–1974.
Oil on cardboard, 31.8 × 45 cm; framed: 46 × 57 cm. Private collection. © Courtesy Sir Selvyn and Kathleen, Lady Walter. Photo: Kenneth M. Milton Fine Arts.

`Fig. 9`
Frank Walter
Complex of Life, 1960.
(from *Milky Way Galaxy* series). Oil on Masonite, 25.5 × 50.5 cm; framed: 33 × 58.5 cm. Private collection. © Courtesy Sir Selvyn and Kathleen, Lady Walter. Photo: Kenneth M. Milton Fine Arts.

`Fig. 10`
Frank Walter
Intergalactic Botany, [n.d.]. Oil on cardboard, 24.5 × 18.2 cm. © Courtesy Sir Selvyn and Kathleen, Lady Walter. Photo: Kenneth M. Milton Fine Arts.

bright red fruit of jumbie bead vines. His gaze was always to the horizon and upward as he witnessed iridescent blue hummingbirds pollinate the lofty flowers. He dwelt in a *merveilleux univers tropical.*

Evidence of this universe can be witnessed in two-dimensional art such as *Intergalactic Botany* (`n.d., fig. 10`), and the six spectacular paintings that make up his *Milky Way Galaxy Series*. *Intergalactic Botany* is linked to the artist's Jupiterian opera, written and composed with guitar, harmonica, and voices (kings, queens, princes, prince, troubadour, etc.) performed by Walter. Walter plays a harmonica solo that is over eight minutes long. Act two is brief, as Walter time-travels through the cosmos in search of his celestial bride. This is followed by a fourteen-minute guitar-and-voice solo, which combines early Roman Catholic chants with the Ashanti Obeah humming he would have heard his grandmother and maiden aunts sing during his childhood in Antigua. The complex vibrations, deep tonal qualities, and rhythm of the music are rooted in Africa. It weaves in European liturgical music drawn from his childhood at St. Joseph's Cathedral in St. John's, as well as his visits to all of the great cathedrals in Europe and England. Walter's crooner-inspired song "I'll Steal You Away to the Moon" brings the audience into a contemporary realm. This highly original opera tells the story of life on Jupiter and intermarriage between members of the royal court there with earth men. Frank Walter, known privily as Charles II, has been selected to marry the daughter of the King of Jupiter, who is concerned about the problems of inbreeding on his planet. The Princess Astrid and her ladies-in-waiting flutter around the universe in stylish astro-cruisers. The opera ends with a grand wedding, and the happy couple fly off in their astro-cruiser with Prince Leopold Archduke of Austria, the consort to Princess Astrid's noble sister. These sleek spacecrafts are depicted in *Intergalactic Botany,* showing how extraterrestrial flowers are pollinated by Jupiterian maidens. The elements, iconographic message, and colour scheme of this figurative work is translated into the abstract in Walter's masterpiece, *Complex of Life*. The stripes represent paths, and the small multi-coloured circles are different races of people clustering together. This painting recalls *Plantation Fields and Workers*, with its stripes of cultivated earth, and humans intentionally staged to complete the canvas.

Physically and emotionally depleted by seven years of manual labour jobs, substandard housing, and the grim reality of starvation, Walter returned to Antigua in 1961. He was again defeated. The sugar industry had collapsed, and there was no prospect of meaningful work for him. Despondent, he relocated to Dominica, where he built the beginnings of Mount Olympus, his agricultural and industrial estate. It was there that he reconnected to Europe and the UK through poetry, music, sculpture, and painting. From his sun-soaked hillside overlooking Prince Rupert Bay, Walter recalled the fog, meadows, mountains, castle battlements, and sense of camaraderie that he encountered in Scotland. Simultaneously, he painted and sculpted local scenes, Antiguan landscapes, and other worlds. Those worlds are expressed over centuries, from Arawaks, Caribs, Christ, and the present to spacemen and future possibilities. Added to this complexity is the fact that the 5,000 paintings in his oeuvre are intricately linked to one another. The two paintings exhibited in *Fragments of Epic Memory* make the case. *Plantation Fields and Workers* finds its parallel in Walter's Scottish series, specifically, *Scottish Agriculture* (n.d., fig. 11) and *Scottish Silviculture* (n.d., fig. 12). Fields and trees are abstracted with a fine brush that captures the chill and cold, foggy atmosphere of the place.

Walter returned to Antigua from Dominica in 1968 and did the bulk of his photography and intricate memory paintings from that time until 1976. He lived in central St. John's and moved to his final destination, a rural property, in 1993. He continued to paint until his death in 2009, focusing on depictions of the natural world (Caribbean, UK, and Europe), figuration, and abstract art. Walter's work is infused with light. He described his dream exhibition as a circuit with paintings on the walls and sculptural pieces in the centre. The main drama of this show would be the play of light activating his art and the way in which the viewer would circulate through the space. Walter's ultimate desire was to impact his audience in a positive way, lifting even the most melancholic and societally bereft to a higher level. Art was his anodyne, and he hoped that it would positively impact others as "some elixir which had been free for the seeing—healthier than an opiate could draw."[3]

Within Walcott's "Epic" address is a lamentation on the "photogenic poverty" and "postcard sadness"

11

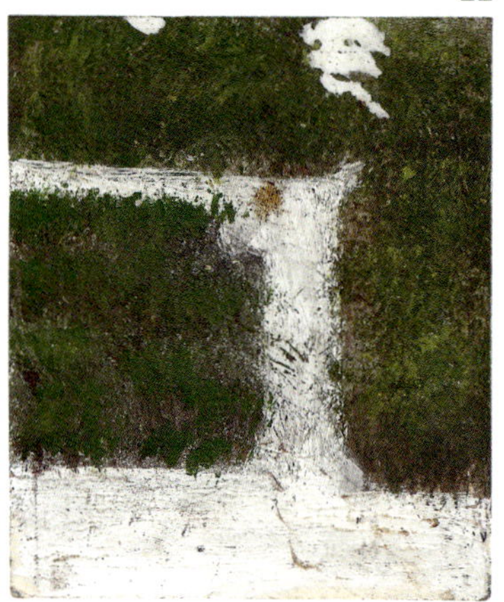

12

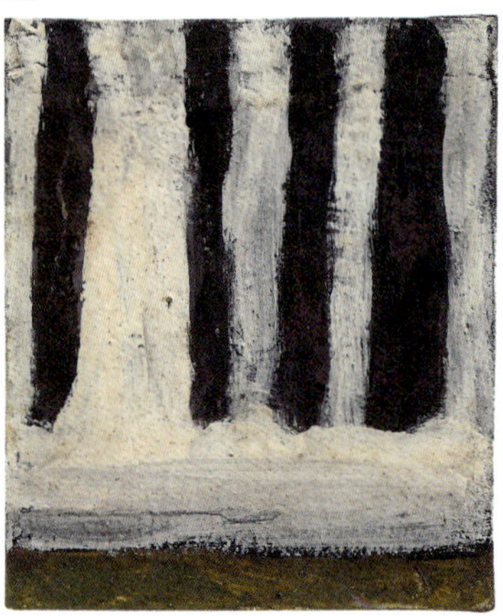

Fig. 11
Frank Walter
Scottish Agriculture
[n.d.]. Oil on Polaroid film cartridge box, 9.8 × 8 cm.
© Courtesy Sir Selvyn and Kathleen, Lady Walter.
Photo: Kenneth M. Milton Fine Arts.

Fig. 12
Frank Walter
Scottish Silviculture
[n.d.]. Oil on Polaroid film cartridge box, 9.8 × 8 cm.
© Courtesy Sir Selvyn and Kathleen, Lady Walter.
Photo: Kenneth M. Milton Fine Arts.

permeating his home. Walcott surmised that "sadly, to sell itself, the Caribbean encourages the delights of mindlessness."[4] Walcott concludes that, for tourists, the poor were there to amuse and were then forgotten like a vacation.[5] There is a more hopeful side to his speech, however, following his statement that Caribbean genius is condemned to contradict itself. He acknowledges the defiant dignity of poor people who live close to the land, and this is the key to understanding Frank Walter and the Caribbean intelligentsia:

> In our tourist brochures the Caribbean is a blue pool into which the republic dangles the extended foot of Florida as inflated rubber islands bob, and drinks with umbrellas float towards her on a raft. This is how the islands from the shame of necessity sell themselves; this is the seasonal erosion of their identity, that high-pitched repetition of the same images of service that cannot distinguish one island from the other, with a future of polluted marinas, land deals negotiated by ministers, and all of this conducted to the music of Happy Hour and the rictus of a smile.
>
> The Caribbean is not an idyll, not to its natives. They draw their working strength from it organically, like trees, like the sea almond or the spice laurel of the heights. Its peasantry and its fishermen are not there to be loved or even photographed; they are trees who sweat, and whose bark is filmed with salt.[6]

For Frank Walter, his countrymen were just that. They were to be treated with respect and honoured, as they were integral to his identity as a key figure in patriarchal society. He identified with Prince Charles and kept a black-and-white photograph of the young prince artistically arranged on the table at the entrance to his house. Walter's curious painting *Adam and Eve* (n.d., fig. 13) features the prince with his wife in a tropical setting, similar to many of his self-portraits as a white man. He believed in his own (imagined) patriarchal duty so strongly that he created the Antigua and Barbuda National Democratic Party and ran a failed campaign for prime minister, losing to his cousin George Walter in 1971. Brown University's Paget Henry

13

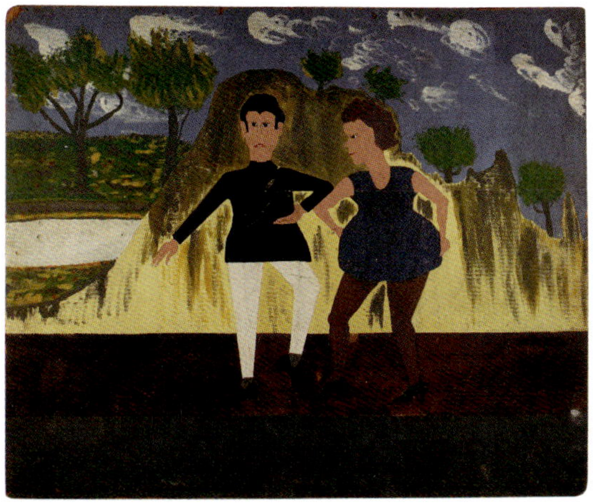

Fig. 13
Frank Walter
Adam and Eve [n.d.].
Oil on Masonite, 60.5 × 71 cm.
© Courtesy Sir Selvyn and Kathleen, Lady Walter. Photo: Kenneth M. Milton Fine Arts.

knew Walter as a youth and was oftentimes confounded by his political and philosophical contradictions. Henry gets to the point of Walter as a "Black Caliban" or self-proclaimed "Europoid" who was ultimately splintered between many worlds, developing a severe case of Frantz Fanon's syndrome of Black skins that wear white masks. Henry describes Walter's art as a kind of upwards sloping graph: "The vertical or y-axis was a highly original spirituality, while the horizontal or x-axis recorded his responses to the racial impact of late colonial society in Antigua and Barbuda on his formation as a young man."[7]

By 1973 Walter had completed over 5,000 paintings, numbering the backs for an exhibition. He felt ready to host an art show and penned many letters to potential "galleries" from 1973 to 1974. His choice of venues was interesting. He solicited the National Coal Board, the Creda Sport & Social Club in Stoke-on-Trent, youth hostels in Düsseldorf, and international cruise ship lines, requesting to have an exhibition on their premises. From a luxurious tourist yacht to a coal mine, Walter was determined to share his memory paintings with a deserving audience. There is a straightforward honesty to Walter's work, and in that form of simplicity there is sophistication. Against staggering odds, Walter's work enlightens the viewer. It is hopeful. Even when Walter was suffering through the torments of nervous breakdowns, his work was intended to have a therapeutic effect and to cure the inner sadness of his audience. Walter's work has universal appeal to this day, as it stitches together every imaginable culture and historical event. In his "Epic" speech, Walcott provides a fitting literary parallel to Walter's unique awareness of the origins that led to his art:

> That is the basis of the Antillean experience, this shipwreck of fragments, these echoes, these shards of a huge tribal vocabulary, these partially remembered customs, and they are not decayed but strong. They survived the Middle Passage.[8]

1 The author wishes to thank Mary-Elisabeth Moore, who assisted with the editing of this article.

2 "The Caribbean is looked at with elegiac pathos, a prolonged sadness to which Lévi-Strauss has supplied an epigraph: *Tristes Tropiques*.... There is something alien and ultimately wrong in the way such a sadness, even a morbidity, is described by English, French, or some of our exiled writers." Derek Walcott, "The Antilles, Fragments of Epic Memory: The 1992 Nobel Lecture," *World Literature Today* 67, no. 2 (1993): 264.

3 Frank Walter, "On Art: A Planter's Feeling" (unpublished poem, August 1–4, 1994), Frank Walter Papers.

4 Walcott, "Fragments of Epic Memory," 263–264.

5 Walcott, "Fragments of Epic Memory," 265.

6 Walcott, "Fragments of Epic Memory," 265–267.

7 Paget Henry, conversation with author, February 22, 2021.

8 Walcott, "Fragments of Epic Memory," 262–263.

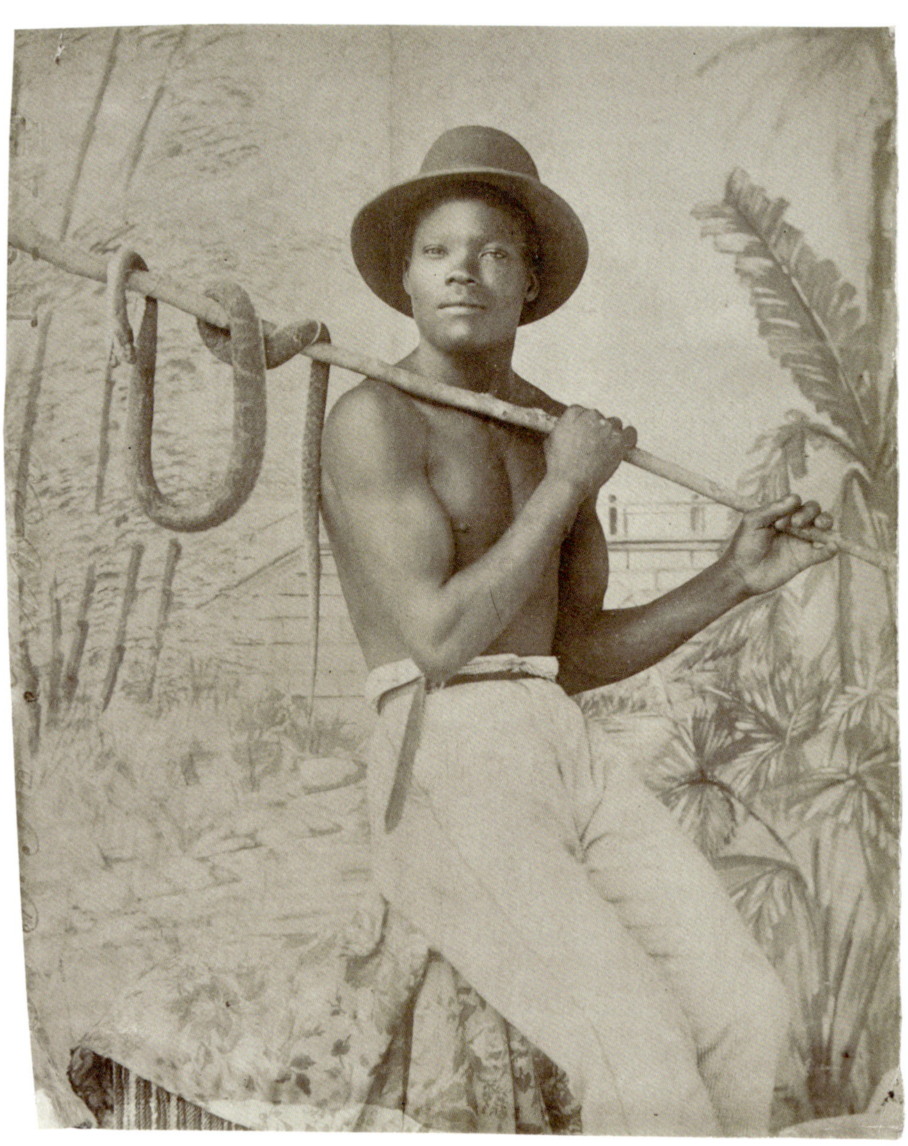

Unknown photographer, *Snake Charmer, Martinique,* c. 1880

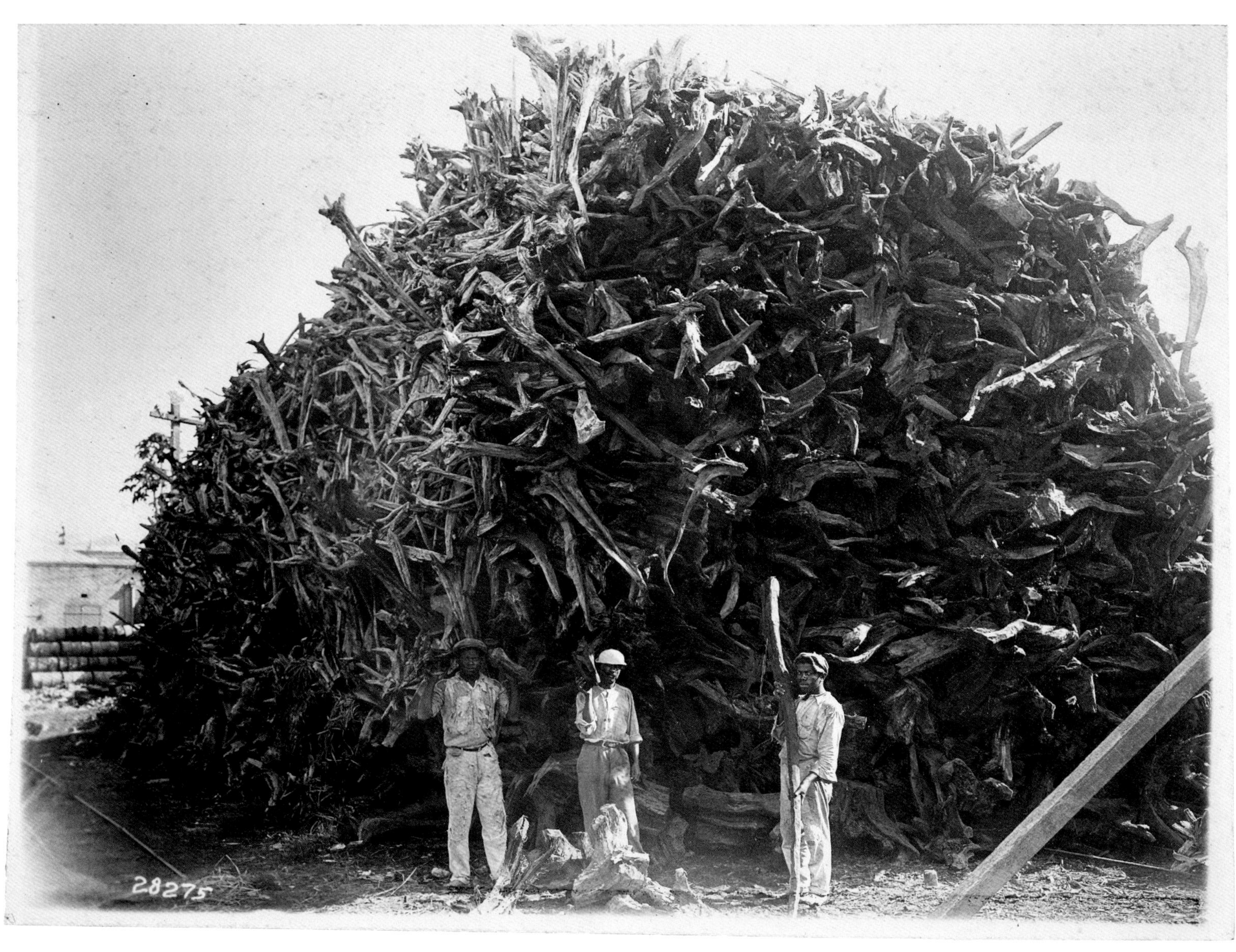

Publishers Photo Service, *Wood Collectors, Kingston, Jamaica*, c. 1920

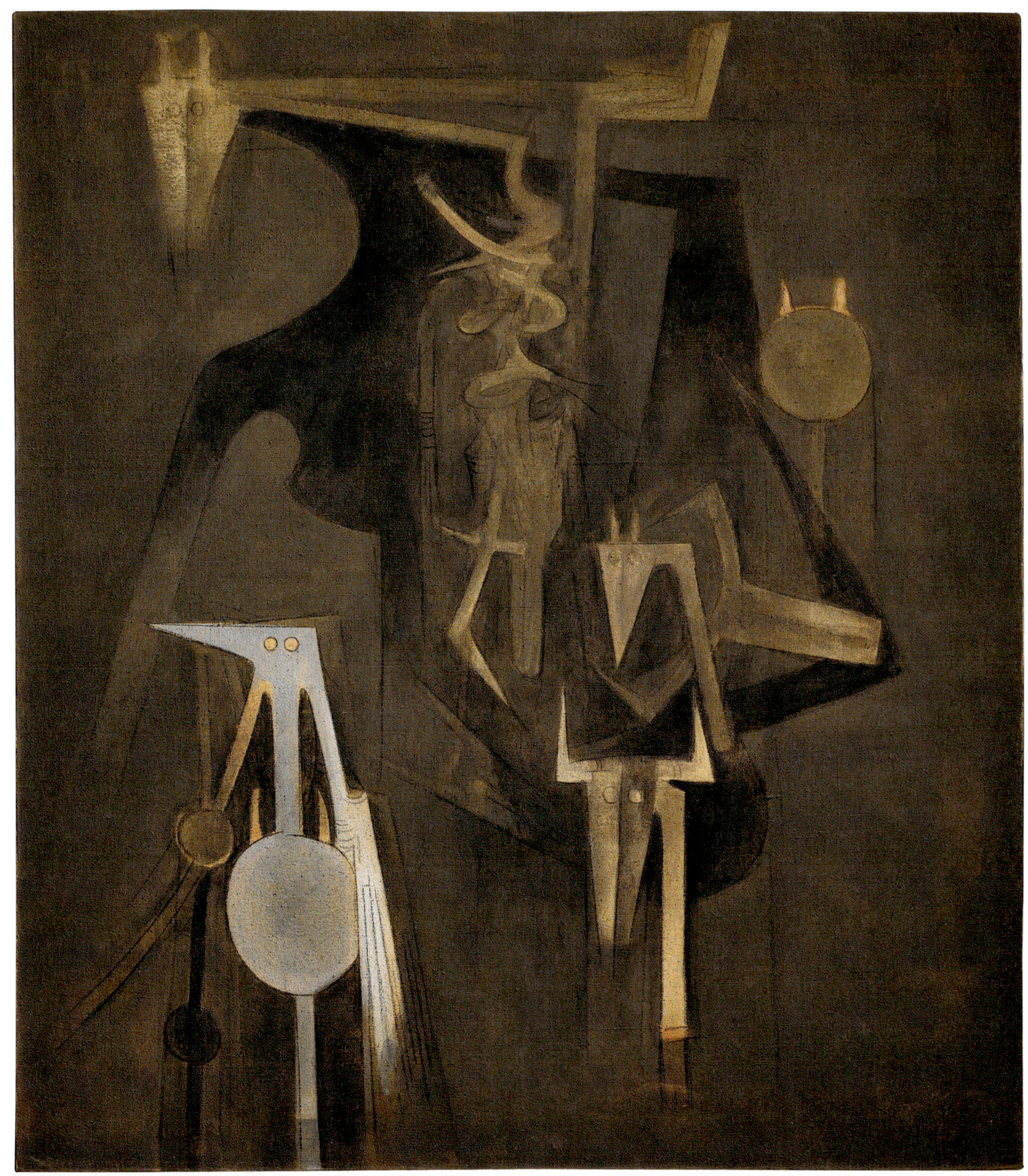

Wifredo Lam, *Mayombè*, 1962

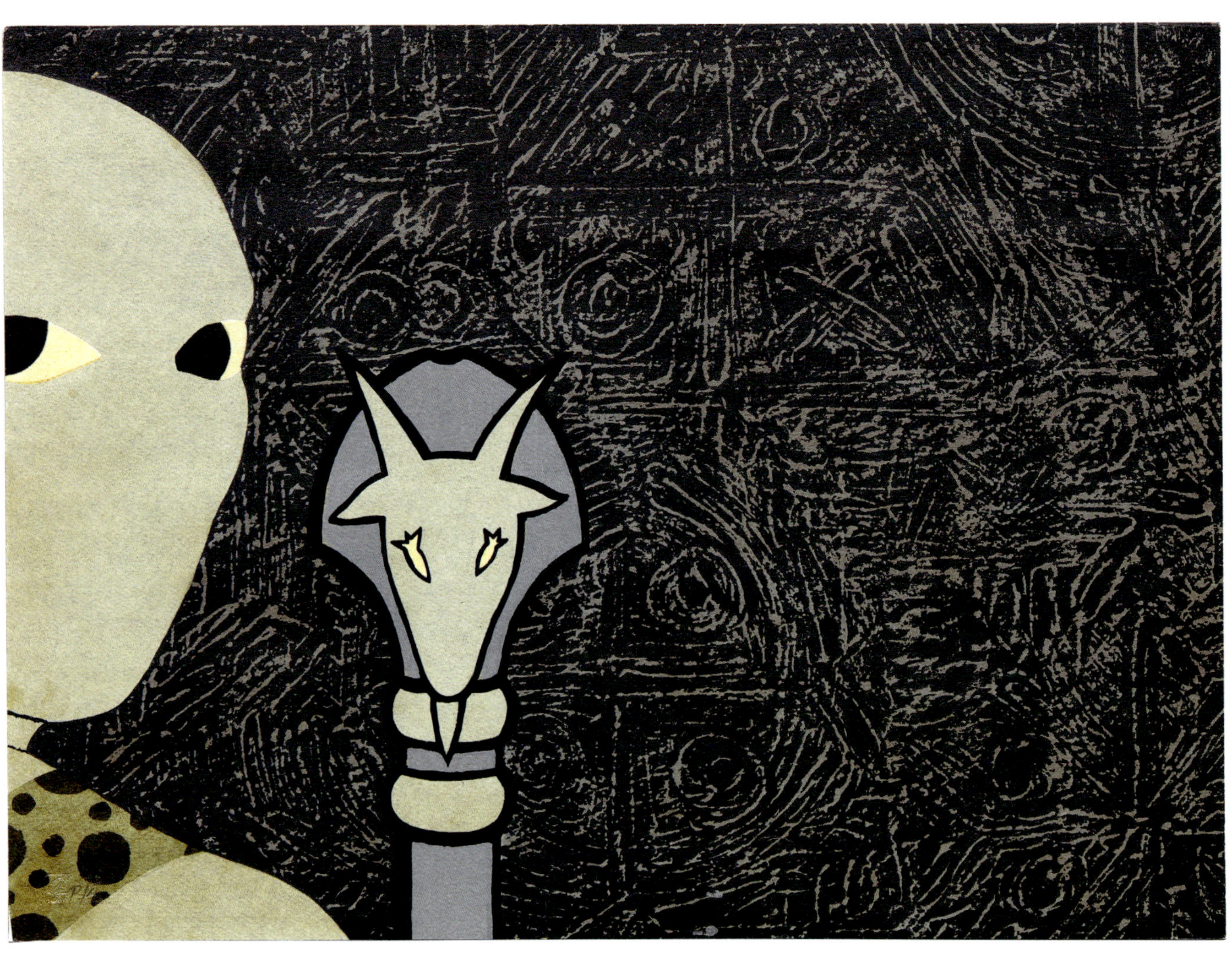

Belkis Ayón, *Untitled (Sikán with staff)*, 1991

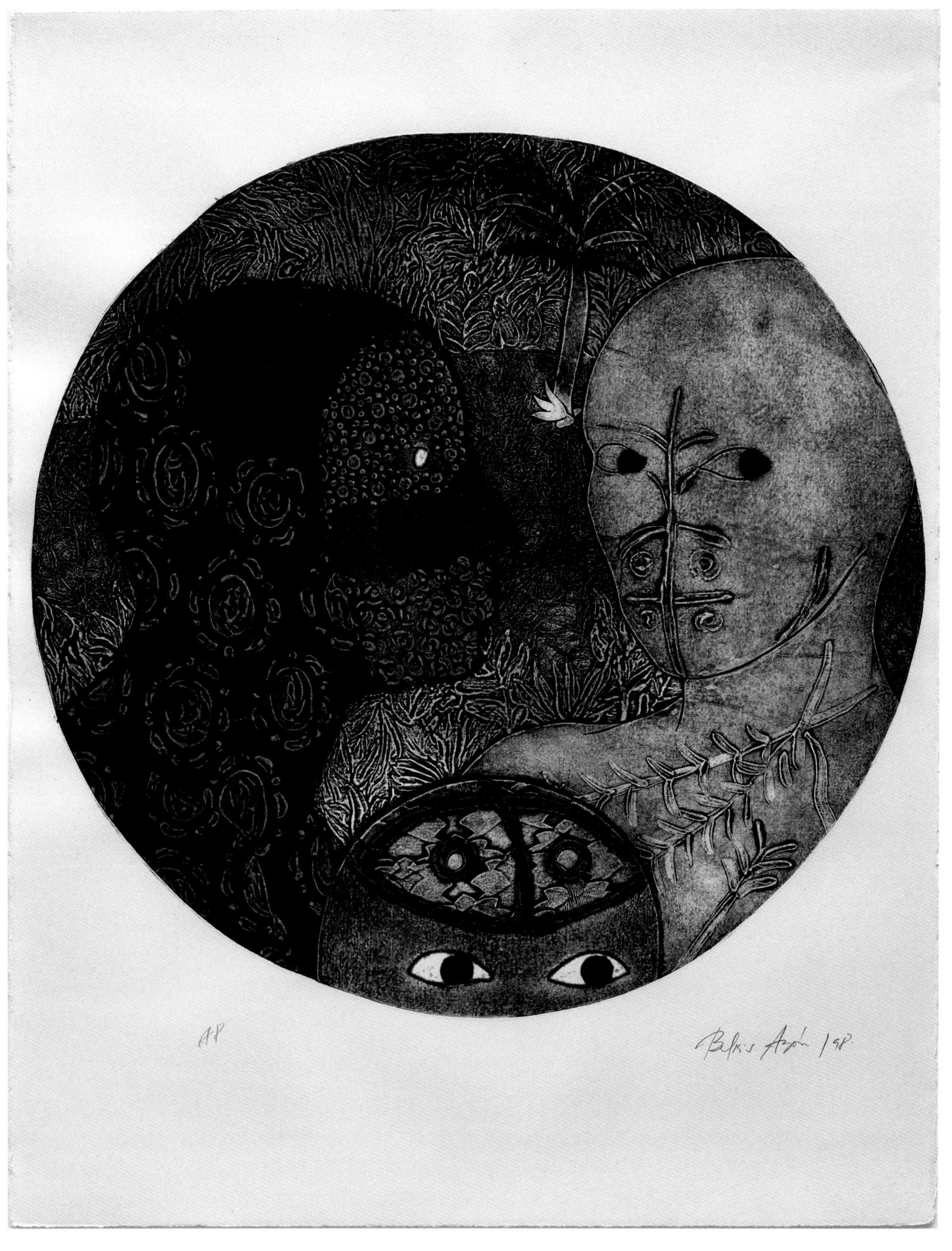

Belkis Ayón, *Untitled*, c. 1998

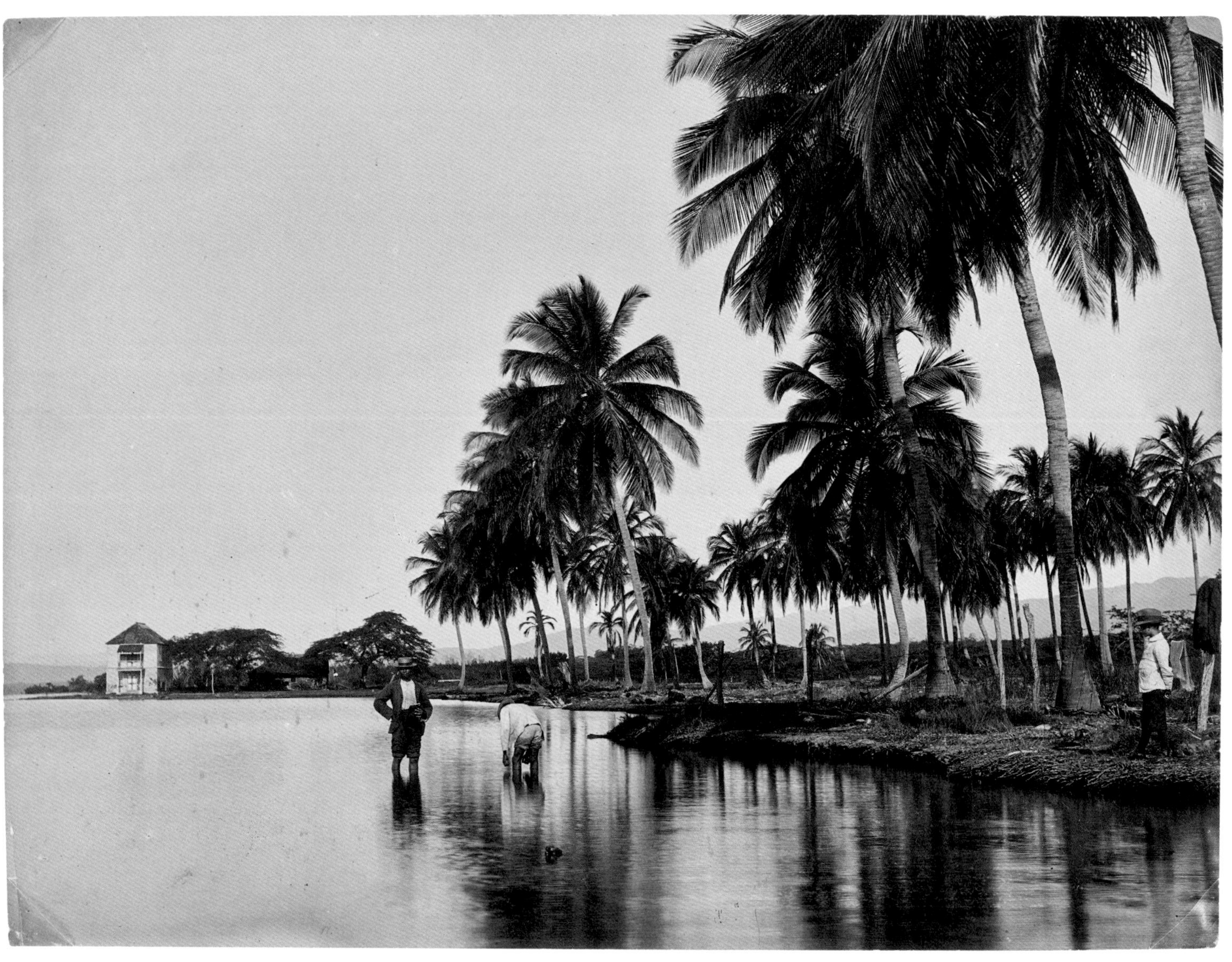

John William Cleary, *Coconut Palms, Kingston Harbour, Jamaica,* c. 1895

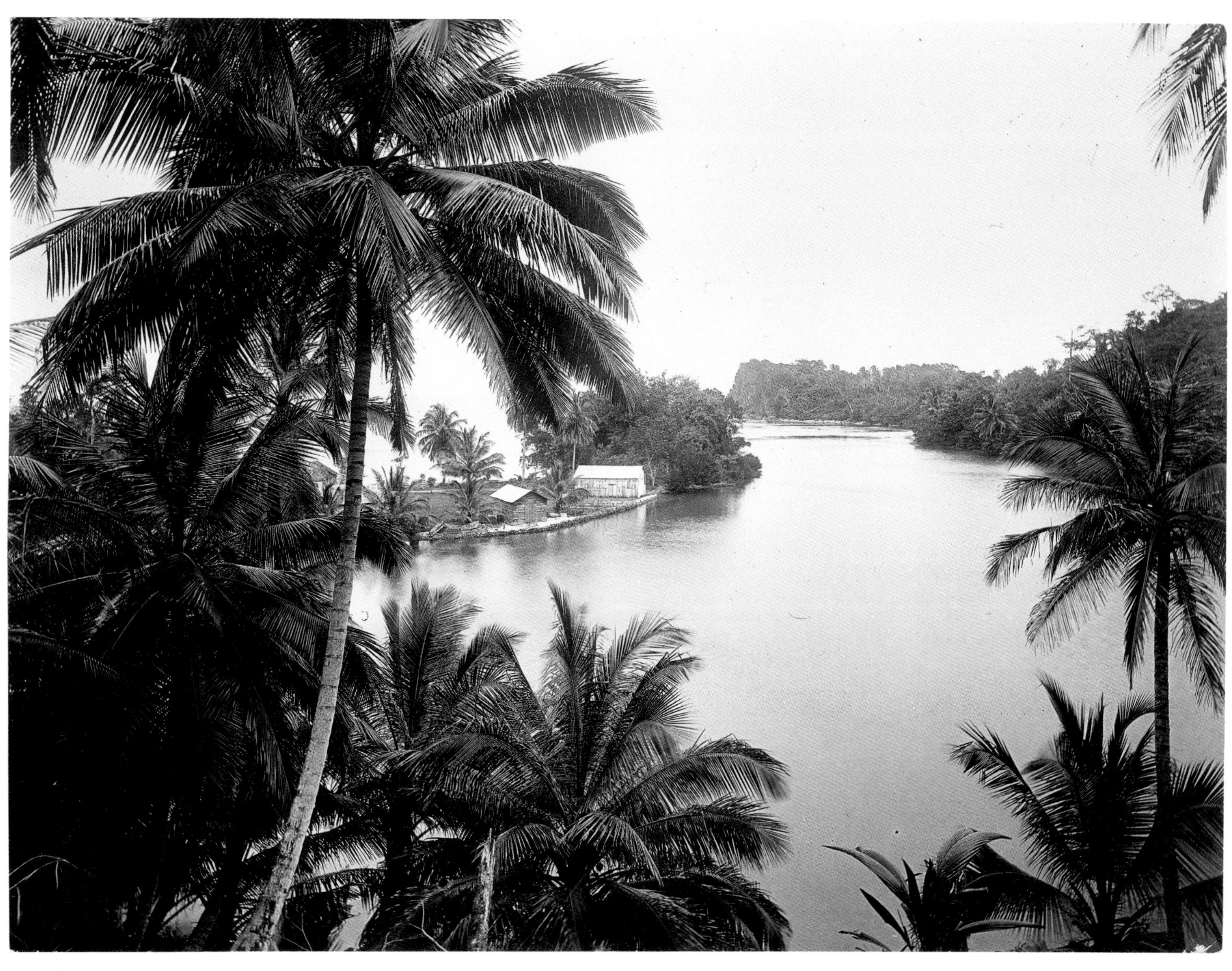

A. Duperly & Sons, *Blue Hole*, *Portland*, *Jamaica*, c. 1900

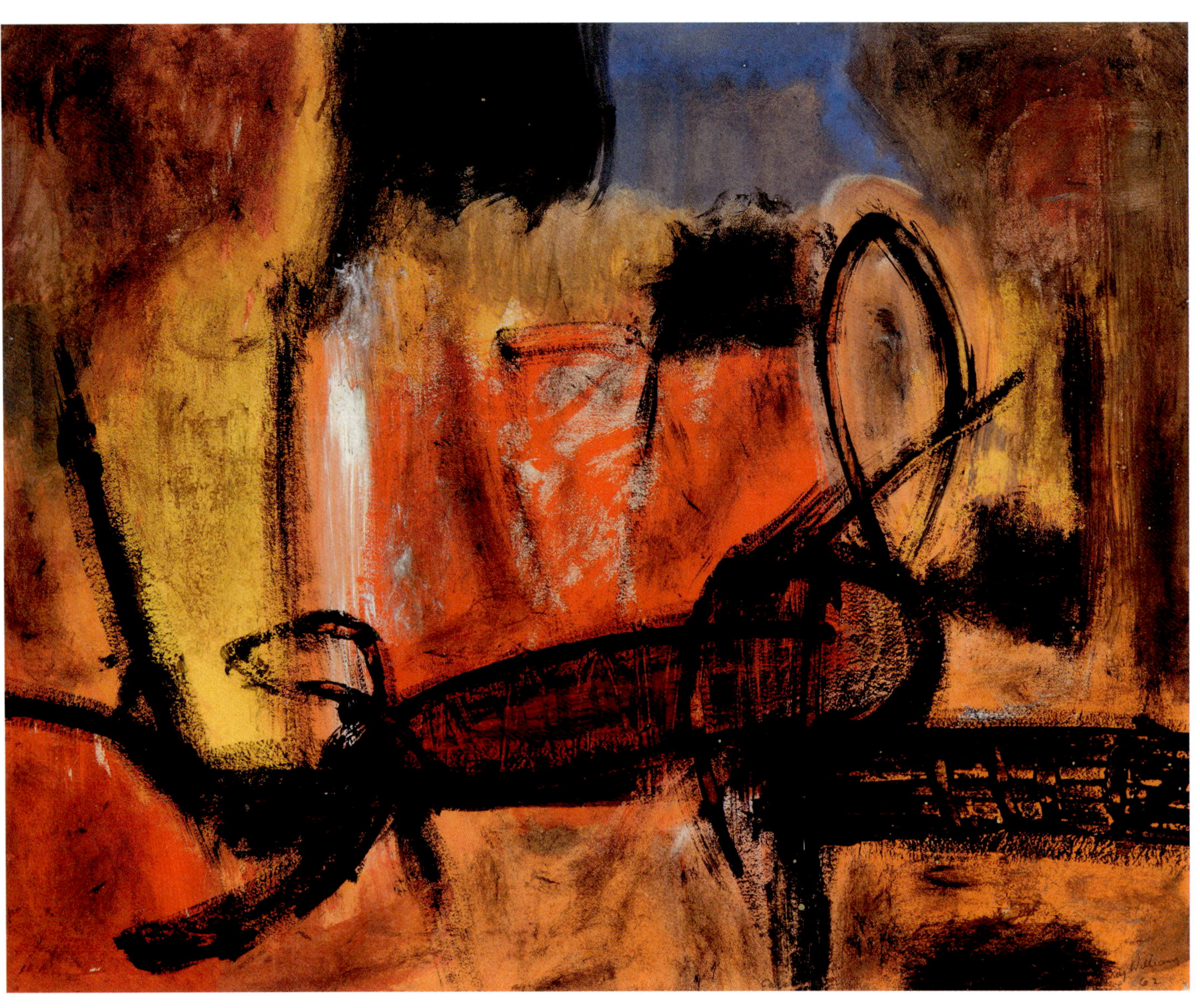

Aubrey Williams, *Carib Form*, 1962

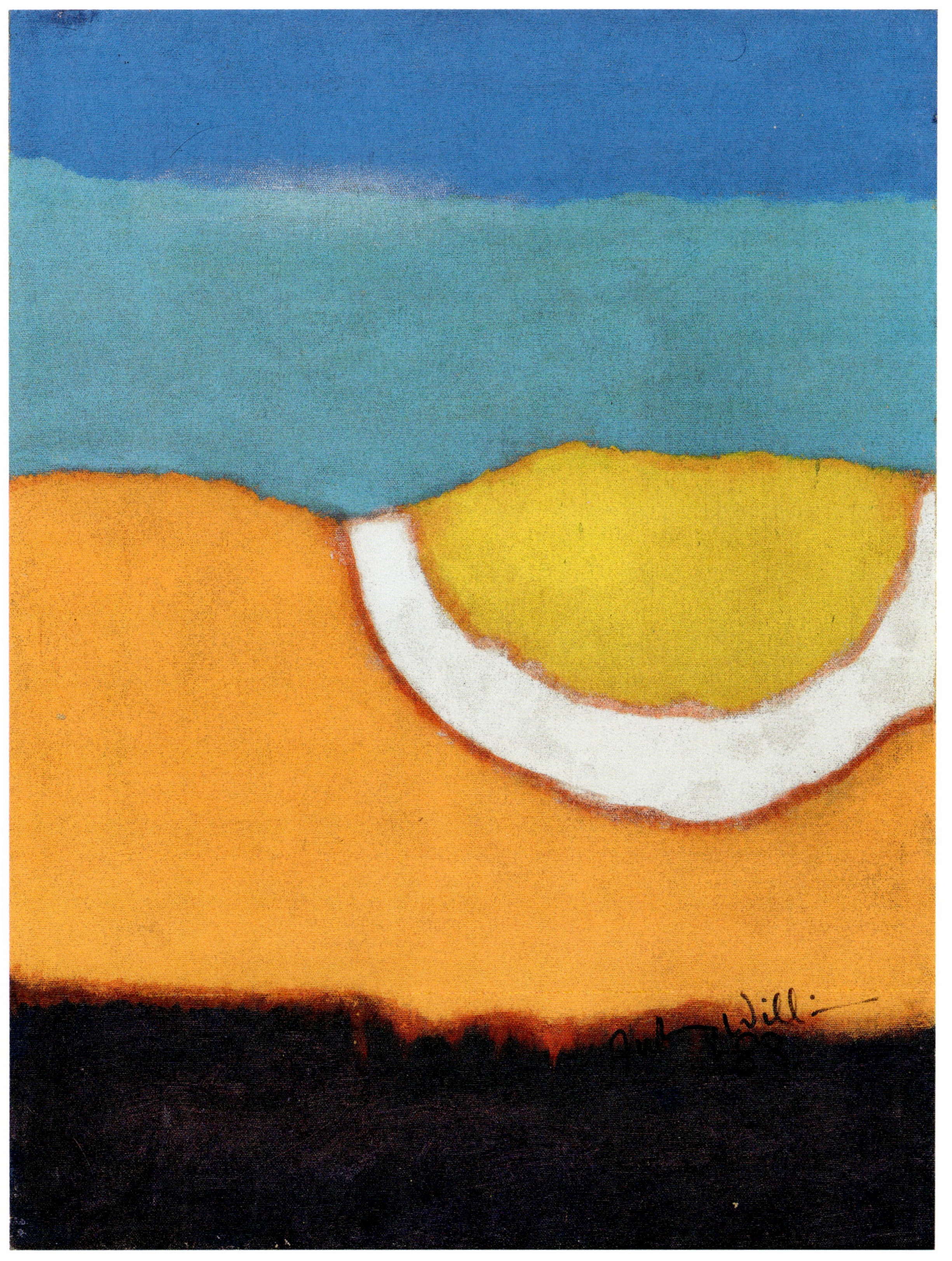

Aubrey Williams, *Solar Rad 1*, 1988

Epilogue

Michel-Rolph Trouillot

I was looking for Columbus, but I knew he would not be there. Down by the shore, Port-au-Prince exposed its wounds to the sun; and Harry Truman Boulevard, once the most beautiful street of Haiti, was now a patchwork of potholes.

The boulevard was built for the bicentennial celebration of Port-au-Prince, which Truman helped finance right between his launching of the North Atlantic Treaty Organization and the start of the Korean War. Now, it looked like a war zone with no memory of the celebrations of which it had been the centre. Only a few of the statues erected for the occasion remained. Its fountains had dried up under two Duvaliers. Its palm trees had shrunk as had Haiti itself.

I turned in front of the French Institute, a living monument to the impact of French culture on the Haitian elites, and drove toward the U.S. embassy, a center of power of a different order. Above a mountain of sandbags, a helmeted black G.I. watched nonchalantly as a crowd of half-naked boys bathed in a puddle left by yesterday's rain. He had probably come with the occupying forces that helped restore President Jean-Bertrand Aristide to power in 1994. The story I was looking for went back to nine years earlier. I drove by.

I stopped the car at safe enough distance from the embassy and started a slow walk on the boulevard. On the buildings around the post office, conflicting graffitis asked the U.S. forces both to stay and to go home. I spotted a statue lying behind a fence across the street.

A peddling artist stood next to it, selling paintings and crafts. I greeted the man and asked him if he knew where the statue of Christopher Columbus was.

I had vague memories of that statue. I only remembered its existence from my adolescent wanderings. The few images I could summon came from Graham Greene's "The Comedians." It was under the watchful eyes of Columbus that the heroes of that story, later played by Richard Burton and Elizabeth Taylor, consummated their illicit love. But the bust on the grass was no Columbus. The painter confirmed my doubts. "No," he said, "this is a statue of Charlemagne Péralte."

Péralte was the leader of a nationalist army that fought the first occupation of Haiti by the United States in the 1920s. From the pictures the Marines took of him after they had crucified him on a door, I knew that he was a thin dark man. The bust on the grass was visibly that of a white male, rather stocky. "You're sure this is Péralte?" I asked again. "Sure is Péralte," replied the painter. I moved closer and read the inscription. The sculpture was a bust of Harry Truman.

"Where is the Columbus one?" I asked.

"I don't know. I am not from Port-au-Prince," replied the man. "Maybe it is the one that used to be near the water."

I walked to the place he indicated. No statue was to be found. The pedestal was still there, but the sculpture itself was missing. Someone had inscribed on the cement: "Charlemagne Péralte Plaza." Truman had become Péralte and Péralte had replaced Columbus.

I stood there for another half hour, asking each passerby if they knew what had happened to the Columbusstatue. I knew the story: I was in Port-au-Prince when Columbus disappeared. I just wanted confirmation, a test of how public memory works and how history takes shape in a country with the lowest literacy rate on this side of the Atlantic.

I was almost ready to give up when a young man recapped for me the events I had first heard about in 1986. In that year, at the fall of Jean-Claude Duvalier's dictatorship, the most miserable people of Haiti's capital had taken to the streets. They had thrown their anger at every monument that they associated with the dictatorship. A number of statues had been broken into pieces; others were simply removed from their bases. This was how Truman came to find himself on the grass.

Columbus had a different fate, for reasons still unknown to me. Perhaps the illiterate demonstrators associated his name with colonialism. The mistake, if mistake there was, is understandable: the word "kolon" in Haitian means both Columbus and a colonist. Perhaps they associated him with the ocean from which he came. At any rate, when the angry crowd from the neighbouring shanty towns rolled down the Harry Truman Boulevard, they took the statue of Columbus, removed it from its pedestal, and dumped it into the sea.

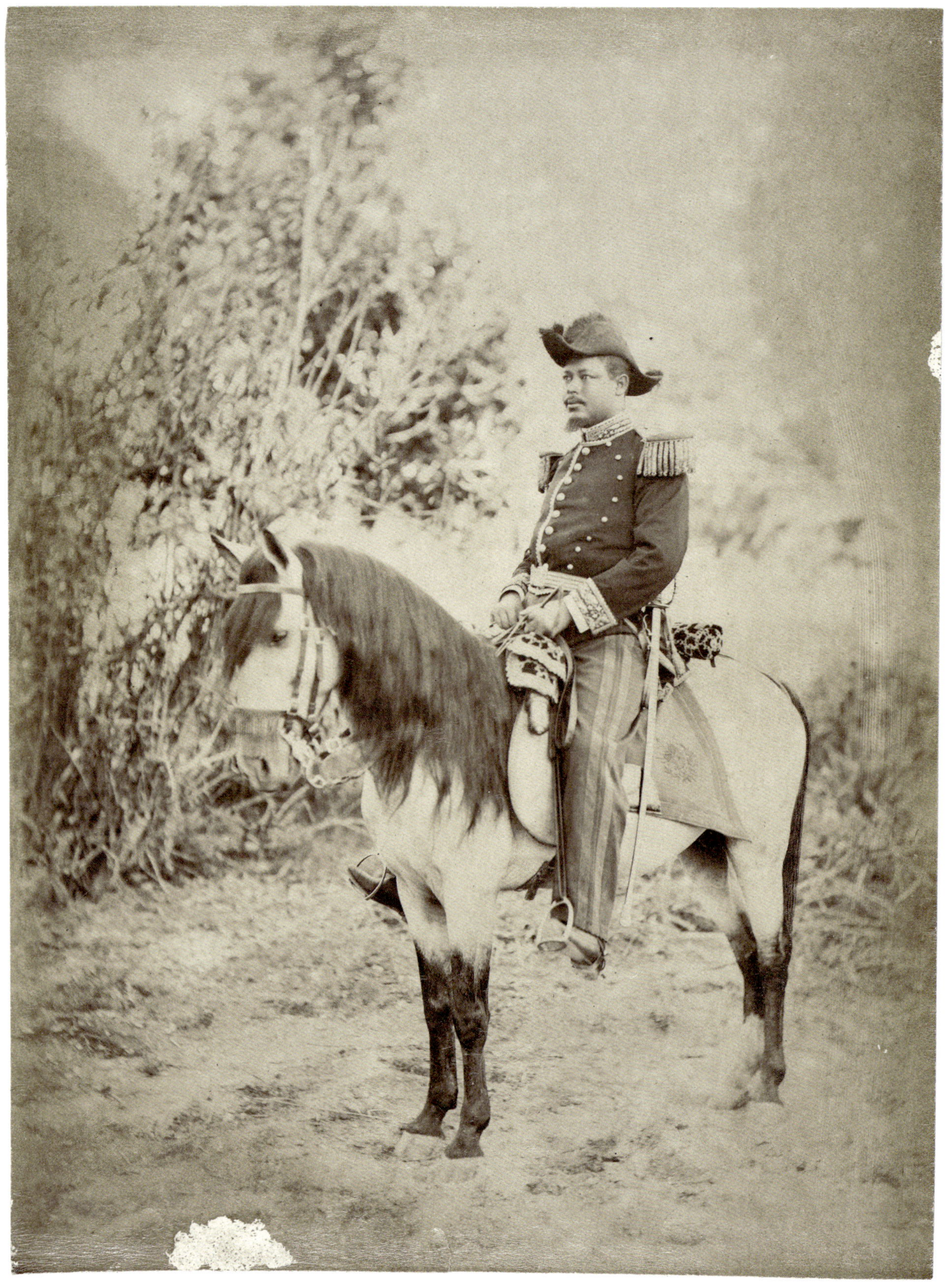

Unknown photographer, *Officer, Haiti*, c. 1880

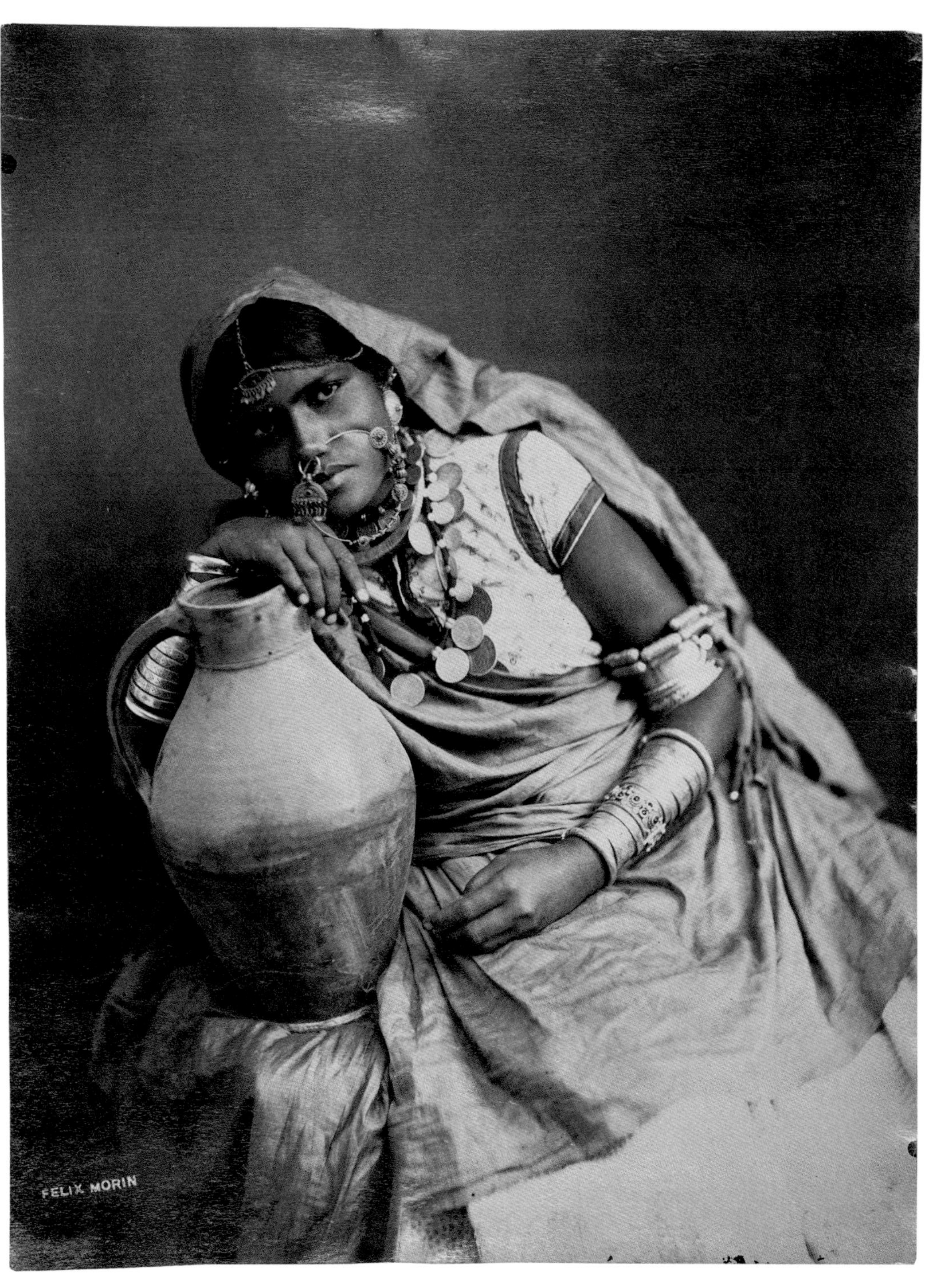

Felix Morin, *Woman with Clay Vessel, Trinidad*, c. 1895

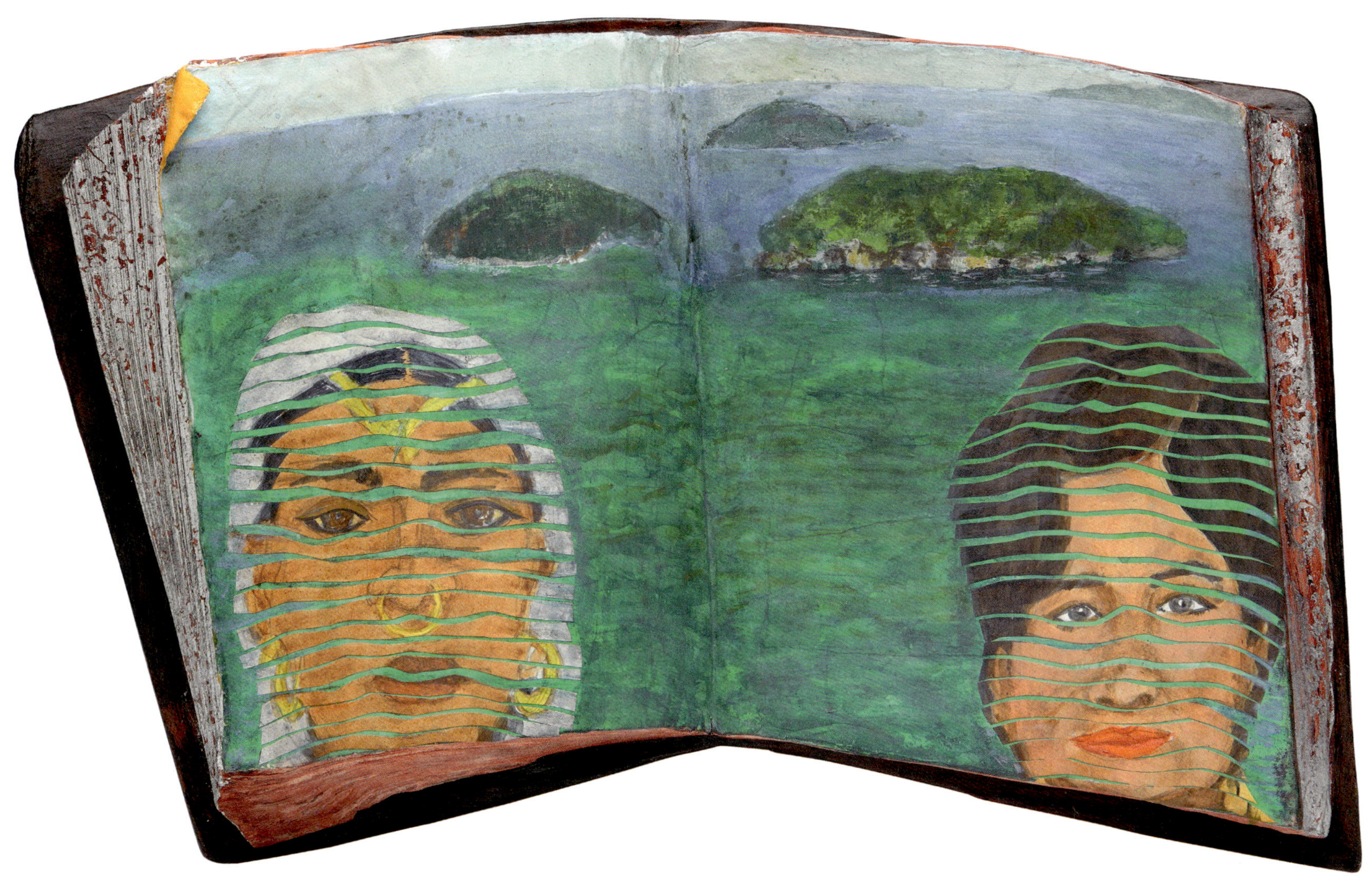

Wendy Nanan, *Nelson Island*, 2012

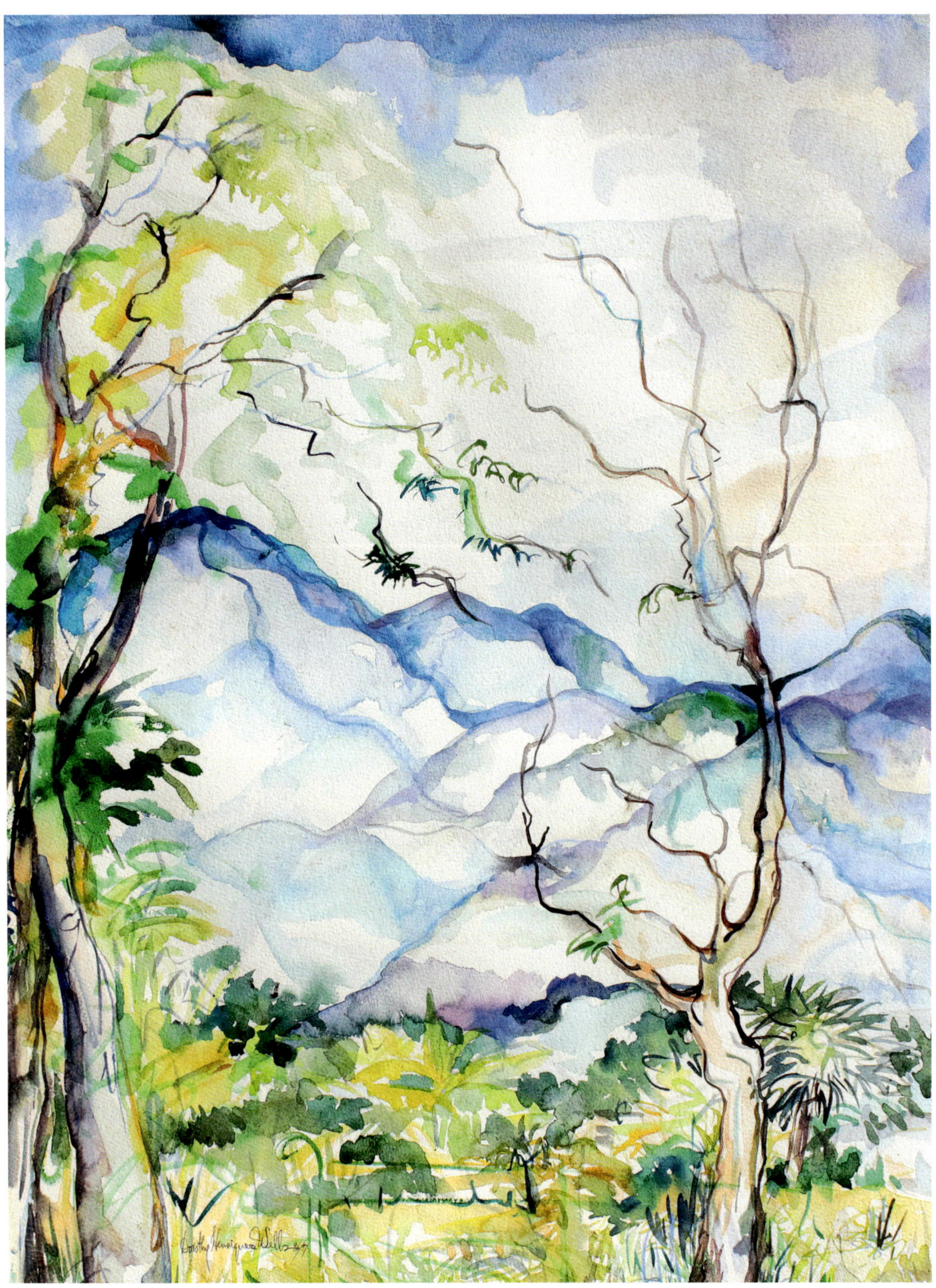

Dorothy Henriques Wells, *The Blue Mountains*, 1996–1997

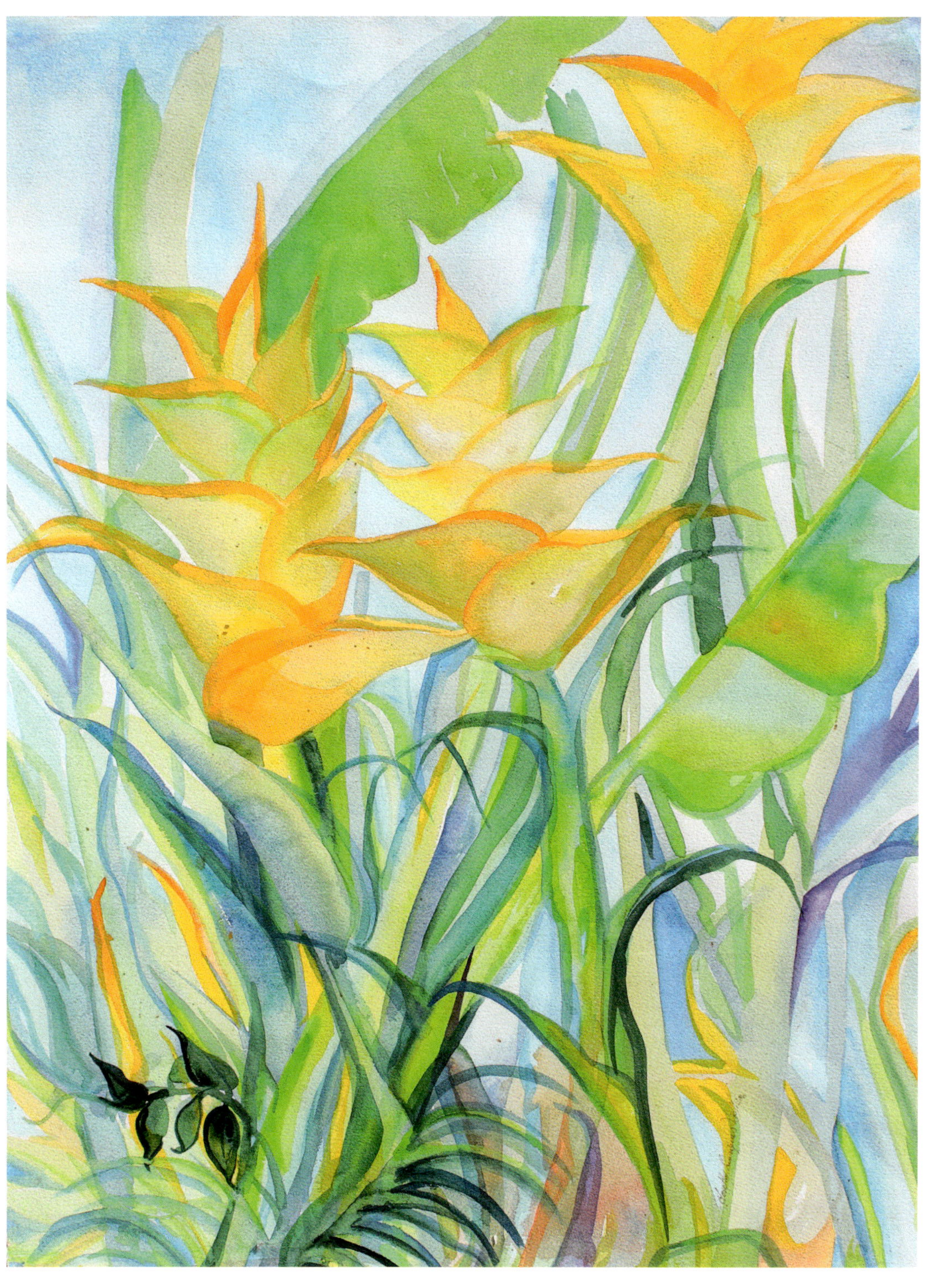

Dorothy Henriques Wells, *Wild Banana*, 1990

My Mother, Dorothy Henriques Wells

Mary Wells, with a preface by Emily Cluett

Preface

Celebrated as "one of the finest watercolourists in the Americas" (to borrow a description from the British art critic Edward Lucie-Smith),[1] the Jamaican artist Dorothy Henriques Wells (1926–2018) was born into a creative family of jewellers and painters who proudly supported her creative endeavours at a young age. Wells grew up in Kingston, which is where her parents met the Armenian artist Koren der Harootian (who occasionally worked in Jamaica); between 1939 and 1943, they arranged for him to give private lessons to their then-teenage daughter. Wells's artistic pursuits took her around the world, beginning in 1947 when she enrolled at what was then known as the Ontario College of Art (now OCAD University), in Toronto, Canada. When she graduated in 1950 she became the college's first Black alumnus. This groundbreaking achievement was an anomaly at the time—with the exception of Wells, OCA's first racialized students graduated in the 1970s.[2]

Wells further developed her artistic practice at the Minneapolis School of Art in the early 1960s before returning to her homeland of Jamaica, where she dedicated herself to the local creative community. In 1968 she opened a commercial gallery, The Art Wheel, and helped establish the Jamaican Artists and Craftsmen Guild, which promoted the country's emerging art scene. Over the following decades, Wells continued working as an artist, travelling to Barbados and Senegal, before she eventually settled in the United States in the mid-1980s.

Though Wells drew inspiration from various places that she travelled to, she always returned to her metaphorical roots and painted the flora of her beloved Jamaica. She rarely strayed from watercolour, her preferred mode of expression, which bolstered her mastery of the notoriously unforgiving medium. As Dr. Wayne Lawrence describes in *The Art of Jamaica: A Prelude,* Wells confidently approached her compositions without the use of preliminary sketches, wielding only paint and brush to convey her vision.

Wells shared her passion for art through teaching. For more than twenty years, she was an instructor at the secondary and post-secondary levels, influencing countless future artists. Her children, whom she also taught, now work in documentary film, architecture, and education. Her legacy continues through them and through the many others she has inspired.
—Emily Cluett

Thanks to Dr. Andrea Fatona, the Tier 2 Canada Research Chair in Canadian Black Diasporic Cultural Production, who has worked to raise awareness of Wells's contributions to Canadian art, and whose essential research has secured a space for this historically significant and under-recognized artist.

1 Edward Lucie-Smith, *Flora: Gardens and Plants in Art and Literature* (New York: Watson-Guptill Publications, 2001).

2 Andrea Fatona, "Welcome Remarks" (presentation, The State of Blackness: From Production to Presentation conference, Toronto, ON, February 21–22, 2014).

My mother painted for more than fifty years. A woman fine artist from the island of Jamaica, she painted quietly, consistently, and passionately, amassing a collection of more than 300 works—mostly large pieces on paper.

I mostly remember her working in wonderful, very informal settings. Her "studio" was mostly her materials: her brush, fine watercolour paper, and paints stretched out on a hard board or low table before her. Sometimes she had a folding stool; the surrounding space could be anywhere. She often worked on a cool veranda facing Jamaica's spectacular Blue Mountains, in front of our old family house, or, at the back, on an old cut-stone porch, under gentle tropical rainforest vines and aged trees that watched and whispered. An adventurer who loved day trips and travel, she could extend her studio into beautiful gardens with a pond or a river nearby. Or she would work on a rustic fishing beach or cross the high seas of the Atlantic into a lush, culturally explosive, and fascinating West African market.

It's in this way that she imparted the importance of stillness, observation, and compassion for the human form and the indelible atmosphere. And we, her children, knew that whatever she was creating, it was very important. Her images of such moments will last forever, soft translucent colours spread across fine rag sheets—sometimes with other media and formats.

It wasn't unusual for me to come home to find posing for her a stranger whom she had just met. The smell of fresh watercolour paper; the paint out of tubes; thick, soft sable brushes; and water bottles—these impressions have never left my memory, along with the effortlessness with which she communicated. During the twenty years that she worked as an art educator, her students, also found her to be an inspiration.

Dorothy was an inclusive, magical free-spirited person whose essence was integral to what she created. Born in St. Andrew, Jamaica, in 1926, she was a graduate of the Ontario College of Art in 1952 and spent a year at the Minneapolis School of Art, from 1961 to 1962. As one of the forerunners of the Jamaican and Caribbean fine art scene, she was awarded the Silver Musgrave Medal for Outstanding Merit in the field of visual arts from the Institute of Jamaica in 1987. She always conveyed that her originality, familiarity, and expertise developed over a lifetime of painting. Her fine works exemplify her unique representational approach, which reflects a particular time and space and mixes styles and mediums, with an emphasis on watercolours and influences from the Impressionist school. She didn't take shortcuts or do any preliminary sketching, as she drew and painted only with her brush in a beautiful free-flowing line. "For those who know watercolour," she once said, "it's very difficult to do that. Once you put down what you want you leave it, as there is no possibility to rework a piece. It has to stay fresh, bright and clear as it's such a beautiful and immediate medium."

My mother exhibited extensively: she showed her work at Jamaica's National Gallery of Art, in private galleries across the Caribbean, and in many international exhibitions and solo shows in the US, the UK, Europe, and Senegal, West Africa, where she once lived. Her work is now found mostly in private and corporate collections around the world. In *Flora: Gardens and Plants in Art and Literature*, one of his many publications, the British art critic and writer Edward Lucie-Smith offers this poignant description of my mother:

> **A senior Jamaican artist, celebrated as one of the finest watercolourists in the Americas. She is greatly influenced by vibrant colours and vegetation of the Caribbean. The freshness of her work is...expressive, lyrical, delicate and sensitive to abstract values.[1]**

I feel her spirit, I hear her voice, I see her working...

—Mary Wells

1 Edward Lucie-Smith, *Flora: Gardens and Plants in Art and Literature* (New York: Watson-Guptill Publications, 2001).

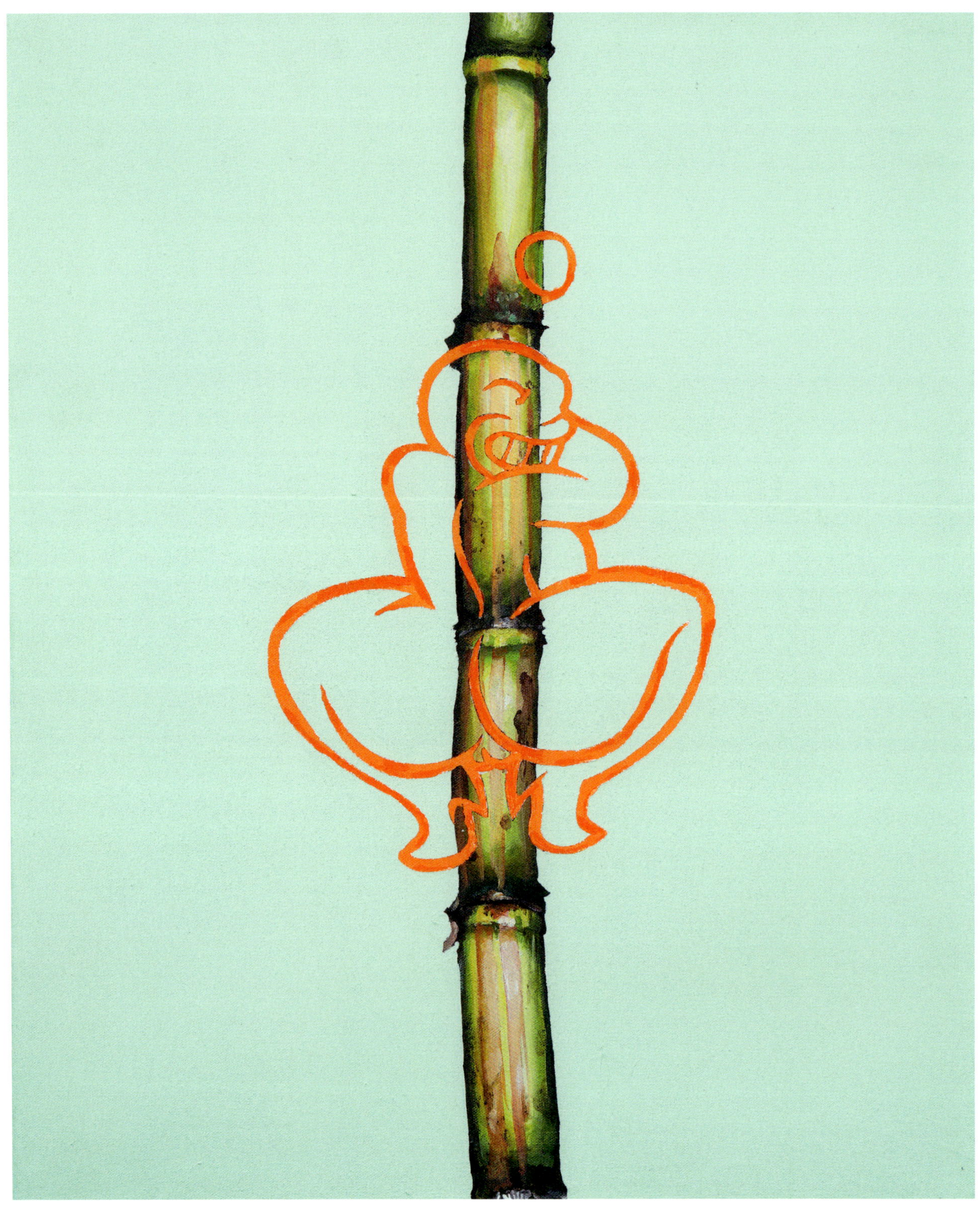

Leasho Johnson, *Sweet Sugarcane (Female Figure)*, 2014

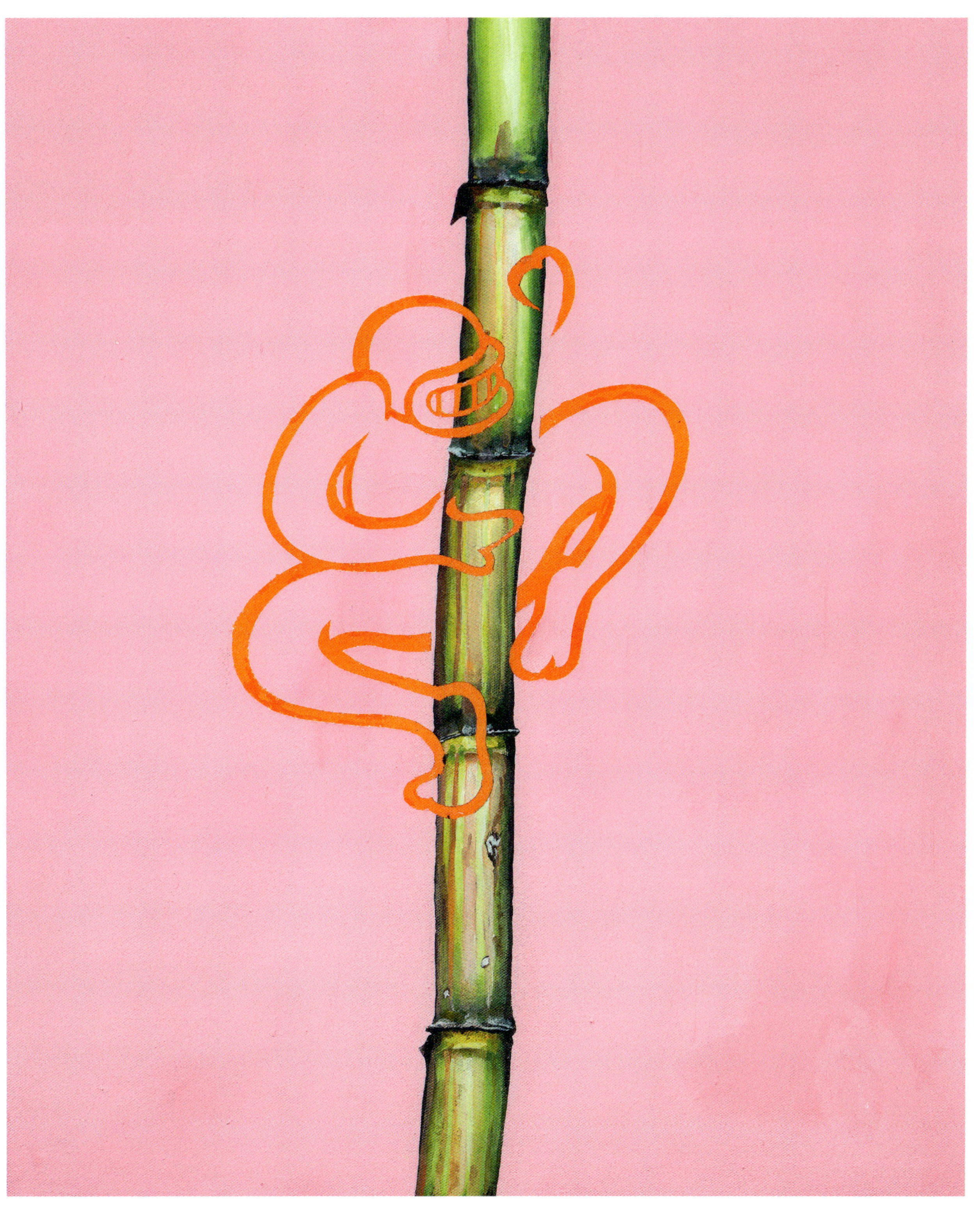

Leasho Johnson, *Sweet Sugarcane (Male Figure)*, 2014

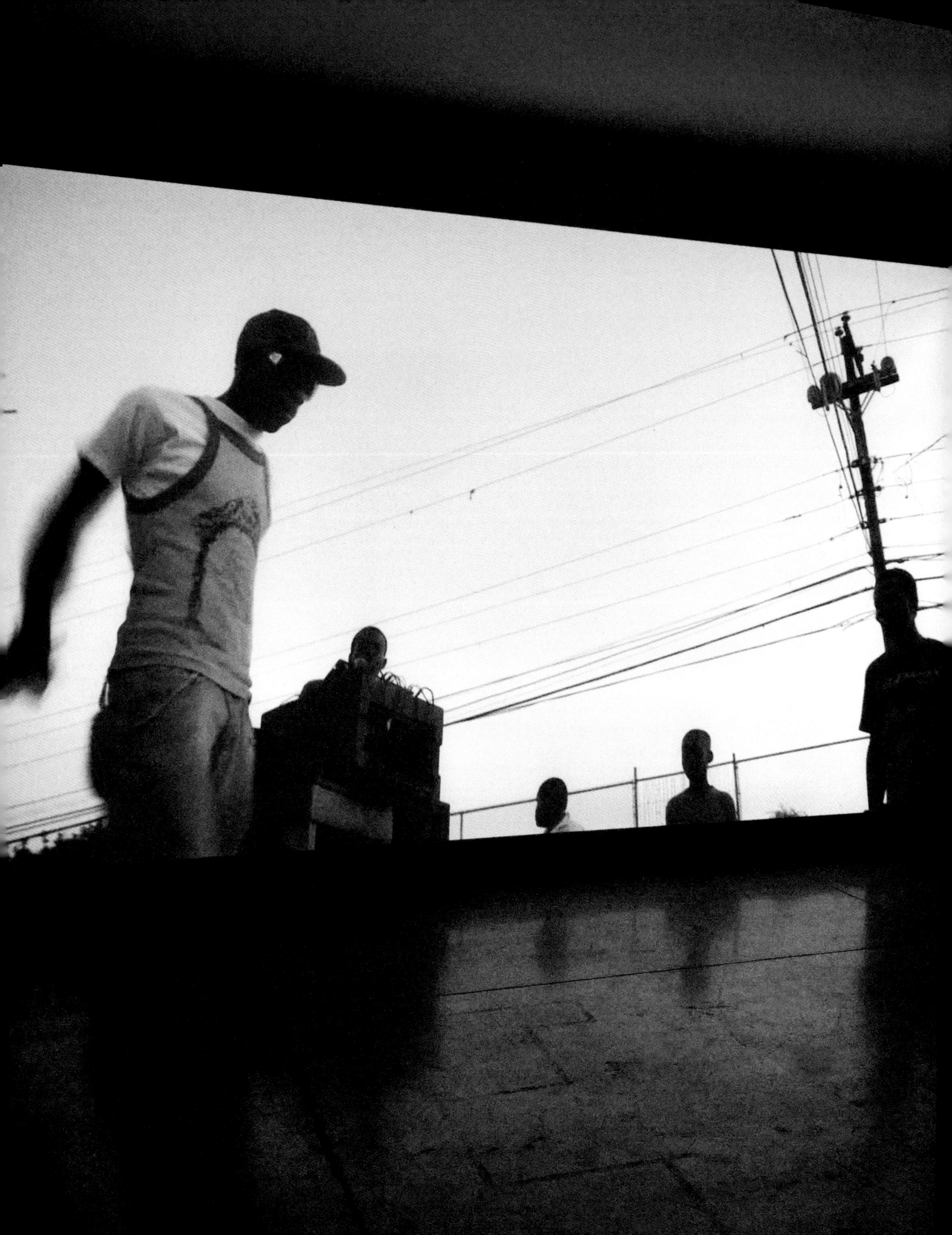

If you falter in times of trouble,
how small is your strength?

Proverbs 24:10

Opposite
Installation view of Peter Dean Rickards / The Afflicted Yard, *Proverbs 24:10*, 2008, at the Art Gallery of Ontario

Above
Peter Dean Rickards / The Afflicted Yard, still from *Proverbs 24:10*, 2008

The Afflicted Gaze of Peter Dean Rickards

Annie Paul

Pd, as we called him, was a notoriously cantankerous young fossil. At his worst he could be a merciless bully, but at his best he was a tender, irrepressible genius with an unerring instinct for the gritty heart of darkness throbbing amid the postcolony. His was a restless, inspired, and influential eye, adept at revealing the necropolitics of present-day Jamaica, whether through the still image, the moving one, or written text. Pd was not just a digital native, he was a digital denizen, a habitué and curator of a potent Jamaican variant of twenty-first-century vernacular realism.

In 2014 photographer Berette Macaulay captured the shape and size of the hole left by Pd's death in this pithy tribute:

> The profession of photography lost a brilliant visionary of style, wit, and talent. This dude Peter Dean Rickards stirred the shit up wherever he could, pissed off many, even frightened a few, and was definitely among the #zerofucksgiven SoulJahs. BUT no one could dispute his talent or resist the laughs.[1]

A full decade in advance of the creeping epidemic we've come to know as "cancel culture," that toxic byproduct of social media, Peter Dean Rickards was cancelled in England. More than one gallery that wanted to show his work was warned against it by powerful rights groups that claimed the right to shut Pd's work down and did so in classic enactments of "performative wokeness at its worst."[2]

In order to *get* the radical nature of PDR's work, an intimate knowledge of the post-colonial contrivance that is Jamaica is needed. A society so resolutely polite that even thieves and rapists are referred to as "ladies" and "gentlemen"; citizens are prosecuted, even killed, by police for the utterance of so-called bad words in public (while corruption and the murder rate soar unchecked); and schoolboys are expelled for wearing pants a shade too tight. In the face of such flagrant humbug, Rickards's brilliant website, *The Afflicted Yard*, was a welcome antidote to the pieties of Christian Jamaica, a virtual oasis or rest stop where weary wayfarers could stop and take the piss.

In a blurb outlining what he called the Afflicted Purpose, Pd made sure his oppositional gaze was manifest. "We mess with everyone and everything. We were those kids who laughed when the space shuttle blew up. We were those guys who got thrown out of class for laughing at the class retard."[3] Peter was a truly original rudie from the wrong side of town (up rather than down).

His images arrest you boldly and directly, stunning you with style, then immersing you in saturated detail if you choose to zoom in for a closer look. Remarkably, Rickards stumbled into digital photography while looking for ways to provide a visual analog to the innovative site *Kingston Signals*—the first Jamaica-based multi-media website to broadcast live, started by Rickards and Downsound Records label boss Josef Bogdanovich circa 2000. According to David Katz, Peter "first picked up a digital camera primarily as a means of providing his rapidly growing online audience with up-to-the-minute visuals to go with the incredibly raw sounds that were emanating from turntables in Kingston."[4] Rickards succinctly summed up the situation: "Now, instead of having to listen to news reports of the latest shootout downtown, we can simply turn on a computer and listen to intercepted radio transmissions of taxi drivers discussing the action live."[5]

Intercepting police radio transmissions became somewhat of a pastime for Pd, which is how in 2005 he was the first photographer on the scene the night Jamaican police killed Christopher "Chris Royal" Coke, twenty-three, in a prominent uptown location in Tivoli. Rickards's shocking photographs of the death scene were viewed in disbelief later the same night by Royal's cousin, notorious don-of-dons Christopher "Dudus" Coke, who was extradited to the US in 2010. Royal's death was part of an extended reprisal that took the lives of five Jamaican policemen before it ended.

Rickards's signature photojournalistic style mingled with the eye of a fashion photographer and a factographic imagination to produce a wealth of electrifying imagery and text. Most of this was made available on *The Afflicted Yard* website but also, starting in late 2004, in the short-lived but vibrantly innovative magazine *FIRST*. With its unorthodox mix of fashion, style, and hardcore reporting from the streets of inner-city Kingston, *FIRST* was truly the first of its kind. Not only did it train its high-tech lenses on the logical subjects of the fashion industry—youth—but in a brilliant editorial move also focused on what is normally considered inherently unfashionable—the elderly. The first

1

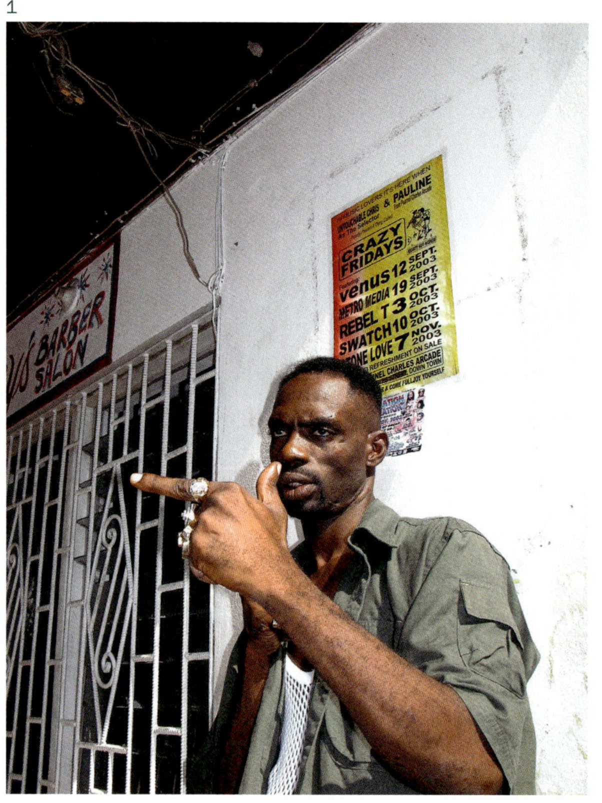

Fig. 1
Peter Dean Rickards /
The Afflicted Yard
Ninjaman, 2003.
© The Estate of Peter Dean Rickards / The Afflicted Yard.

issue of the magazine, subtitled *Splash*, featured "Classic People, Classic Cars," a photo essay about senior citizens who refused to relinquish the style and dash of their youth, personified by their aging but beautifully maintained cars. As the text elaborated, "If you take the time to notice these people, you might be transported back to a time when style mattered more than size and quality mattered more than quantity. These are the former Kingston 'hot foots' in their mature prime. Still fascinating, still stylish and still running things."[6]

Rickards could also be relentlessly scathing in his denunciation of perceived predators, no matter how powerful. The athletic footwear brand Puma found itself skewered in the pages of *FIRST* after its much-hyped publicity campaign about its entry into the Jamaican market. A feature titled "When Puma Ruled the World" detailed the debacle:

> 23: People who admitted wearing Puma trainers in 2002, one year before Jamaican colours, flags and slogans were slapped all over them...
> 2: Number of seconds it took Helen Sweeney-Dougan to storm off after being asked by Entertainment Report at the party if Puma had actually invested anything in Jamaica besides a few free trainers and wristbands...
> 0: Number of basketball courts (or anything) built by Puma in Jamaica before, during or after their 2003 invasion.[7]

In 2008, Peter picked up a video camera and the plot took another twist as he moved to combine his trademark imagery with his unique brand of social commentary and storytelling in video format. His first video work, *The System*, made for Waterhouse musical artist Terry Lynn, was shot in eight hours at a slaughterhouse in Mandeville, Jamaica, using a borrowed camcorder, a twelve-dollar tripod, and available light. The video was called "brutally effective" by *The Guardian* and went on to receive accolades from the likes of *Pitchfork* and *Spin* magazine, which included the video in their "Best of 2008" roundups.

Two more video projects followed in 2008, *Kingston Logic 2.0* and *Proverbs 24:10*, the latter a two-and-a-half-minute clip that was featured in *Rockstone and Bootheel*, a 2009 exhibition at Real Art Ways (Hartford, Connecticut).

Also in 2009, Peter created his first short feature, *DiMaggio: The Last Don*, a television pilot about American record producer Josef Bogdanovich and his trials working in the bizarre world of Jamaican dancehall. It was at the premiere of *The Last Don* in Kingston that Rickards realized his true calling was film.

The Brazilian film *Cidade de Deus* (*City of God*, 2002) made a huge impression on Pd, who held several screenings of the movie in Kingston. He was a great aficionado of the TV series *The Office*, and by 2011 was on the verge of launching a TV series himself titled *The Afflicted Yard*: "the only theme that remains consistent throughout its 22-minutes of circus-like mayhem will be its stylized cinematography and the famous motto of its star—expect the unexpected."[8] The star was to be ace DJ Vybz Kartel, and the series was slated to debut on Halloween 2011. The treatment for the series gives insights into Pd's overall modus operandi and the intentionality behind his unique transmedial work:

> Underlining the programme is the intent of its creators to translate and communicate the wildness of Kartel's life as an over-the-top dancehall star as well as his environment for both Jamaicans and foreigners who may not have any knowledge of dancehall (or even Jamaica).
>
> It will be this ability to translate and communicate the adrenaline, female sexuality, dark humor, randomness, violence, hypocrisy, language and geography of modern urban Jamaica from a Jamaican standpoint that will make the Vybz Kartel Show successful.[9]

Alas, the series would not see the light of day. In September 2011, Vybz Kartel was arrested for murder and, in 2014, was sentenced to thirty-five years in prison.

But there were other compelling subjects around. By 2012 Pd had started work on the film he thought would be his magnum opus. Simply titled *GORGON*, the ninety-minute feature was to document the life and times of the paradigmatic bad man of dancehall, DJ Ninjaman or Desmond Ballantyne. Filming had already begun and Rickards was hyper-excited about the project, often arriving unannounced from a shoot with rushes to share and savour. All the top dancehall DJs—Kartel, Sizzla, Bounty Killer,

2

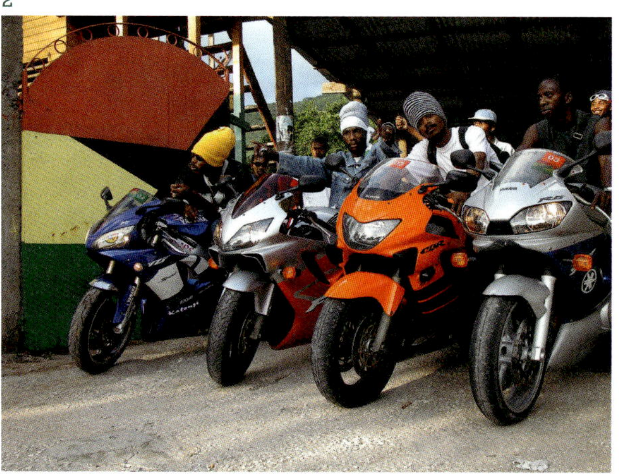

Fig. 2
Peter Dean Rickards /
The Afflicted Yard
Sizzla, 2003.

Buju Banton—had borrowed from Ninja according to Rickards, and were fundamentally formed by this hardcore, brilliant, verging-on-violent vernacular genius. Pd was determined to create the definitive vehicle through which Ninjaman could be articulated, could articulate himself—a kind of Ninja uncut. Today, Ninjaman too is in prison serving a life sentence for murder.

In the few years that Peter practised his craft(s) he created a valuable archive documenting diverse aspects of contemporary Jamaican life; fashion models frolicking in the toxic waste of Jamaica's famed bauxite industry; DJs advertising their infatuation with guns; old folks cruising in faded glory; tender glimpses of social outcasts; slaughterhouses in Babylon; the green beauty of ganja fields; behind the scenes in Jamdown's most feared garrison community, Tivoli. All the images not fit to print were casually collected and displayed by Rickards in cyberspace and on video.

3

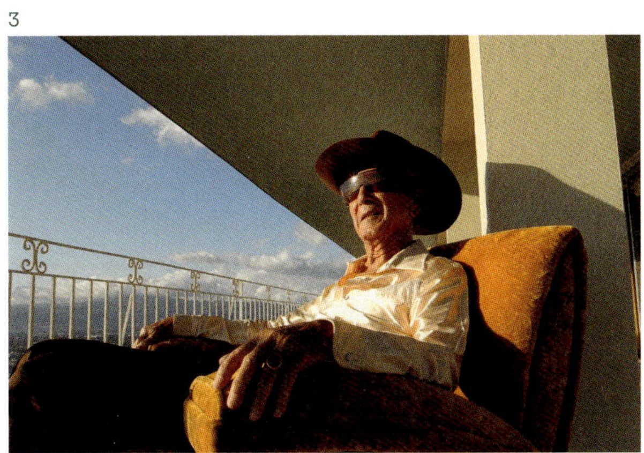

Fig. 3
Peter Dean Rickards /
The Afflicted Yard
Percy Lee, 2004.
© The Estate of Peter Dean Rickards / The Afflicted Yard.

Peter Dean Rickards was a disruptor extraordinaire, the body of work he left behind an unparalleled examination and documentation of the poetics of precarity, and its politics—the eternally fascinating, hardcore beauty of Jamaicans reinventing the ordinary. Yet Pd's refusal to avert his afflicted gaze and hold his criticism meant that he could never rely on a steady income or post-colonial spoils coming his way ("We really don't care what you think unless you're going to pay us and even then we'll probably still make fun of you behind your back.")[10]

Towards the end of his time in Kingston, when he realized the extent of his illness, the "Bad man red nigga" (as he jokingly referred to himself) was seriously considering setting up a wedding photography service titled Marry Me in Jamaica Dot Com, or something similar, to fund himself and projects such as *GORGON*. Regrettably, as Russell Hergert tweeted on December 31, 2014: "Saddest thing is Jamaica lost its most important artist today and they don't even realise it."

One likes to think that, if he were around today, Pd would have minted a profane NFT[11] or two solving his cash-flow problem once and for all.

In the final reckoning, as Edgar Lewis, a long-time friend and spar of his said, Peter Dean's true legacy was "the cadre of people that he pushed to the limit—people he got to think outside the box and outside themselves. This is what a true artist is supposed to do—influence generations through his creations and creativity, and that is what Peter Rickards did—that's his legacy."[12]

1 Originally posted on Berette Macaulay's Facebook page (December 31, 2014). This and other tributes to Rickards collected in Annie Paul, "'I'm dead. No returns.': The Afflicted One Checks Out," January 3, 2015, anniepaul.net/2015/01/03.

2 This evocative phrase is borrowed from Evan Moffitt, who used it in a slightly different context. Andrew Durbin, Amy Sherlock, Evan Moffitt, Pablo Larios, and Terence Trouillot, "Frieze Editors Discuss What the Art World Has Learned in 2020," December 14, 2020, frieze.com/article/frieze-editors-discuss-what-art-world-has-learned-2020.

3 Peter Dean Rickards, "The Afflicted Purpose," *The Afflicted Yard*, 1999, afflictedyard.com/thepurpose.htm.

4 David Katz, "The Afflicted Yard: Peter Dean Rickards RIP," January 12, 2015, daily.redbullmusicacademy.com/2015/01/peter-dean-rickards-rip.

5 Rickards, "The Afflicted Purpose."

6 Peter Dean Rickards, "Classic People, Classic Cars," *FIRST*, no. 1, 2004, 11.

7 This excerpt, from a much longer list, is a sample of the mocking spirit that came naturally to Rickards. Puma was a non-entity in Jamaica and perhaps much of the world till it decided to become Usain Bolt's sponsor, to give it credit, long before Bolt became a global superstar. Puma brand manager Helen Sweeney-Dougan's discomfiture at the pointed questions asked by local media was irresistible fodder for Rickards. Needless to say, his barbed critique could have been levelled at any global corporation's attempt to enter new markets; Puma merely provided the instant case. Peter Dean Rickards, "When Puma Ruled the World," *FIRST*, no. 4, 2005, 124.

8 Unpublished treatment for *The Afflicted Yard* TV series, 2011.

9 Ibid.

10 "The Afflicted Purpose."

11 Non-fungible token. NFTs or one-of-a-kind digital artworks/assets, are gaining popularity as a way for artists and other creators to sell their work digitally.

12 Posted on Edgar Lewis's private Facebook page, c. January 2015.

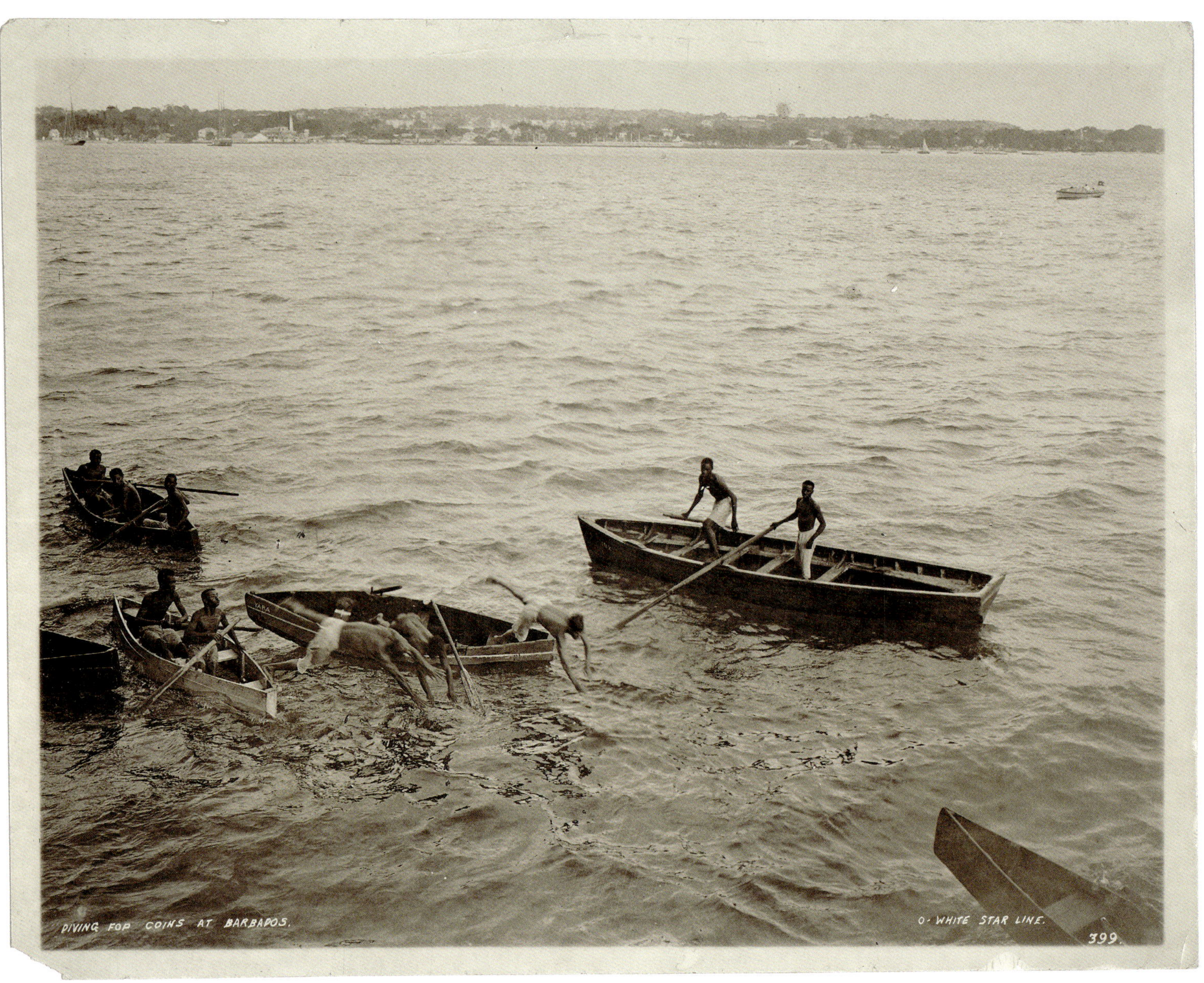

Unknown photographer for White Star Line, *Diving for Coins, Barbados*, c. 1890

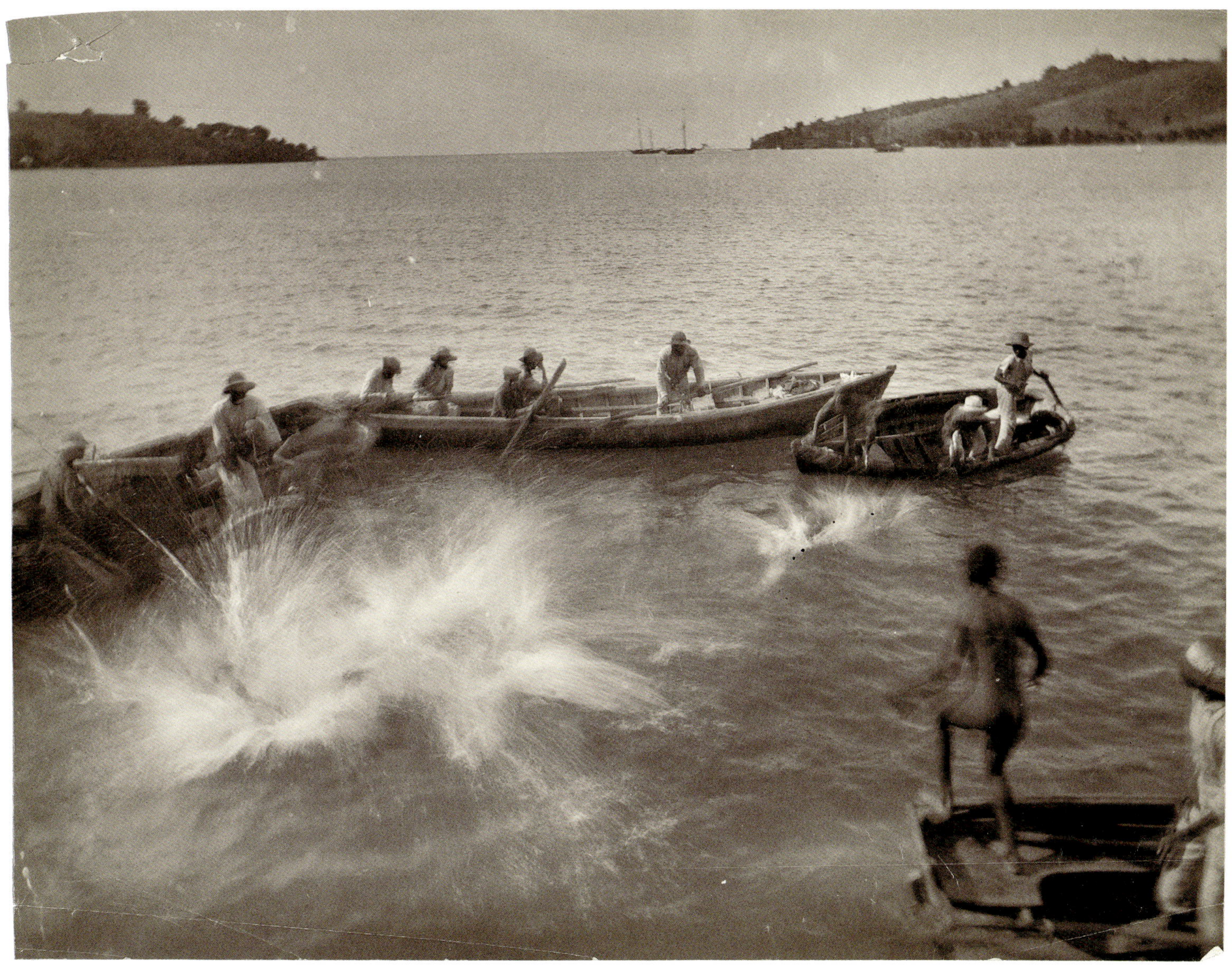

Unknown photographer, *Boys Diving For Coins, St. Lucia*, c. 1887

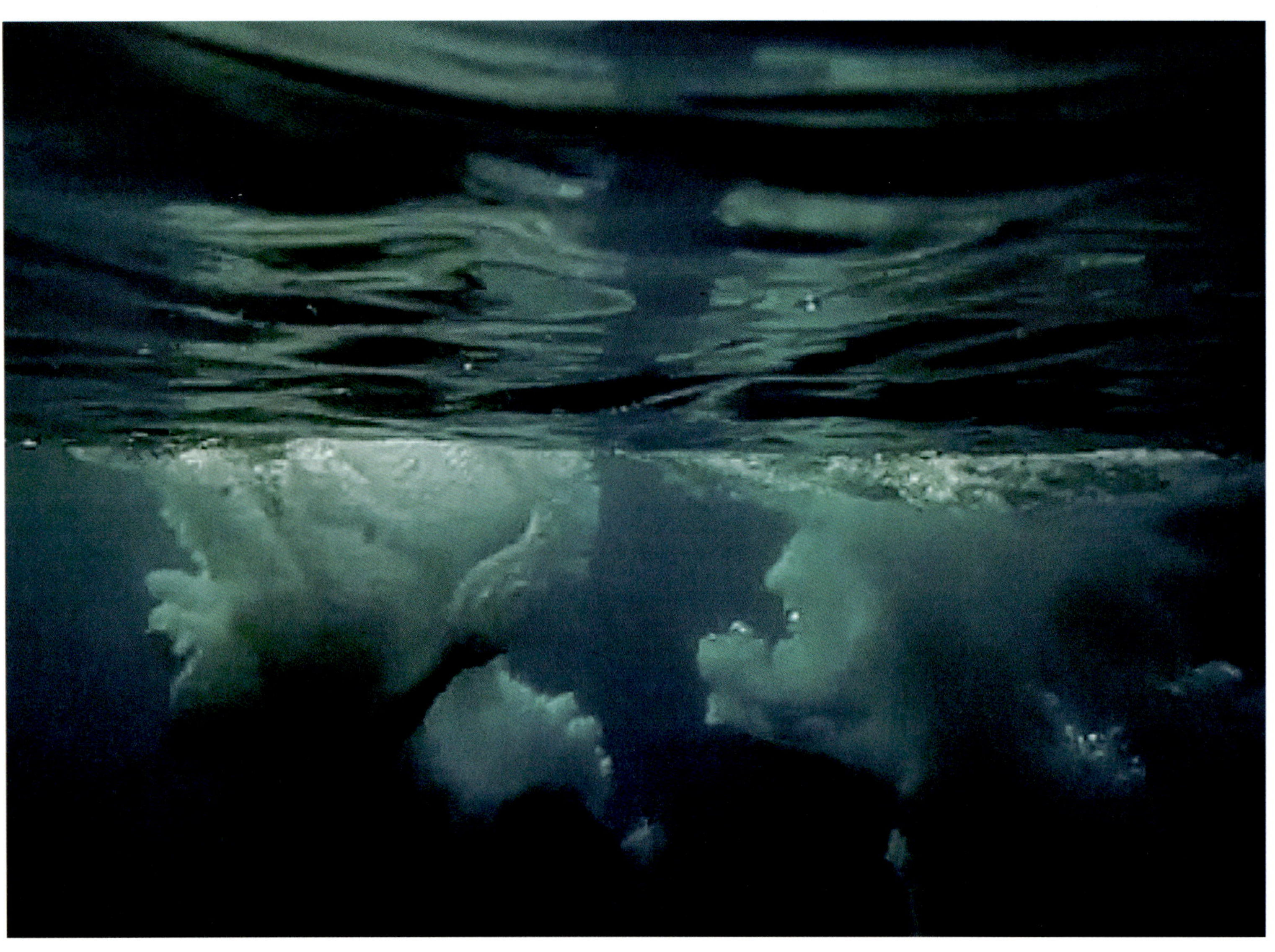

Above
Nadia Huggins, still from *Circa no future*, 2016–2019

Opposite
Installation view of Nadia Huggins, *Circa no future*, 2016–2019, at the Art Gallery of Ontario

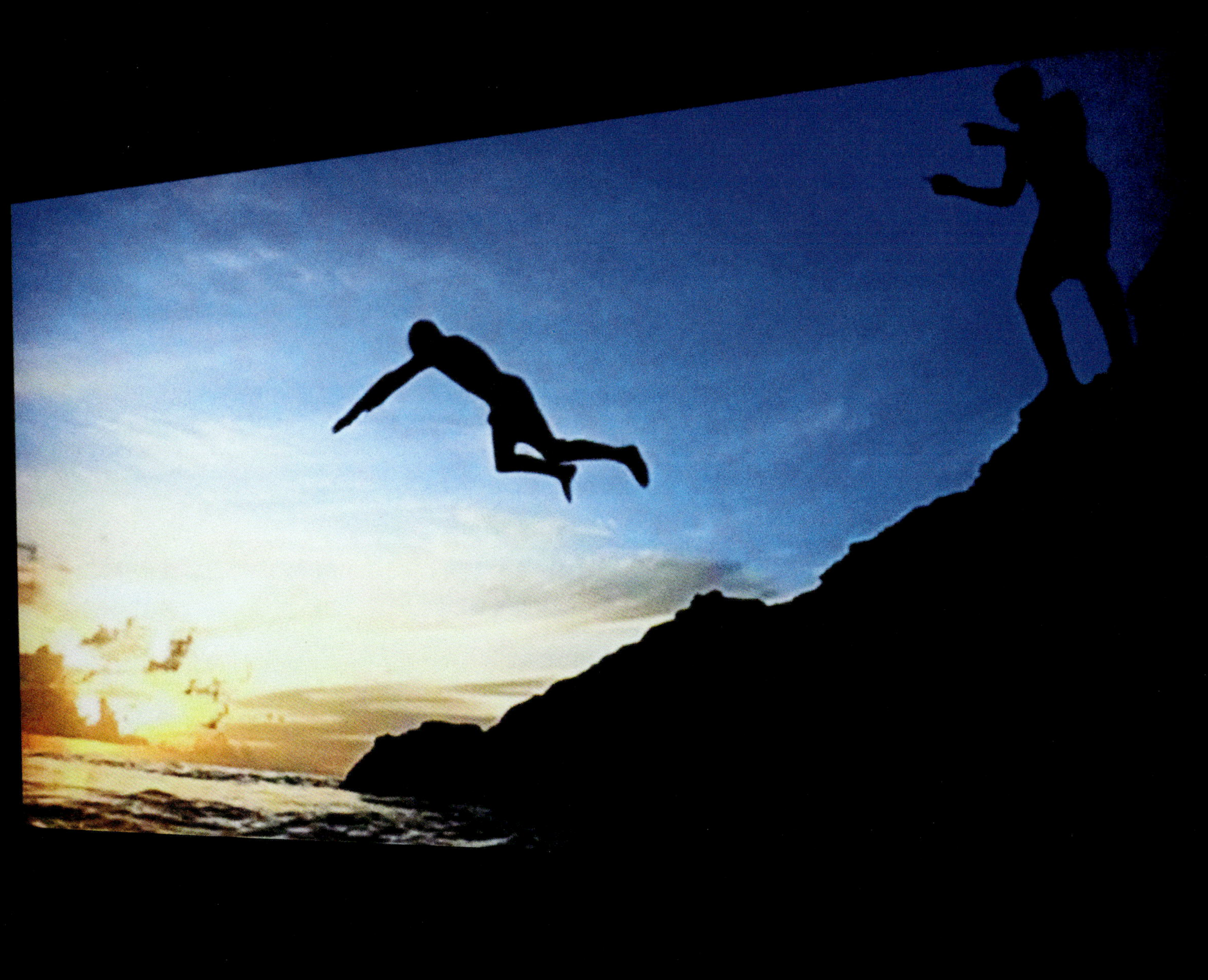

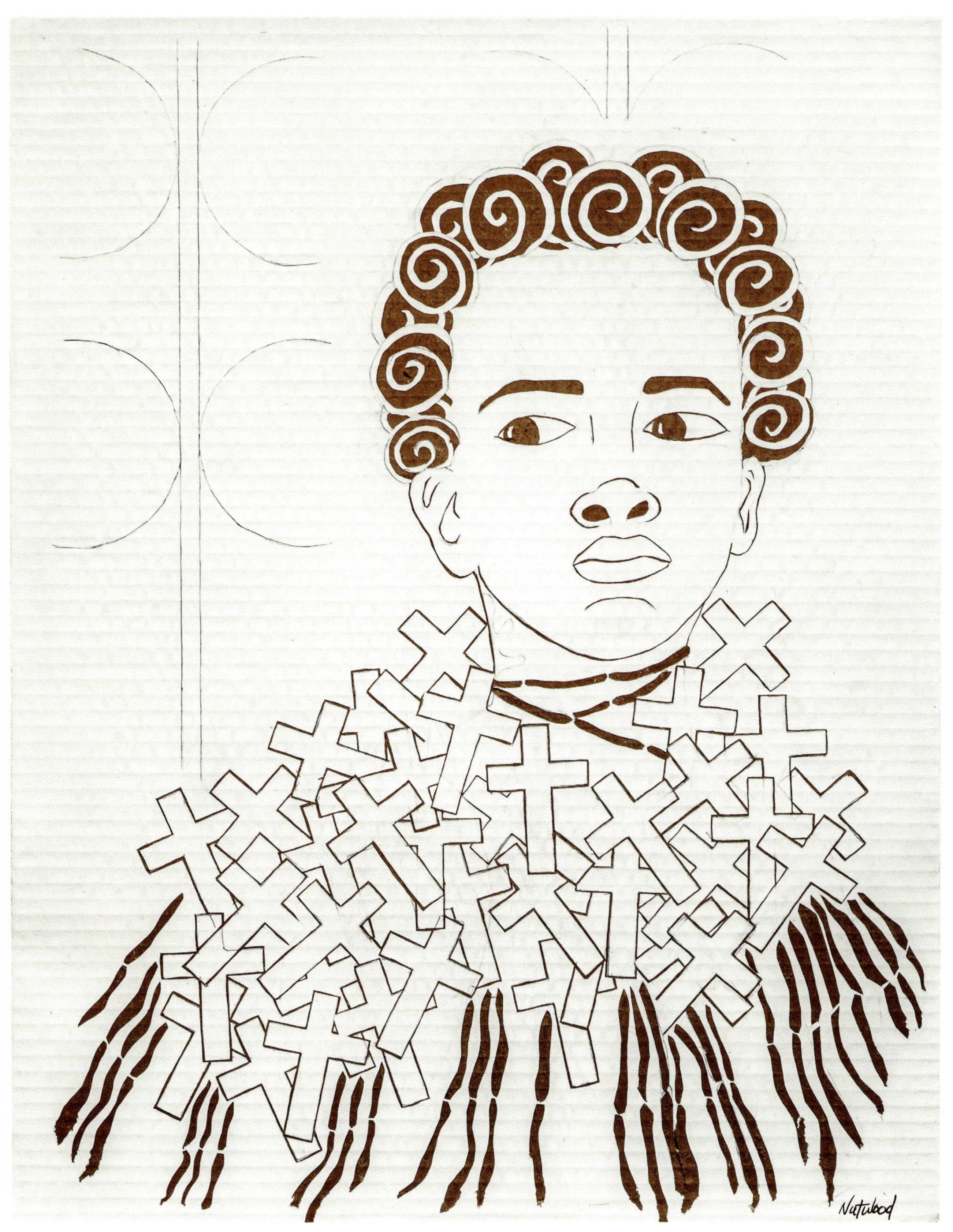

Natalie Wood, *Mazalee (crossed)*, 2012

The Cartographer Tries to Map a Way to Zion

Kei Miller

i. in which the cartographer explains himself

You might say
my job is not
to lose myself exactly
but to imagine
what loss might feel like–
the sudden creeping pace,
the consultation with trees and blue
fences and whatever else
might prove a landmark.
My job is to imagine the widening
of the unfamiliar and also
the widening ache of it;
to anticipate the ironic

question: how did we find
ourselves here? My job is
to untangle the tangled,
to unworry the concerned,
to guide you out from cul-de-sacs
into which you may have wrongly turned.

ii. in which the rastaman disagrees

The rastaman has another reasoning.
He says–now that man's job is never straightforward or easy. Him work is to make thin and crushable
all that is big and as real as ourselves; is to make flat
all that is high and rolling; is to make invisible and wutliss
plenty things that poor people cyaa do without–like board
houses, and the corner shop from which Miss Katie sell
her famous peanut porridge. And then again
the mapmaker's work is to make visible
all them things that shoulda never exist in the first place
like the conquest of pirates, like borders,
like the viral spread of governments

iii.

The cartographer says
no–
What I do is science. I show
the earth as it is, without bias.
I never fall in love. I never get involved
with the muddy affairs of land.
Too much passion unsteadies the hand.
I aim to show the full
of a place in just a glance.

iv.

The rastaman thinks, draw me a map of what you see
then I will draw a map of what you never see
and guess me whose map will be bigger than whose?
Guess me whose map will tell the larger truth?

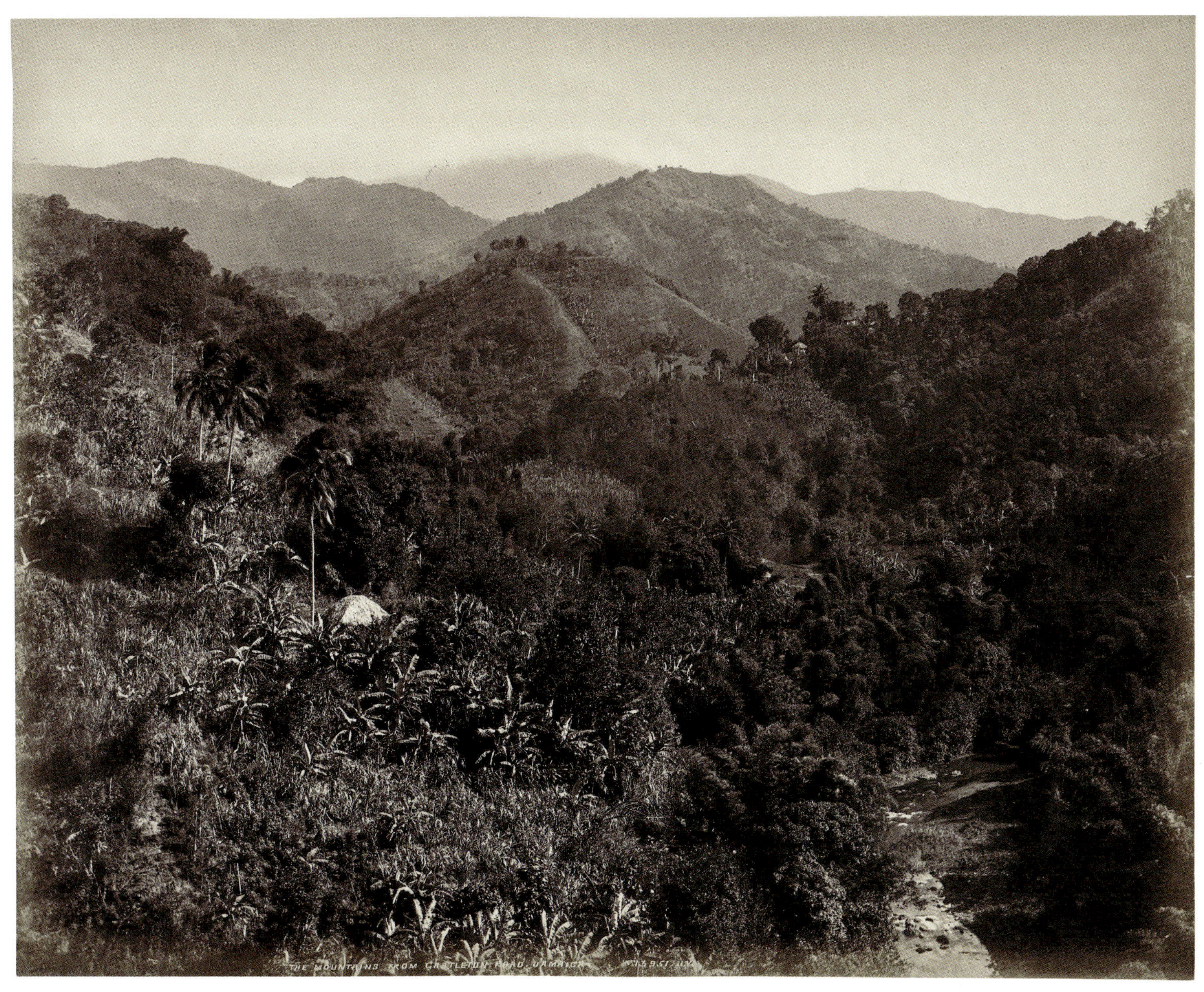

J. Valentine & Sons, *The Mountains from Castleton Road, Jamaica*, 1891

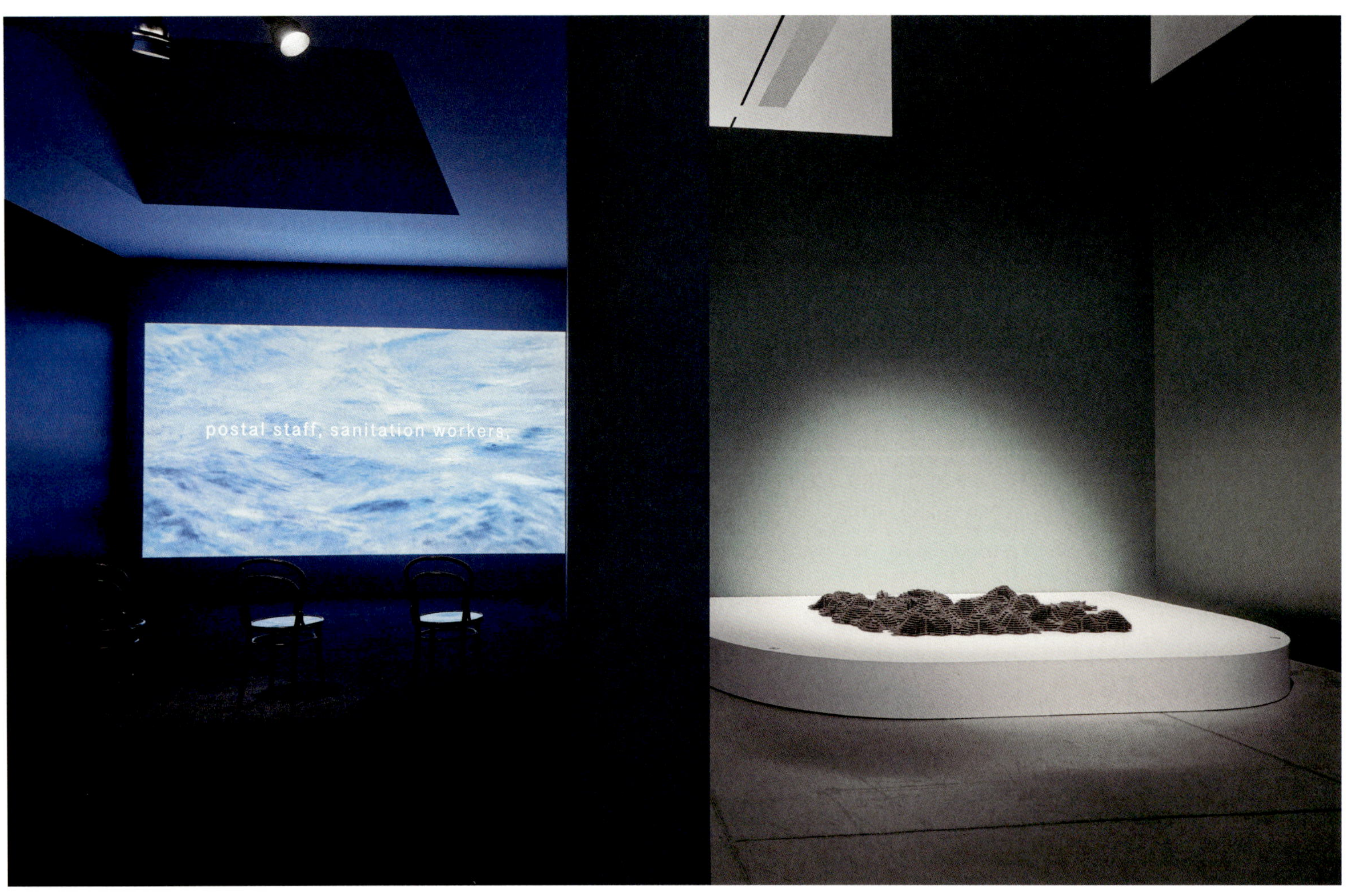

Above
Installation view of Charles Campbell, *Maroonscape 1: Cockpit Archipelago*, 2019, and Alberta Whittle, *business as usual: hostile environment*, 2020, at the Art Gallery of Ontario

Opposite
Charles Campbell, *Maroonscape 1: Cockpit Archipelago* (detail), 2019

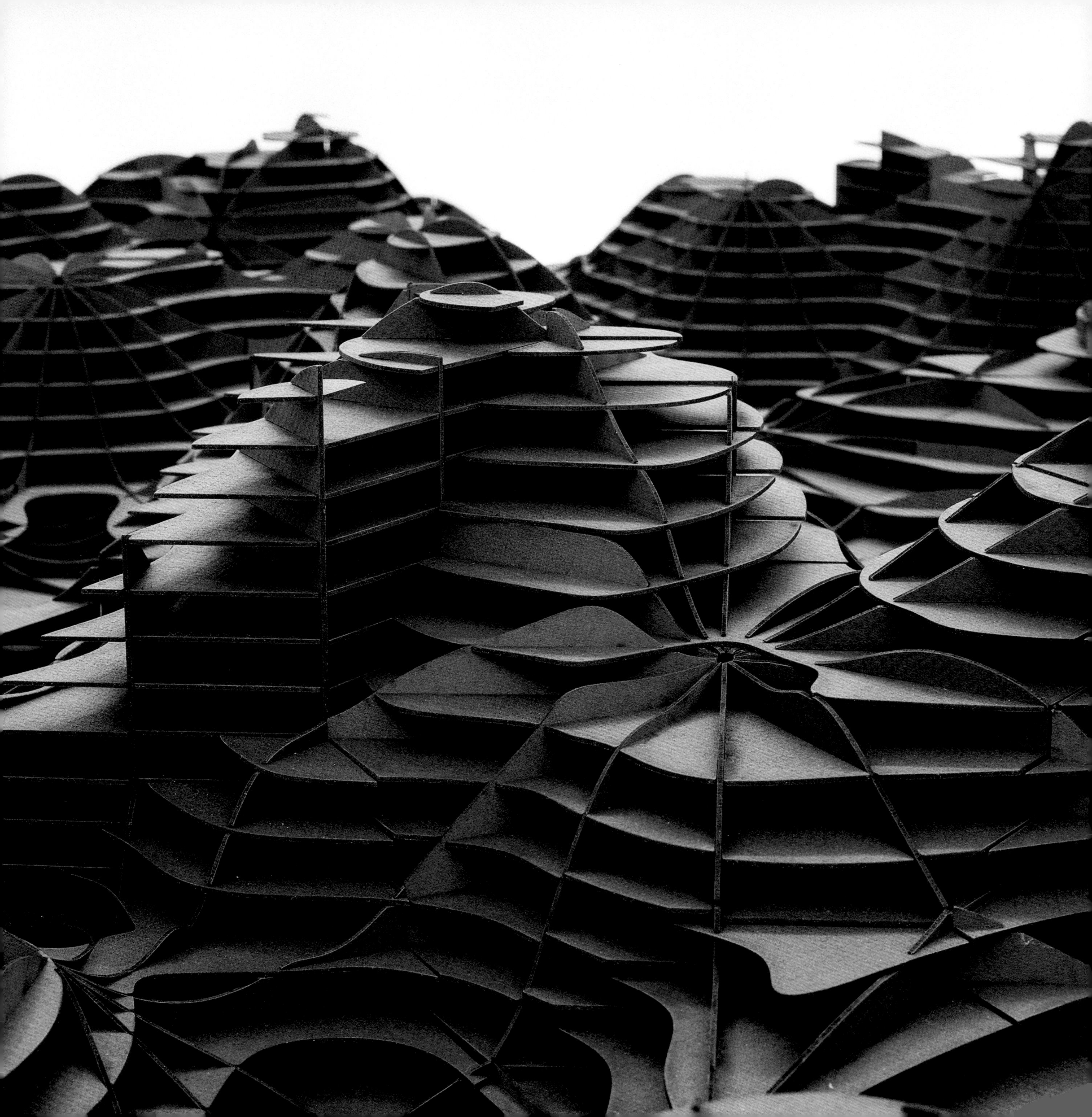

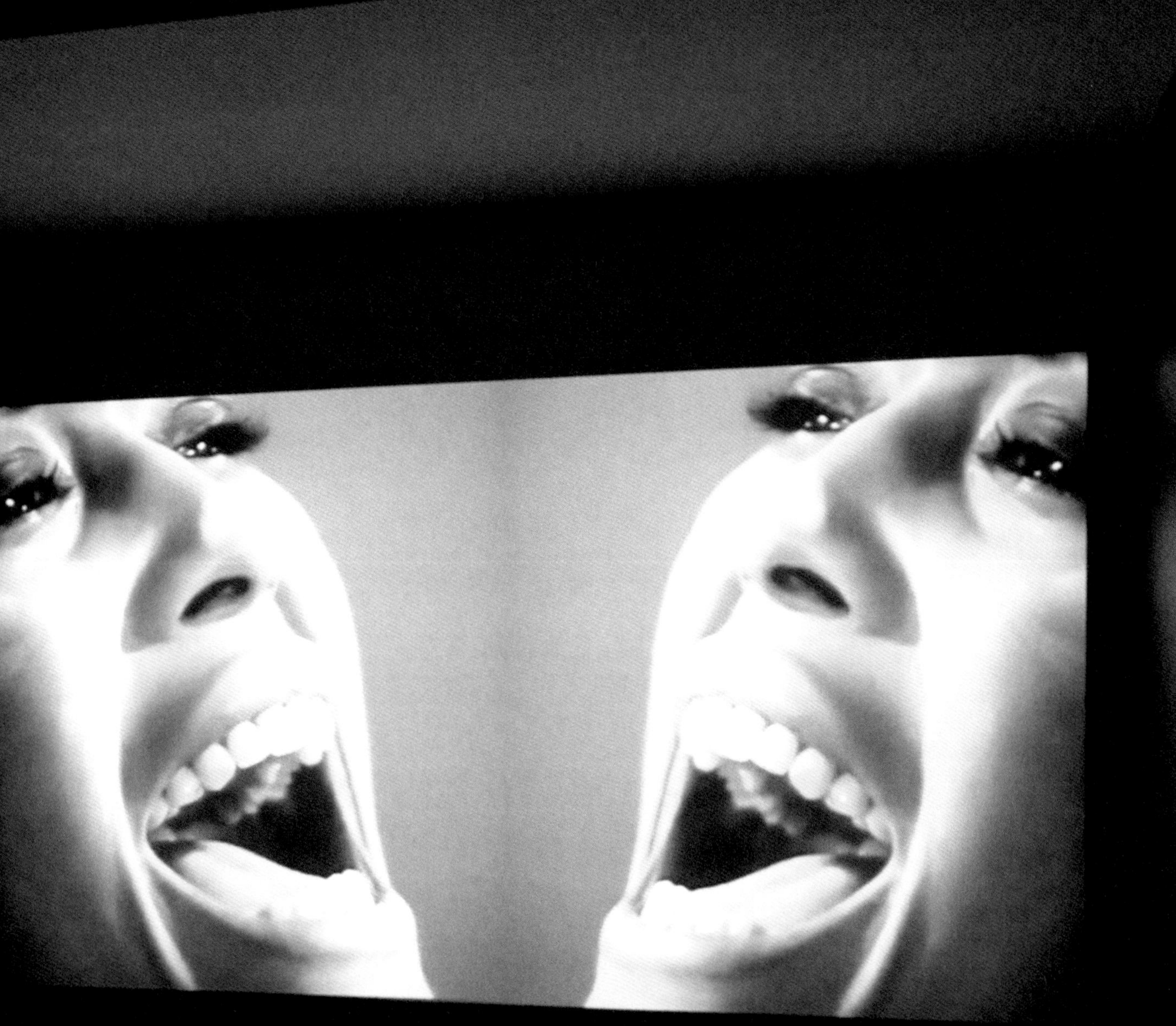

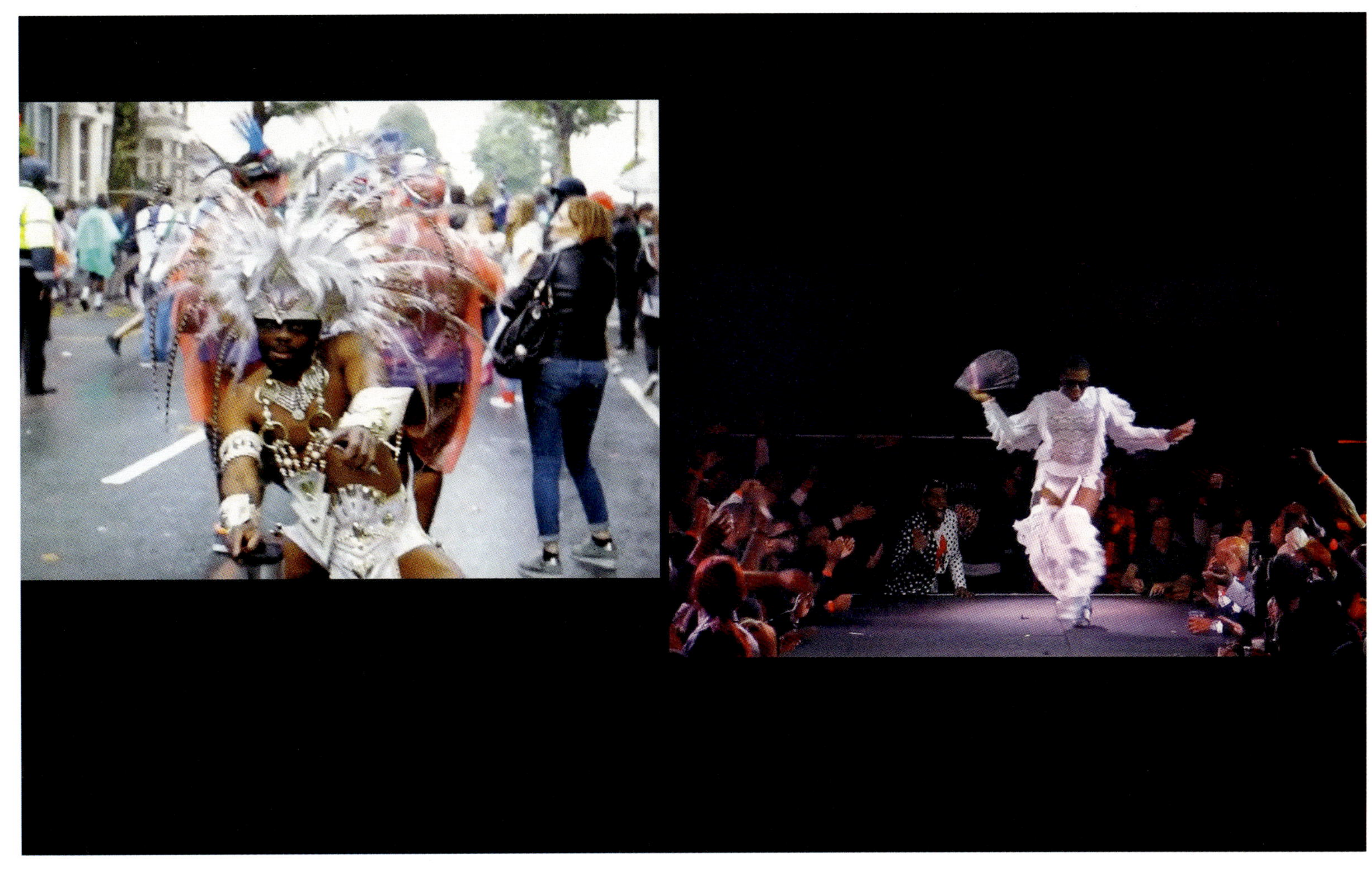

Opposite
Installation view of Alberta Whittle, *business as usual: hostile environment*, 2020, at the Art Gallery of Ontario

Above
Alberta Whittle, still from *business as usual: hostile environment*, 2020

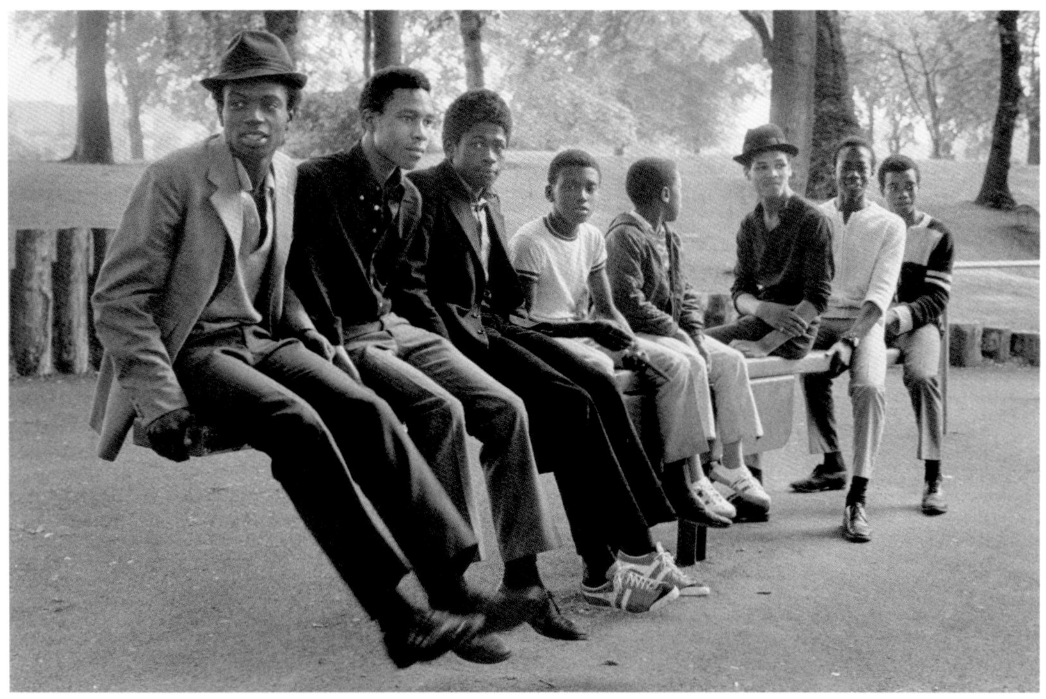

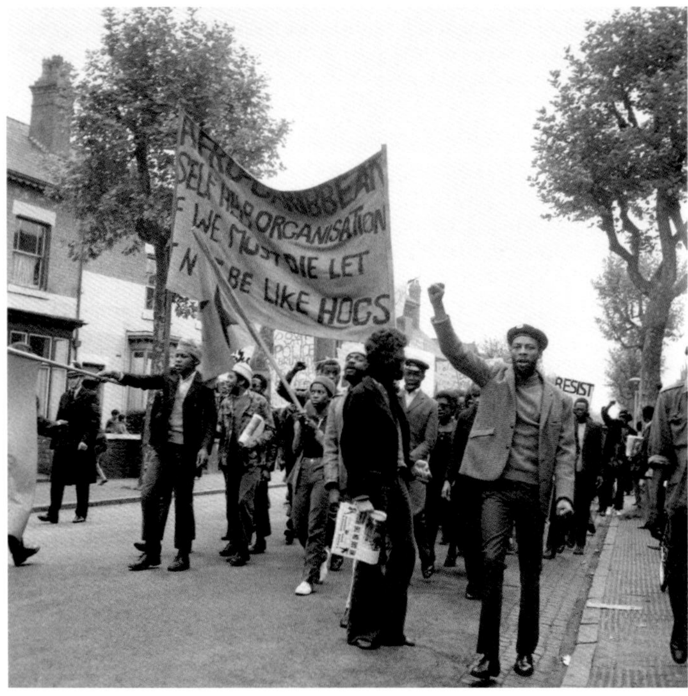

Top
Vanley Burke, *Young men on a see-saw in Handsworth Park*, 1984

Bottom
Vanley Burke, *Protesting against racism and police brutality*, 1972

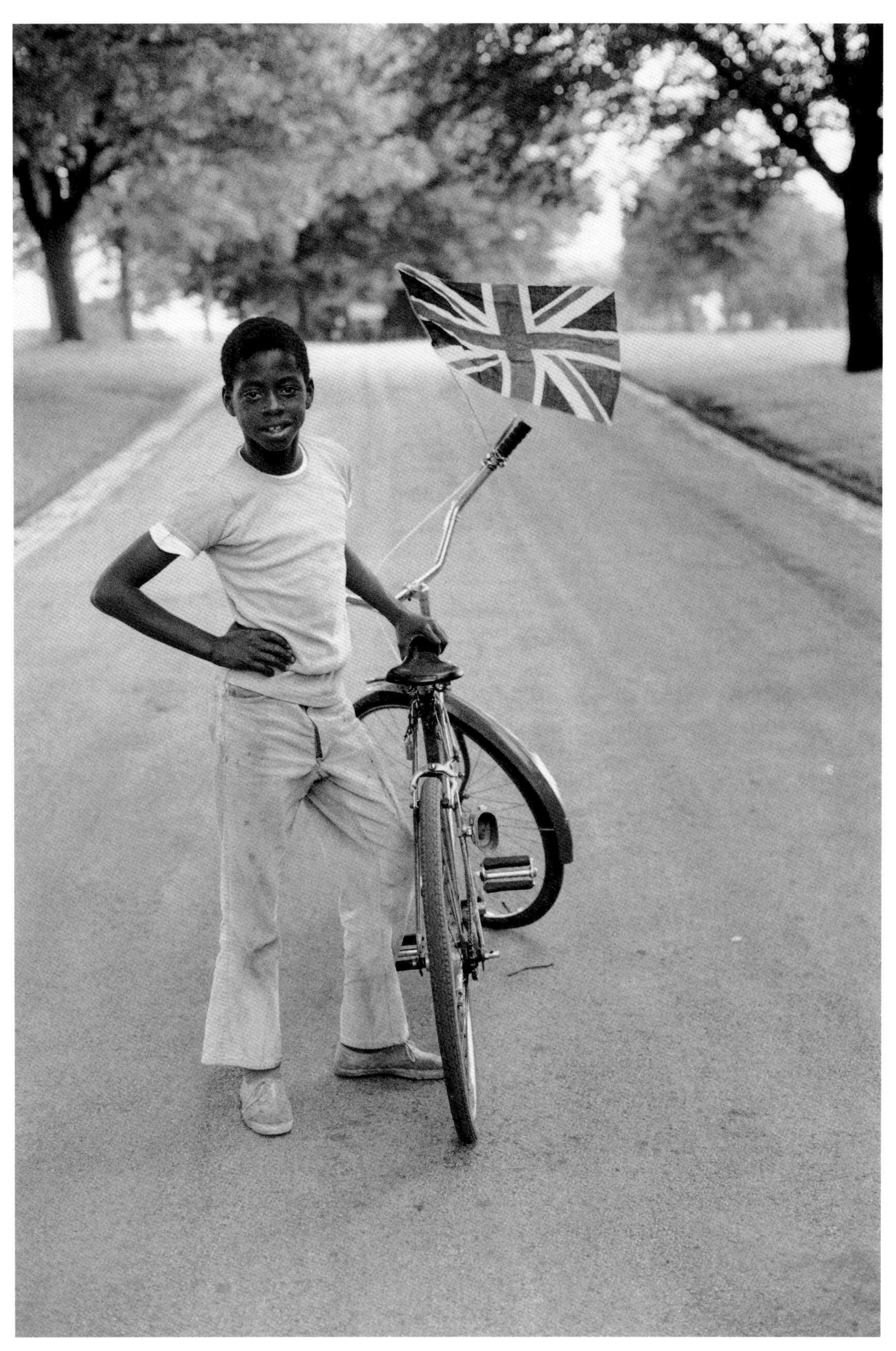

Vanley Burke, *Boy with flag, Winford in Handsworth Park*, 1970

Reimagining History as Narrative in Contemporary Art

Marsha Pearce

History may be understood in many ways, but it is its invocation *as narrative* that finds critical resonance in a discourse on contemporary art from the Caribbean. As narrative, history is made distinct from the past. Historian Alun Munslow sheds light on this difference: "While the past defined as a period of time during which many things happened is not invented, history, on the other hand, is a constructed narrative representation (a narration) *of* it."[1] The past may be gone, but Caribbean people live with narratives—many built from viewpoints outside the region. Questions about point of view remain critical in efforts to narrate time and experiences in a space that bears the weight of a colonial gaze and history—a given or legacy narrative that continues to throb in the passage of years we know today as the *post*-colonial. Yet, in the post-colonial context, time is less precise than we might think. If the colonial time span comprised discernible periods of enslavement, apprenticeship, emancipation, and indentureship—cardinal points that could be identified, mapped, narrated—the post-colonial is a long moment; a perpetual after-ness, with no clear beginning and no end in sight.[2] How to find one's bearings? How to construct a narrative representation of something that has no distinct contours? And, what might be the role of contemporary art in such a context? This essay considers contemporary art's particular functionality within a Caribbean post-colonial milieu. It draws examples from artists who presented work as part of the exhibition *Fragments of Epic Memory* (2021). In some cases, discussions of specific works go beyond those included in the exhibition.

Writing in the 1990s, Trinidad-based contemporary artist Christopher Cozier contemplates art practice in the Caribbean. He articulates his own sense of disorientation and post-colonial tensions:

> I used to always feel that I was born into a sort of after-everythingness: after independence, after the Federal moment, after the 1970 events, after Jamaica in the seventies and so forth. The only thing that I experienced as an adult was the looting and the rampage of the attempted coup in Trinidad in 1990. Again, however, that event seemed like the end result of some series of interactions yet to be revealed. This is why the term 'narrative' attracted me.

I felt that I lived in a space outside of a clear narrative with a clear point of origin and destination or point of arrival. I felt that I was in motion between non-discernible points. So, as an artist, I begun to wonder whether my work was defining its own point of view and the means to articulate it or whether the work was merely an illustration, an interpretation of a given viewpoint.[3]

Cozier's thoughts hint at how contemporary art can function as a way of approaching a "space outside of a clear narrative." In that space, prescribed or "given" narratives have to be tested, rather than described, and new ways of seeing crafted. How one composes a history of last week, yesterday, or even five minutes ago, within the uncharted and dizzying time-space of "after," requires fresh vantage points (fig. 1).

Over the years, contemporary art production in the Caribbean and its diaspora has demonstrated features of self-determined perspectives and an experimentation with modes of expression. Such artistic activity has also shown a consciousness of its own fluidity. Suchitra Mattai's work is one example of a malleable practice that yields new configurations in her exploration of found materials—each with its own history (fig. 2). The ongoing nature of the post-colonial moment suggests that narrative representations remain open-ended and subject to re-articulation. This is where the labour of memory resides. The work of recall in contemporary art practice is not simply a task of looking back on experiences; neither is it only an exercise in re-membering—a putting together of fragments of time and encounters. Rather, the artist *recalls*—as in revoking or negating—fixity. In a place often perceived in the rigid terms of sun, sea, and sand, contemporary art rejects set paradigms in favour of a Caribbean mutability.

Through contemporary art practice and the medium of memory, history—as a constructed narrative representation—is re-engaged and re-written from new points of view that are informed by experiences of this post-colonial present continuous. In the work of Nadia Huggins, for example, the photographer proposes a new way of seeing that positions the viewer underwater (fig. 3). She takes us below the surface of postcard seascapes hemmed in by shoreline and horizon. In her images, the body finds

1

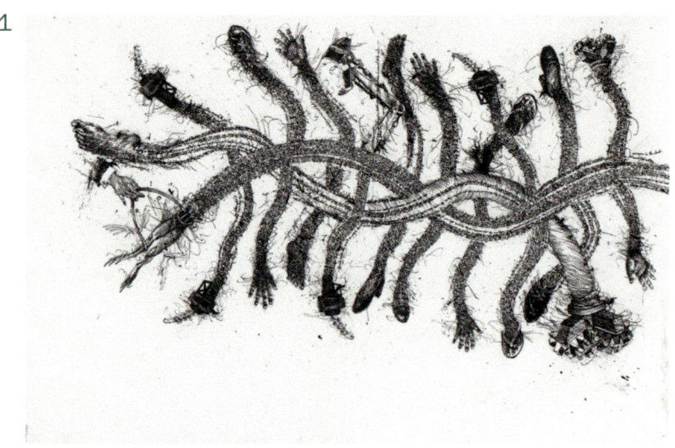

2

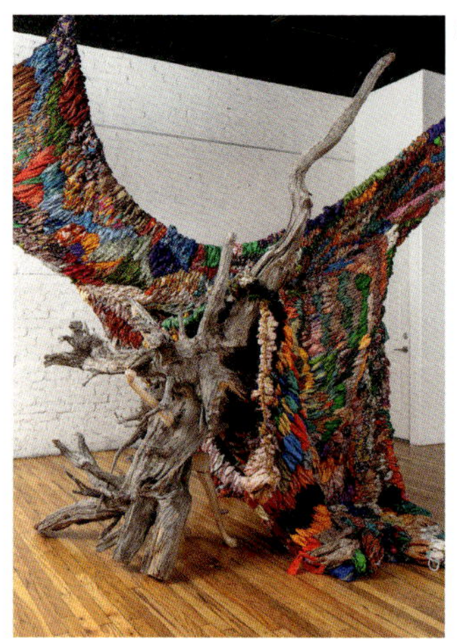

3

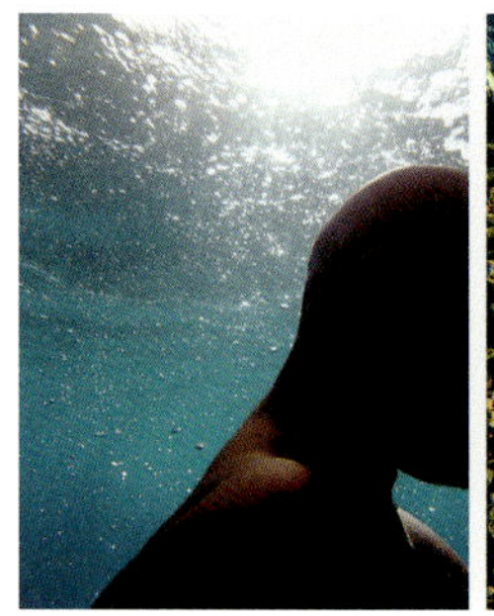

Fig. 1
Christopher Cozier
Entanglements (Dem Things Does Bite Too?), 2015.
Ink on paper, 76.2 × 111.8 cm.
© Christopher Cozier.
Image courtesy of the artist.

Fig. 2
Suchitra Mattai
Breathing Room, 2020.
Vintage saris, driftwood, and table legs, dimensions variable. © Suchitra Mattai.
Photo: Wes Magyar.

Fig. 3
Nadia Huggins
Transformations No. 7, 2016. Digital photograph, 76.2 × 118.1 cm.
© Nadia Huggins. Image courtesy of the artist, 2021.

4

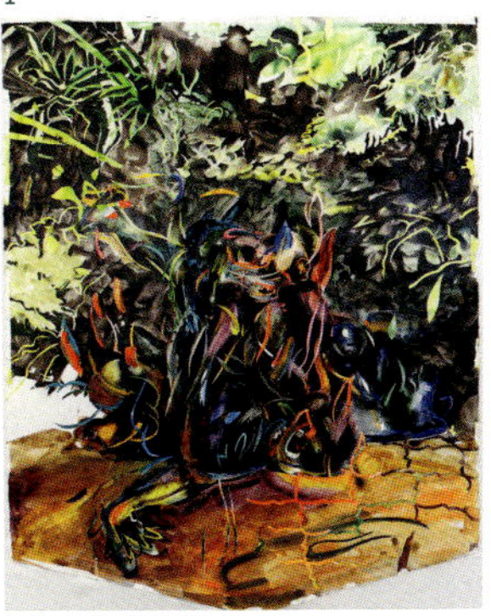

5

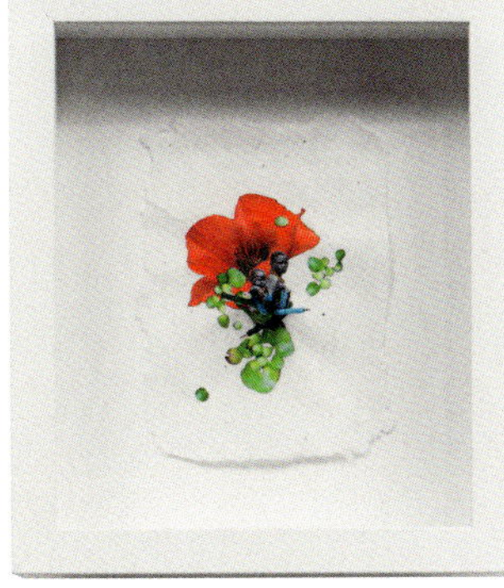

6

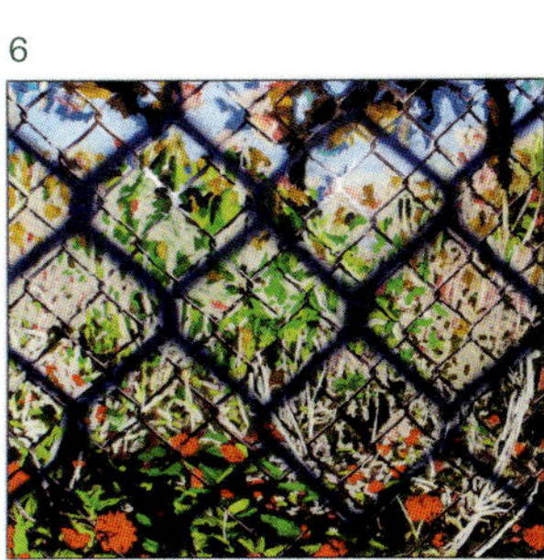

Fig. 4
Leasho Johnson
Anansi: A place where no one can hear us, where no one can see us cry, 2020.
Charcoal, distemper, watercolour, ink, coffee, acrylic, oil, oil stick, and gesso on paper, 129.54 × 170.18 cm.
© Leasho Johnson.
Image courtesy of the artist.

Fig. 5
Andrea Chung
Vex IX, 2020.
Collage, ink, and beads on paper, handmade from traditional birthing cloth, 24.13 × 20.32 cm. Private collection. © Andrea Chung.
Image courtesy of the artist, Klowden Mann, and Tyler Park Presents, Los Angeles; photo: Michael Underwood.

Fig. 6
Paul Anthony Smith
Untitled (Dreams Deferred), 2020. Oil stick and spray paint on inkjet print, mounted on Sintra, 207.01 × 186.69 × 6.35 cm.
© Paul Anthony Smith.
Image courtesy of the artist and Jack Shainman Gallery, New York.

agency; it is free from historical constructs of gender, race, and class. Her portraits, which put the human body in an intimate dialogue with marine life, are at once windows to a self in flux and a reconsideration of an ecological poetics in a context where "the brutality of the plantation system produced a particular relationship to the natural world."[4]

Recent work by Leasho Johnson also addresses the notion of the surface (fig. 4). In his portraits, the artist abandons a pursuit of likeness, looking instead at what lies beneath the surface of Black flesh. His investigations reveal a metaphysical state. If the "colonialists believed that the bodies of the enslaved were shrouded in blackness, which they saw not only as a color but also as evidence of a congenital and moral failing,"[5] then Johnson disrupts this narrative with his own viewpoint; re-presenting blackness in less definite terms. His forms are rendered amorphous, unfamiliar, unapologetic, and liberated from facile readings.

Similarly, work by Andrea Chung and Paul Anthony Smith trouble perspectives, and therefore destabilize established histories. In her new collage series *Vex* (2020, fig. 5), Chung re-imagines ethnographic photographs taken of women from the African diaspora. Considering the narratives of these images, she shares:

> Many of these [photographs] were used to make cartes de visite. They were taken by photographers and turned into postcards.... [People visiting a place] would find a card... and then would write something on the back and mail it to a friend to say, 'I was here.' There is something really perverse about that.[6]

Chung's art resists this perversion by questioning whether the women wanted their pictures taken. Using the aesthetic and meaning of the Congo practice of nkisi nkondi, she reclaims their power. A nkisi is a carved wooden figure; a potent spirit carrier used to resolve human affairs. It can protect or destroy, and is typically identified by numerous sharp objects inserted into its surface. Chung echoes this act by driving needles into the archival photographs. In this way, she shifts the framework of representation. Experiencing the work is further complicated by an obscuring of vision—and a forestalling of quick interpretations—with the needles serving as a barrier between the viewer and the subject of the photographs.

Smith's mottled picture planes also check easy access to his images (fig. 6). He gouges the surface of his photographs in a technique called picotage. The result is a textured layer that both hides and reveals the subject matter. The photographs appear to dance in defiance of stillness—daring the viewer's gaze to match their movements. As angles change, new narratives open up in Smith's work. This sense of motion is equally palpable in Sandra Brewster's art. Her *Blur* (2015-18, figs. 7 & 8) series provides a glimpse of her subjects traversing places and spaces. Our eyes are never settled.

Zak Ové's work sets up its own address of history. Through his references to Trinidad Carnival and acts of masking, Ové initiates a process of "demasking" (to borrow Gerard Aching's term) narratives of self (fig. 9). Encounters with his art are less about an "unmasking, which tends to be laden with the meaning that the mask is removed from someone else" and more about removing an ideological mask from oneself; a "self-recognition... that is brought on by contact with a masked subject."[7] Ové re-presents historically defined identities and ushers alternative possibilities of being in the contemporary moment.

Other ways of seeing are interrogated in artworks by Peter Dean Rickards, Ebony G. Patterson, Wendy Nanan, and Kelly Sinnapah Mary. Rickards's photographs peer at the raw underbelly of Jamaica, offering sensitive counter-narratives to the histories of place and people told by the mainstream media. Patterson's lush, multidimensional works draw the viewer into their patterned depths. With a grammar of beads, sequins, flowers, lace, and glitter, she presents bold recontextualizations of existing narratives—teasing out layers and rendering audible the silences in history. Sinnapah Mary's visual language embraces multiple identities in her revisiting and assessment of violence, domination, and narratives of indentureship, and Nanan brings a trenchant eye to a history of dependence. Her manipulation of papier-mâché gives shape to an aesthetic of syncretism, with varying signifiers, practices, and viewpoints becoming interlocuters in fluid conversations about resourcefulness and self-reliance in our present time.

This attention to a plurality of vision is also witnessed in contemporary works by Roshini Kempadoo and Jeannette Ehlers—artists who both underscore the cumulative force

7

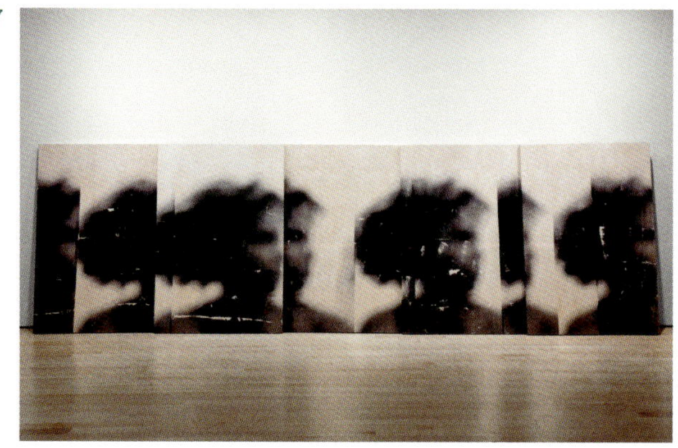

8

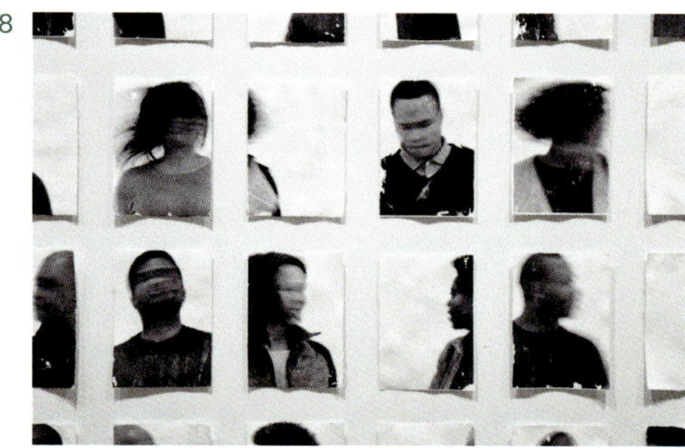

Fig. 7
Sandra Brewster
Untitled, 2015–2016.
Photo-based gel transfer on wood, each: 152.4 × 101.6 cm. Courtesy of the artist and Georgia Scherman Projects. Installation view of *Sandra Brewster: Blur* at the Art Gallery of Ontario, 2019–2020. © Sandra Brewster. Photo: Art Gallery of Ontario.

Fig. 8
Sandra Brewster
Untitled, 2016–2018.
Photo-based gel transfer on archival paper, each: 25.4 × 17.8 cm. Courtesy of the artist and Georgia Scherman Projects. Installation view of *Sandra Brewster: Blur* at the Art Gallery of Ontario, 2019–2020. © Sandra Brewster. Photo: Art Gallery of Ontario.

of multiple lenses through which experiences can be considered. Kempadoo's strategic use of montage, and Ehlers's liminal positioning between installation, video, photography, sculpture, and performance, create nuanced representations that confront monolithic histories.

The various practices by these artists from the Caribbean make manifest Christopher Cozier's observation that "artistic activity is not merely an embroidery or embellishment upon a fixed narrative."[8] The statement finds as much resonance among a number of creative practitioners today as it does in his own work. His output has been, and remains, a tangible effort to develop personal vocabularies that probe how we experience this "now" moment, and the ways in which history as a constructed narrative representation is summoned and given fresh utterance in the making of what is called art.

Contemporary art may be the art of the present, but its production is not solely reliant on present time. A recognition of lingering histories/narratives unlocks a space of potential for alternative ontologies or, as art historian Terry Smith puts it: "Seeing the present historically is disjunctive: it is freed from determination's concrete channelling, from the rolling thunder of inevitability, and from the subtler straitjacket of probability."[9] In contemporary art from the Caribbean and its diaspora, history is constantly being leveraged and reimagined as part of a process of identifying new vantage points, and memory (as a particular kind of recall) is put to service in ensuring that the region and its diaspora are routed rather than rooted in time. The *post*-colonial context comes with its own temporal complexities that demand an alertness to the interplay of the historical and the contemporary. The challenging of the taken-for-granted—the given narratives—is the work of the artist in a Caribbean (happily) ever *after*.

9

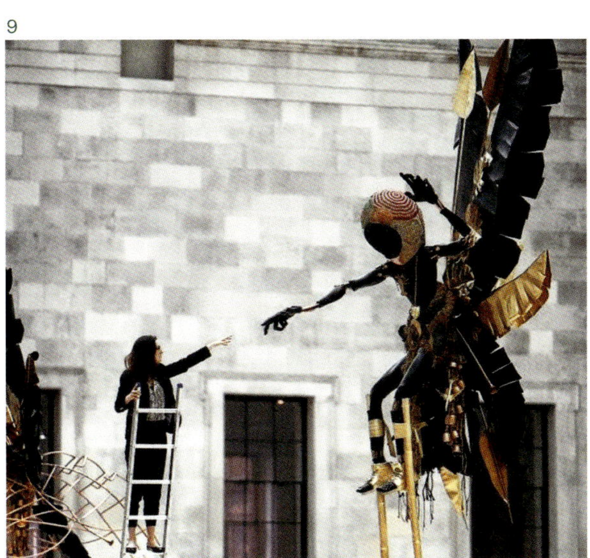

Fig. 9
Zak Ové
Moko Jumbie (Katie Morais poses with a *Moko Jumbie* sculpture), 2015.
Mixed media, dimensions variable. © Zak Ové.
Image courtesy of the artist and Vigo Gallery.

1 Alun Munslow, *Narrative and History* (London: Red Globe Press, 2019), 4.

2 The notion of the post-colonial is understood in different temporal terms, making it a contested period of time with a shifting starting point. For example, Chadwick Allen notes that its common hyphenated form, *post-colonial*, identifies "an attention to historical periodization" while the run-together *postcolonial* emphasizes "ideological continuity." Chadwick Allen, "Who Put the 'Post' in Postcolonial?," *NOVEL: A Forum on Fiction* 32, no. 1 (Autumn 1998): 144–146.

3 Christopher Cozier, "Between Narratives and Other Spaces," *Small Axe* 6 (September 1999): 20–21.

4 Elizabeth M. DeLoughrey, Renée K. Gosson, and George B. Handley, eds., *Caribbean Literature and the Environment: Between Nature and Culture* (Charlottesville: University of Virginia Press, 2005), 2.

5 Dawn P. Harris, *Punishing the Black Body: Marking Social and Racial Structures in Barbados and Jamaica* (Athens: University of Georgia Press, 2017), 16.

6 Andrea Chung, "Andrea Chung with HereIn," interviewed by HereIn, October 16, 2020, hereinjournal.org/conversations/andrea-chung-with-herein.

7 Gerard Aching, *Masking and Power: Carnival and Popular Culture in the Caribbean* (Minneapolis: University of Minnesota Press, 2002), 6.

8 Cozier, "Between Narratives," 22.

9 Terry Smith, *Art to Come: Histories of Contemporary Art* (Durham, NC: Duke University Press, 2019), 6.

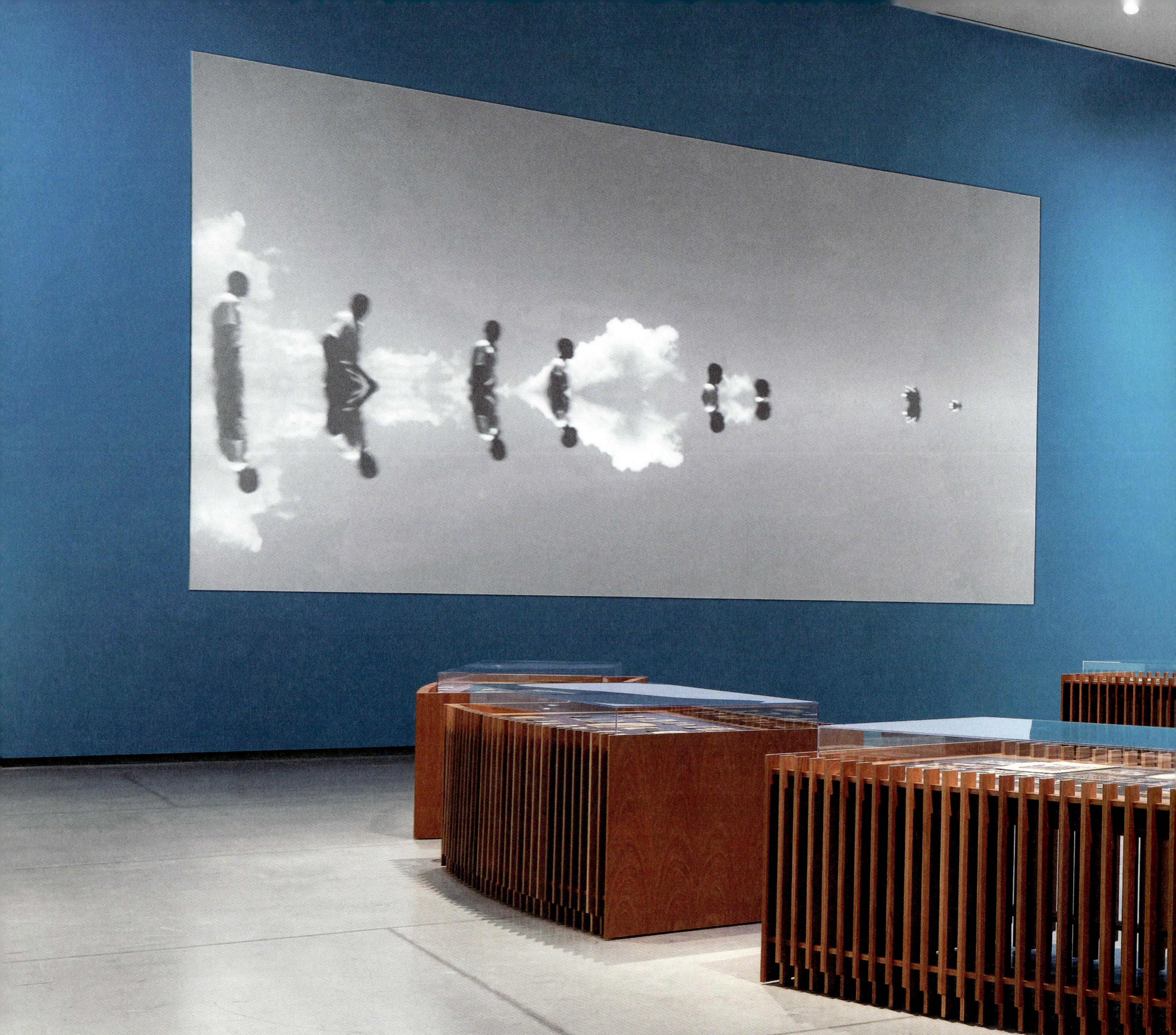

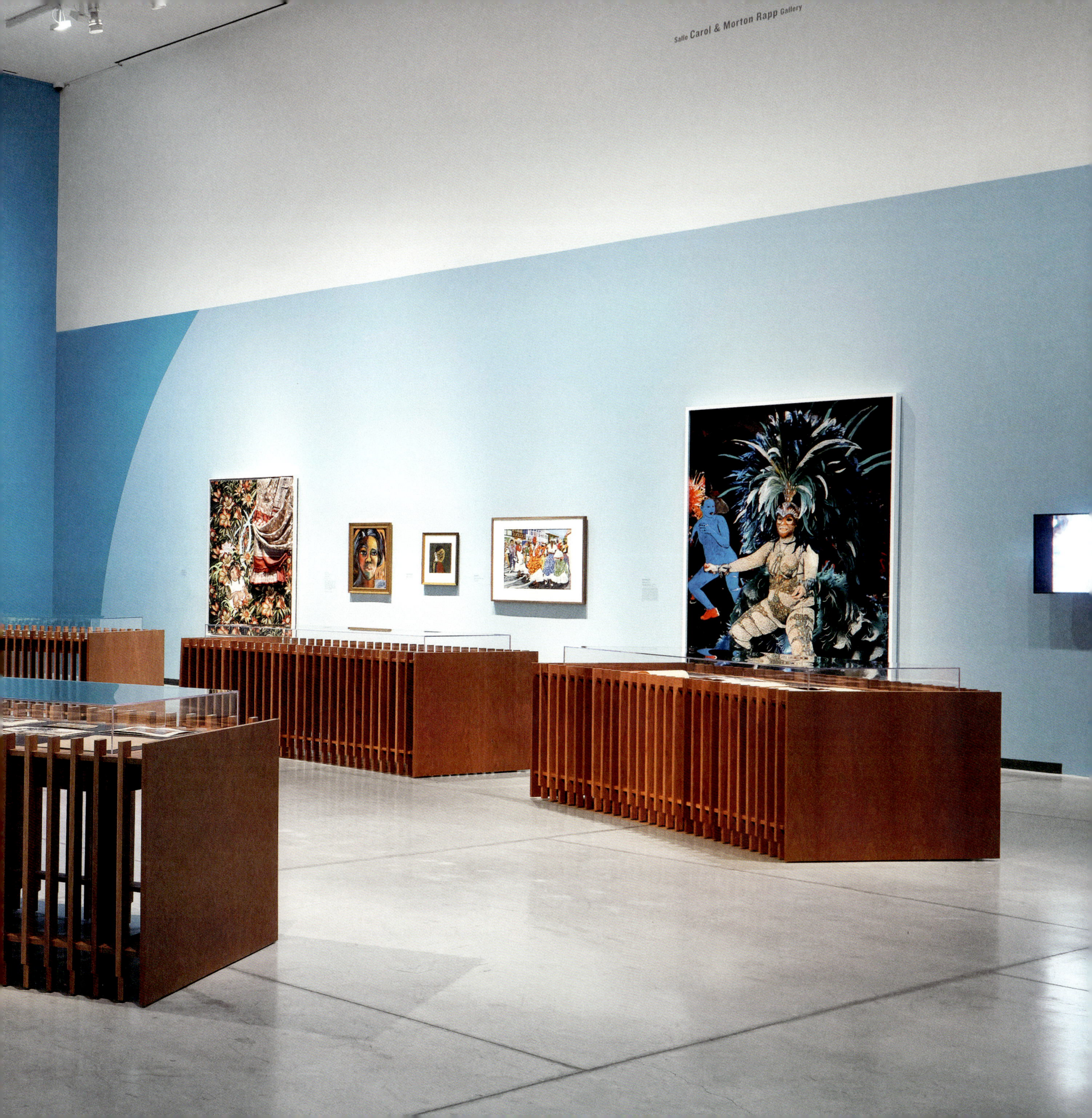
Salle Carol & Morton Rapp Gallery

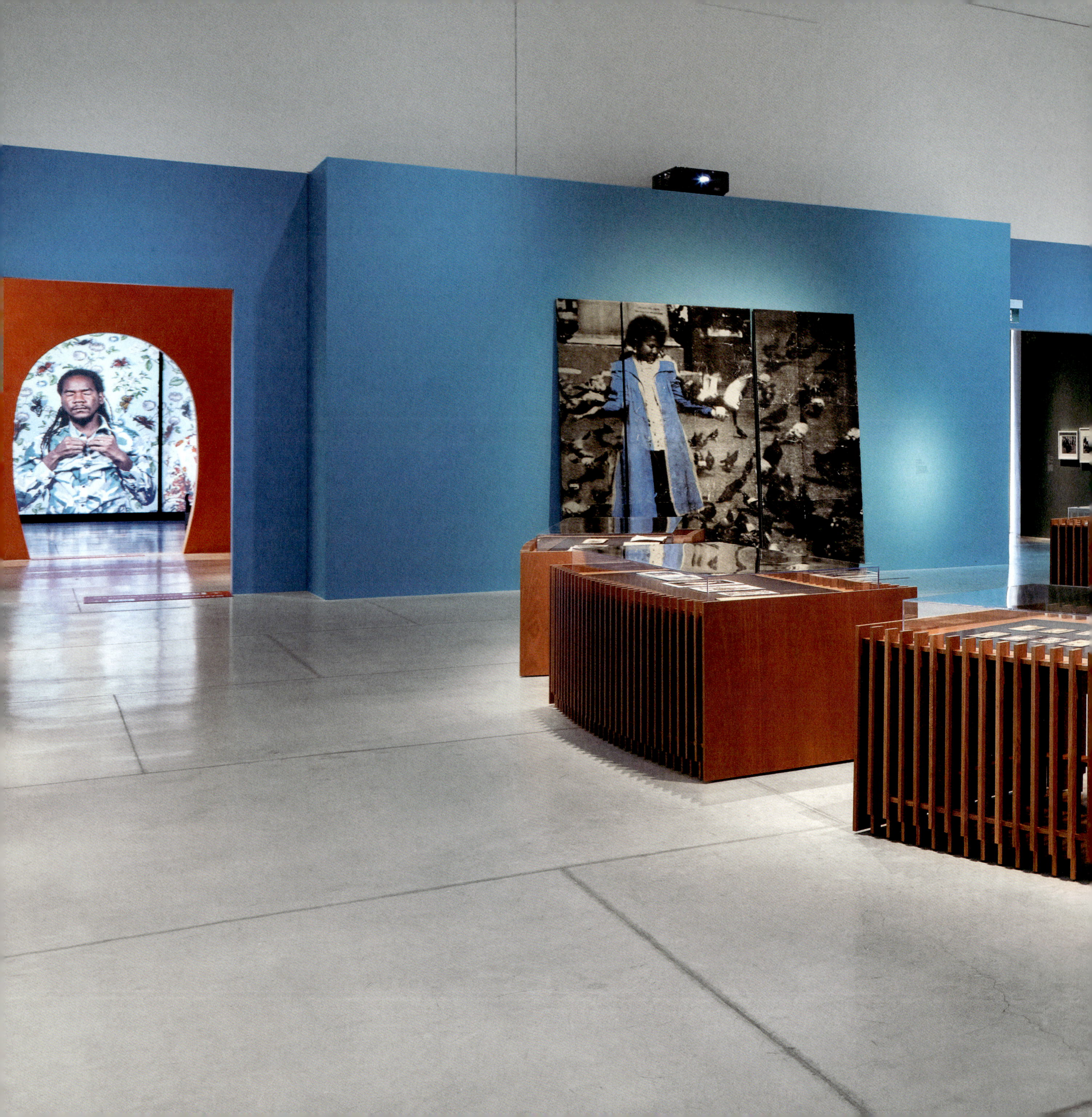

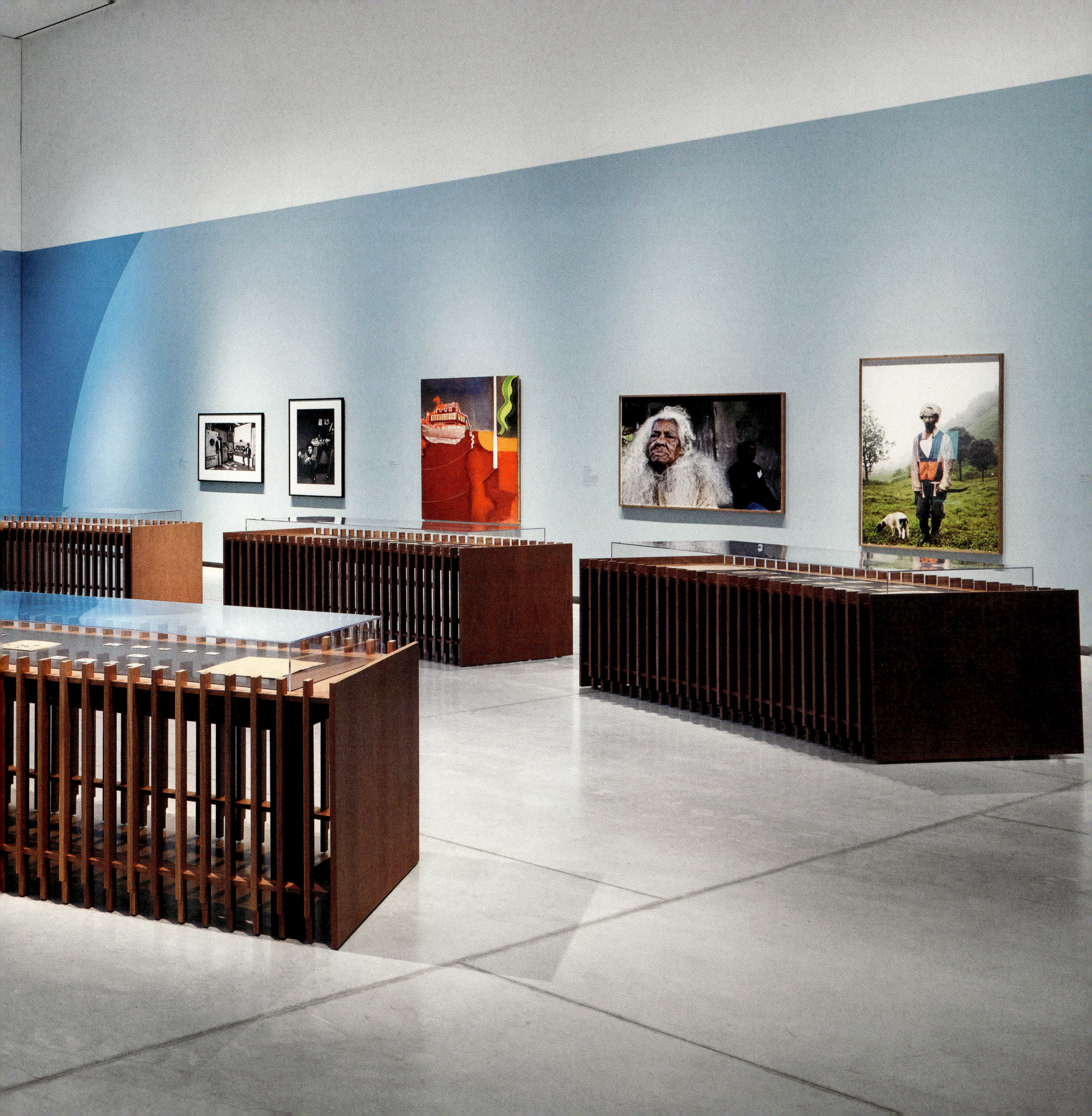

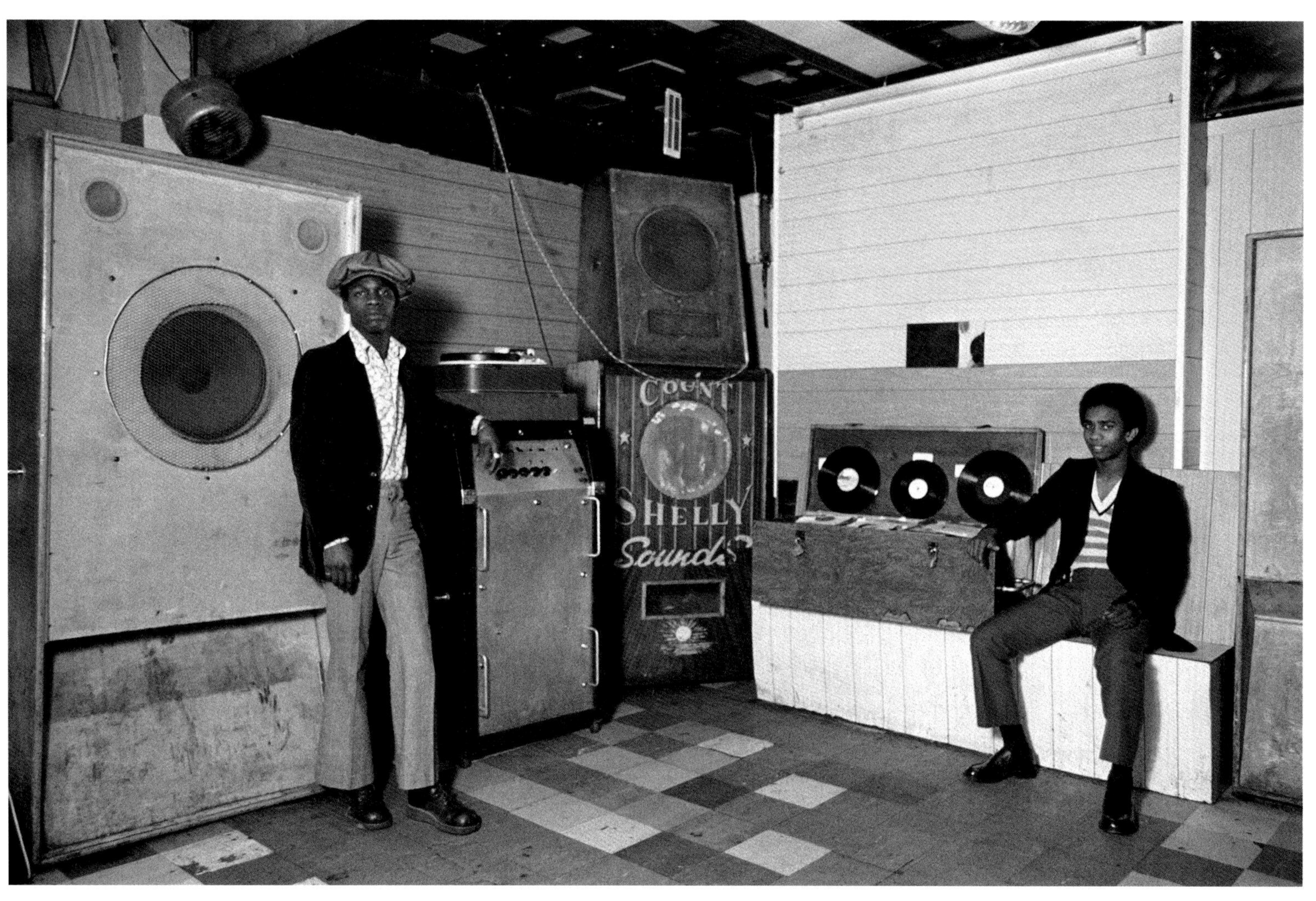

Dennis Morris, *MC & Selector – Count Shelly Sound System*, 1972

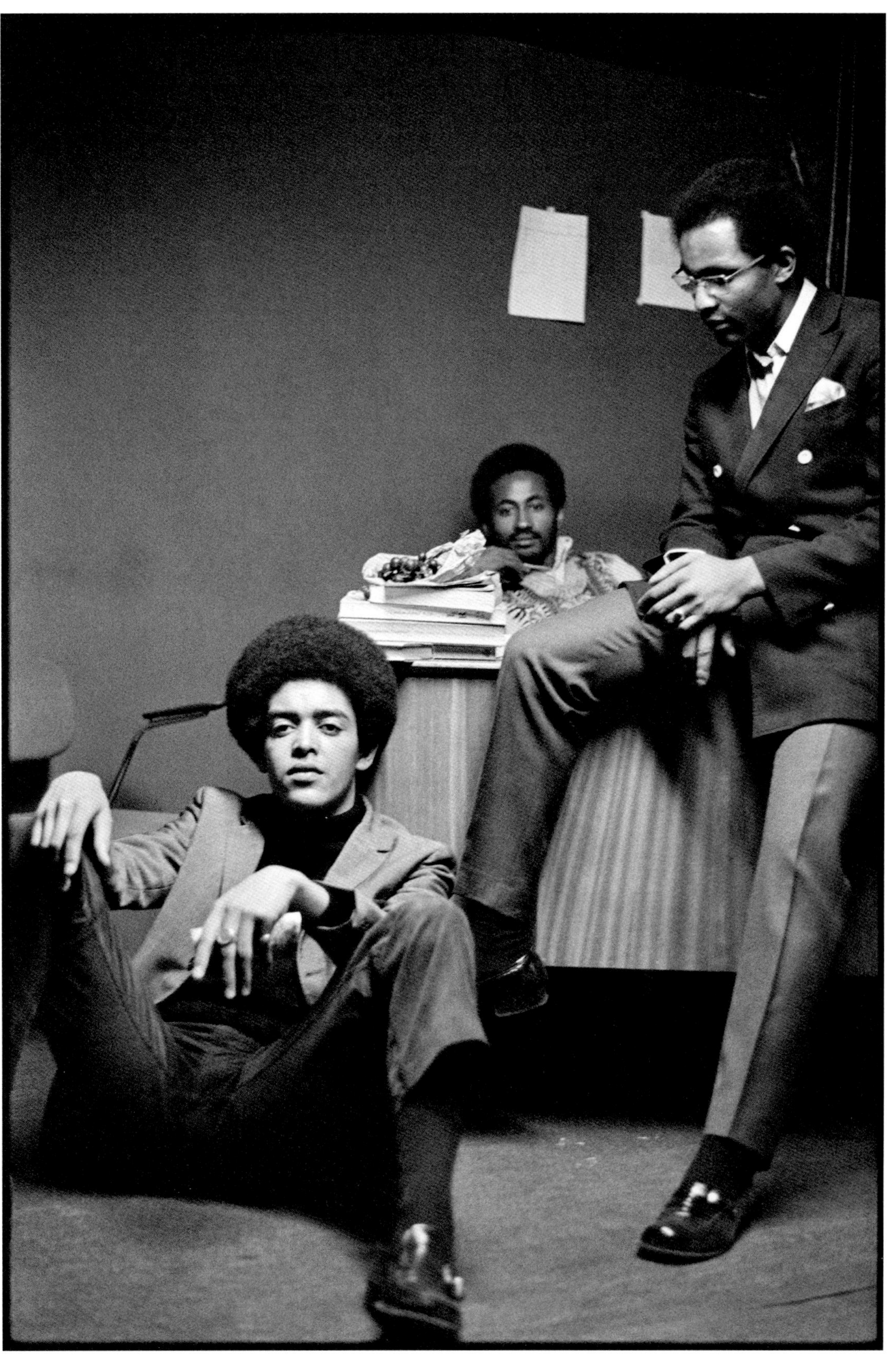

Dennis Morris, *The Brothers at the Black House*, 1972

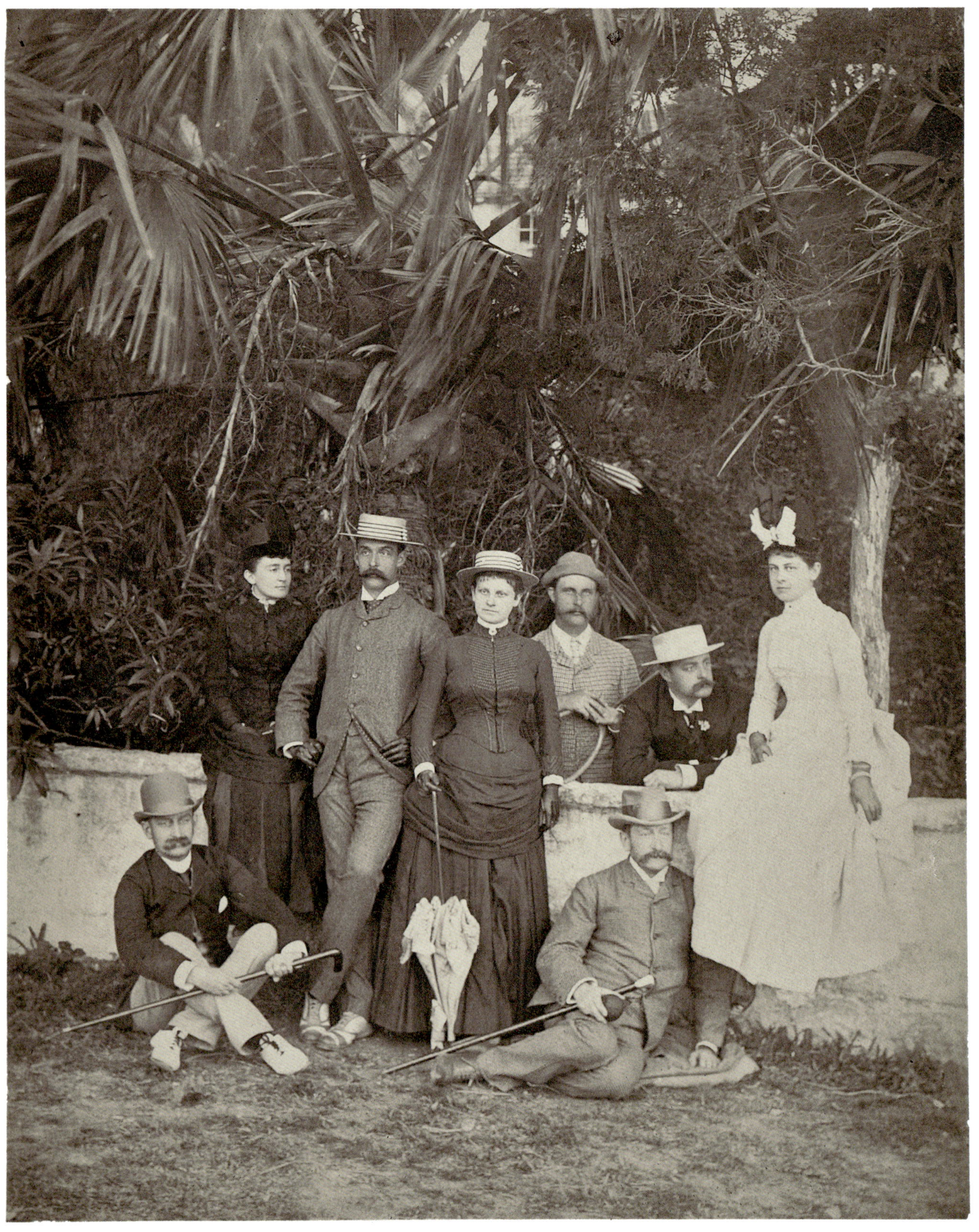

Unknown photographer, *Family Picnic, Bermuda*, 1887

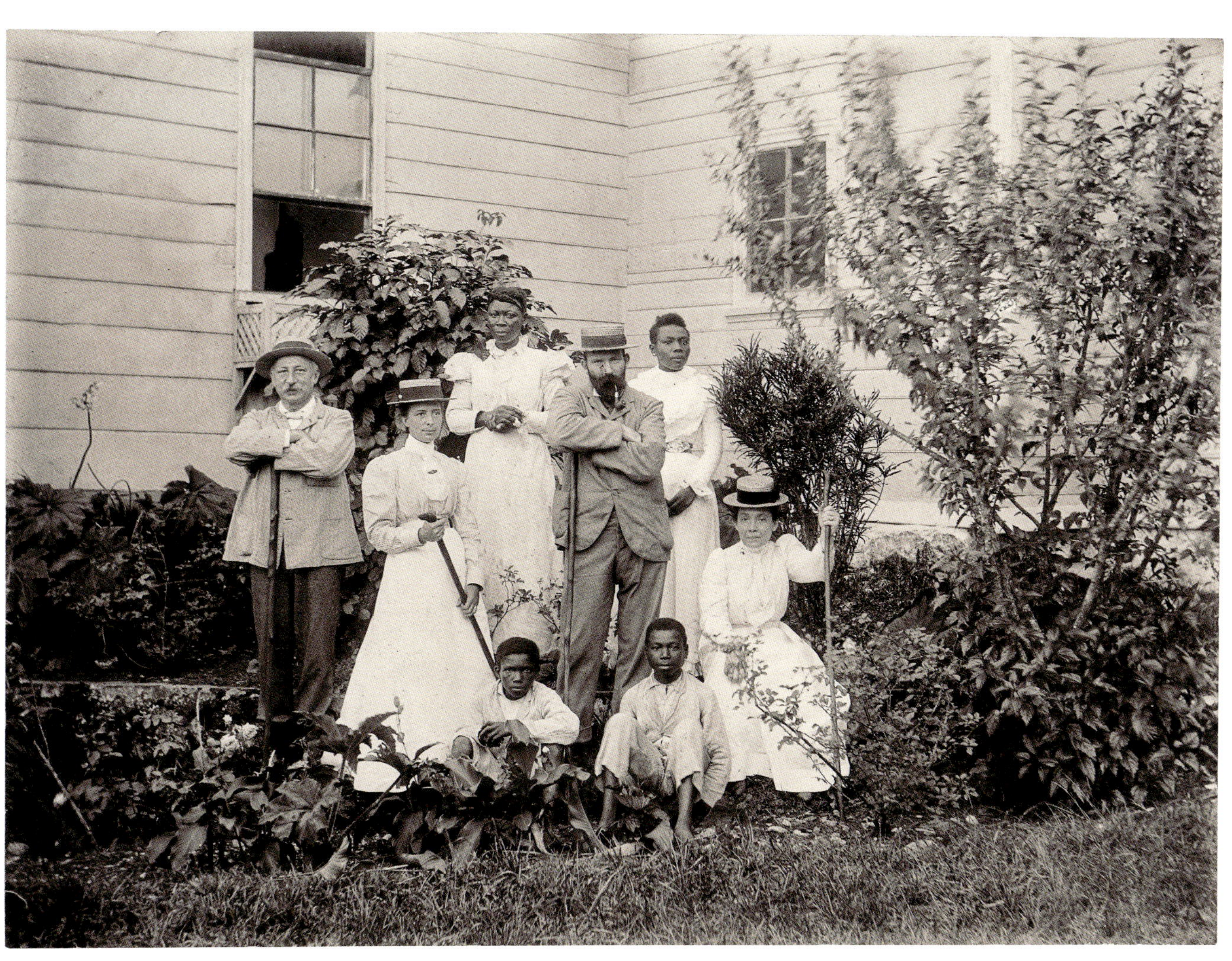

Unknown photographer, *Family in Garden, Jamaica*, c. 1890

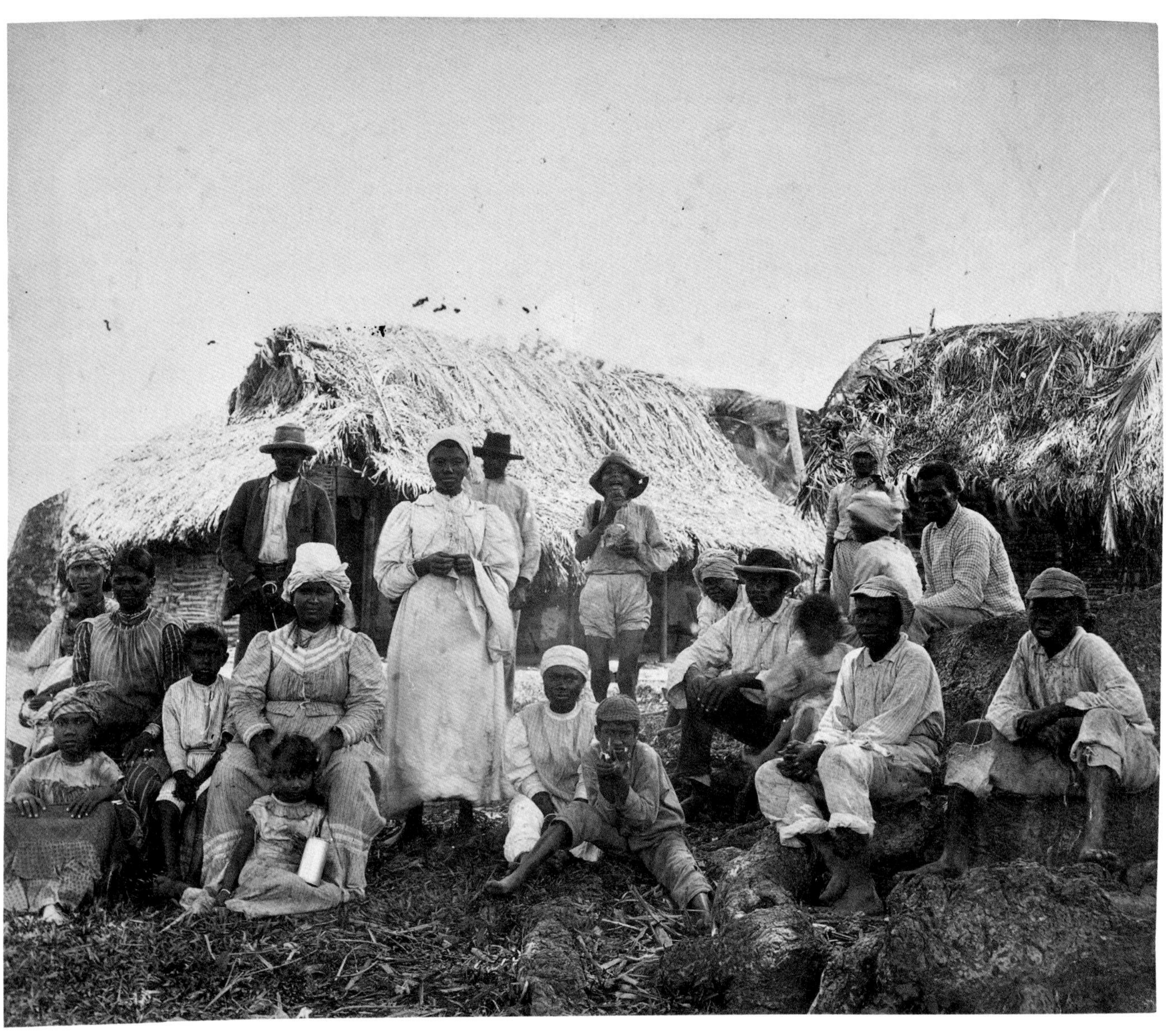

Unknown photographer, *Family at Home, Blue Mountains, Jamaica*, c. 1890

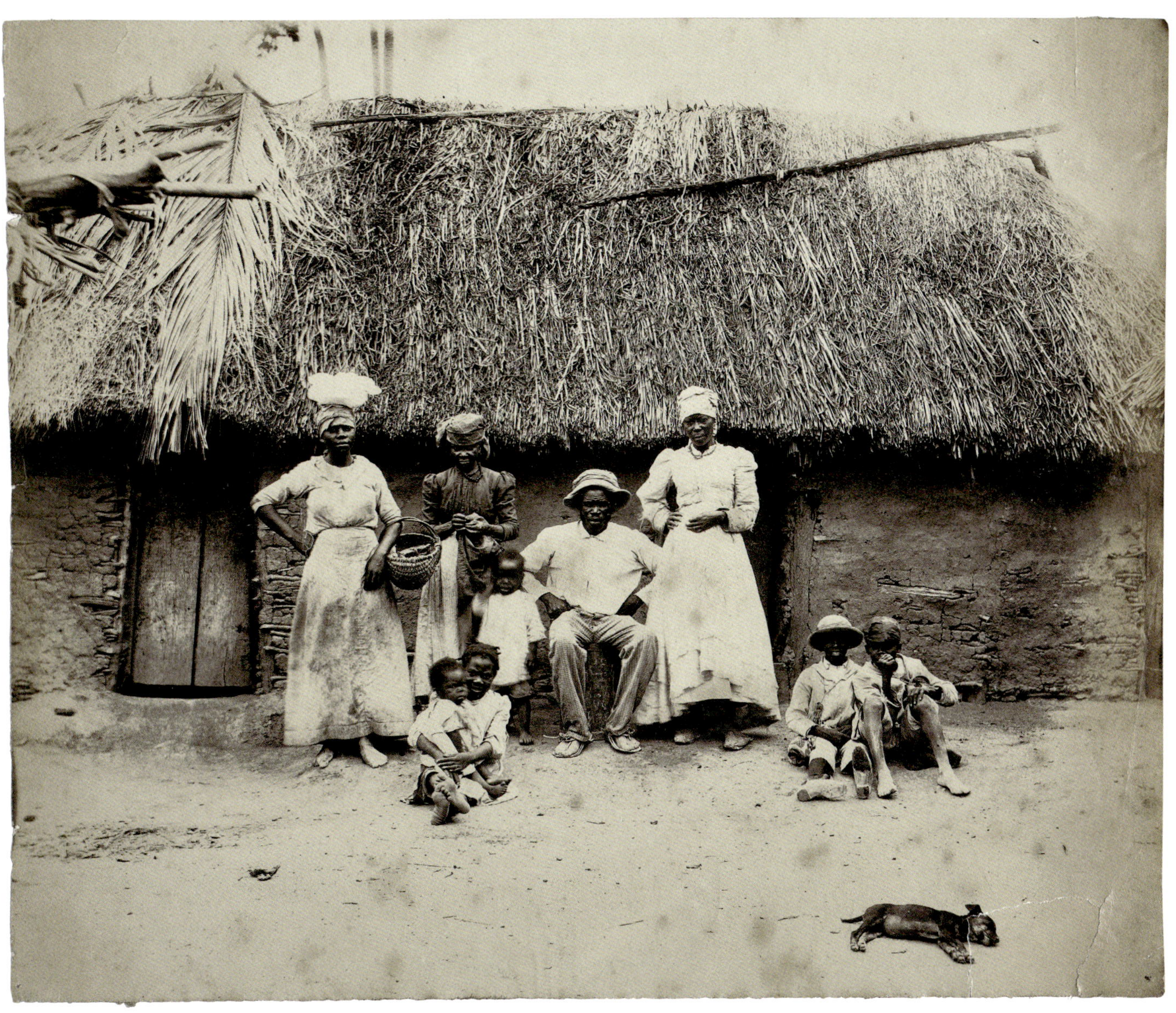

John William Cleary, *A Family, Jamaica*, c. 1890

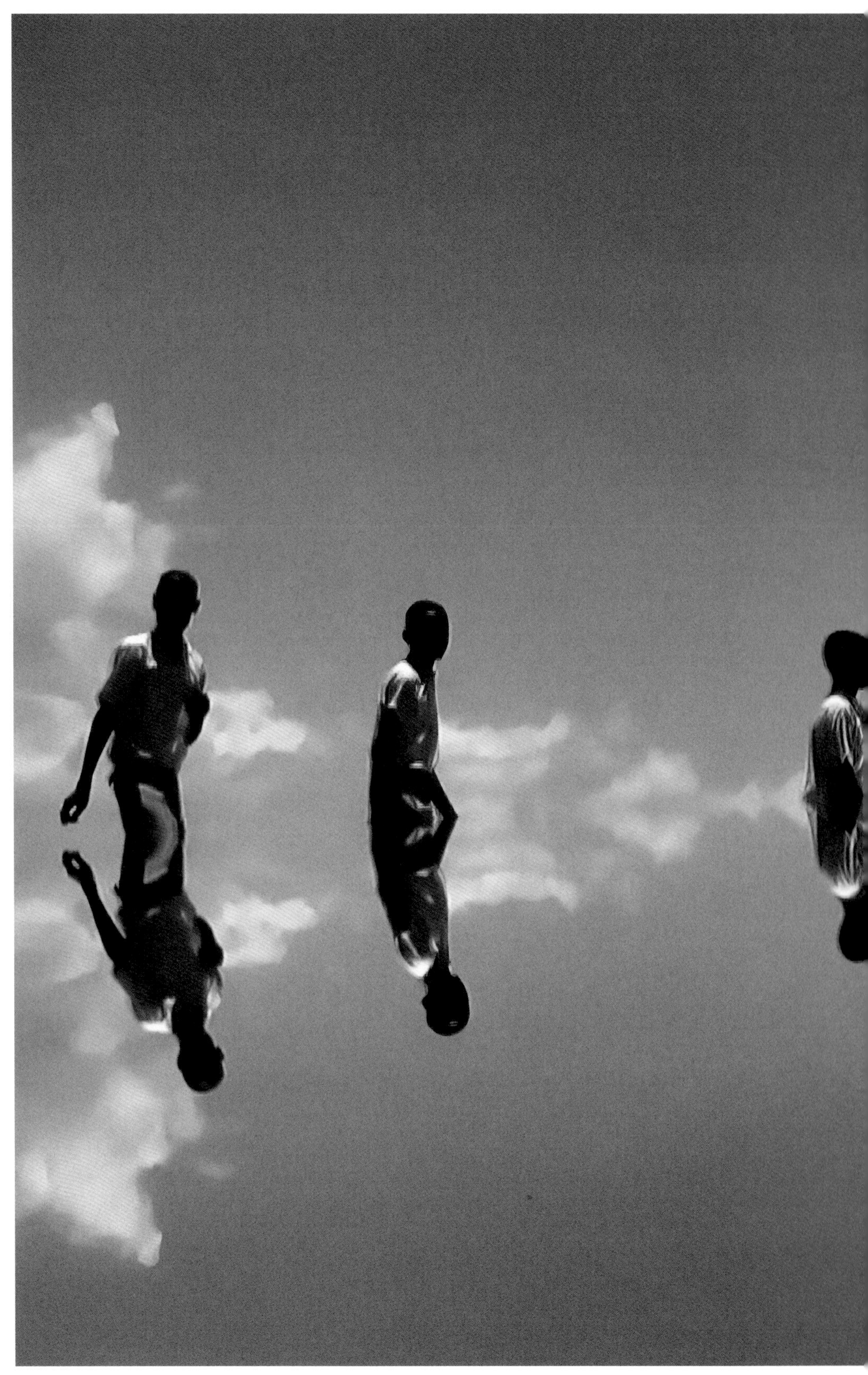

Jeannette Ehlers, still from *Black Bullets*, 2012

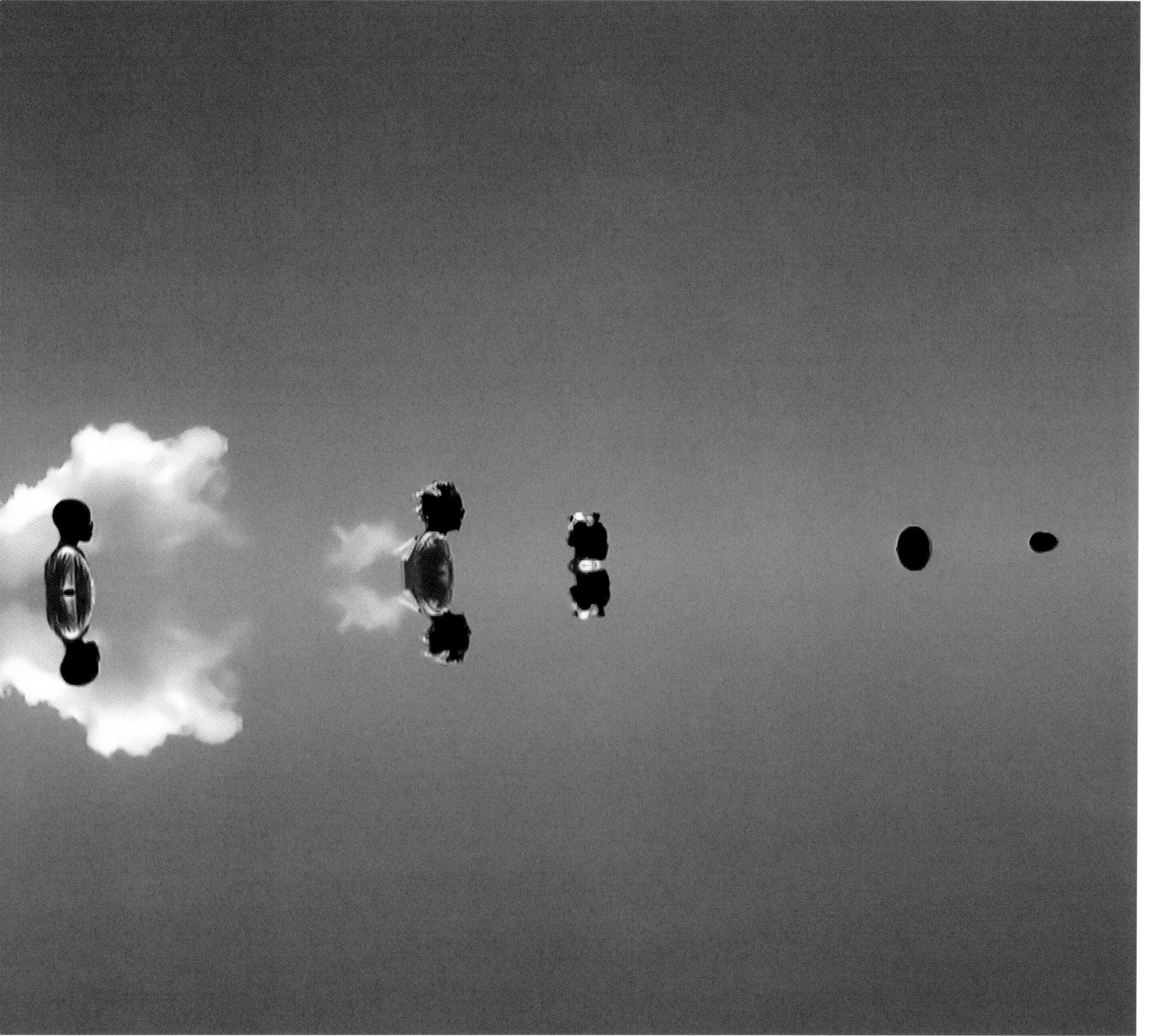

The San Domingo Masses Begin

C.L.R. James

Eh ! Eh ! Bomba ! Heu ! Heu !
Canga, bafio té !
Canga, mouné de lé !
Canga, do ki la !
Canga, li !

The slaves worked on the land, and, like revolutionary peasants everywhere, they aimed at the extermination of their oppressors. But working and living together in gangs of hundreds on the huge sugar-factories which covered the North Plain, they were closer to a modern proletariat than any group of workers in existence at the time, and the rising was, therefore, a thoroughly prepared and organized mass movement. By hard experience they had learnt that isolated efforts were doomed to failure, and in the early months of 1791 in and around Le Cap they were organizing for revolution. Voodoo was the medium of the conspiracy. In spite of all prohibitions, the slaves travelled miles to sing and dance and practice the rites and talk; and now, since the revolution, to hear the political news and make their plans. Boukman, a Papaloi or High Priest, a gigantic Negro, was the leader. He was headman of a plantation and followed the political situation both among the whites and among the Mulattoes. By the end of July 1791, the blacks in and around Le Cap were ready and waiting. The plan was conceived on a massive scale and they aimed at exterminating the whites and taking the colony for themselves. There were perhaps 12,000 slaves in Le Cap, 6,000 of them men. One night the slaves in the suburbs and outskirts of Le Cap were to fire the plantations. At this signal the slaves in the town would massacre the whites and the slaves on the plain would complete the destruction. They had travelled a long, long way since the grandiose poisoning schemes of Mackandal.

The plan did not succeed in its entirety. But it very nearly did, and the scope and organization of this revolt shows Boukman to be the first of that line of great leaders whom the slaves were to throw up in such profusion and rapidity during the years which followed. That so vast a conspiracy was not discovered until it had actually broken out is a testimony to their solidarity. In early August the slaves in Limbé, then and to the end of the revolution one of the storm-centres, rose prematurely and were crushed. This Limbé rising showed that it was dangerous to delay. Three days after, representatives from parishes all over the plain assembled to fix the day. Deputies on their way to Le Cap for the first session of the Colonial Assembly, to begin on August 25, met throngs of slaves on the road who abused and even attacked them. On August 21 some prisoners were taken and de Blanchelande, the Governor, examined them himself the next day. He did not get much from them, but he understood vaguely that there was to be some sort of rising. He took precautions to safeguard the city from the slaves within and he ordered patrols to cover the outskirts. But these whites despised the slaves too much to believe them capable of organizing a mass movement on a grand scale. They could not get from the prisoners the names of the leaders, and what precautions could they take against the thousands of slaves on the hundreds of plantations? Some of the white rabble in Le Cap, always ready for loot and pillage, were revealed as being connected with a plot of some sort. De Blanchelande was more concerned about these than about the Negroes.

On the night of the 22 a tropical storm raged, with lightning and gusts of wind and heavy showers of rain. Carrying torches to light their way, the leaders of the revolt met in an open space in the thick forests of the Morne Rouge, a mountain overlooking Le Cap. There Boukman gave the last instructions and, after Voodoo incantations and the sucking of the blood of a stuck pig, he stimulated his followers by a prayer spoken in creole, which, like so much spoken on such occasions, has remained. “The god who created the sun which gives us light, who rouses the waves and rules the storm, though hidden in the clouds, he watches us. He sees all that the white man does. The god of the white man inspires him with crime, but our god calls upon us to do good works. Our god who is good to us orders us to revenge our wrongs. He will direct our arms and aid us. Throw away the symbol of the god of the whites who has so often caused us to weep, and listen to the voice of liberty, which speaks in the hearts of us all."

The symbol of the god of the whites was the cross which, as Catholics, they wore around their necks.

That very night they began. The slaves on the Gallifet plantation were so well treated that "happy as the Negroes of Gallifet" was a slave proverb. Yet by a phenomenon noticed in all revolutions it was they who led the way. Each slave-gang murdered its masters and burnt the plantation to the ground. The precautions that de Blanchelande had taken saved Le Cap, but the preparation otherwise had been thorough and complete, and in a few days one-half of the famous North Plain was a flaming ruin. From Le Cap the whole horizon was a wall of fire. From this wall continually rose thick black volumes of smoke, through which came tongues of flame leaping to the very sky. For nearly three weeks the people of Le Cap could barely distinguish day from night, while a rain of burning cane straw, driven before the wind like flakes of snow, flew over the city and the shipping in the harbour, threatening both with destruction.

The slaves destroyed tirelessly. Like the peasants in the Jacquerie or the Luddite wreckers, they were seeking their salvation in the most obvious way, the destruction of what they knew was the cause of their sufferings; and if they destroyed much it was because they had suffered much. They knew that as long as these plantations stood their lot would be to labour on them until they dropped. The only thing was to destroy them. From their masters they had known rape, torture, degradation, and, at the slightest provocation, death. They returned in kind. For two centuries the higher civilization had shown them that power was used for wreaking your will on those whom you controlled. Now that they held power they did as they had been taught. In the frenzy of the first encounters they killed all, yet they spared the priests whom they feared and the surgeons who had been kind to them. They, whose women had undergone countless violations, violated all the women who fell into their hands, often on the bodies of their still bleeding husbands, fathers and brothers. "Vengeance! Vengeance!" was their war-cry, and one of them carried a white child on a pike as a standard.

And yet they were surprisingly moderate,[1] then and afterwards, far more humane than their masters had been or would ever be to them. They did not maintain this revengeful spirit for long. The cruelties of property and privilege are always more ferocious than the revenges of poverty and oppression. For the one aims at perpetuating resented injustice, the other is merely a momentary passion soon appeased. As the revolution gained territory, they spared many of the men, women, and children whom they surprised on plantations. To prisoners of war alone they remained merciless. They tore out their flesh with red-hot pincers, they roasted them on slow fires, they sawed a carpenter between two of his boards. Yet in all the records of that time there is no single instance of such fiendish tortures as burying white men up to the neck and smearing the holes in their faces to attract insects, or blowing them up with gun-powder, or any of the thousand and one bestialities to which they had been subjected. Compared with what their masters had done to them in cold blood, what they did was negligible, and they were spurred on by the ferocity with which the whites in Le Cap treated all slave prisoners who fell into their hands.

As usual the strength of the mass movement dragged in its wake revolutionary sections of those classes nearest to it. Free blacks joined them. A planter of Port Magot had taught his black foreman to read and write, had made him free, had left him in his will 10,000 francs, had given to the foreman's mother land on which she had made a coffee plantation. But this black raised the slaves on the plantations of his master and his own mother, set them on fire, and joined the revolution, which gave him a high command. The Mulattoes hated the black slaves because they were slaves and because they were blacks. But when they actually saw the slaves taking action on such a grand scale, numbers of young Mulattoes from Le Cap and round about rushed to join the hitherto despised blacks and fight against the common enemy.

They were fortunate in that the troops in Le Cap were few, and de Blanchelande, afraid of the slaves and the white rabble in the town, preferred to act on the defensive. One attack was made by the regulars, who drove the slaves before them, but de Blanchelande, yielding to the nervous fears awakened in the city, recalled the detachment. This left the revolution master of the countryside. Gaining courage, the blacks extended their destruction over the plain. If they had had the slightest material interest in the plantations, they would not have destroyed so wantonly. But they had none. After a few weeks they stopped for a moment to organize themselves. It is at this period, one month after the revolt had begun, that Toussaint Bréda joined them, and made an unobtrusive entrance into history.

It seems certain that he had been in secret communication with the leaders, but like so many men of better education than the rank and file, he lacked their boldness at the moment of action and waited to see how things would go. Meanwhile, hating destruction, he kept his master's slaves in order and prevented the revolutionary labourers from setting fire to the plantation. While all t he other whites in the neighbourhood made a dash for Le Cap, Madame Bayou de Libertas remained on the plantation, protected by Toussaint. Bayou de Libertas himself was with a camp of planters not far off, on guard against the slaves, but came every day to the plantation. Toussaint, then as always master of himself and of all near to him, maintained this untenable situation for over a month. But as the insurrection grew, worn out by the strain of defending the property, his master and his mistress, and learning that Madame de Libertas' life was now in danger, he decided that the old life was over and a new one had begun. He told Madame de Libertas that the time had come for her to go to Le Cap, packed her and some valuables in a carriage and sent her off under the care of his brother, Paul. He sent his own wife and the two children of the household into a safe spot in Spanish San Domingo. Then he slowly made his way to the camp of the revolted slaves.

The man who so deliberately decided to join the revolution was 45 years of age, an advanced age for those times, grey already, and known to everyone as Old Toussaint. Out of the chaos in San Domingo that existed then and for years to follow, he would lay the foundations of a Negro State that lasts to this day. From the moment he joined the revolution he was a leader, and moved without serious rivalry to the first rank. We have clearly stated the vast impersonal forces at work in the crisis of San Domingo. But men make history, and Toussaint made the history that he made because he was the man he was.

He had had exceptional opportunities, and both in mind and body was far beyond the average slave. Slavery dulls the intellect and degrades the character of the slave. There was nothing of that dullness or degradation in Toussaint.

His post as steward of the livestock had given him experience in administration, authority, and intercourse with those who ran the plantation. Men who, by sheer ability and character, find themselves occupying positions usually reserved for persons of a different upbringing, education, and class, usually perform those duties with exceptional care and devoted labour. In addition to this practical education, he had, as we have seen, been able to read a little. He had read Caesar's Commentaries, which had given him some idea of politics and the military art and the connection between them. Having read and re-read the long volume by the Abbé Raynal on the East and West Indies, he had a thorough grounding in the economics and politics, not only of San Domingo, but of all the great empires of Europe which were engaged in colonial expansion and trade. Finally, he had had the exceptional experience of the last three years of the revolution in San Domingo. The plantation was only two miles from Le Cap, and his duties took him often into the town. The masses of the people learn much during a revolution, far more a man like Toussaint. His superb intellect had therefore had some opportunity of cultivating itself in general affairs at home and abroad: from the very beginning he manoeuvred with an uncanny certainty not only between local parties in San Domingo but between the international forces at work.

An important thing for his future was that his character was quite unwarped. Since his childhood he had probably never been whipped as so many slaves had been whipped. He himself tells us that he and his wife were among the fortunate few who had acquired a modest competence and used to go hand in hand and very happy to work on the little plot of land which some of the slaves cultivated for themselves. Besides his knowledge and experience, through natural strength of character he had acquired a formidable mastery over himself, both mind and body. As a boy he was so frail and delicate that his parents had not expected him to live, and he was nicknamed “Little Stick.” While still a child he determined to acquire not only knowledge but a strong body, and he strengthened himself by the severest exercises, so that by the time he was 12 he had surpassed all the boys of his age on the plantation in athletic feats. He could swim across a dangerous river, jump on a horse at full speed and do what he liked with it. When he was nearly sixty, he was still the finest rider in San Domingo, habitually rode 125 miles a day, and sat his horse with such ease and grace that he was known as the Centaur of the Savannahs.

As a young man he had run after women. Then he decided to settle down. Refusing to live in the concubinage which was so widely prevalent among all classes in San Domingo, but particularly among the slaves, he married a woman who already had a son. She bore Toussaint one child, and he and his wife lived together in the greatest harmony and friendship, when he was master of all San Domingo just as in the days when he was an ordinary slave. For the life that so many lived in the colony, for the reputation that he had among the blacks and the opportunities that his position offered, this was an unusual thing for a man who had begun life as Toussaint had, and who, in the days of his greatness, was partial to the society of attractive women.

From childhood he had been taciturn, which singled him out among his countrymen, a talkative, argumentative people. He was very small, ugly, and ill-shaped, but although his general expression was one of benevolence, he had eyes like steel and no one ever laughed in his presence. His comparative learning, his success in life, his character, and personality gave him an immense prestige among all the Negroes who knew him, and he was a man of some consequence among the slaves long before the revolution. Knowing his superiority, he never had the slightest doubt that his destiny was to be their leader, nor would those with whom he came in contact take long to recognize it.

Excerpted from "The San Domingo Masses Begin," in The Black Jacobins: Toussaint L'Ouverture and the San Domingo Revolution, *2nd ed., rev. (New York: Vintage Books, 1989; first published by Penguin Random House, Inc., 1963), 85–117.*

1 This statement has been criticized. I stand by it. —C.L.R.J.

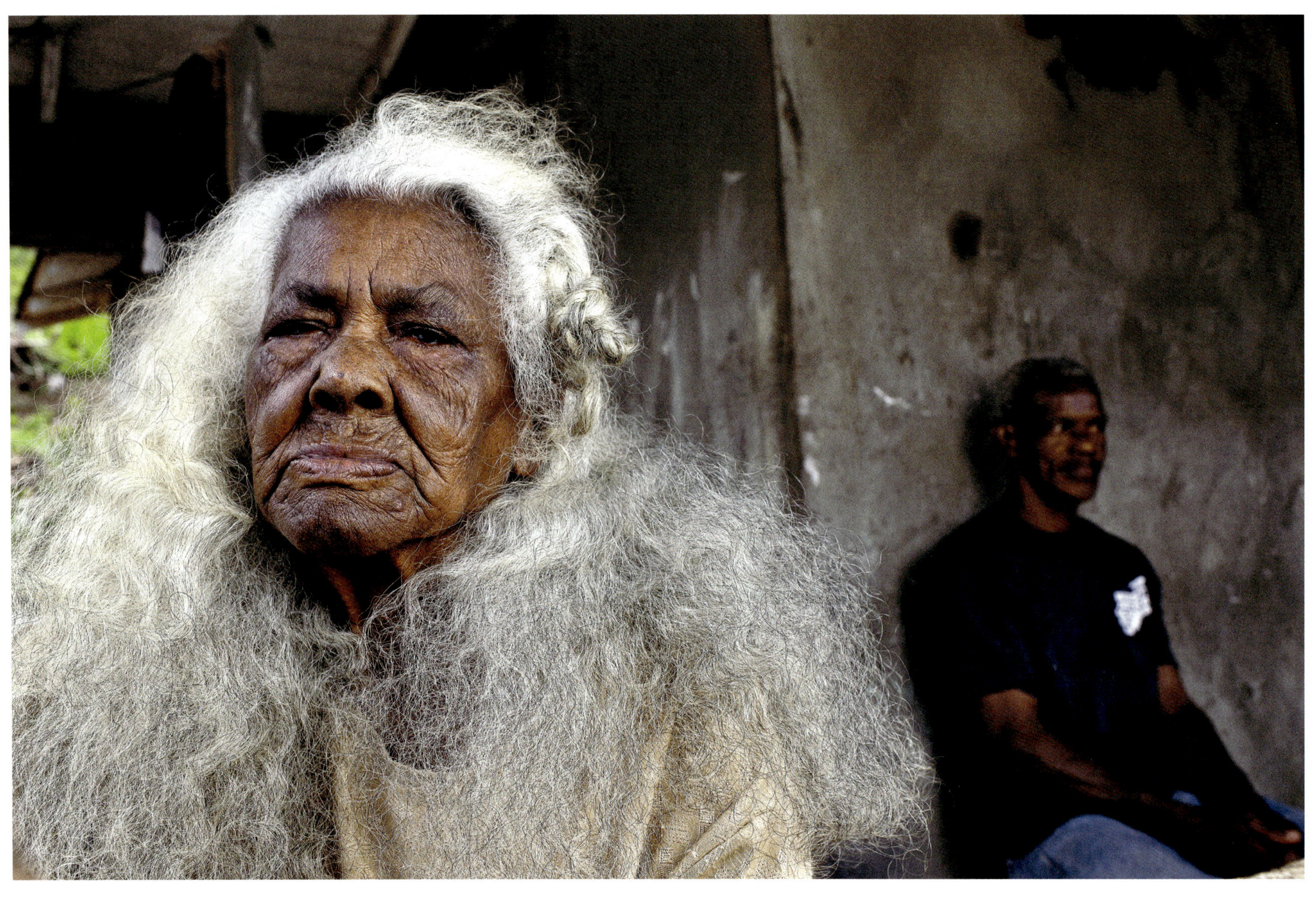

Robert Charlotte, *Luci Collins and Son*, 2014, from *Garifuna Indigenous*

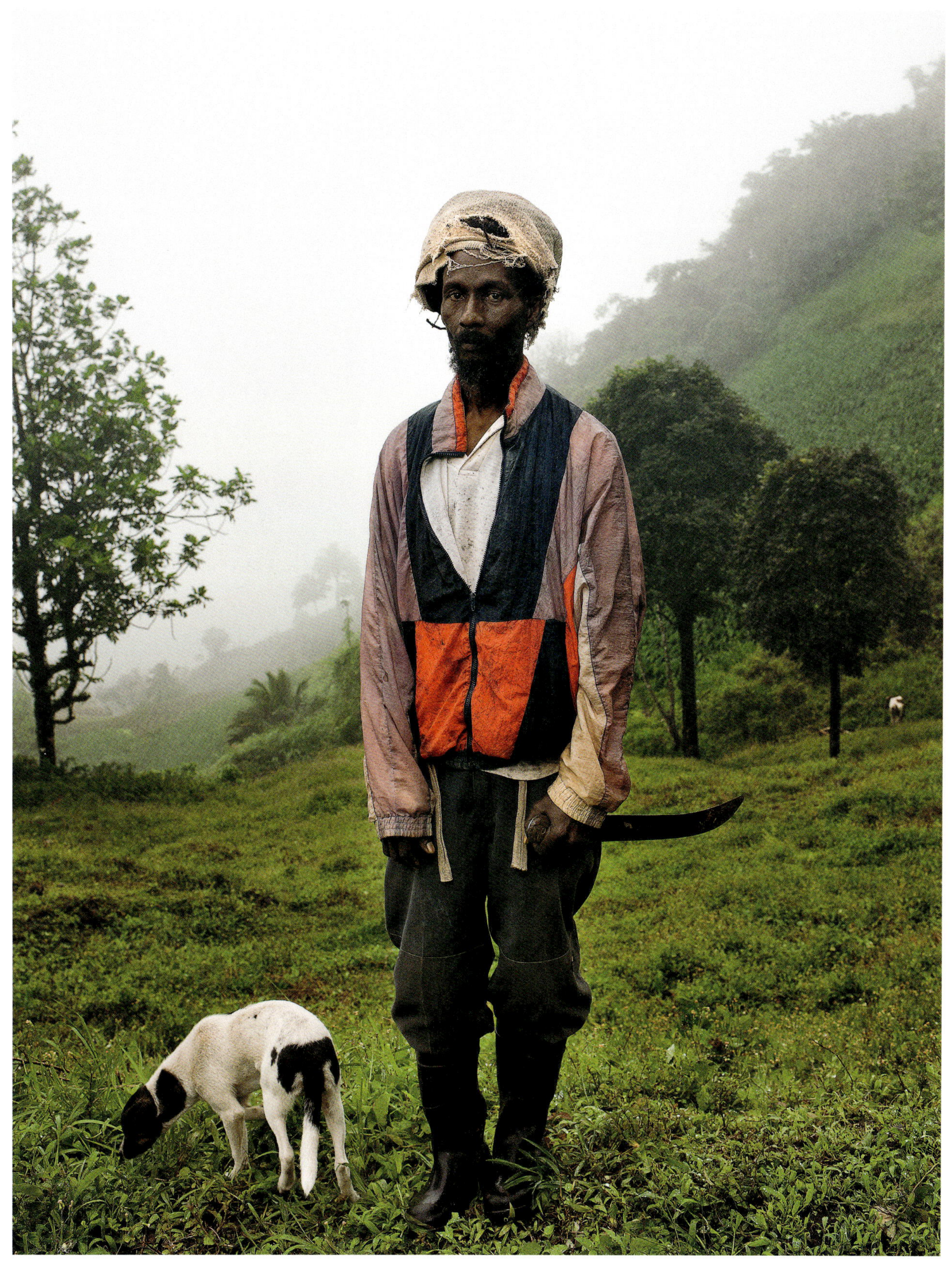

Robert Charlotte, *Farmer with Dog*, 2014, from *Garifuna Indigenous*

"*The* Qui*ntessential* C*a*r*i*bb*ean* P*e*opl*e*":

The Garifuna of St. Vincent and the Grenadines... and the World

Melanie J. Newton

Belizean elder and anthropologist Joseph Palacio once described his people, the Garifuna, as the inheritors of a tradition of "geographical multiplicity… the continuation of a tradition spanning more than 2,000 years." For Palacio, the Garifuna are "the quintessential Caribbean people," who exhibit an "ability in the past and present to synchronize daily actions across different places and cultures," even as a deep connection to village life and ancestral communities remains central to Garifuna understandings of *home*.[1] These inherently multi-sited, quotidian cultural and economic strategies emerged millennia ago, born of the Garifuna peoples' ancestral home in the Lesser Antilles, an intimate world of islands connected by ocean currents and waterways. Colonialism transformed these ancient practices into necessary strategies of survival in the face of immense odds. Today, Garifuna resilience involves a renewed struggle to safeguard their ancestral homeland in the Lesser Antilles through and alongside the mobilization of both local and transnational circuits of migration, exile, and return.

The Vincentian Garifuna people in Martinican photographer Robert Charlotte's powerful and moving portraits, some of which are included in the exhibition *Fragments of Epic Memory* (2021), embody this Garifuna heritage—an epic journey of diaspora and rootedness, at once tragic and triumphant, transregional and local. The Garifuna or Garinagu are the descendants of African fugitives from slavery and the Indigenous people of the Lesser Antilles, whom Europeans misnamed the "Caribs." The multi-island state of St. Vincent and the Grenadines (SVG) is the yurumei (homeland) of Garifuna people, but today most Garifuna live across several countries of Central America (Belize, Honduras, Guatemala, Nicaragua, and El Salvador), as well as across North America and the Lesser Antilles. In both continental America and SVG, Garifuna people endure economic and political marginalization. They fight to protect their sacred and ancestral lands from private land sales, tourism, and resource development projects from which they do not benefit and about which they are not consulted; to pass their Afro-Indigenous language, religion, and cultural traditions down to younger generations in the face of anti-Black and anti-Indigenous racism; and to gain meaningful recognition as Indigenous people from the national governments under which they live.[2]

In the late fifteenth and early sixteenth centuries, the Indigenous peoples of the Lesser Antilles successfully fought off Spanish efforts to establish settlements east of Puerto Rico and north of Trinidad. Even though they staved off colonization, Spanish slave raiding cost unknown numbers of people their freedom, while epidemic diseases brought from the so-called Old World to the New cost countless lives. At the same time, the people of the Lesser Antilles established trade relationships with Spain's rivals in the early colonial era, other Europeans such as the French, English, and Dutch. Once these nations gained a foothold in the Lesser Antilles, European-Indigenous relationships that had often begun as relatively equal interactions underwent a catastrophic transformation. Over the decades of the seventeenth and early eighteenth centuries, European settlers engaged in a large-scale transition to a model of colonization based on the capture, enslavement, and forced migration of Africans to cultivate sugar and other colonial crops on plantations in the Caribbean.

The expansion of European plantations, environmental destruction, inter-imperial violence, and African enslavement violently dispossessed Indigenous people of their homelands. Yet Indigenous Antilleans adapted, in part by adopting European, African, and Indigenous fugitives from elsewhere in the region into their communities. European chroniclers recorded names for Indigenous societies, including Kalinago and Callipuna/Karífuna/Kaliphuna, lexical cognates for Garinagu and Garifuna.[3] By the early eighteenth century, the Windward island of St. Vincent was the home of an Indigenous society of mixed heritage, the result of centuries of ethnogenesis. Because of their visibly African and Indigenous heritage, the French and the British who dominated the Lesser Antilles sought to dismiss the Garifuna as African fugitives from slavery who were only pretending to be Indigenous and referred to them pejoratively as "Black Caribs." Nevertheless, for much of the late seventeenth and early eighteenth centuries, St. Vincent remained a Garifuna-controlled island. Through military prowess, diplomatic skill, and superior understanding of the region's waterways and islandscapes, the Garifuna forced European colonists to negotiate with them as equals.

Indigenous freedom on St. Vincent came under threat after the Seven Years' War of 1756–1763, when France "ceded" St. Vincent, along with several other territories, to Great Britain.[4] Planning to transform St. Vincent into its next sugar island, the British imperial government invited speculators to gobble up land in St. Vincent, but the Garifuna refused to sell. By the 1790s imperial administrators had, through violence, disregard for previous agreements, and deceit, reduced Garifuna territory to the north of the island, where many Garifuna communities remain to this day. Between 1795 and 1797, the final war between the French, British, and Indigenous Vincentians ended in genocide for St. Vincent's Indigenous people. The British massacred the populations of entire villages, rounded up others whom they captured, and separated the few whom they considered to be light-complexioned enough to be "real Caribs" from those whom they deemed "Black," and therefore not true Caribs. The "Blacks," 4,476 of them, were exiled to Balliceaux, a barren island in the Grenadines, which became an internment camp where half of the prisoners died in a few months. In 1797 the 2,248 survivors were then exiled to Roatán, off the coast of Central America, where they struggled to eke out a living.

Over the course of the early nineteenth century, the Garifuna made their way to mainland Central America. November 19, 1802, is celebrated by Belizean Garifuna today as Garifuna Settlement Day, commemorating their ancestors' journey to the mainland from Roatán. Today, across Central America and St. Vincent, Garifuna people continue to organize for their cultural and territorial rights. The language, dance, and music of the Garifuna of Belize, Guatemala, Honduras, and Nicaragua is recognized by UNESCO as part of the intangible cultural heritage of humanity. On March 14, 2002, the SVG government recognized Chief Joseph Chatoyer, who led the fight against the British and died in combat in 1795, as the country's first National Hero. Garifuna spiritual leaders, activists, and elders are fighting to protect Balliceaux island, a sacred site of pilgrimage and memory for the Garifuna diaspora. Increasingly, non-Garifuna scholars and reparations activists see Balliceaux's protection as critical to a global effort to confront the racist legacies of slavery and Indigenous displacement.

Since 1492, the Garifuna and their ancestors have defied the violent and deracinating logic of formal European colonialism and its neocolonial aftermath. Garifuna communities face very real challenges, including poverty; climate change; a lack of state support to preserve their language, land, and traditions; and, at the time of writing, mass displacement from their villages in northern St. Vincent because of the eruption of the Soufrière volcano. What is certain—and what shines through in Robert Charlotte's photographs—is that their ancestors have bequeathed a legacy of cultural vibrancy, ingenuity, determination, and pride. With this rich inheritance, today's Garifuna celebrate their past, challenge their dispossession in the present, and turn their eyes towards the future.

1 Joseph O. Palacio, ed., *The Garifuna: A Nation Across Borders; Essays in Social Anthropology* (Benque Viejo del Carmen, Belize: Cubola, 2005). Palacio describes the Garifuna as "the quintessential Caribbean people" in the volume's "Introduction," 11. For his discussion of Garifuna "geographical multiplicity" see Chapter 5, "The Multifaceted Garifuna: Juggling Cultural Spaces in the 21st Century," 105–122.

2 Sharlene Mollett, "Mapping Deception: The Politics of Mapping Miskito and Garifuna Space in Honduras," *Annals of the Association of American Geographers* 103, no. 5 (September 2013): 1227–1241.

3 Seventeenth-century French missionaries claimed that "Kalinago" was used for men and "Callipuna" for women, a claim that has been repeated by many scholars over the years but not deeply investigated. Others highlight a distinction that has nothing to do with gender, observing that each word has been used interchangeably across the centuries in Dominica and St. Vincent to distinguish between Indigenous Lesser Antillean *people* on the one hand, and the *language* that they spoke on the other (see for example Julian S. Granberry and Gary S. Vescelius, *Languages of the Pre-Columbian Antilles* [Tuscaloosa: University of Alabama Press, 200], 61). Dominica's Indigenous people today use "Kalinago," while those of St. Vincent refer to themselves as Garifuna.

4 Several critics questioned France's authority to cede Indigenous territory in St. Vincent to Great Britain in the 1763 Treaty of Paris. Anglo-Jamaican planter and late eighteenth-century historian Bryan Edwards noted that the treaty was silent about "the Charaibes... as if no such people existed" (Bryan Edwards, *The History, Civil and Commercial, of the British Colonies in the West Indies*, vol. 1 [Dublin, 1793], 377).

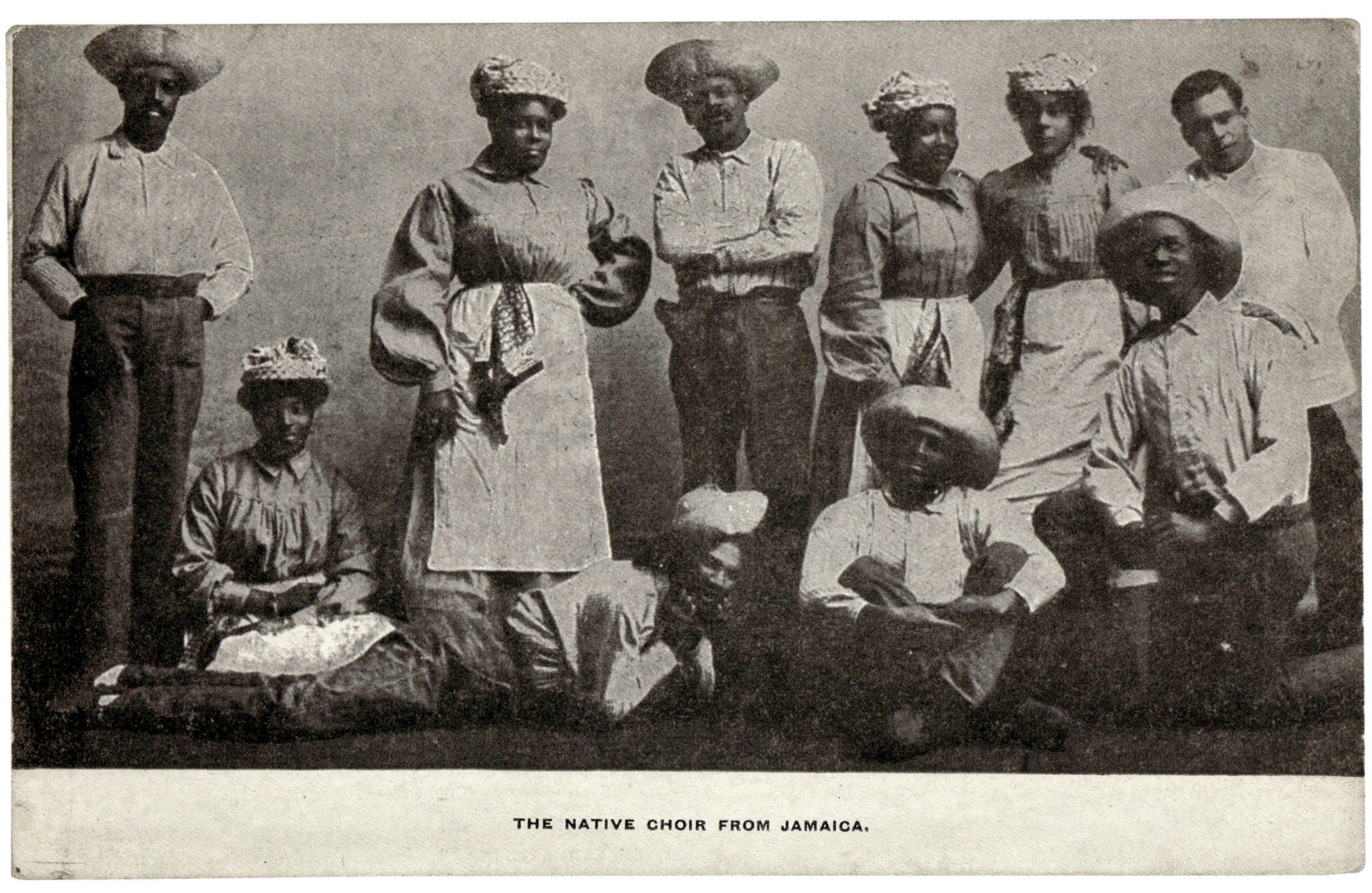

Unknown photographer, *The Choir from Jamaica*, c. 1905

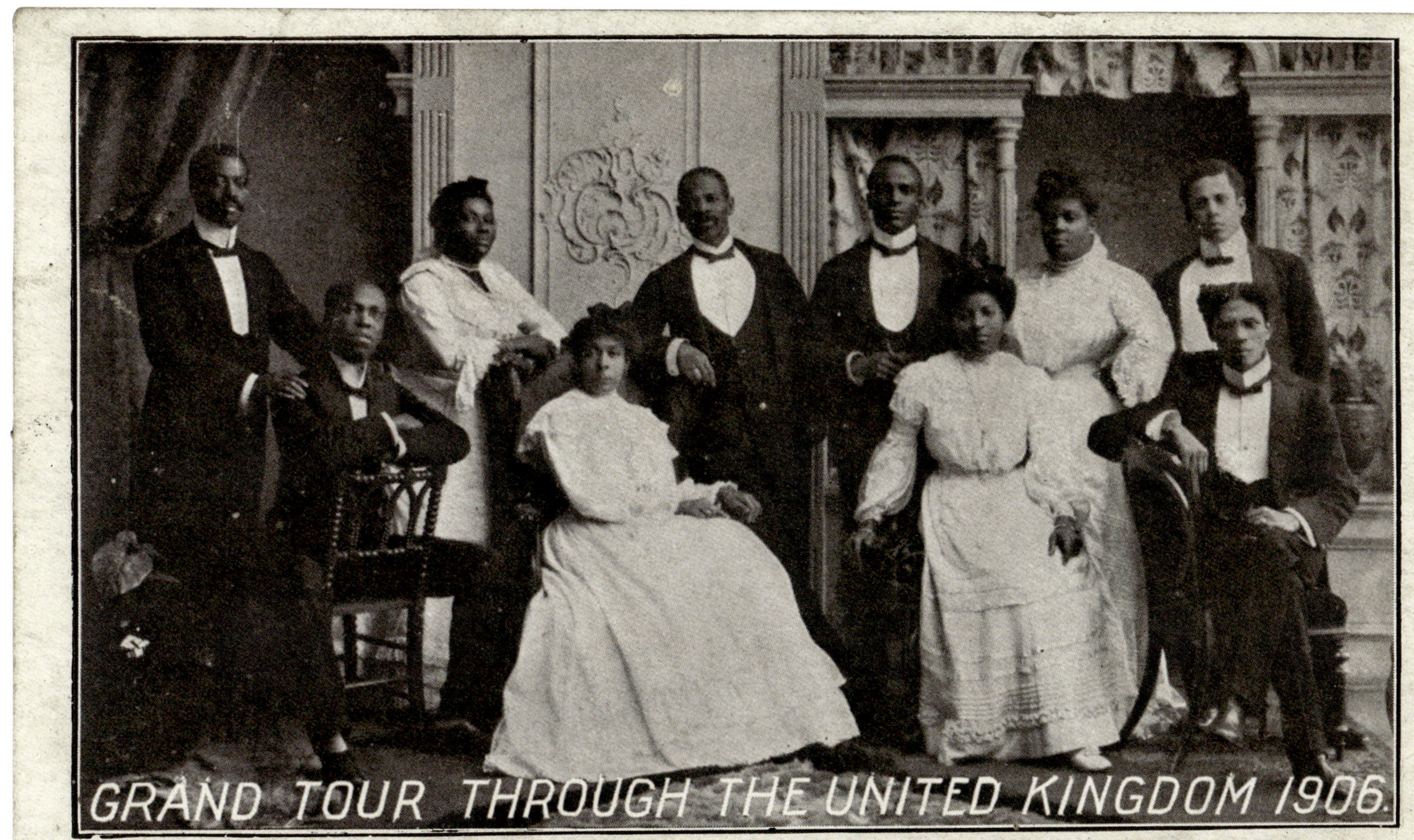

Unknown photographer, *Grand Tour through the United Kingdom*, 1906

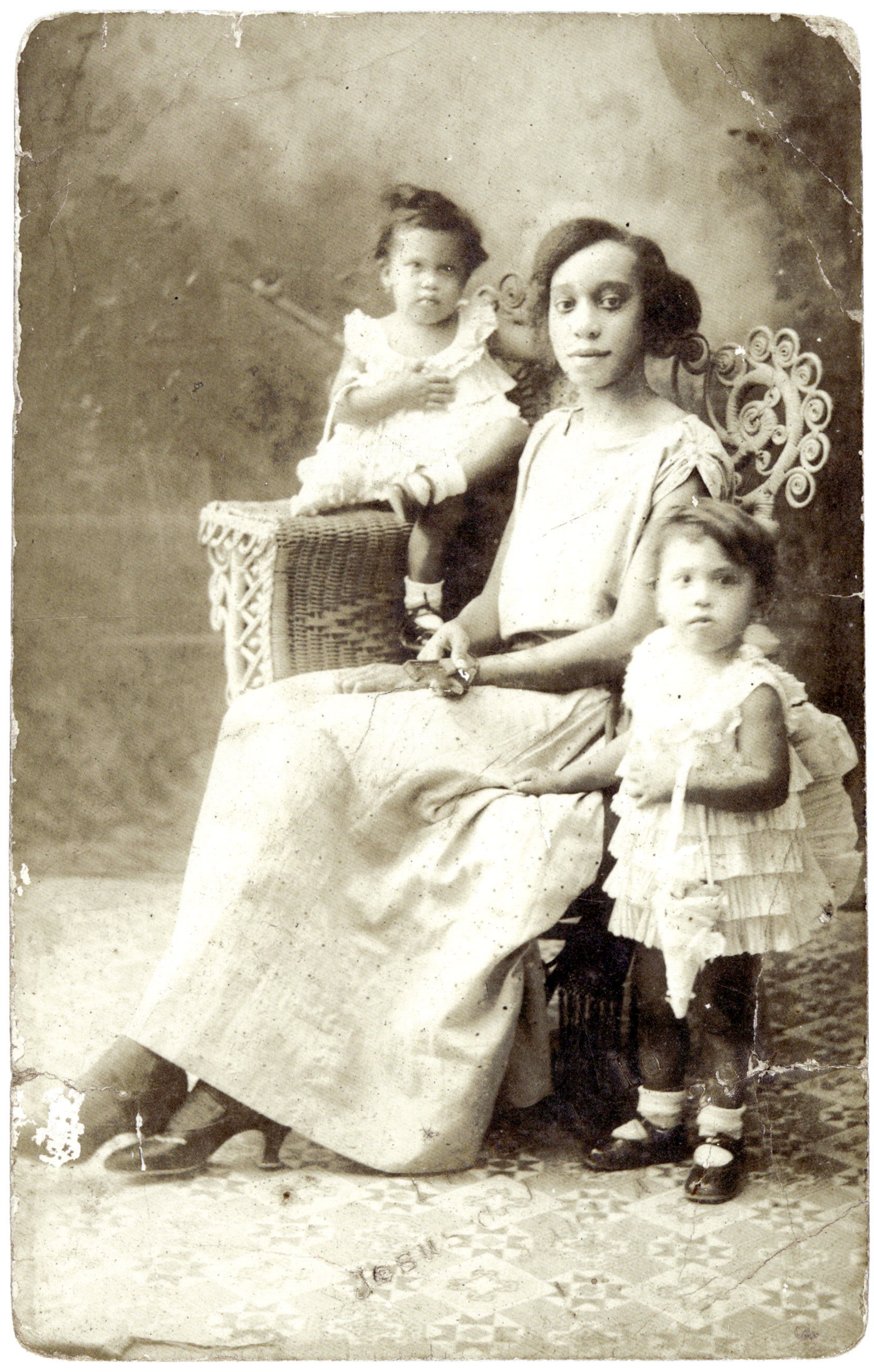

Foto Apolo, *Woman with Two Young Girls*, c. 1905

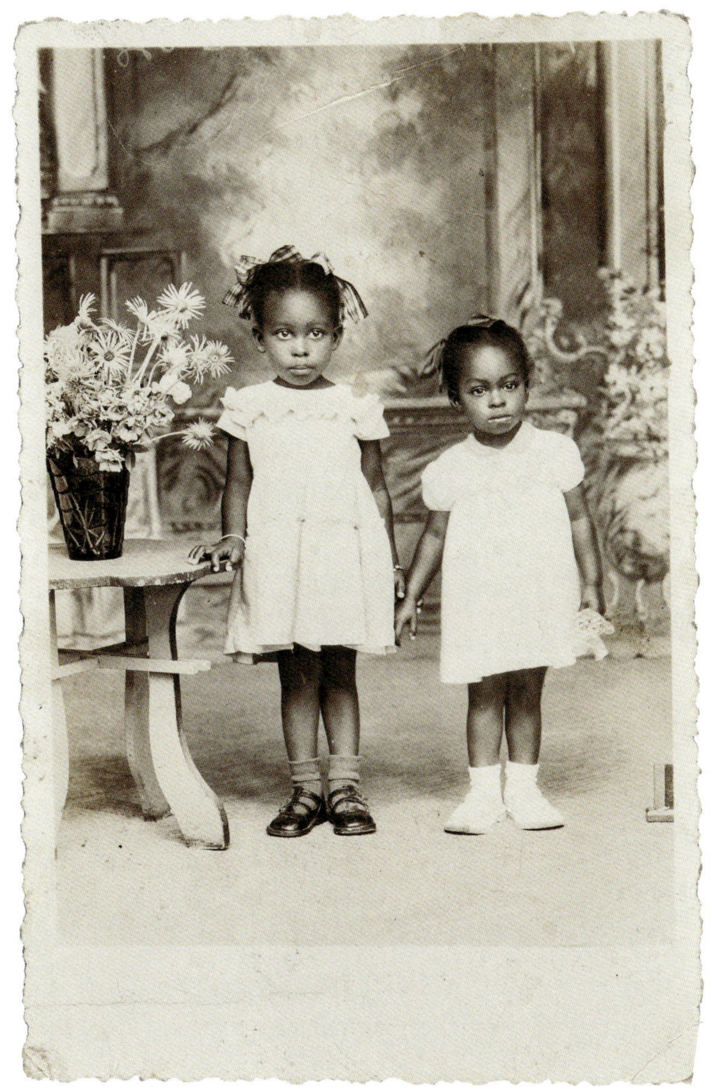

Unknown photographer, *Sisters*,
c. 1940

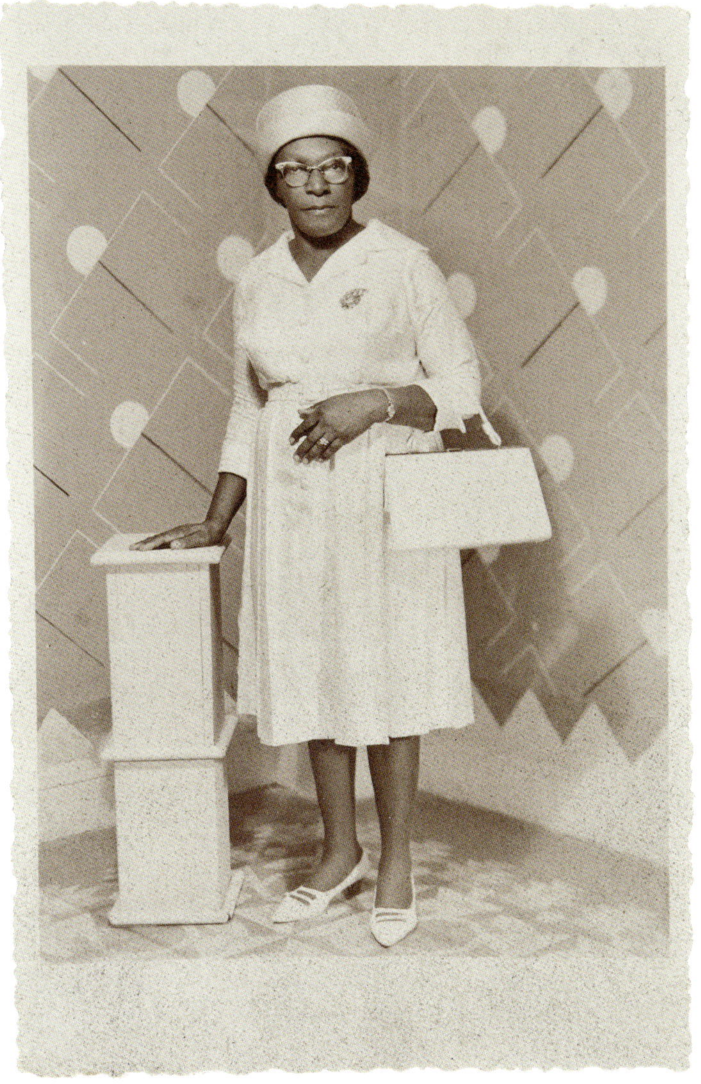

Unknown photographer, *Aunt Doris*,
c. 1940

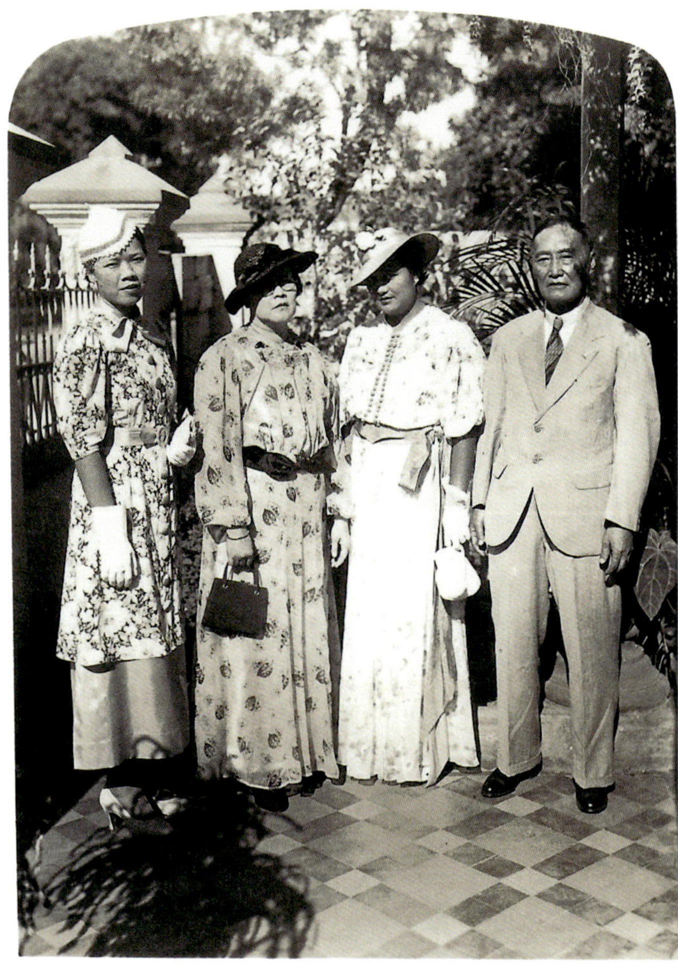

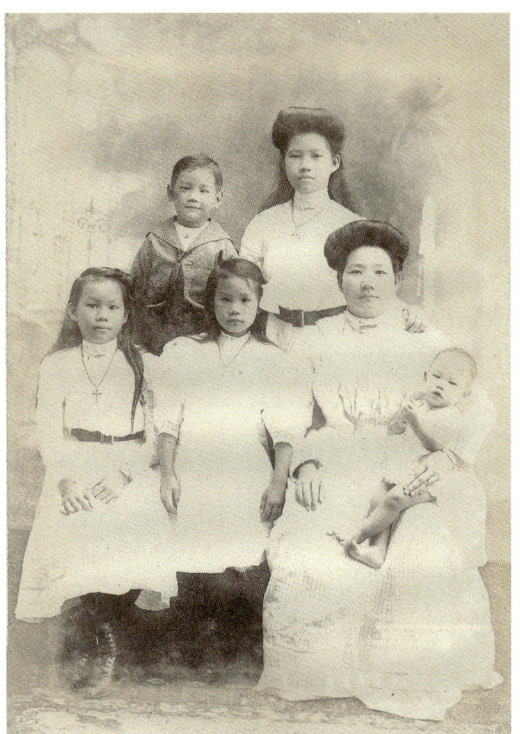

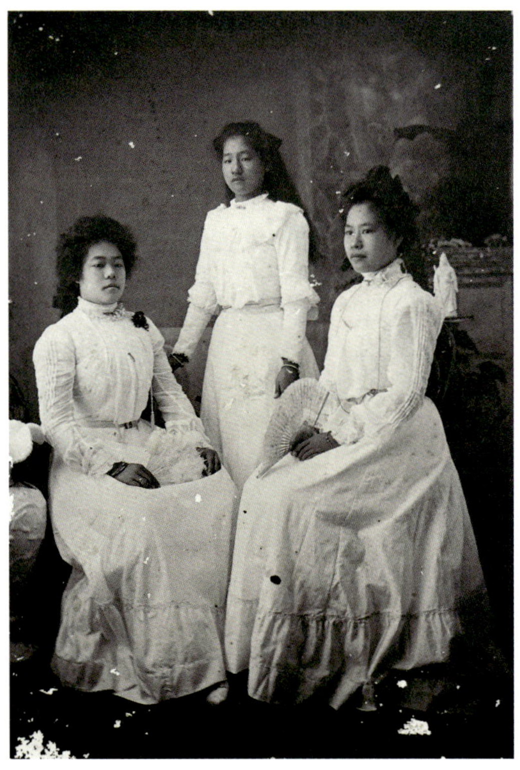

Above
Unknown photographer, *Sybil Atteck Going to a Wedding*, April 22, 1937

Top
Sellier's Studio, *George Peter McLean Family*, 1890

Bottom
George Adhar, *Three Chinese Girls in Trinidad*, c. 1900

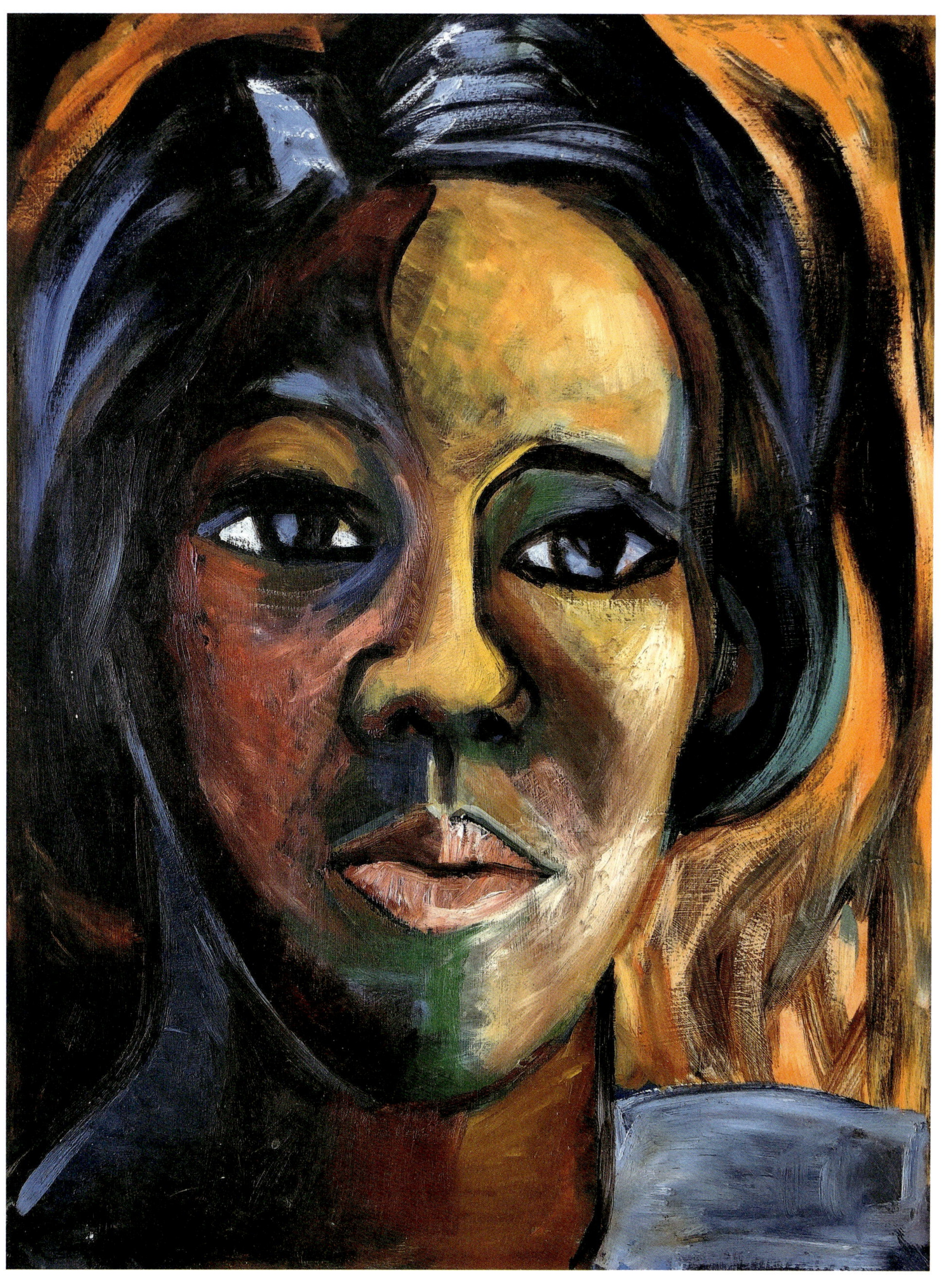

Sybil Atteck, *Self-Portrait*, 1973

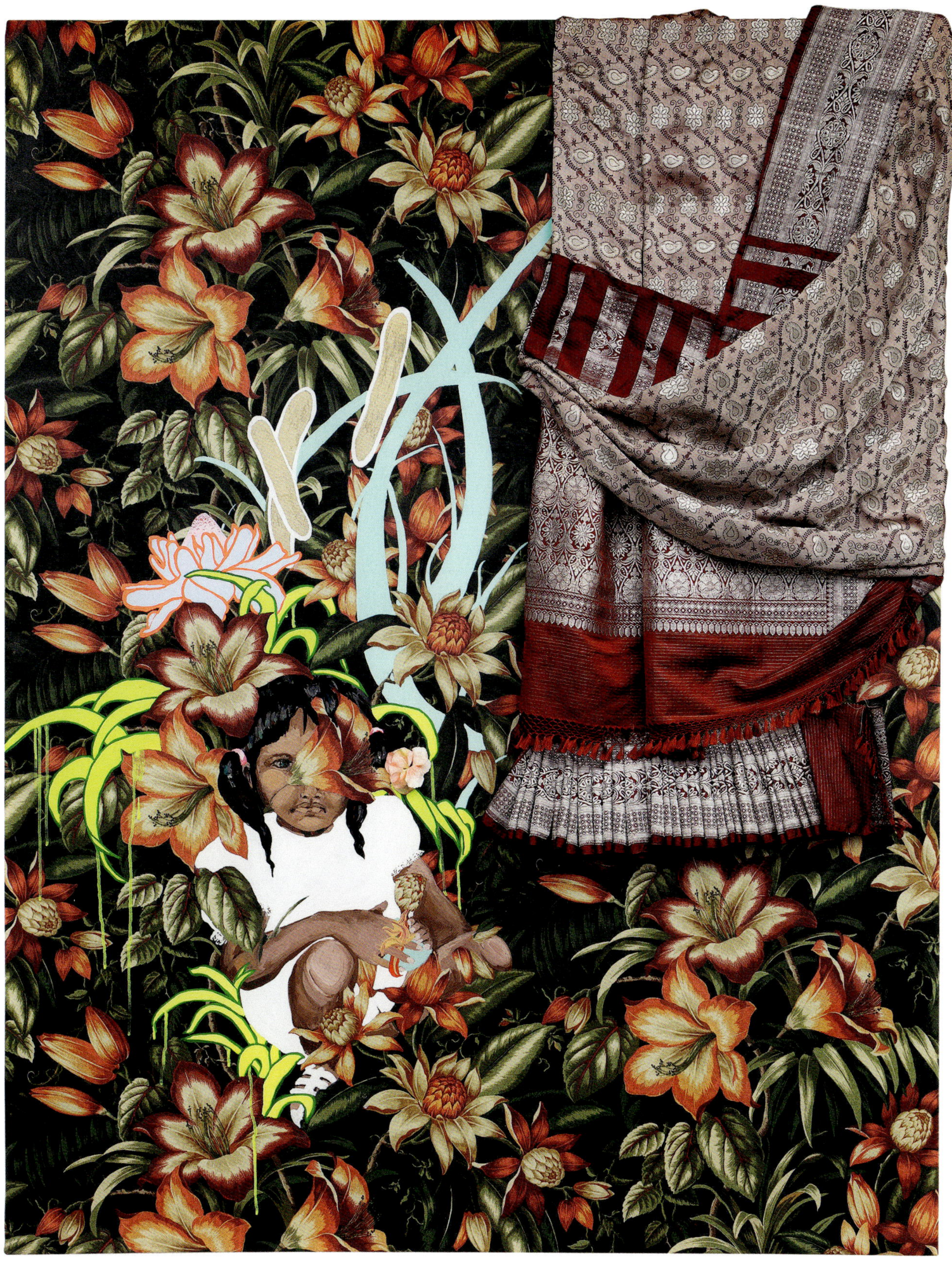

Suchitra Mattai, *Demerara Dreams*, 2019

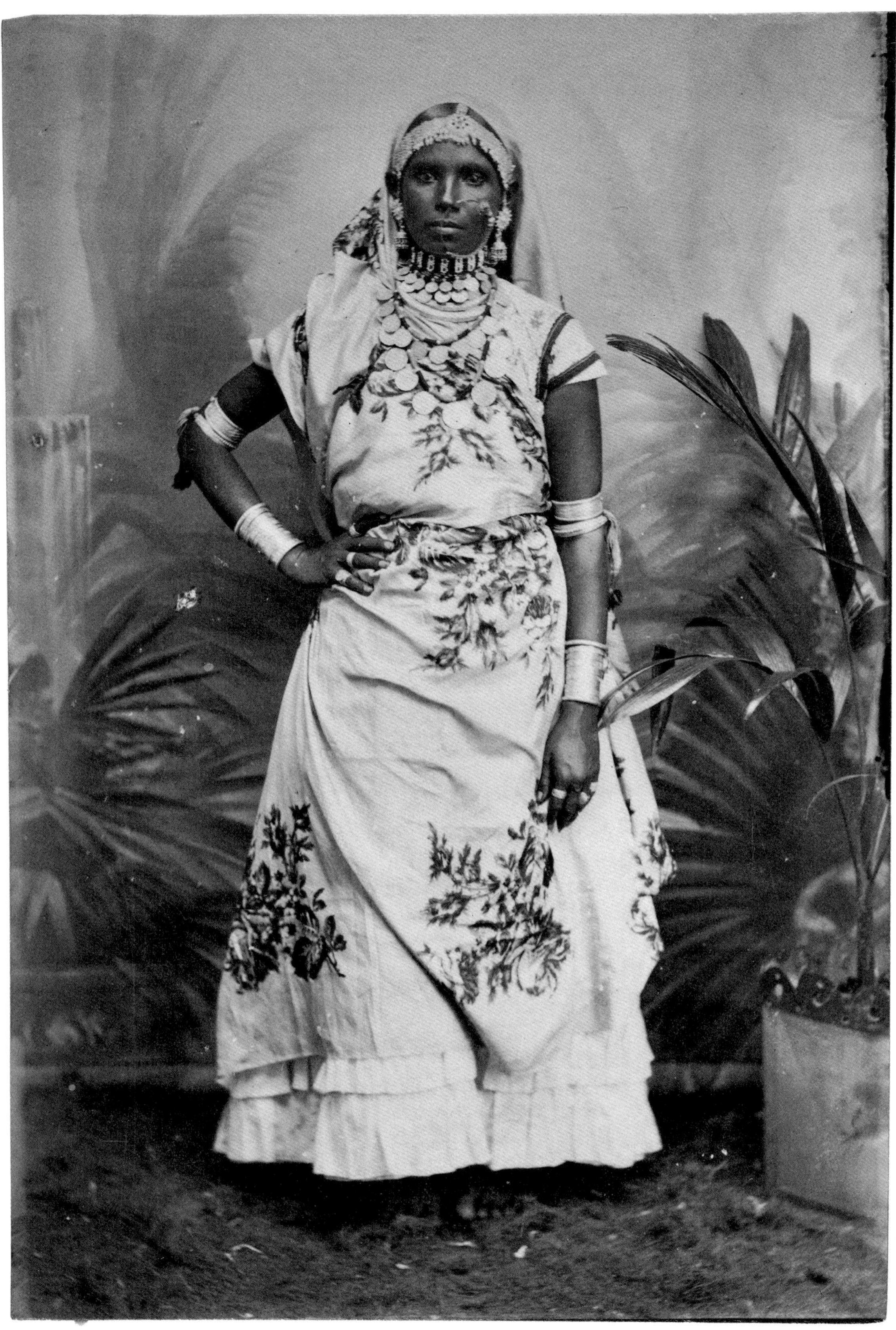

Unknown photographer, *Woman*, *Trinidad*, c. 1890

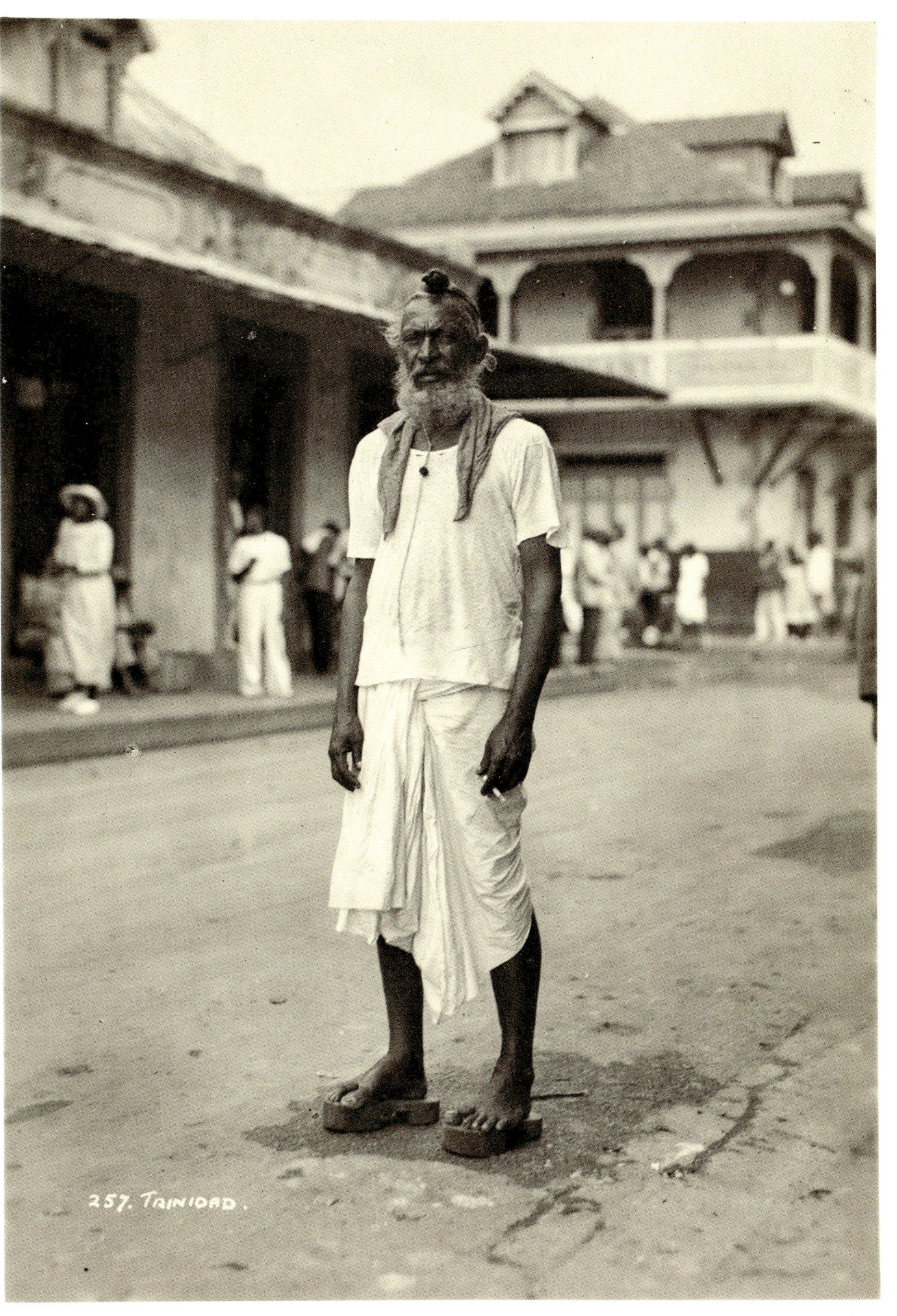

Unknown photographer, *Old Man, Trinidad*, c. 1900

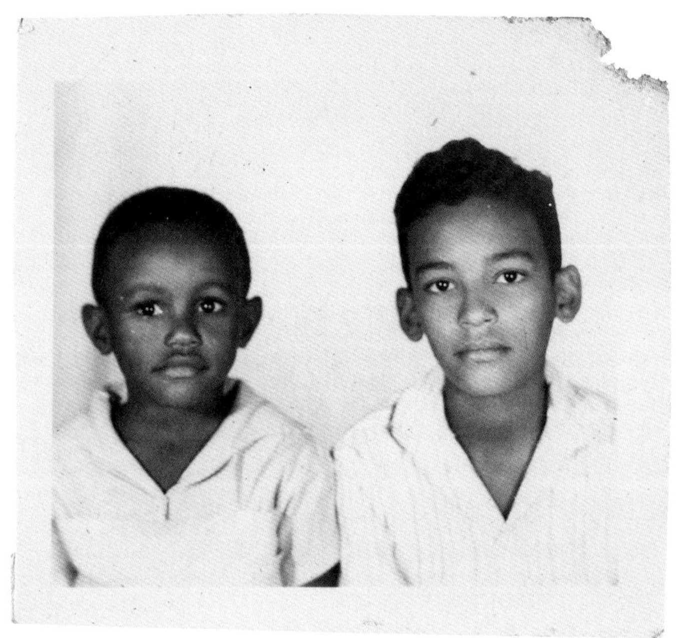

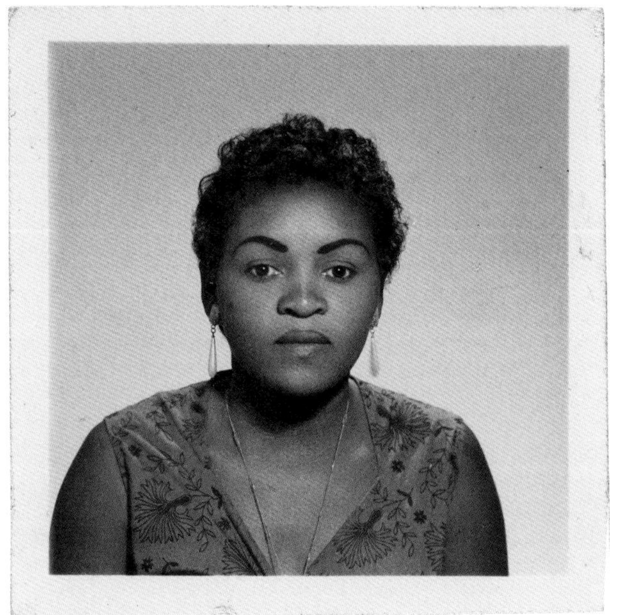

Unknown photographer(s), *Passport photographs of Haitian immigrant workers in Cuba*, 1957–1960

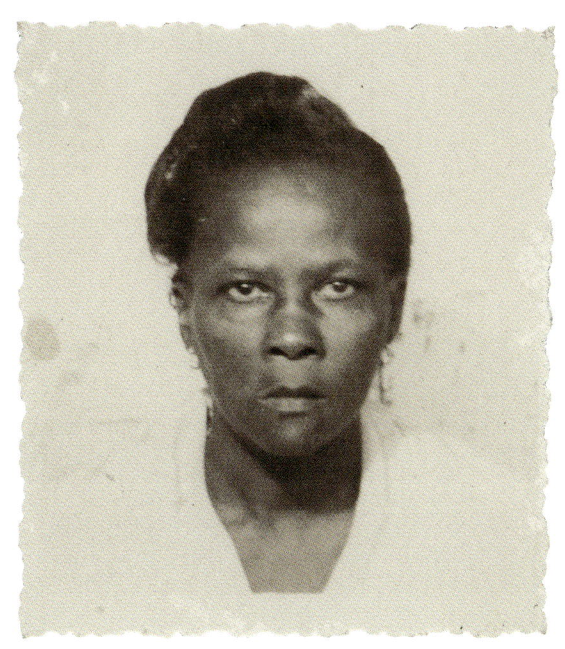

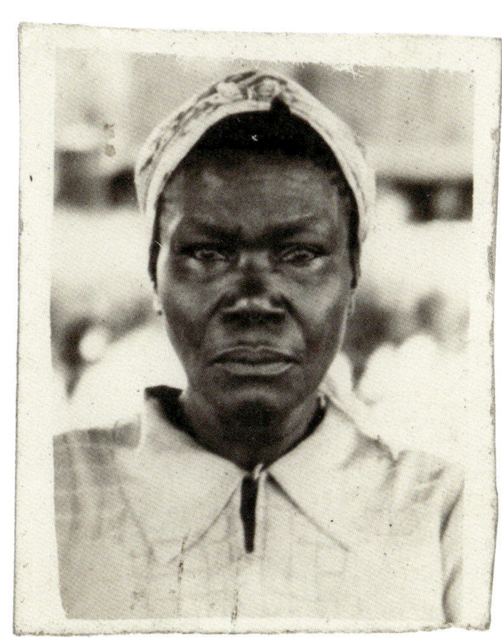

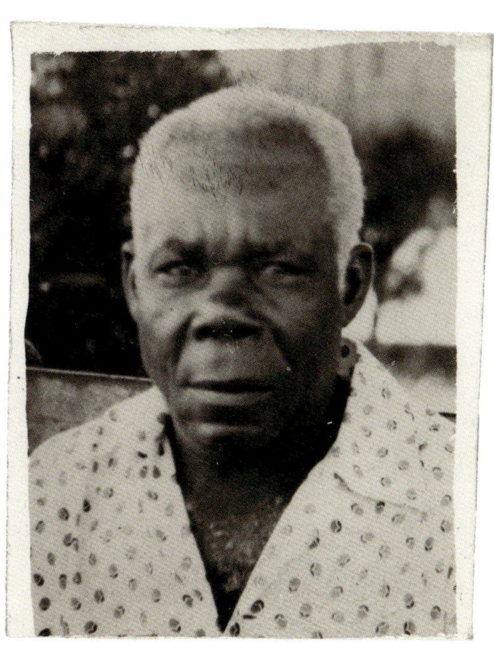

Bl*a*cklight*t*

Christian Campbell

Look 1
Birdsong, birdsong, and a close-up of what could only be a banana leaf, tattooed with yellow-brown streaks and white and black spots from pests and disease, but still green. The leaf heaves lung-like I want to say, but this heaving is not in time, so it's better to say that the leaf heaves ship-like. Everything is pitched by the sea, the leaves, the ghost birds, the sea, which I can sense and hear in these seconds. We never see the birds but their tweeting fades or is engulfed by a crescendo of voices gathering into a cacophony. It's a film trick I know from my head, at times its own Tower of Babel, which reminds me how a space can suddenly be crowded by ancestors.

Cut to sudden silence and the sky above a grove of trees, that leaf's actual family, then a voice begins to recite Walcott as the scene of Caribbean trees dissolves to England: a young man walking in a houndstooth blazer clutching a book, Walcott's *The Prodigal*. But the poem in the voiceover is "Exile," from another Walcott book, *The Gulf*.

Cut to the waves going-going crescendo until the sea-sound becomes the sound of change, wiping to black screen. Cut to a clean-faced youth walking on the shore, on a mound of slate sand, in a red long-sleeved button-down shirt and black pants, loose enough for the wind to make of him a small flag:

Wind-haired, mufflered
against dawn, you watched the herd
of migrants ring the deck
from steerage. Only the funnel
bellowing, the gulls who peck
waste from the plowed channel
knew that you had not come
to England; you were home.

The sea does its thing and the piano does its thing, and birds too, another "herd / of migrants," flying over the sea rocking a lonely boat. It's a stock Caribbean scene. Cut to brown hands holding a copy of *The Gulf*, with its black-and-white cover photograph of a sailboat on the sea. Cut again to the actual sea, this time with the chiaroscuro of dusk. What is the representation? What is the thing itself? And I am in that cover too, writing this from the Gulf Coast.

> Even her wretched weather
> was poetry. Your scarred leather
> suitcase held that first
> indenture, to her Word,
> but, among cattle docking, that rehearsed
> calm meant to mark you from the herd
> shook, calflike, in her cold.

Two boys marine-crawl in the shallow of a Caribbean river, laughing. They become, it seems, the elegant young men in tailored blazers at a university away, going or coming from tutorial or the library, books in hand; reciting poetry; sifting through archival documents; playing the piano.

Then the piano gives way to a shimmering music, dream-life. A voice begins reciting Walcott's "Star" like a mantra. It is moulting music, things change shape—the sea, the land, countries, bodies. We are always becoming something else.

Look 2

Cut to the Caribbean
Cut to Europe
Cut to the Caribbean
Cut to Europe
Cut to the Caribbean
Cut to Europe
Cut up the Caribbean
Cut up Europe
The sea the sea the sea

Look 3

Cut to my hands holding a copy of *The Prodigal,* a manila-covered advance review copy of his book that he had gifted to me in St. Lucia. He was in London and I couldn't miss it. I hopped on the X90 bus from Oxford to London dressed in dark blue jeans and an embroidered Ethiopian shirt beneath a grey wool blazer. His partner, Sigrid, told me, "You just keep turning up like a bad penny." I waited in line to get my book signed and to give him a gift—a wooden book stand emblazoned with the image of Ganesh.

Cut to Dara's room in Trinity—it was neither "Star" nor "Exile" that we recited during our regular groundings on poetry and survival, but rather "Ruins of a Great House": "Stones only, the disjecta membra of this Great House"; Brathwaite's "Stone": "When the stone fall that morning out of the johncrow sky"; Carter, Goodison, Keats, Auden, Hopkins, beloved Hopkins.

Look 4

"My generation had looked at life with black skins and blue eyes, but only our own painful, strenuous looking, the learning of looking could find meaning in life around us, only our own hearing, the hearing of our hearing, could make sense of the sounds we made."

— Derek Walcott, *What the Twilight Says*

The Wales Bonner Collection A/W 2021 is called "Black Sunlight," perhaps a reference to the novel *Black Sunlight* by Dambudzo Marechera, a radical Black South African writer who was expelled from Oxford in the 1980s.

Grace Wales Bonner, a thirty-year-old artist and designer of Black Jamaican and white British parentage, is the founder of the label Wales Bonner, which is distinguished by its commitment to craft, thought, and poetic vision through the complex style languages of the Black world. "Black Sunlight" completes Wales Bonner's trilogy, "revealing threads between Britain and the Caribbean" with a focus on Black Oxford.

Look 5
Though we corresponded over the years, I only met Kamau Brathwaite once, by chance. I was a grad student attending my first academic conference in New York City and he seemed to suddenly appear on the street—the unmistakable face, the tam, beard, glasses. He was wearing a denim jacket and had his arm around his wife, Beverly, the two striding purposefully, a nice New York gait. They seemed to carry a light. I was in my academic conference get-up—a pale-coloured dress shirt and dark pants, toting one of those professorial leather briefcases I would later abandon. I stopped Kamau, shook his hand, and thanked him for his work, then watched them stride off to where they had to go.

Look 6

> Guided by the expansive language of Saint Lucian poet Derek Walcott—there is eloquence, fluidity and reimagining in the crafting of the offering. A tailored sensibility is cut with ease and softness, underlying a relaxed self-possession throughout the collection which, showing a balance of men's and womenswear, combines cotton cashmere oxford shirts, luxurious wool overcoats, soft shearling shawl jackets and brushed cotton and raw denim uniforms. Hand printed shirting created in collaboration with the artist Joy Gregory, whose study of plants in Jamaican culture results in captivating flowers of resistance, exalt the magic of discovery.
>
> — Wales Bonner website

Look 7
"Break a vase," Derek Walcott famously instructs in "Fragments of Epic Memory":

> and the love that reassembles the fragments is stronger than that love which took its symmetry for granted when it was whole. The glue that fits the pieces is the sealing of its original shape. It is such a love that reassembles our African and Asiatic fragments, the cracked heirlooms whose restoration shows its white scars. This gathering of broken pieces is the care and pain of the Antilles, and if the pieces are disparate, ill-fitting, they contain more pain than their original sculpture, those icons and sacred vessels taken for granted in their ancestral places. Antillean art is this restoration of our shattered histories, our shards of vocabulary, our archipelago becoming a synonym for pieces broken off from the original continent.

Here, out of breaking and loving, Walcott offers what I would call a diasporic theory of reassemblage. This is a *visual* practice that is kin with the ancient Japanese art of ceramic repair, kintsugi, in which the sites of fracture are sustained and illuminated in gold. It is a specifically Caribbean survivalist ethics of imaginative possibility.

Look 8
Stones only, the disjecta membra of this Great House.

The university was carceral; it was modelled after the militarized state. Each of its forty-five colleges was a little territory; every border was policed, arranged by shame. Prestige was precarious, unbearable, like a medallion that branded the chest. One moment you could be served port to toast in a bizarre rite (*To the Founder! To the Queen!*), and the next, denied entry to your own college. “Where then is the nigger’s/home?” asks the speaker in Kamau Brathwaite’s “Postlude/Home”:

In Paris Brixton Kingston
Rome?

Here?
Or in Heaven?

Who could answer Brathwaite’s questions?

In the strange anthropology of Oxford’s plantocracy, the college porter positions seemed to adhere to a specific phenotype—usually a clean-cut, white, middle-aged man with an acquired RP accent, like the tall porter-thug at Balliol, my own college, who “carded” me every week. But there were exceptions—the Christchurch porter-troll had a decidedly working-class regional accent; he was white with a face full of warts and he always stunk of drink. Their practice was casual, relentless, pernicious, innate. They set on us like hounds. What is the dress, what is the style then, for survival in brutal constraint?

Look 10

Did you hear?, I asked. Yeah, my friend said. And then we were quiet. Someone at my college hung themselves. “Graves grow no green that you can use,” Gwendolyn Brooks spoke to me from a poem. I just wanted to sleep. And sleep. But for how long?

Who or what lodged a bit of rock into the back of my head, stone from the college, built by whom? You would have to cut into me to remove it.

Look 11

Status of the father: “Peer, Esquire, Gentleman, Cleric, Plebeian”

Look 1: a female model in a tailored black tuxedo with a midnight blue stripe down the side and lapel paired with a red dress shirt, wide collar and black leather shoes.

Look 6: a male model in a houndstooth blazer with leather collar and pocket, dark pants and Adidas shoes.

Look 9: a male model in a pin-stripe cotton print kurta peaking out beneath a royal blue Adidas track-suit with brown leather shoes.

Look 14: a female model in a black leather A-line skirt with brown buttons and stitching, with a blue, red, and white cardigan and white Adidas sneakers with brown stripes, grey socks.

Look 12

If you get dressed up one day, a Bahamian might tell you, “You look like people.”

Wales Bonner draws from a specifically Caribbean sense of form and formality, a kind of Afro-Victorian aesthetic. At the same time, she’s also interested in a Caribbean aesthetics of rebellion. She’s confronting another sense of dramatic formality at Oxford, where dress code continues to be inextricably linked to colonial power and order—*sub fusc*, the dark suits and skirts, et al. What moves me about the collection is her careful attending to the personhood of black Oxford students in clothes that are once stately and understated. She softens and offsets some of that Oxonian rigidity with her own reassemblage—playing with multiple registers in unexpected combinations, Adidas sneakers, subtle embroidery and embellishments, colour.

Look 13

Kim-Marie was the style maven. She would rock clothes in a way that was all her own, like a shortened sari over jeans. To be English would be abhorrent, she once told me. M.J. could go from hip-hop to a more formal look that we could only call *clean*, in labels I couldn’t afford.

At times I would wear a ruddy-brown corduroy suit, white dress shirt, and a red, yellow, and green scarf as a cravat.

Is dignity, a tricky word, totally interior or is it partly conferred? Do you need an other, a viewer?

Look 14

What is the kinship between the cut of clothes, the cut of film, and the cut of poetry?

In *The Light of Black Sunlight*, the "film memory of the collection" made in collaboration between Wales Bonner and Jeano Edwards, the characters model the collection and reveal Wales Bonner's archive by reciting Walcott poems, and displaying and reading Walcott's *The Gulf* and *The Prodigal*, and Kamau Brathwaite's *Black and Blues*, as well as a photograph of Stuart Hall et al.

When the film cuts, it moves between psychic geographies. Edwards uses the cut, the dissolve, and superimposition without worrying about whether those techniques feel old fashioned. He needs a way of travelling, like Walcott and Brathwaite, between landscapes, across the sea. The poetry of these giants offers *forms* for dreaming multiple places at once.

Look 15

Derek said to me once,

> The presence of that landscape, or seascape, inside you is superior to whatever language you speak, it is stronger than the language you speak. A mountain, a bay, a beach, a tree, is stronger than anything you write. It's a physical, beautiful thing.... But I'm telling you though that you can't separate the rhythm of Marley from the hills of Jamaica. They are powerfully related. And you don't need the Marley, because the hills are there, really.
> But ultimately they are only manifestations of praise.

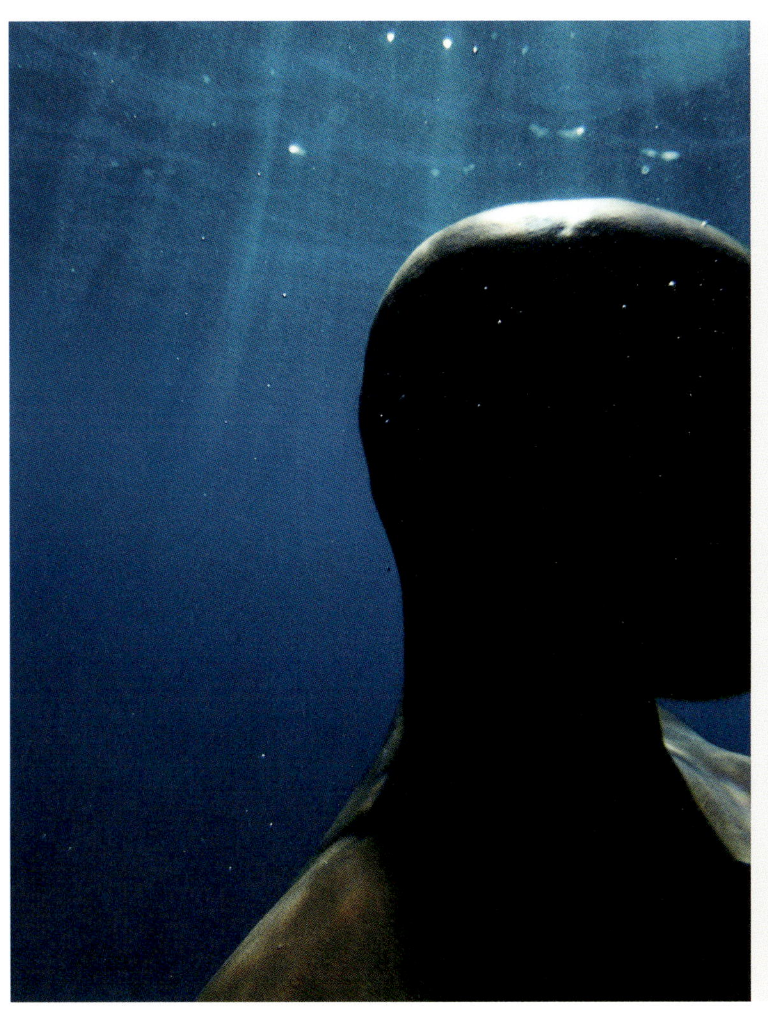

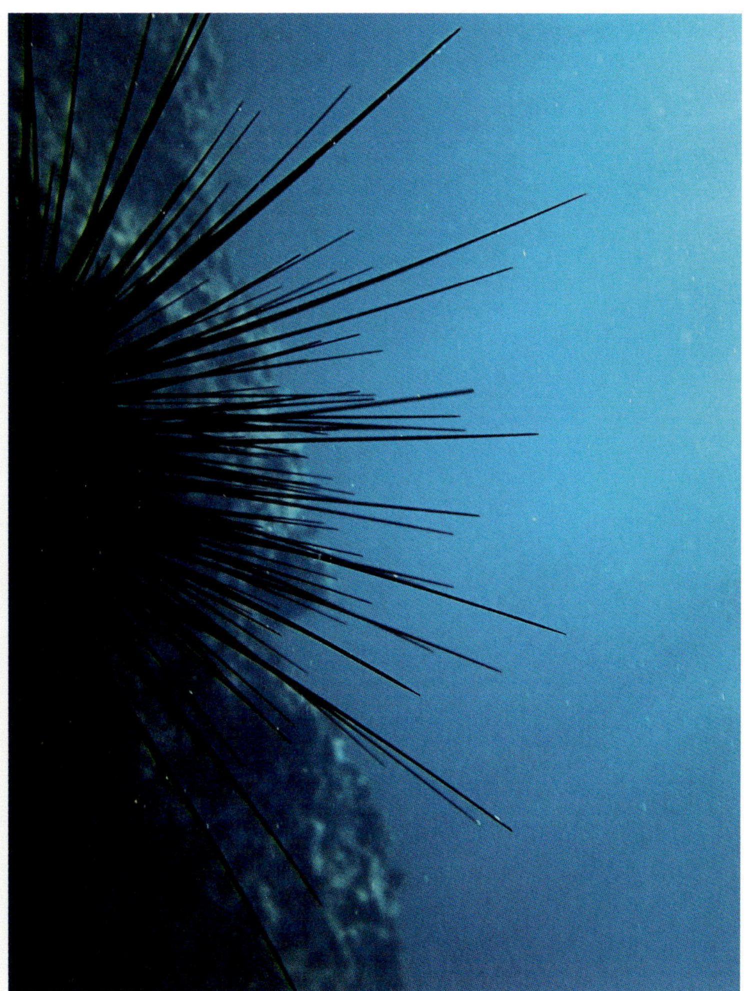

Nadia Huggins, *Transformations No. 1*, 2015

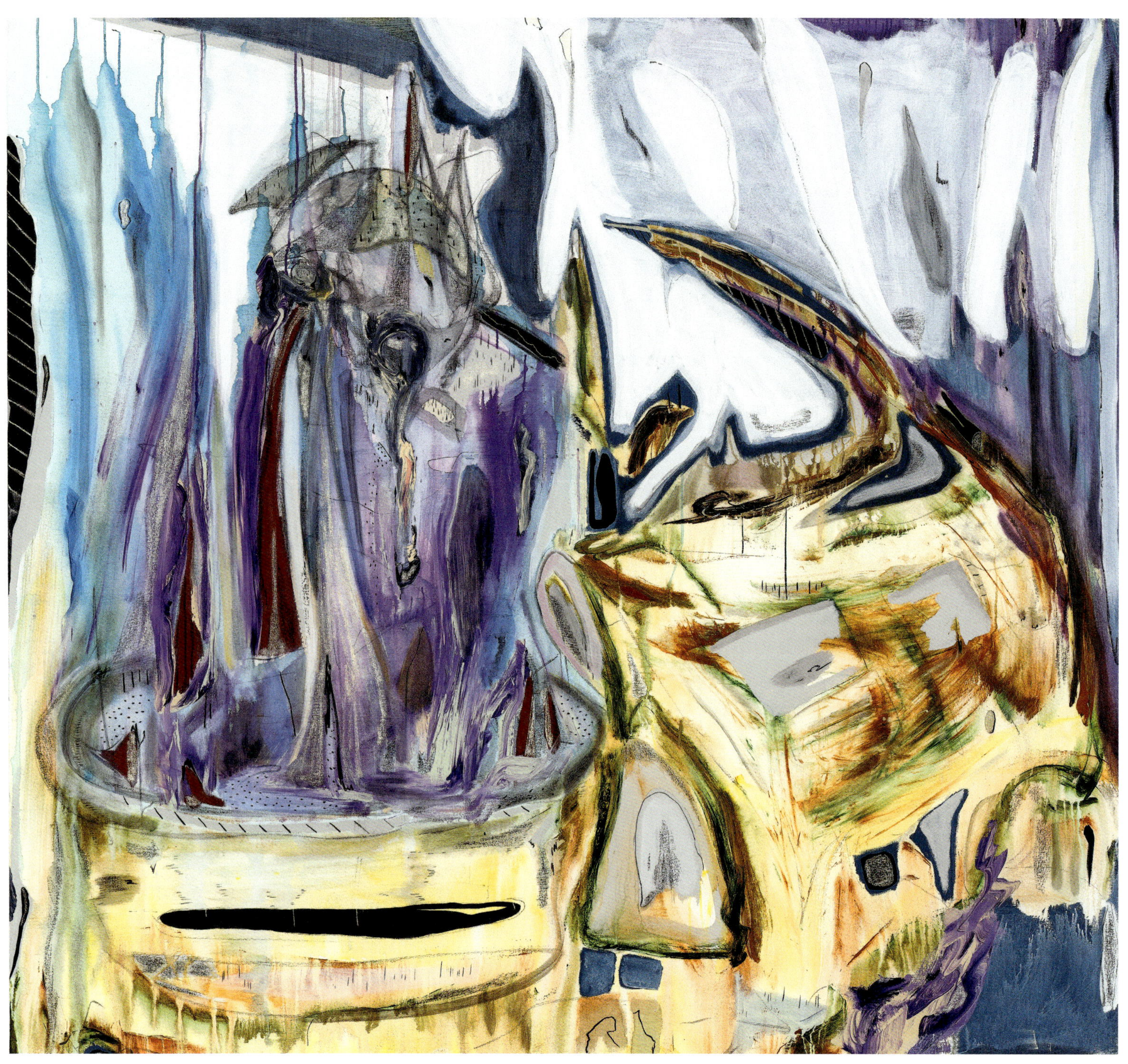

Manuel Matthieu, *Lye*, 2018

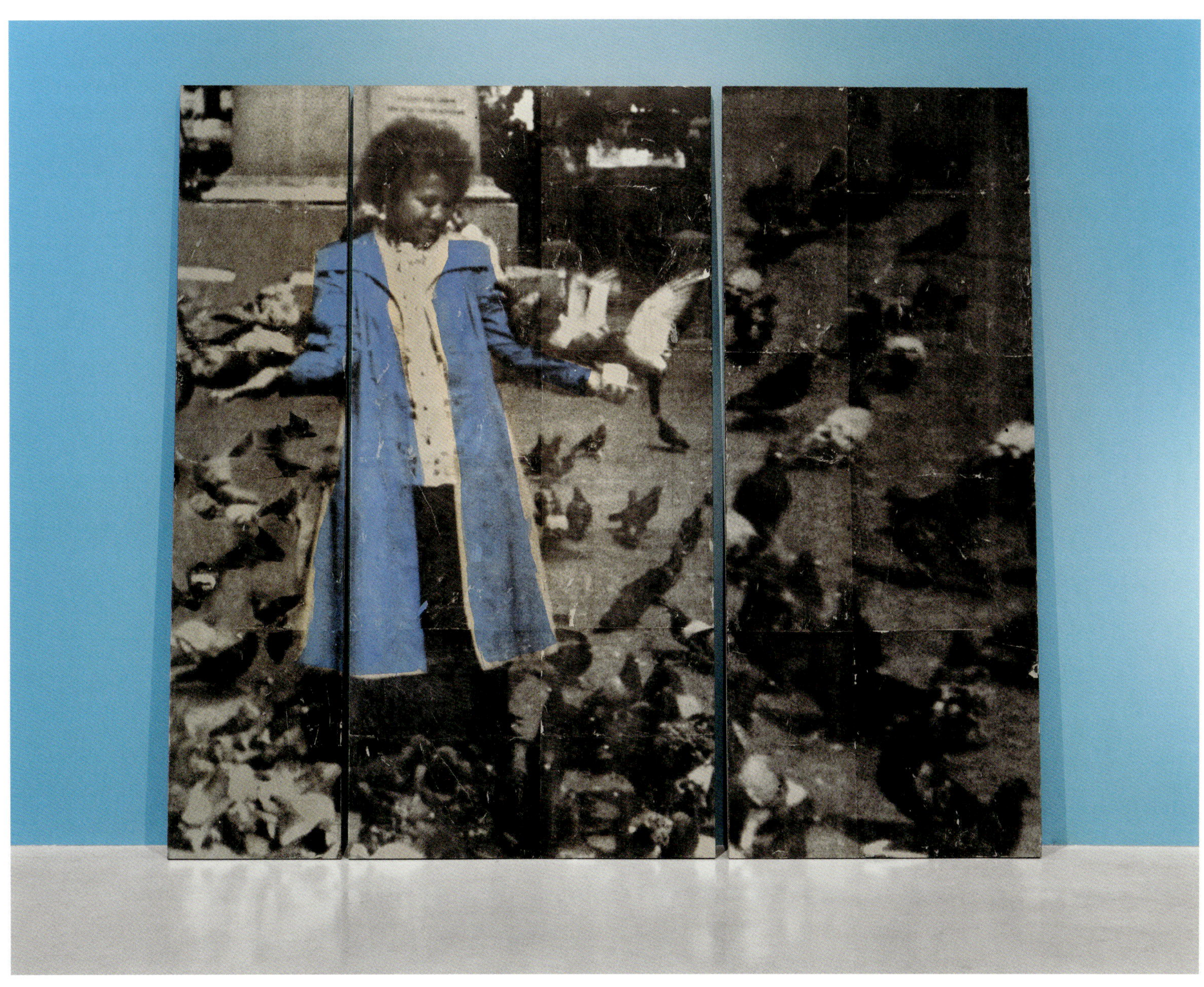

Sandra Brewster, *Feeding Trafalgar Square*, 2021

Poetic Images and Political Places:

The Work of Caribbean-Canadian Artists Sandra Brewster and Manuel Mathieu

Dominique Fontaine

The Caribbean is not a region with defined borders. Its borders shift, and today ... with migration, the Caribbean is present in large urban centres in the West; in New York and Montreal, Toronto and London, Miami and Paris. It takes form in many small Caribbeans (Little Haiti or Little Havana).

— **Frantz Voltaire**
"Territoires de l'imaginaire"[1]

How can we construct a history of Canadian contemporary art by drawing on artistic realities in tune with the Caribbean? How can we build a visual culture that maintains the historical continuity of individual and collective experiences connected by descent?

Be anchored in the history of Canadian contemporary art. Transform the artistic landscape. It seems that with each new decade, we see renewed interest in the work of artists from particular ethnocultural groups—especially Black artists—who are often excluded from the contemporary Canadian artistic landscape. We are compelled to applaud this kind of transformation, which provides access to a multiplicity of stories and gives new life to visual culture in the country. Such recognition, even as it comes late, helps ground Canadian artists of African descent in art history. Although these artists have long been marginalized by institutions, this sudden visibility certainly works toward making up for the lack of representation in an art world that has long been in need of an overhaul of this sort. Moreover, we can see that the growing interest in artists of African and Caribbean descent is prompting museums to purchase and exhibit their work.

Political places. This unprecedented moment in the history of this country's art is exemplified through group and solo exhibitions showcasing the work of Canadian artists of Caribbean descent. Consider Charmaine Lurch, Anique Jordan, Camille Turner, and Eddy Firmin, each of whom has been the subject of a solo exhibition. We might also look to the group exhibitions *Here We Are Here: Black Canadian Contemporary Art* and *New-Found-Lands: An Art Project Exploring Historical and Contemporary Connections between Newfoundland and the Caribbean Diaspora* (to mention just two among several such shows), which were presented in well-known galleries and museums. Each of these exhibitions has, in its own way, made it possible to create other networks of resonance by situating the featured works within the cultures and the social and political contexts in which these artists developed their practices. Members of the Caribbean diaspora address their dual identities as well as questions of invisibility; for many of these artists, concepts such as movement, displacement, and belonging assume important artistic functions. These approaches enrich and contribute to the renewal of this country's artistic discourse.

Poetic images. Sandra Brewster and Manuel Mathieu are two of the artists forging this network of resonance, the magnetically linked chain of meaning that helps construct this shifting contemporary visual language. Their respective artistic practices, like the Creole languages of the Caribbean, proceed "by traces to constitute their lexical and syntactic corpus."[2] In this way, both artists turn to a mode of creation that relies on "traces"—subtle nuances that distinguish themselves from systemic thought—to produce conceptually fascinating bodies of work.

Migratory movement. For Sandra Brewster, movement does not have a rigid end purpose. Hers is a vision of movement as a landing without a destination (to borrow a concept from Dionne Brand).[3] Brewster's ideas are anchored by movement as a motif and as a philosophy. For twenty years she has been using her unique visual vocabulary to explore collective Black experiences, experiences of both belonging to and alienation from the nation of Canada. Born in Toronto to Caribbean parents, Brewster advocates for movement as a way of conceptualizing migration. Her figurative work, inspired by traditional portraiture, includes drawings, paintings, and mixed media. Her most recent photographs and videos interrogate the context in which her community is situated and raise questions around identity related to the place of the Black body in Canadian society. Brewster is particularly interested in the experiences of members of African and Caribbean diasporas. Consequently, she seeks to highlight stories that have been ignored or disrupted (for individual and societal reasons) of Black migration to Canada, which include experiences of settling in large cities and the effects of migratory displacements on subsequent generations. In the 1960s, Brewster's family immigrated to Canada from Guyana and settled in Toronto, where the artist currently resides and where many of her subjects are located.

1

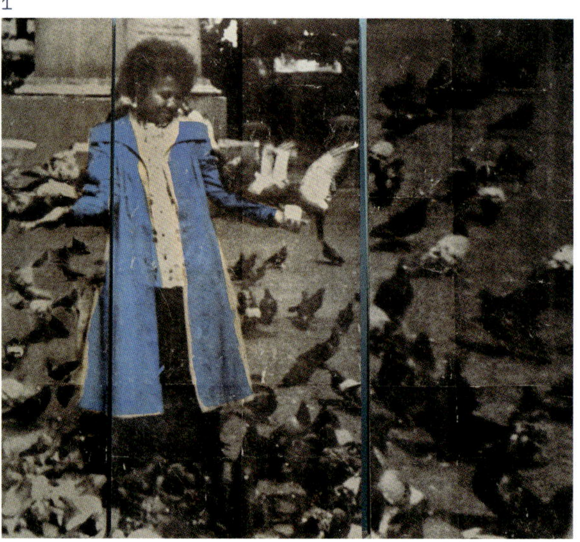

Fig. 1
Sandra Brewster
Feeding Trafalgar Square, 2021.
Gel medium photo transfer, charcoal, and acrylic on wood, 3 panels: 304.8 × 66 cm; 304.8 × 142.2 cm; 304.8 × 121.9 cm.
Art Gallery of Ontario, commission, with funds from the Women's Art Initiative, 2021. 2021/71.
© Sandra Brewster.
Photo: Art Gallery of Ontario.

2

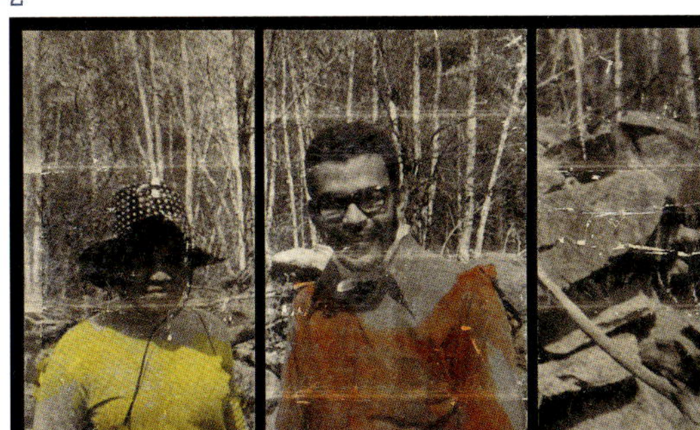

3

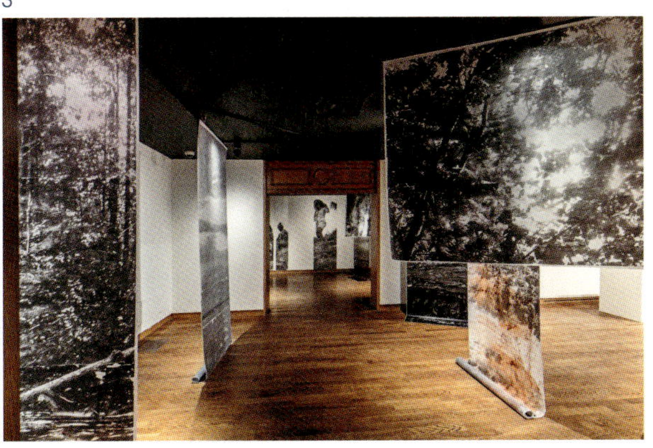

Fig. 2
Sandra Brewster
Hiking Black Creek, 2018.
Gel medium photo transfer, charcoal, acrylic on wood, 3 panels: 335.3 × 142.2 cm; 335.3 × 162.6 cm; 335.3 × 101.6 cm. Art Gallery of Ontario, purchase, with funds by exchange from a gift in memory of J.G. Althouse from Isobel Althouse Wilkinson and John Provost Wilkinson, 2020. 2020/17. © Sandra Brewster. Photo: Art Gallery of Ontario.

Fig. 3
Sandra Brewster
In the Wake of Demerara-Essequibo, 2017. Photo-based gel transfer on Mylar, dimensions variable. Installation view of Sandra Brewster, *A Trace | Evidence of Time Past* at Art Museum, Toronto. March 24–April 15, 2017. © Sandra Brewster. Photo: Toni Hafkenscheid.

For the installation *Feeding Trafalgar Square* (2021, fig. 1), Brewster uses the gel transfer process, a technical strategy she used in her photographic series *Hiking Black Creek* (2018, fig. 2). As in that series, she also draws on her family photo album. The work is based on a photograph of Brewster's mother taken while she was visiting London's Trafalgar Square as a tourist. The artist has long been captivated by her mother's ease among the birds and the joy she radiates in the centre of the image. The geographical context of the original photograph draws attention to the connections between the Caribbean, Europe, and the Americas. The viewer must use their own reading of the work to bring together all the information provided by the artist—notably, the implication is that Caribbean culture is not bounded by a geographical region (fig. 3).

Plural geographies. Magnetic connections. The artist Manuel Mathieu, who has resided in Montreal for the past fifteen years, is informed by intersecting racial, geographic, and cultural identities. In his work, he draws on a long artistic tradition—that of Haiti, his birthplace, and the pioneers of Caribbean abstract painting, such as the Guyanese- born English artist Frank Bowling. Mathieu fuses abstraction and figurative representation, incorporating his own memories as well as quotidian and historical stories (fig. 4). In his multidisciplinary practice, he creates a world of poetry and contrast; his creative process emphasizes certain key characteristics: the use of colour, light, forms, and movement, and the ways in which issues, ideas, and symbols are codified.

His painting *Lye* (2018, fig. 5) illustrates this approach, which is steeped in Haiti's visual culture. Indeed, the source image for this painting is that of a woman crouching near a spring. *Lye* features an archetypal figure—the fruit seller or street merchant, characteristic of the Haitian visual trope of women absorbed in their daily activities. Through a kind of detour, we are led back to the original meaning of the image, which evokes access to water as well as the socio-economic status of the subject. In Haiti, doing one's laundry in public (as in the scene depicted) is indicative of the scarcity of water. Aside from that allusion, the painting also highlights an everyday moment of meditation, escape, imagination, and daydreaming in the life of this woman. In his work, it seems, Mathieu wants to discover the essence of every being—of every *thing*—so that this essence can illuminate all that is pictured.

Sandra Brewster and Manuel Mathieu both succeed in making one thing out of many; and out of the smallest part of that one thing, they manage to make a world, all while exploring notions of identity, representation, and memory. What, then, can we take away from the work of these two individuals and other Canadian artists of Caribbean descent? Perhaps it's that the Caribbean does not lie on the periphery of art history, as the poet Joël Des Rosiers explains: "Modern, contemporary, since 1492 the Caribbean has determined the destiny of all the Americas."[4] Perhaps the destiny of Canadian contemporary art derives from the artistic language being employed today in the work of Canadian artists of Caribbean descent. Perhaps now, even in our urban archipelagos, we are all connected back to the Caribbean?

4

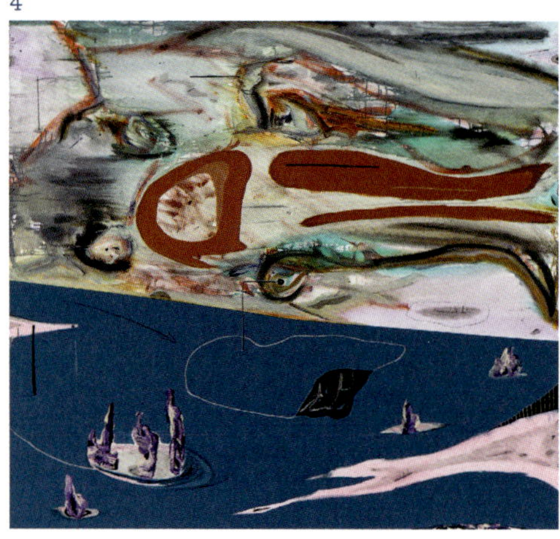

5

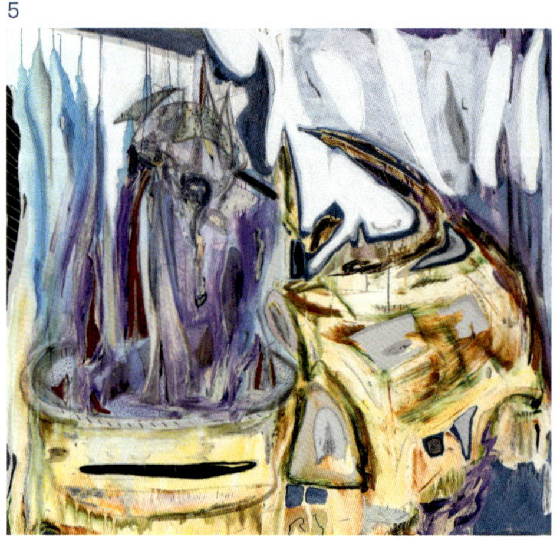

1 Frantz Voltaire, "Territoires de l'imaginaire," *Liberté* 330 (Spring 2021): 37–39.

2 Édouard Glissant, *Une nouvelle région du monde, Esthétique I* (Paris: Gallimard, 2006), 189.

3 Dionne Brand, quoted in Nalini Mohabir, *The Potential of Movement,* exhibition brochure (Montreal: Optica, 2020), 7.

4 Joël Des Rosiers, *Théories caraïbes: Poétique du déracinement* (Montreal: Triptyque, 1996).

Fig. 4
Manuel Mathieu
Fractures 1, 2019.
Acrylic, chalk, charcoal, and tape, 190.5 × 203.2 cm.
Courtesy of the artist.
© Manuel Mathieu.
Photo: Guy L'Heureux.

Fig. 5
Manuel Mathieu
Lye, 2018.
Acrylic, oil stick, charcoal, spray paint, tape, and chalk on canvas, 190.5 × 203.2 cm.
Hydro-Québec Collection.
© Manuel Mathieu.
Photo: Guy L'Heureux.

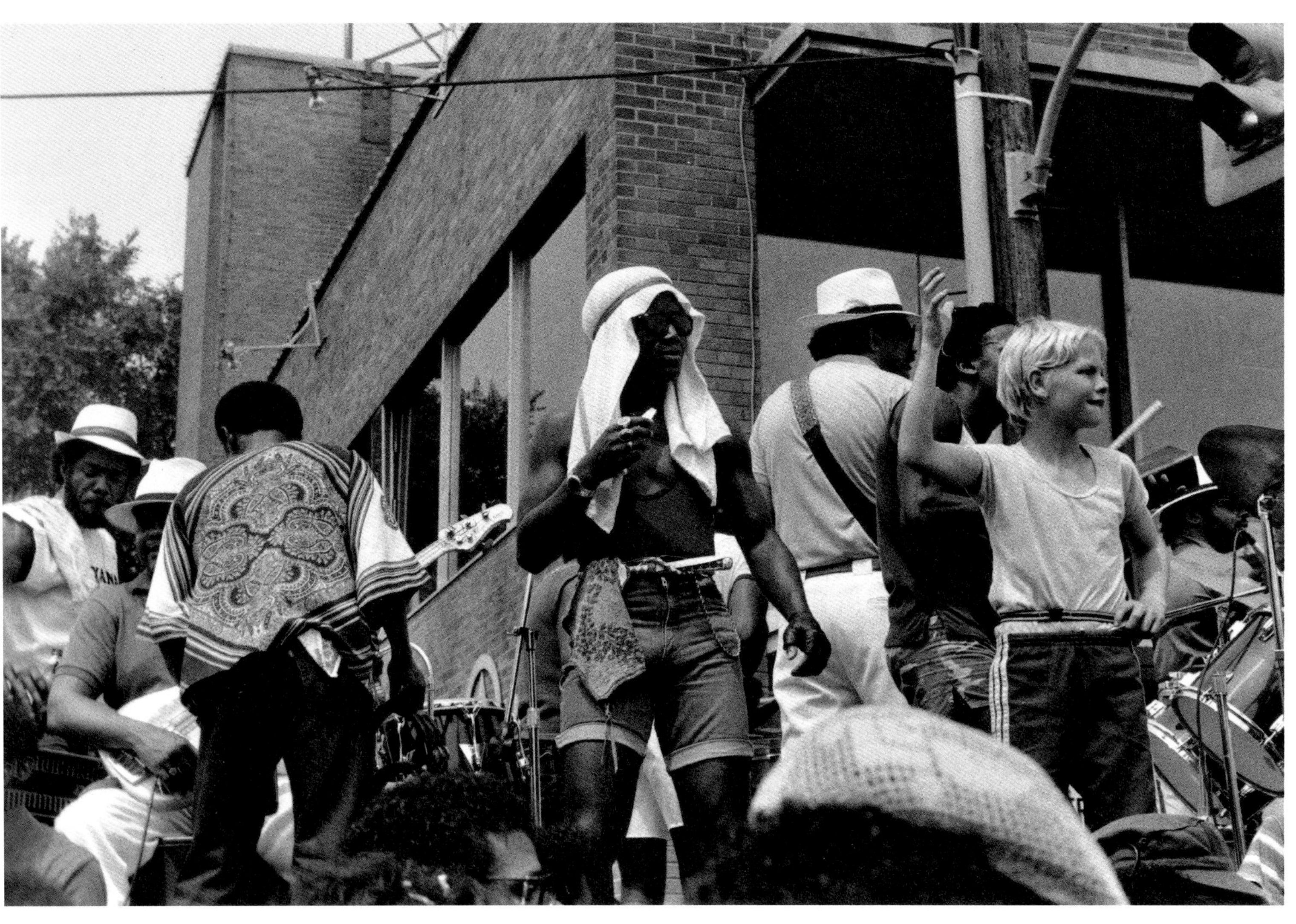

June Clark, *Untitled*, 1972

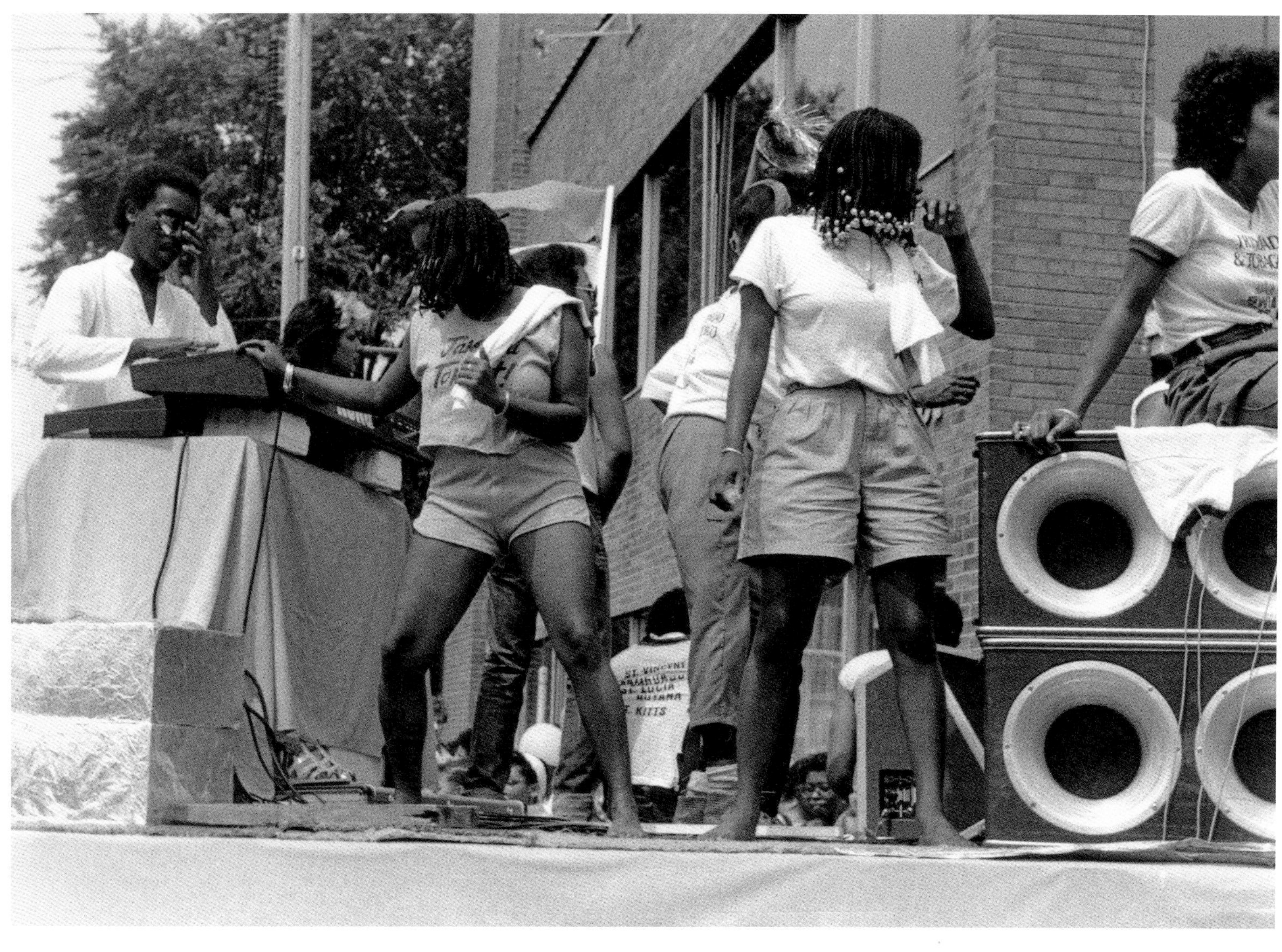

June Clark, *Untitled*, 1972

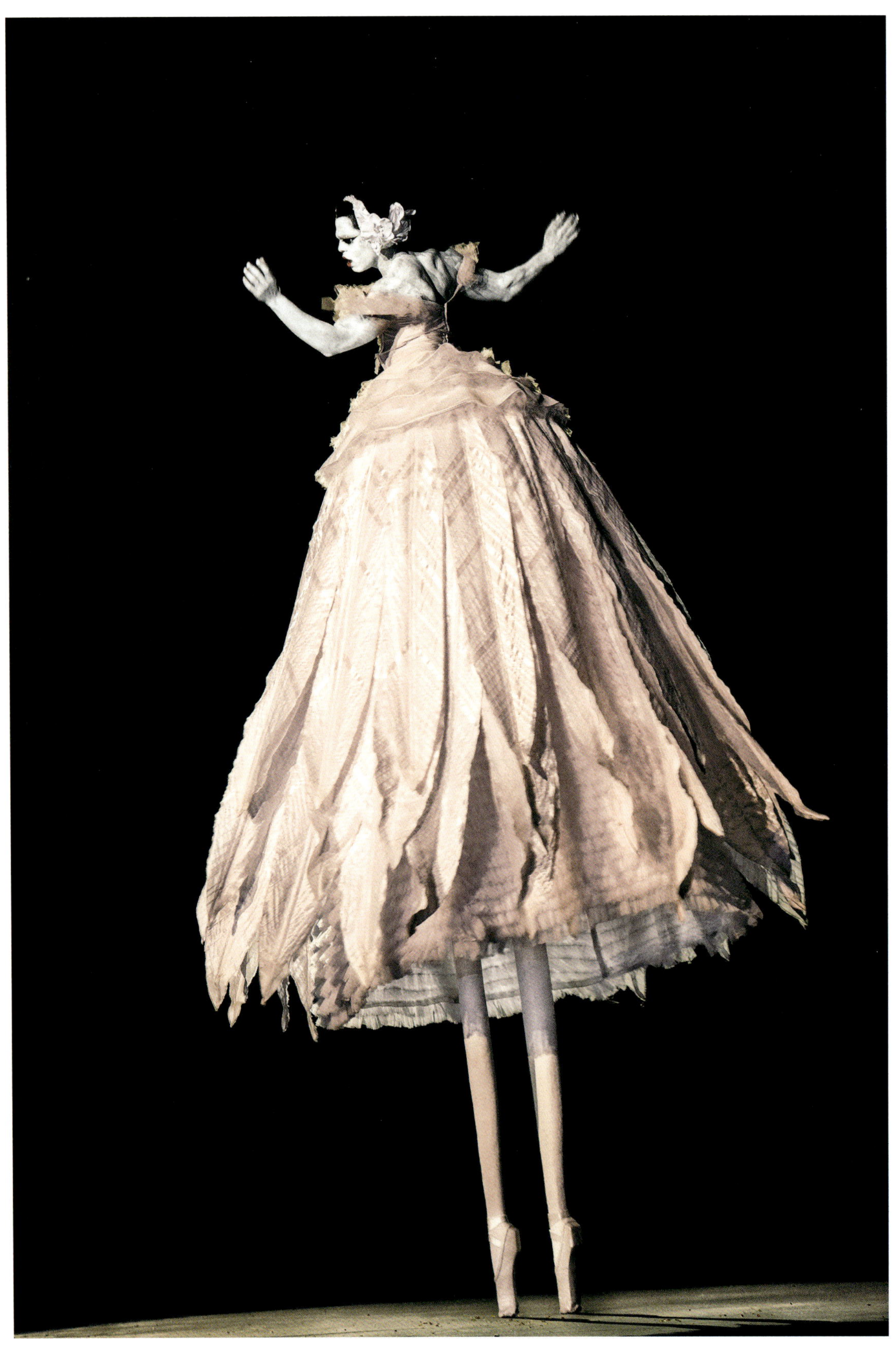

Abigail Hadeed, *The Dying Swan – Ras Nijinsky in Drag as Pavlova*, 2016; printed 2021

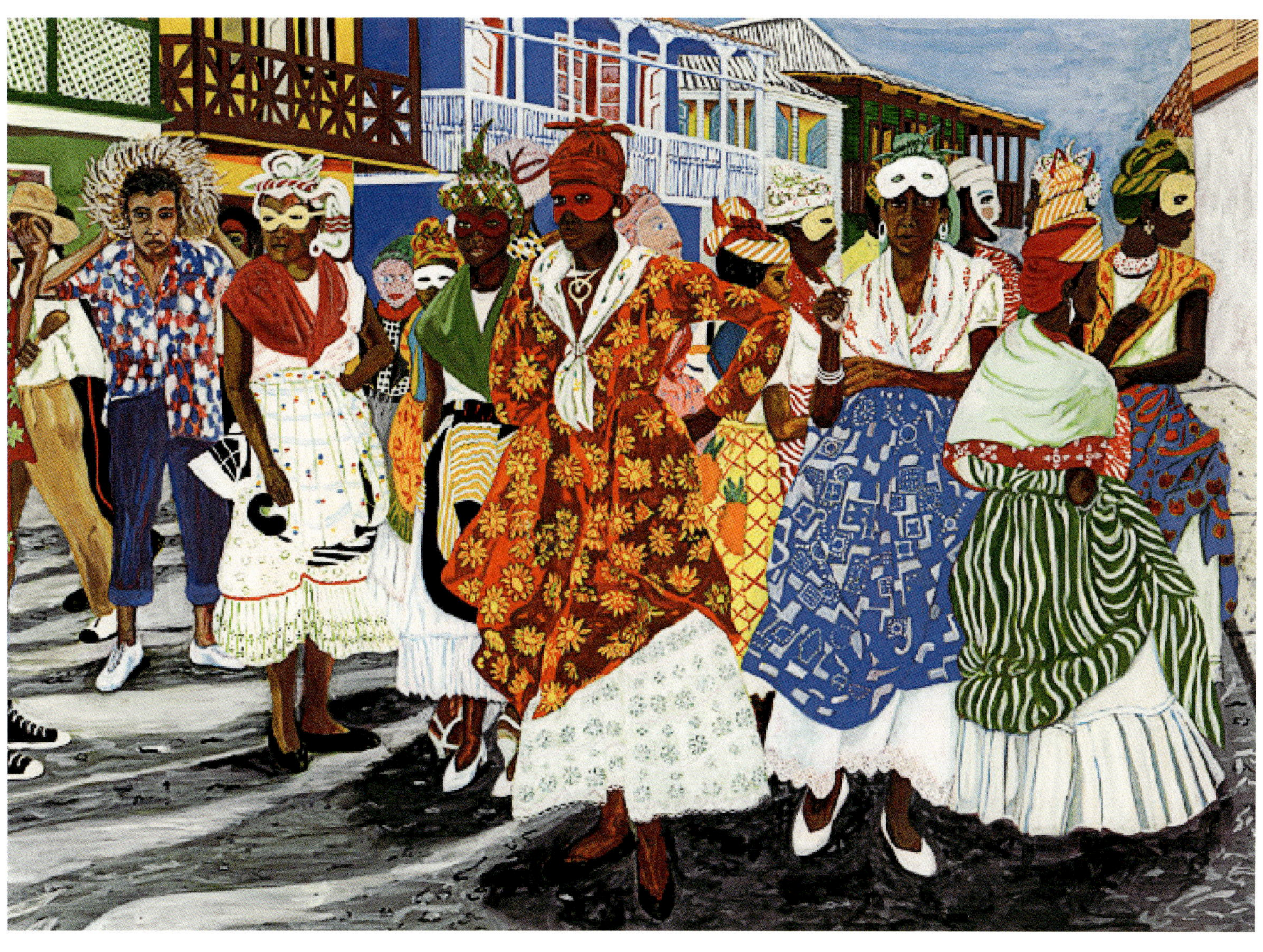

Gomo George, *Women's Carnival Group*, 1996

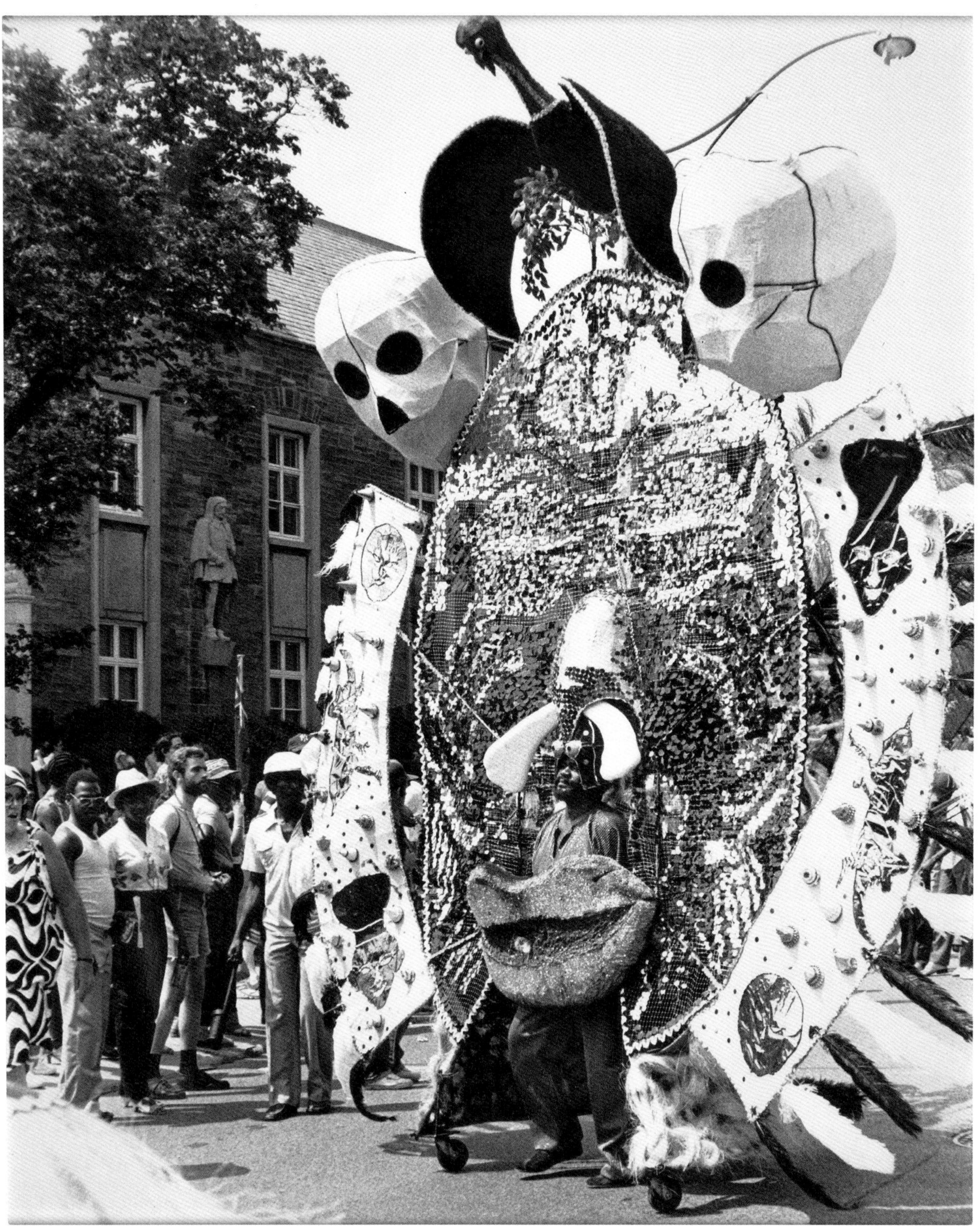

Diane Liverpool, *"He came out to play Mas" – Caribana parade on University Avenue*, 1981

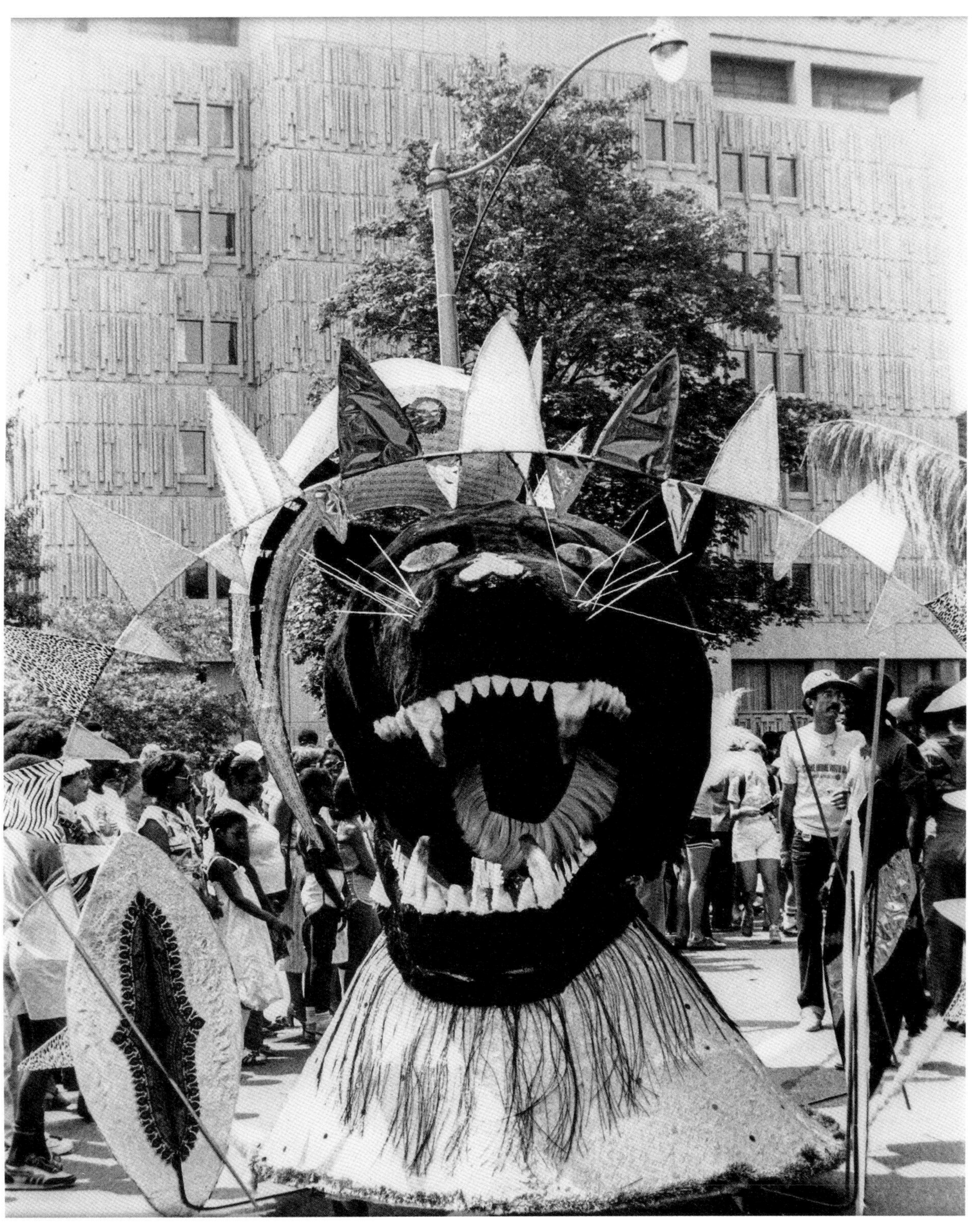

Diane Liverpool, *"Face of the Panther Mas" – Caribana parade on University Avenue,* 1981

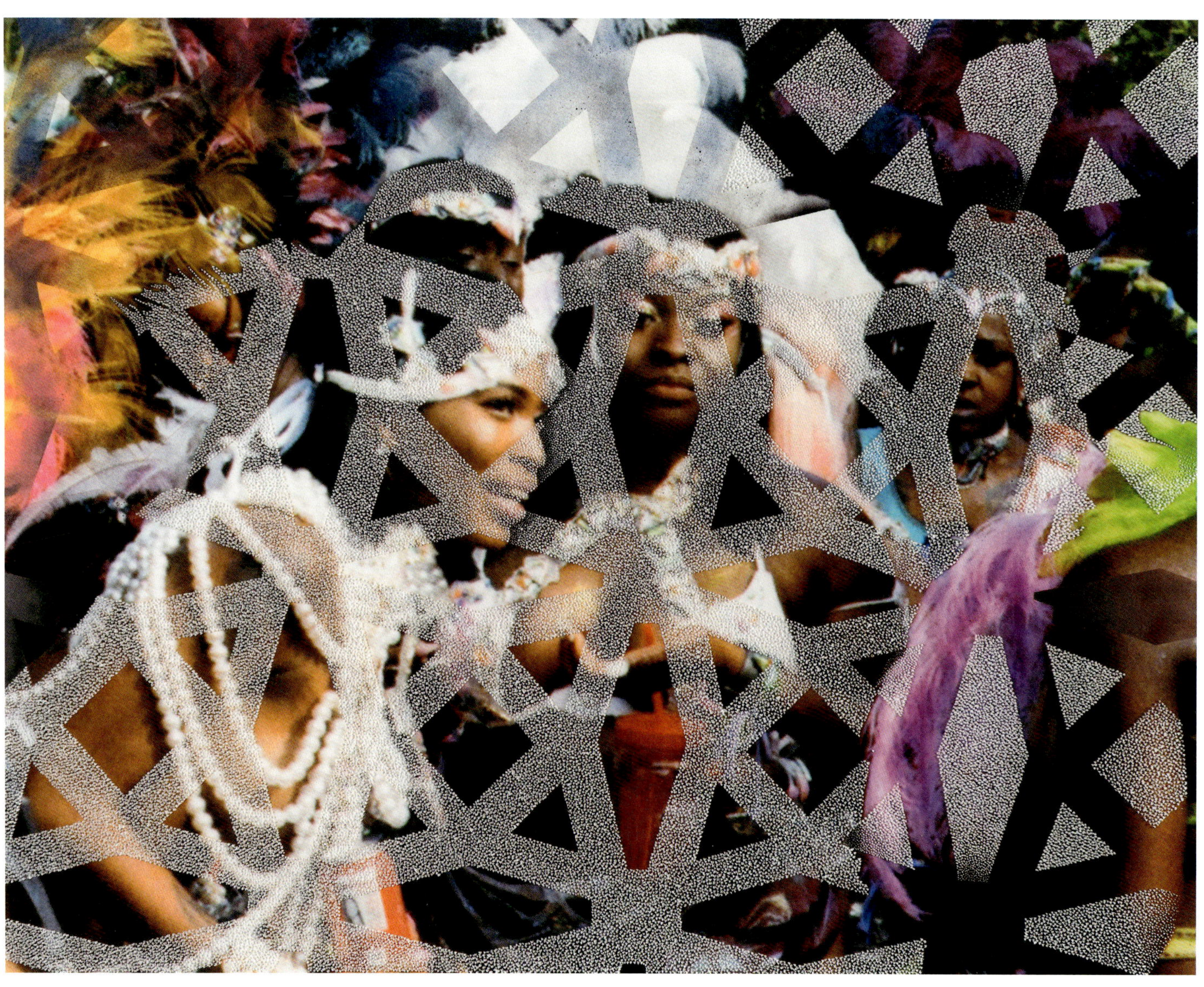

Paul Anthony Smith, *Untitled, 7 Women*, 2019

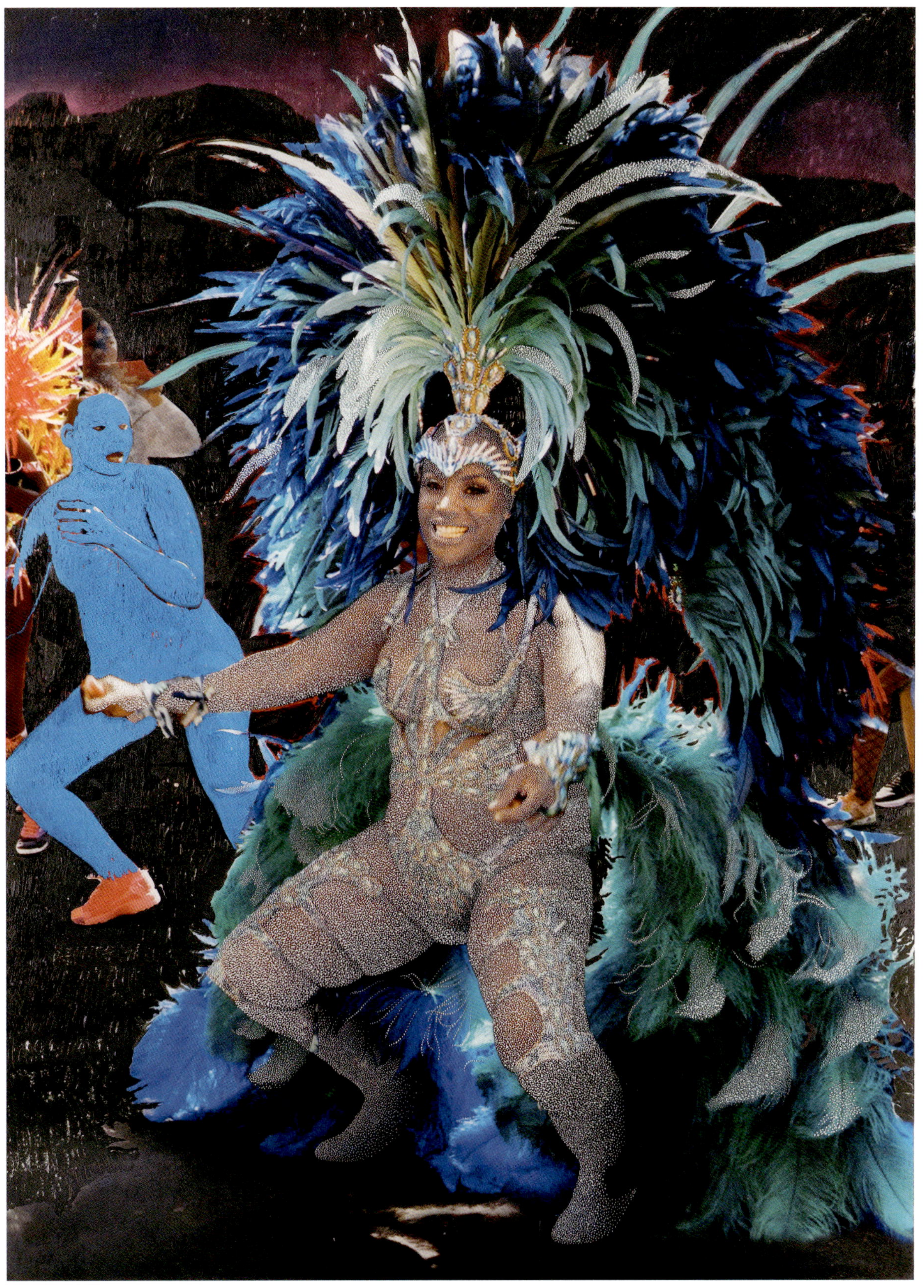

Paul Anthony Smith, *Midnight Blue*, 2020

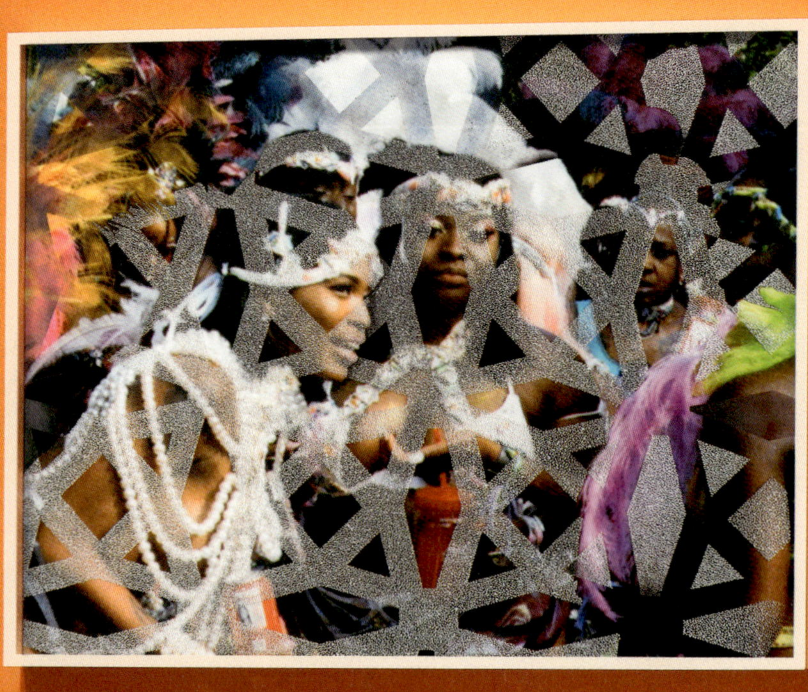

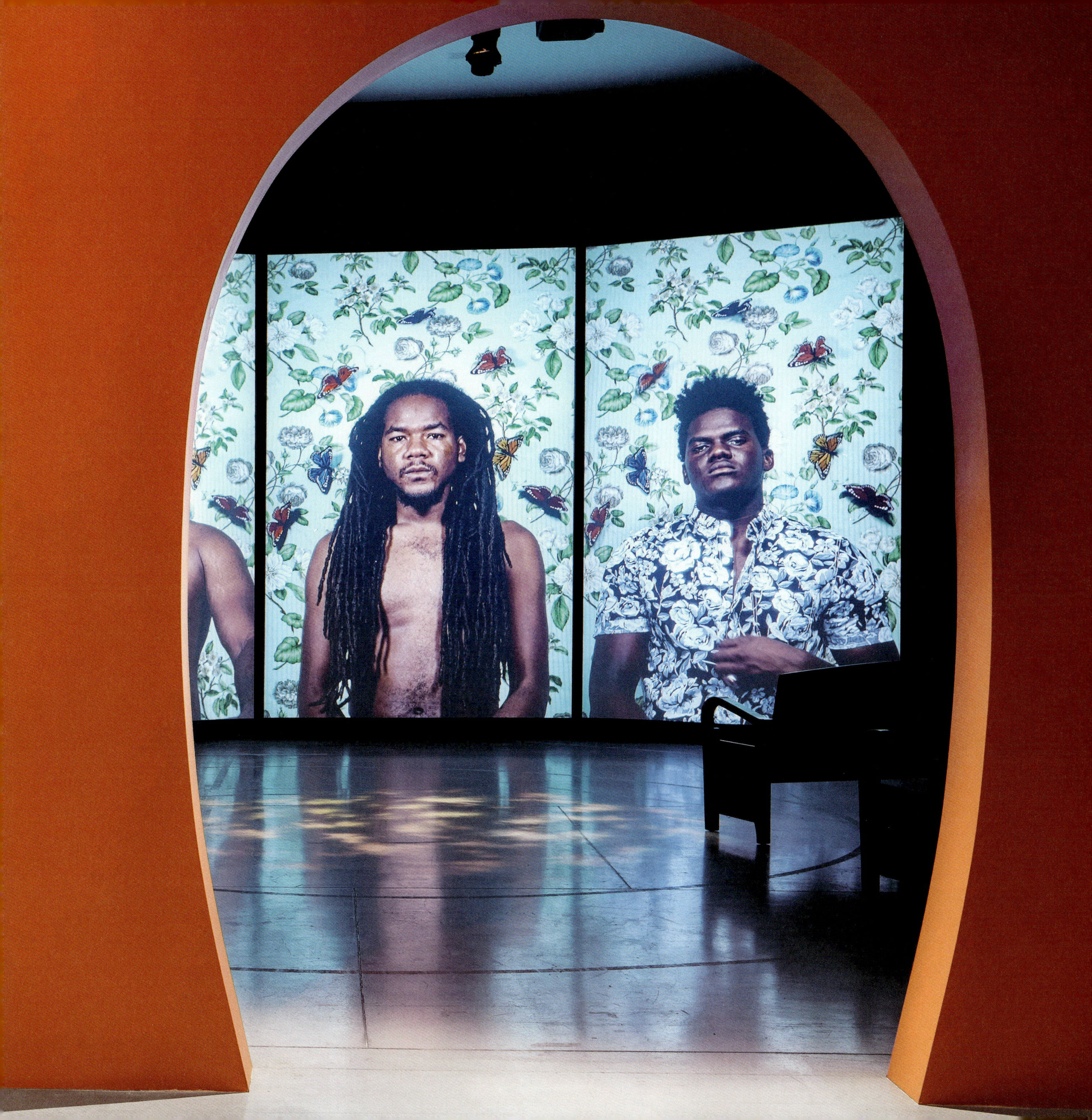

How to Kill a Soundboy: A Conversation with Leasho Johnson

O'Neil Lawrence

O'Neil Lawrence is an artist and the Chief Curator at the National Gallery of Jamaica. His research interests include race, gender, and sexuality in Caribbean and African diasporal art and visual culture; memory, identity, and hidden archives; and photography as a medium and a social vehicle. In 2018, he served on the Board of the Davidoff Art Initiative and he is currently on the Advisory Council of the Caribbean Art Initiative.

Leasho Johnson is a Jamaican-born artist who uses a wide range of media to create his art, which takes the form of paintings, collages, murals, street art, and sculpture. In his work, which is often sardonic in tone, he addresses topics that are contentious in Jamaican society, such as gender, homosexuality, and violence, and explores subcultures such as dancehall. Johnson creates characters that live on the edge of perception, visible and invisible at the same time.

The following conversation between Lawrence and Johnson is part of a series of Lawrence's ongoing dialogues with queer Caribbean artists about the nature of their varying experiences as queer people in the Caribbean as well as their artistic practices. It has been edited and condensed.

O'Neil Lawrence (OL): I want to begin by talking about your exhibition *Belisario and the Soundboy*[1] and how it connects with the *Back-fi-a-bend* (2015) installation in New Kingston; for me, these works necessarily disrupt a particular historical narrative. Walk me through those works and why you chose to take on that history.

Leasho Johnson (LJ): At that time, I was reading Krista Thompson's book *An Eye for the Tropics*[2] and I began to look at photography and what happened pre-photography. When I stumbled upon J.B. Kidd's work and saw recognizable places in Jamaica, there was the question of how much of these depictions is factual. The depictions are not from a photographer's lens—rather, a moment in time captured in light. It's now translated through this artist's understanding. I began to interrogate the inception of who we are and what Jamaica is, and to do that, I had to think about the land and the people separately. Looking at these paintings and photographs, between the spaces, the landscape, the people, to figure out where in history queerness exists, in Blackness, in the Caribbean. Where do I exist? Where do people like me exist?

I used a photograph by A. Duperly and Sons—*Women Sitting with Their Products*—to create *Back-fi-a-bend* (2015, fig. 1) as almost a direct channel between the present and the past. I used the character [pumpum][3] (fig. 2) as a method of disrupting what was presented in these photographs and watercolour paintings, [bringing it] in dialogue with the present. The way we were taught history in high school makes it seem that our inception started with slavery, and that is a poor foundation to build identity on. [Following from that,] certain ideas were filtered down to us in a particular, rigid way as well, so of course we can't negotiate queerness or feminine power, and it's problematic to negotiate masculinity. The interrogation of that way of thinking was through re-painting, cutting up, and collaging images and digitizing them with the avatar to ask the question "Is this who we were—who we *really* were?"

and put it in conversation with who we are now (fig. 3). With *Belisario and the Soundboy*,[4] I was thinking of two observers, with the Soundboy as the maestro of a street scene in dialogue with Belisario as the colonial perspective, and the resulting artwork being a "clash"[5] to bring attention to this "fake" history. With the absence of cameras in the seventeenth century, there is a very pliable method of visually propagating how something might have happened.

OL: Why did you choose to use these cute, quirky—but also disruptive—cartoon-like figures in your work, as opposed to more realistic depictions?

LJ: I've always been aware of how cartoons and caricatures change things. When I created these characters, I thought about how Japanese popular culture translates the historical and factual to become a cute thing that is sellable and collectible. When I began to assess my own space in Jamaica, there seemed to be this demeaning of imagination; Jamaicans tend to gravitate towards realism. Post-independence, the more popular representations of Jamaican life were wrapped in realism. I grew up in the 1990s without the Internet but when [it] came, people started to look at themselves in different ways. My exposure to anime was also [being exposed] to a reimagination of reality: the technology was "real" and the emotions were "real," but the characters had huge eyes and tiny mouths. It made me think, "How can we reimagine ourselves?" The creation of the character was my attempt at that, but I needed to reference something real. When I did the series *Church Is in Session* (2012), I was looking at dancehall and the ridiculousness of the caricature [in that work] ([the character] Spice, with her legs spread east and west) represented in dancehall. I thought I've never seen these cute kawaii Japanese characters do something like that, and when I created them, it became its own thing.

Of course, there are many other artists who have done that, like KAWS, for example. They use these ready-go-to characters that they invented; I thought, "Why can't *we* do that?" Of course, I didn't have plastic so I approximated it with my use of colour; once it is absorbed by white, earthenware looks like plastic. It was also an attempt to challenge or understand what Blackness is. There is this literalness about depictions of Blackness, and I'm now becoming more appreciative of the many different ways this can be done.

1

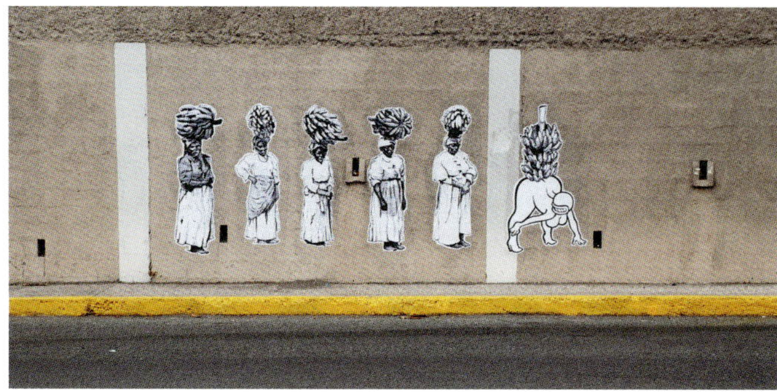

2

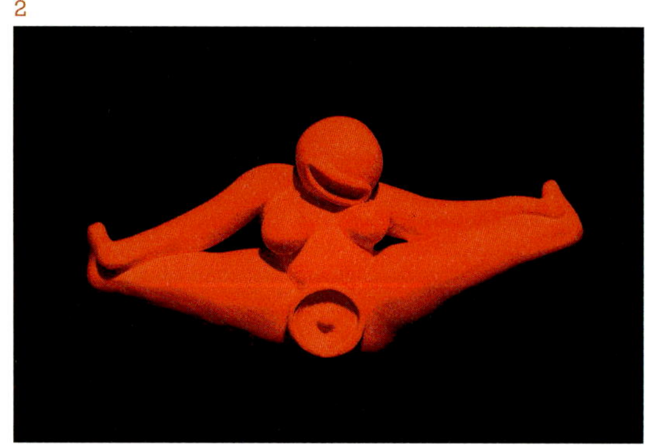

Fig. 1
Leasho Johnson
Back-fi-a-bend, 2015.
Digital print on bond paper and yeast paste, dimensions variable. View at Trafalgar Road, New Kingston, Jamaica, installation. © Leasho Johnson. Image courtesy of the artist.

Fig. 2
Leasho Johnson
Pum-pum Tun-up East and West, 2012 (from *The Church Is in Session* series).
Earthenware and spray paint, 30.48 × 12.7 × 20.32 cm.
© Leasho Johnson.
Image courtesy of the artist.

3

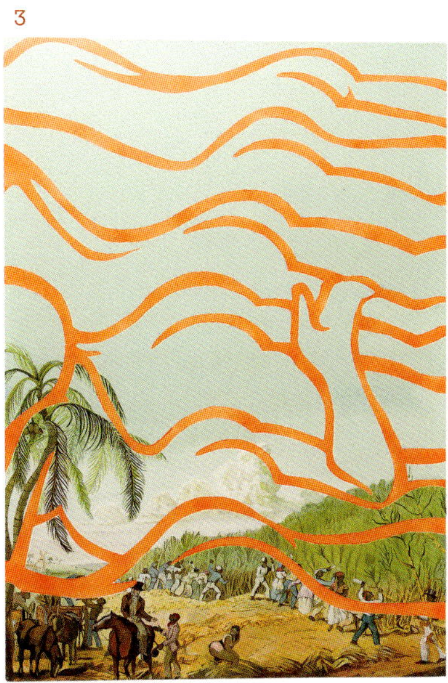

4

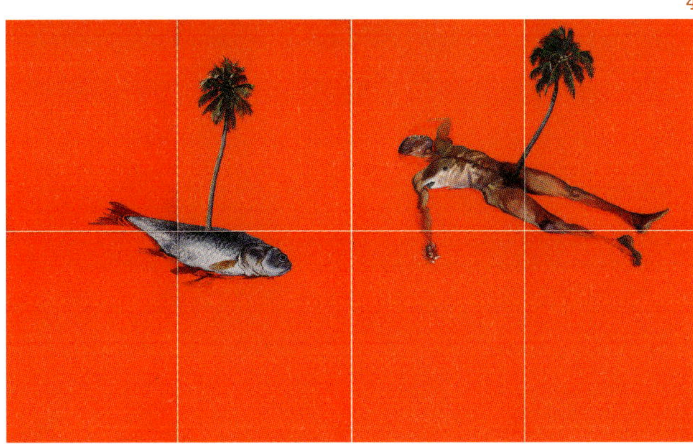

Fig. 3
Leasho Johnson
Rude to Your Parents, 2017.
Acrylic and spray paint on canvas, 137.16 × 93.98 cm.
© Leasho Johnson.
Image courtesy of the artist.

Fig. 4
Leasho Johnson
Land of Big Hood and Water, 2015. Acrylic on canvas (polyptych), 127 x 203.2 cm. Caribbean Queer Visualities (CQV).
© Leasho Johnson. Image courtesy of the artist.

It's harder to satirize something when it is realistically depicted; with this character, you're forced to contend with what is presented because there's this play between it being realistic, but not realistic.

Look at the rejected public monuments [in Jamaica]: the recent Marcus Garvey bust[6] and the Bob Marley monument (1982) by Christopher Gonzales. People rejected them because the works were negotiating an identity and it was art bumping up against society. For my public work, I needed people to see themselves and critique and understand, but despite the publicity, it only seemed that people were doing it privately. Trying to negotiate space—which is the intent of the work—is personal and I have to deal with my own [psyche] and myself.

I've been having conversations [with artists here in Chicago] about how unsafe it feels for me to be in Jamaica. The fact that I can pass as a straight man is something that I use to my advantage, and people don't ask questions. I have had to negotiate the fact that Jamaican culture is homophobic and if you want to be outwardly queer, you have to leave. My work only makes incremental moves to show [that it is about queerness], largely because of the fear of exposure. As opposed to works in public, the gallery is a safe space for the work and I don't feel exposed.

OL: Your work hasn't just been about queerness; there are a lot of other social issues that you've addressed, like sexual tourism. I told you some time ago that the work you did for the Caribbean Queer Visualities project was some of your most powerful…

LJ: But it never got shown in Jamaica. That version of *Land of Big Hood and Water* (2015, fig. 4) was a polyptych painting and I strategically did not show it in Jamaica. I wasn't ready for the questions that would arise from showing that work. Yes, it was powerful. But I was almost attacked while at art school because I'm gay—in what was supposed to be a space with open-minded people—and that made me uncomfortable about showing that work.

OL: Is that why you felt more comfortable returning to the use of your avatars to tackle some of the same issues in the 2016 installation of *Land of Big Hood and Water* (fig. 5)?

LJ: The avatars are really pacifiers; in their "cartoonishness" they make [the subject matter] more approachable.

The moment that the renderings become real, it becomes problematic, and you can see that in the street version.... A lawyer told me I could have been arrested for indecent exposure. The person who owned the wall wanted me convicted for putting the work on "his" wall. The lawyer told me that the only thing that protected me was that there were trees in place of the figures' penises.

OL: The conversations I've been having with other queer artists in the Caribbean have made me contemplate my own journey as an artist through my work. There is a question I've asked several times: As queer artists, who are we talking to with our work? The responses have been very different each time. I was never really having a conversation with anyone besides myself. My work was a visualization of an internal narrative that was easier to articulate through my photography.

LJ: We all envision a solution for ourselves and we are trying to solve this through art. It's probably the most flawed methodology to fix anything but it's providing a [kind of] fulfillment we can't get from reality. I use my work as a way of learning about, understanding, and negotiating with myself and negotiating with my audience; there is violence, too, in its creation and there is a battle going on in my head. For me, people looking at and understanding a work helps to complete the work. I've been using the character to almost test the psyche of my audience, which is important because, for me, queerness is this constant state of negotiation with society. If there weren't society's "norms," there wouldn't be queerness. My works have always been my thermometer and I know when my characters begin to push against the norms of society—like *How to Kill a Soundboy* [particularly because the sculpture has male genitals] (fig. 6).

OL: I'd like to use *How to Kill a Soundboy* (2017) to talk more about lives lived on the periphery of the periphery. That work was a turning point—less so for you, but more of a turning point for my interface with your work because it seemed to explicitly deal with transgender lives. What I found interesting was the way the records cut through the figures. It was almost reminiscent of the scene in *The Seven Year Itch* when Marilyn Monroe's skirt is blown up. The use of the records was a provocative way of revealing what was underneath the

5

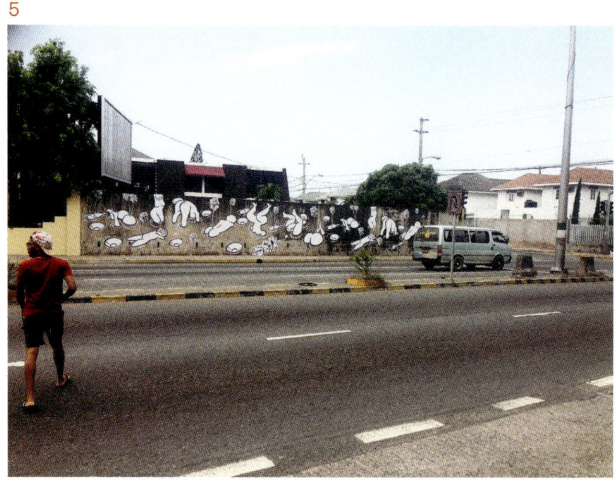

6

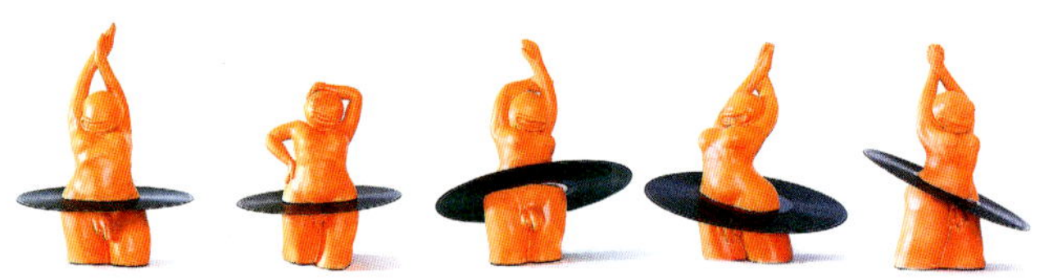

Fig. 5
Leasho Johnson
Land of Big Hood and Water, 2016.
Digital print on bond paper and yeast paste on wall, 2072.64 × 243.84 cm.
View at Hope Road, Kingston, Jamaica, installation.
© Leasho Johnson. Image courtesy of the artist.

Fig. 6
Leasho Johnson
How to Kill a Soundboy, 2017. Earthenware, spray paint, and vinyl records, approx. 30.48 × 30.48 x 33.02 cm each. © Leasho Johnson. Image courtesy of the artist.

rhetoric of dancehall music[7] and how it disrupts and cuts through these lives. It was important for me that this work was exhibited in Montego Bay [in *I Shall Return Again*[8]] because of the savage 2013 killing of a transgender teen in that city and the lack of public outcry in Jamaica.[9]

LJ: When I did that piece, I wasn't specifically thinking about trans lives, but about queer life in general and how those lives exist in Jamaica. I wanted to create a series with records cutting through the figures not only horizontally but also vertically. The character/avatar called "pumpum" is an object of desire and the reciprocal/receptacle of violence acting as a mirror of Jamaican society and culture, and a reflection of how it inflicts its own damage on Black bodies—and not just Black bodies, but the bodies of Black women specifically. *How to Kill a Soundboy* (2018) coexisted with other works in that exhibition like *Sugar Daddy* (2018); reinforcing and inspecting a particular type of masculinity was its real purpose. It ended up being this poetic play on what is in the music, which, for me, isn't discussed enough. Creating this work was part of the process of distilling and trying to [understand] what is really in the music and the culture. There was a whole period in my life of demystifying and then distilling the music to understand the culture that it represents. The work sits in this uncomfortable spot between queerness, Blackness, and masculinity. The philosophies behind our image of ourselves as men and women stem from Christianity, and Christianity renders some people invisible. I created this character as a solidification of how we see gender, femininity, and masculinity, and the male genitalia was meant to disturb—the character made people feel comfortable and, in playing with gender, the character began to collapse. Trying to collapse the character in my painting became more of an amalgamation of clashing elements. That collapse has disrupted the appearance of the character, and my work now is literally a destruction of the character. I knew I needed to destroy the character for the audience I have been creating this work for, and Montego Bay was the perfect venue for that, since it was the first place I ever saw transgender women and transgender men.

OL: Why did you feel the need at this point in your work to destroy a character that you have created and that you've made complicated for so long?

LJ: The character, for me, was [initially] more of a reflection of a society. But what happened was that the character was becoming a reflection of myself, of my interior and the way I feel, and it had to be a sacrificial lamb. The reputation of the character was, in a way, an illustration of Jamaican culture through the lens of dancehall. It's almost like revenge: I am trying to reclaim myself. There was, and still is, lots of hiding of the aspects of myself that I'm not comfortable revealing. The character [in the work] became the avatar for those things: revealing a reimagining of myself as both male and female: I can be both at any time and the character performs this through its body. It can become a receptor of hate and love and ultimately, of acceptance. It's less violent than taking that on for myself; I had to prepare myself psychologically to deal with the repercussions of how I really feel about society. There had begun this merging of myself and the character—there had to be a breakdown of something and I'm not going to martyr myself, so it had to be the character.

OL: I have one final question in terms of your current work, particularly because of your use of the word *destroy*. It's almost as if the current work is *Yeng Yeng* (2018, fig. 7) collapsed upon itself. Do you see the next stage yet or are you still working through this stage of collapsing, destroying, and reconfiguring the character?

LJ: Yes, I am still working through that [stage] because it is a space I can own. I'm trying to go as far as I can. If there is anything that is going to survive this stage, it will be my sculpture. I'm reconfiguring how I am going to present [that work] as well as how I am going to extend some of these conversations through performance and photography. If I go back into ceramics, how would it work with the characters now that they have been destroyed in a certain way? What kind of dialogues would I be having now in relation to artifacts and images? How do I revise working on walls? The only thing that is clear is how I am working on my painting. It is a slower process now. I feel as if I went [to] negative one hundred on a number line and I'm now working my way back to one hundred on the other side of the scale.

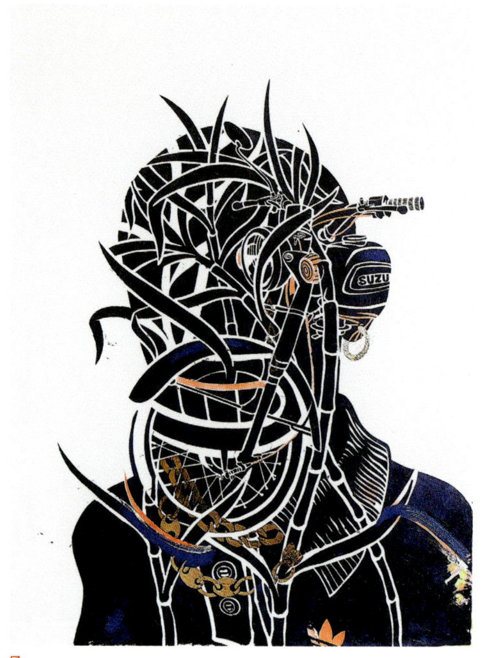

7

Fig. 7
Leasho Johnson
Yeng Yeng, 2018. Oil paint, gold leaf, spray paint, vinyl, and gesso on watercolour paper, 152.4 × 127 cm.
© Leasho Johnson. Image courtesy of the artist.

1 The exhibition *Belisario and the Soundboy* was presented at New Local Space in Kingston, Jamaica, and ran from February 4–24, 2017.

2 Krista Thompson, *An Eye for the Tropics: Tourism, Photography, and Framing the Caribbean Picturesque* (Durham, NC: Duke University Press, 2006).

3 "Pumpum" is named after the Jamaican patois term for the vagina featured in several of Johnson's earlier works. With her fixed, minstrel-like smile, voluptuous body and oversimplified features, she is a caricature used to critique the objectification of the Black female body in dancehall culture.

4 *Belisario and the Soundboy*, presented at New Local Space, Kingston, Jamaica (February 4–24, 2017).

5 "The sound clash is one of the most creative forces in dancehall culture, maintaining a hierarchy among sound systems. The selector's strategies of moving the crowd in favour of his sound during a clash is a highly refined and complicated affair. To win a clash, a sound must have a good collection of the dubs with the hottest artists running the road. The crowd's response is the final judge of which system is victorious." Norman C. Stolzoff, *Wake the Town and Tell the People* (Durham, NC, and London: Duke University Press, 2000), 201.

6 A controversial bust of Marcus Garvey (2017) by Raymond Watson, commissioned by the University of the West Indies. Paul H. Williams, "No disrespect meant—Sculptor Raymond Watson upset that people are angry over his bust of Marcus Garvey," *Daily Gleaner* (Kingston, Jamaica), June 12, 2017.

7 "A progeny of reggae, contemporary dancehall music is now Jamaica's most popular indigenous music, and the sociocultural manifestations around its consumption constitute Jamaica's premier street theatre." Sonjah Stanley-Niaah, *Dancehall: From Slave Ship to Ghetto* (Ottawa: University of Ottawa Press, 2010), 2.

8 *I Shall Return Again*, presented at National Gallery West, Montego Bay (September 2018–April 2019).

9 David McFadden, "In Jamaica, transgender teen killed by mob," *AP News*, August 11, 2013. Accessed May 26, 2021, apnews.com/article/ba0683d026e-c41e58a1f1589a7de7f8a

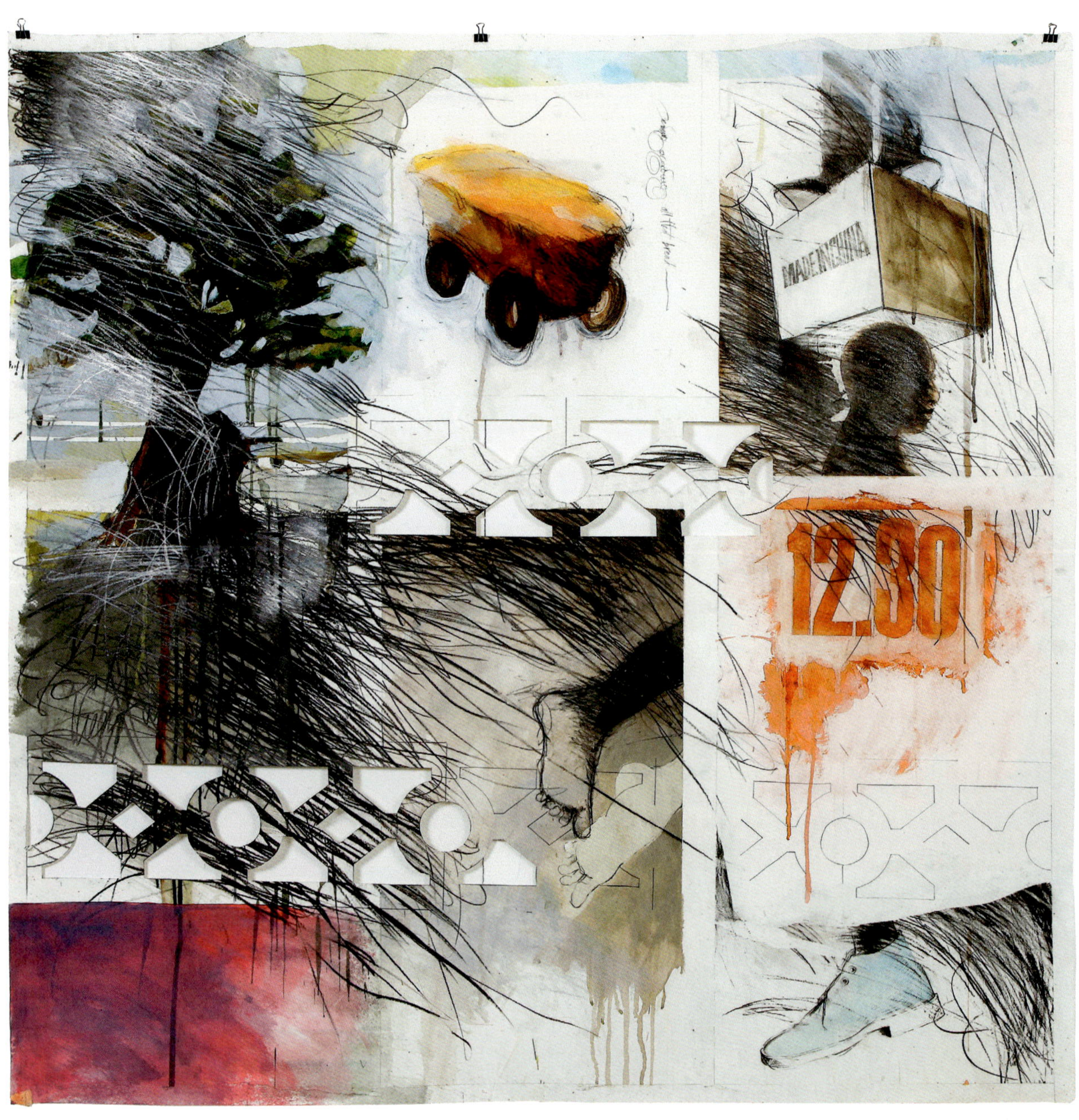

 Christopher Cozier, *NOW SHOWING 12:30*, 2010–2012

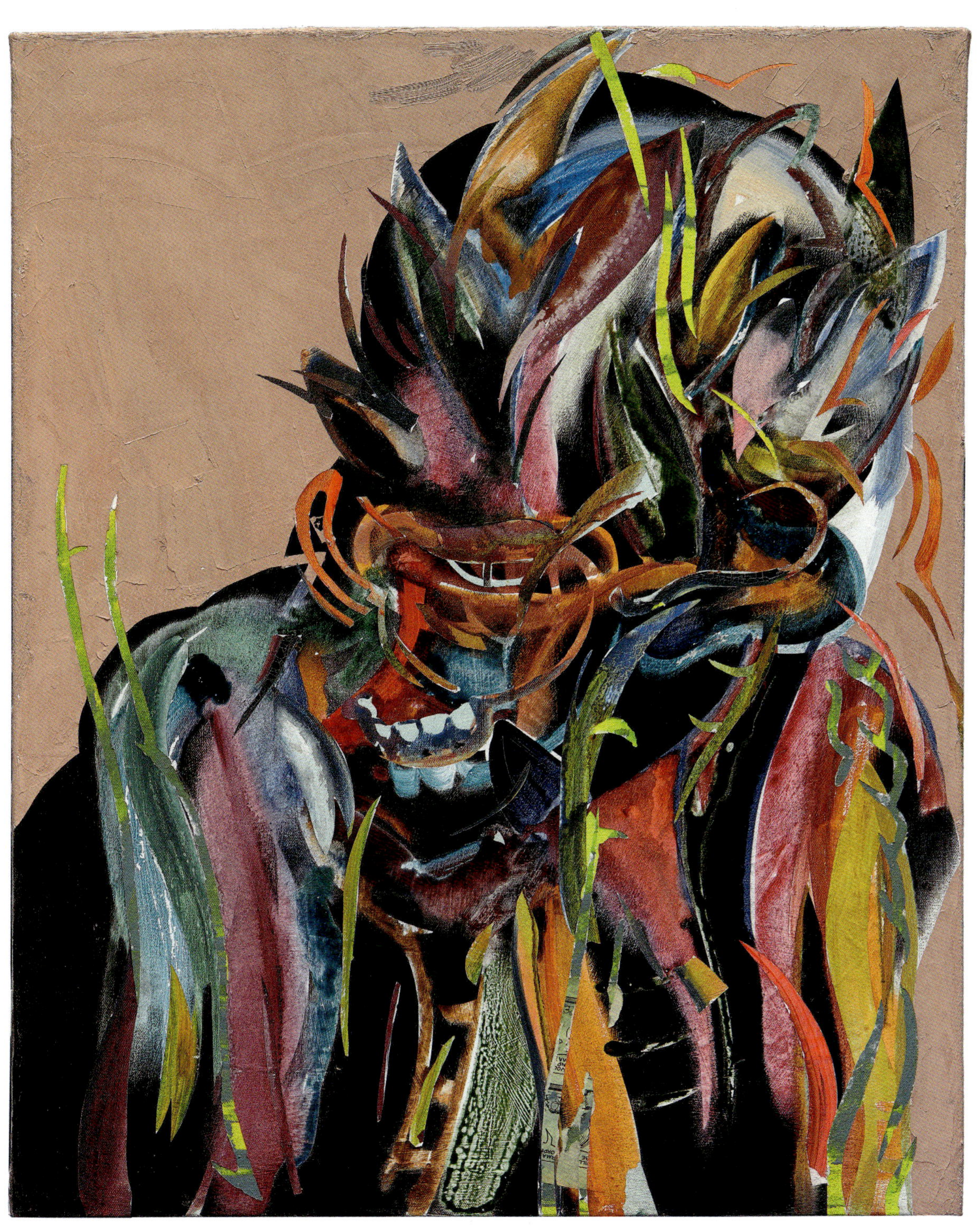

Leasho Johnson, *Jaw bone (man looking back at the cane fields)*, 2019

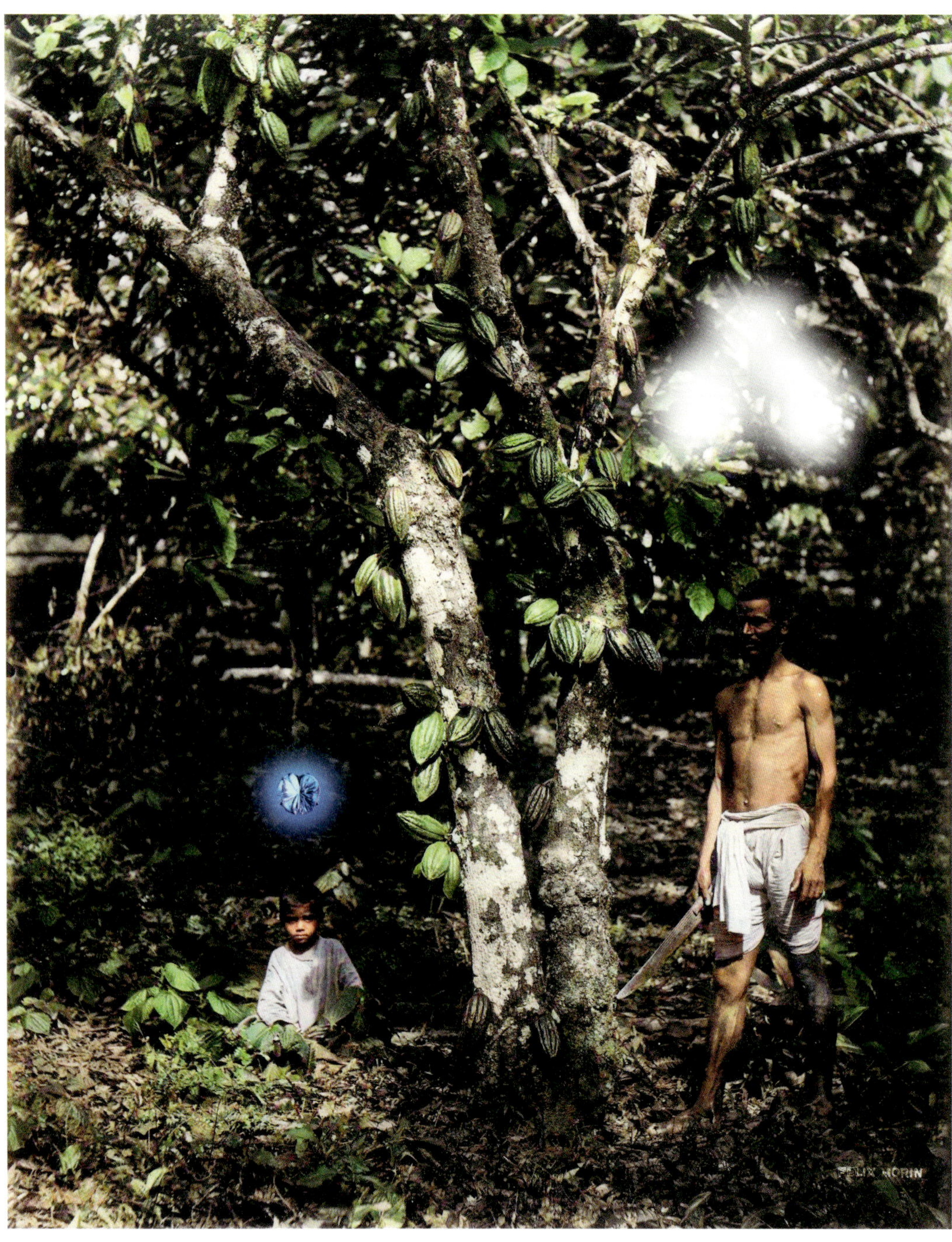

Rodell Warner, *Augmented Archive 021* (colourized), 2021

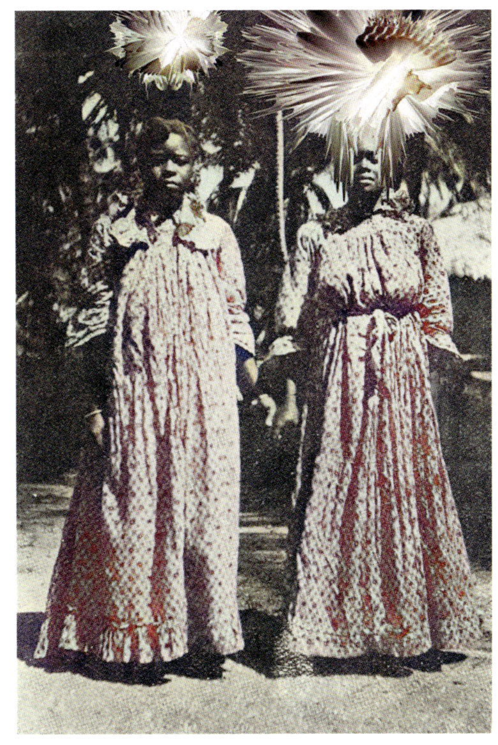

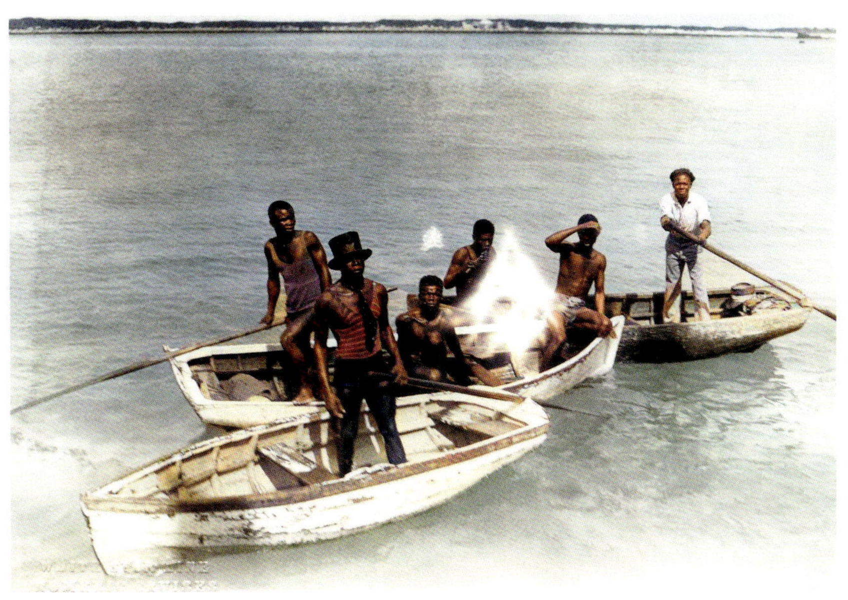

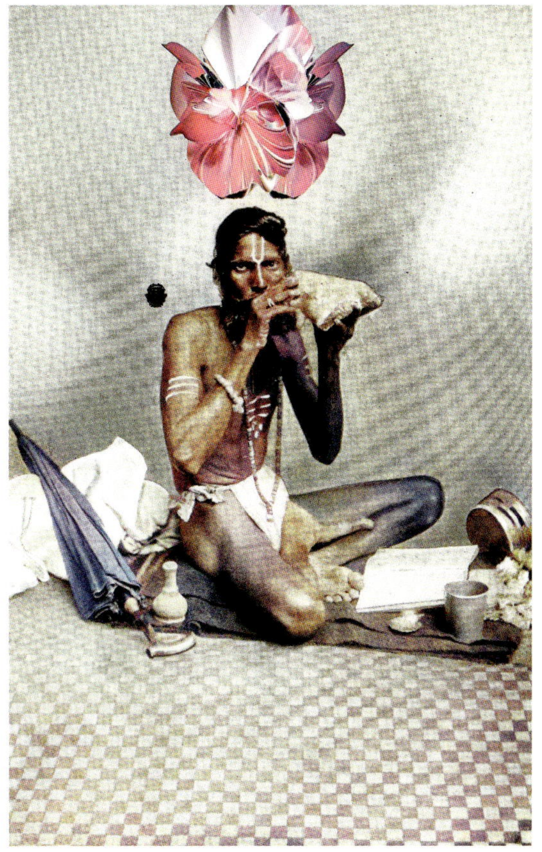

Clockwise from top
Rodell Warner
Augmented Archive 015
(colourized), 2020

Augmented Archive 011
(colourized), 2020

Augmented Archive 020
(colourized), 2021

Installation view of Ebony G. Patterson, *...three kings weep...*, 2018, at the Art Gallery of Ontario

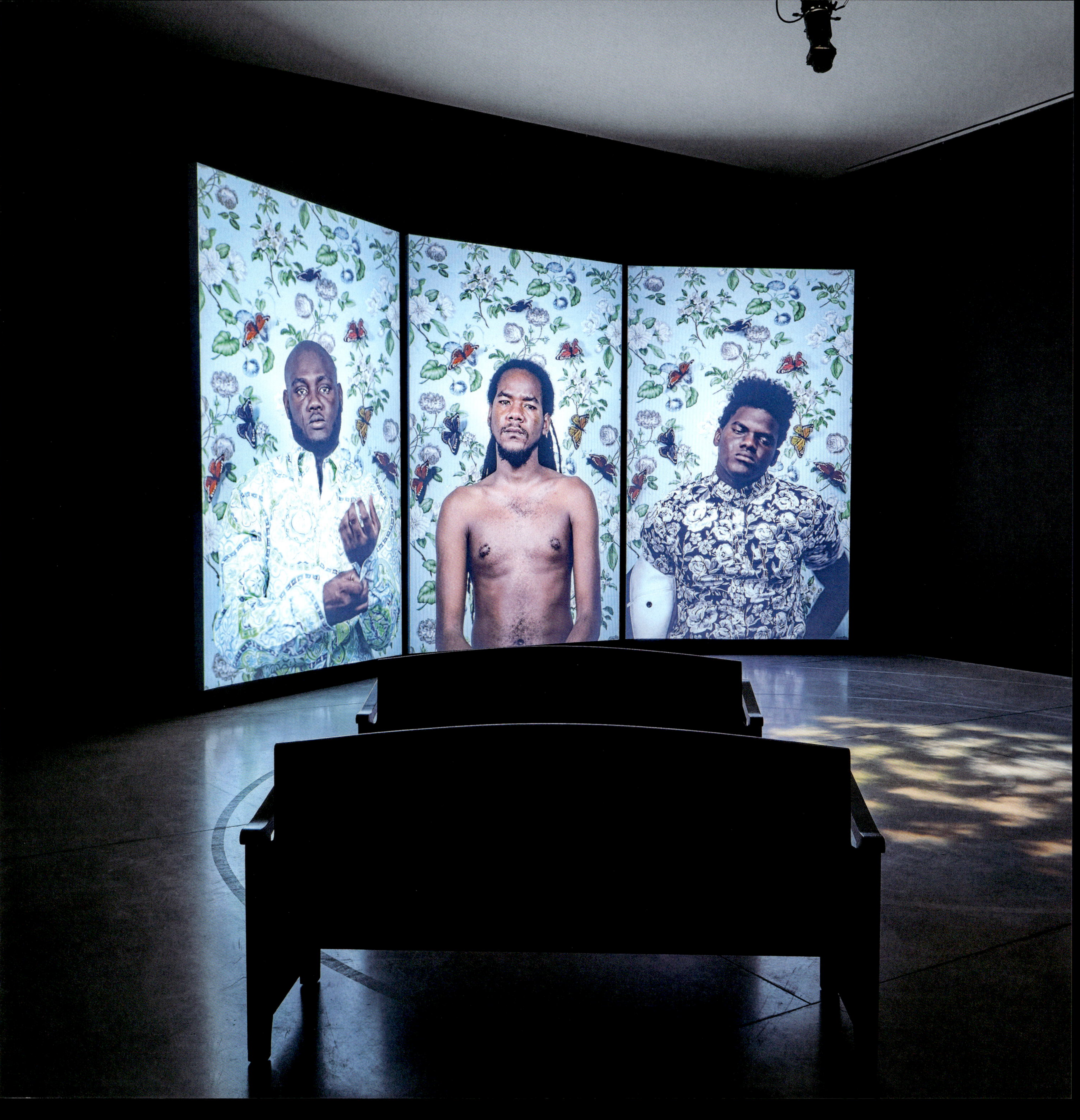

If We Must Die

Claude McKay

If we must die, let it not be like hogs
Hunted and penned in an inglorious spot,
While round us bark the mad and hungry dogs,
Making their mock at our accursèd lot.
If we must die, O let us nobly die,
So that our precious blood may not be shed
In vain; then even the monsters we defy
Shall be constrained to honor us though dead!
O kinsmen! we must meet the common foe!
Though far outnumbered let us show us brave,
And for their thousand blows deal one death-blow!
What though before us lies the open grave?
Like men we'll face the murderous, cowardly pack,
Pressed to the wall, dying, but fighting back!

Courtesy of Representative Poetry Online (RPO) University of Toronto Libraries, Editor: Ian Lancashire.

A 1 2 3 Portrait of a Legend

Josefina Báez

Our deity Ciguapa arrived in New York too.

The subway steps changed her nature.
In the ups and downs to and from the silver-grey fast worms,
her feet became as everybody else's in the rush hour crowd.

She did not notice the drastic change.

This was the first sign of assimilation
-a concept not to be understood but experienced.

And Ciguapa cut her hair.
Maybe to be in vogue or just to simplify her rituals.

Her lover was not a hunter as the legend goes.
He was a medical doctor by profession
turned taxi driver by necessity.

He, the gypsy Caribbean, worked for an uptown car service: La Base Tuya.
In this base, our deity was codified to a mere 10-13.
It meant mistress or wife.
We never knew
and she never cared.

Their love was filled with few words, passionate actions,
fast merengues, tasty sancochos and predictable trips
to la remesa El Sol Sale Para Todos.

Todos. Todos! Todos?

Anyways,
These trips energized by green dollars reforested the island.

Ciguapa works in a factory making pinkish dolls.
Dolls that she never had.
Dolls dulled by the unique smell of new.
Earning less than the minimum,
she managed to pay an immigration lawyer that she never met.

She got her green card.
It was not green.

Now she prepared herself to visit the Dominican Republic.
What a triumph!!
She made it.
She made it! She made it?

Huge suitcases, bought at 14th Street were filled with unthinkable,
unnecessary items.
Items to be sold at laughable prices.
Prices calculated in dollars, paid in pesos.
Laughable reality.
She whose laugh is based on
a constant and bitter cry.

Constant nostalgia.
Bitter reality.
Unheard cry.

Here is no man's land.
Here is no woman's stand.
You can become what you are not
by circumstances, opportunity, luck, unluck, karma.

You can become a saint
or
forget your divinity.

Excerpted from Callaloo, *23, no. 3,* Dominican Republic Literature and Culture *(Summer 2000): 1038–40.*

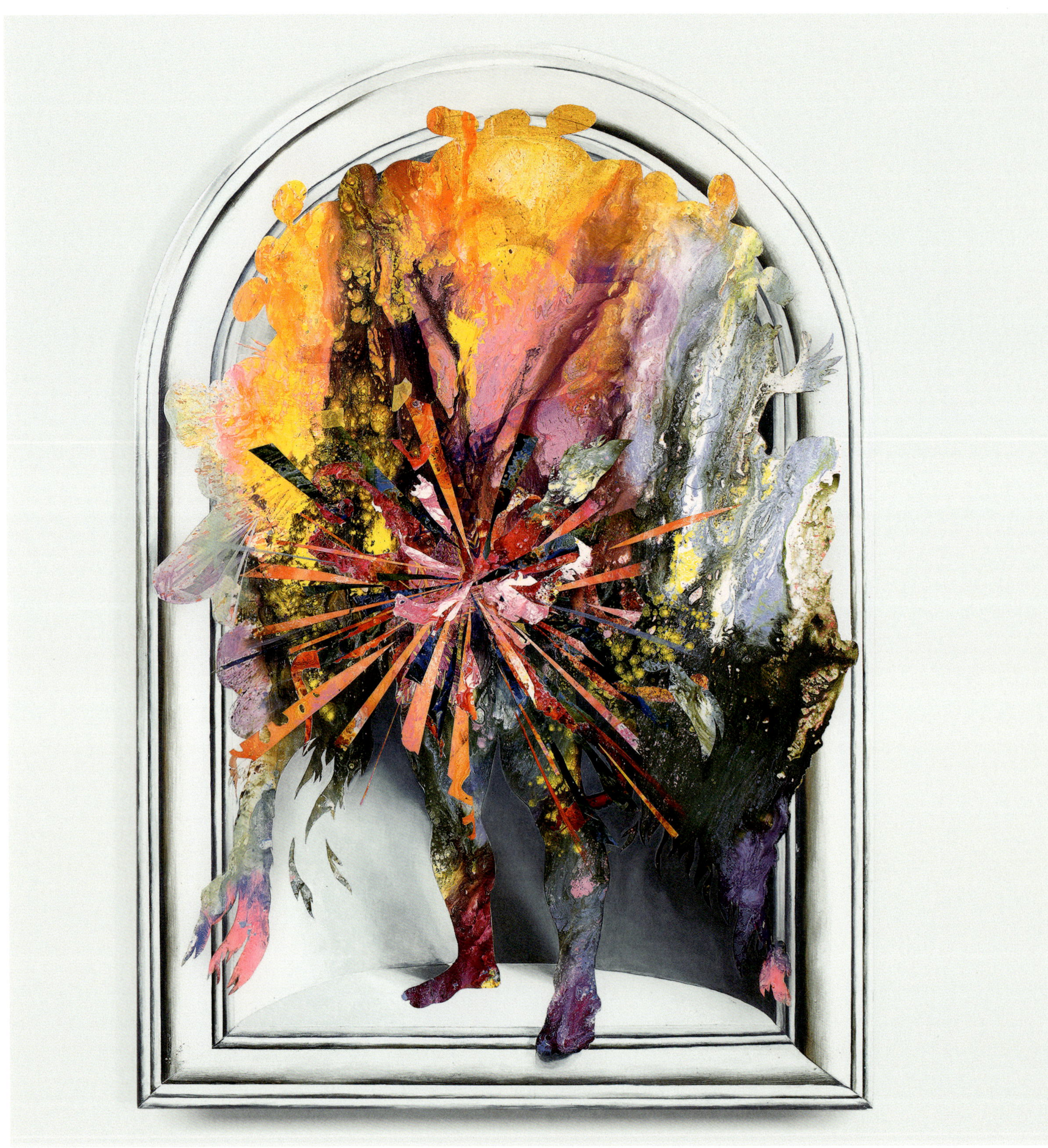

Firelei Báez, *Adjusting the Moon (The right to non-imperative clarities): Waxing,* 2019–2020

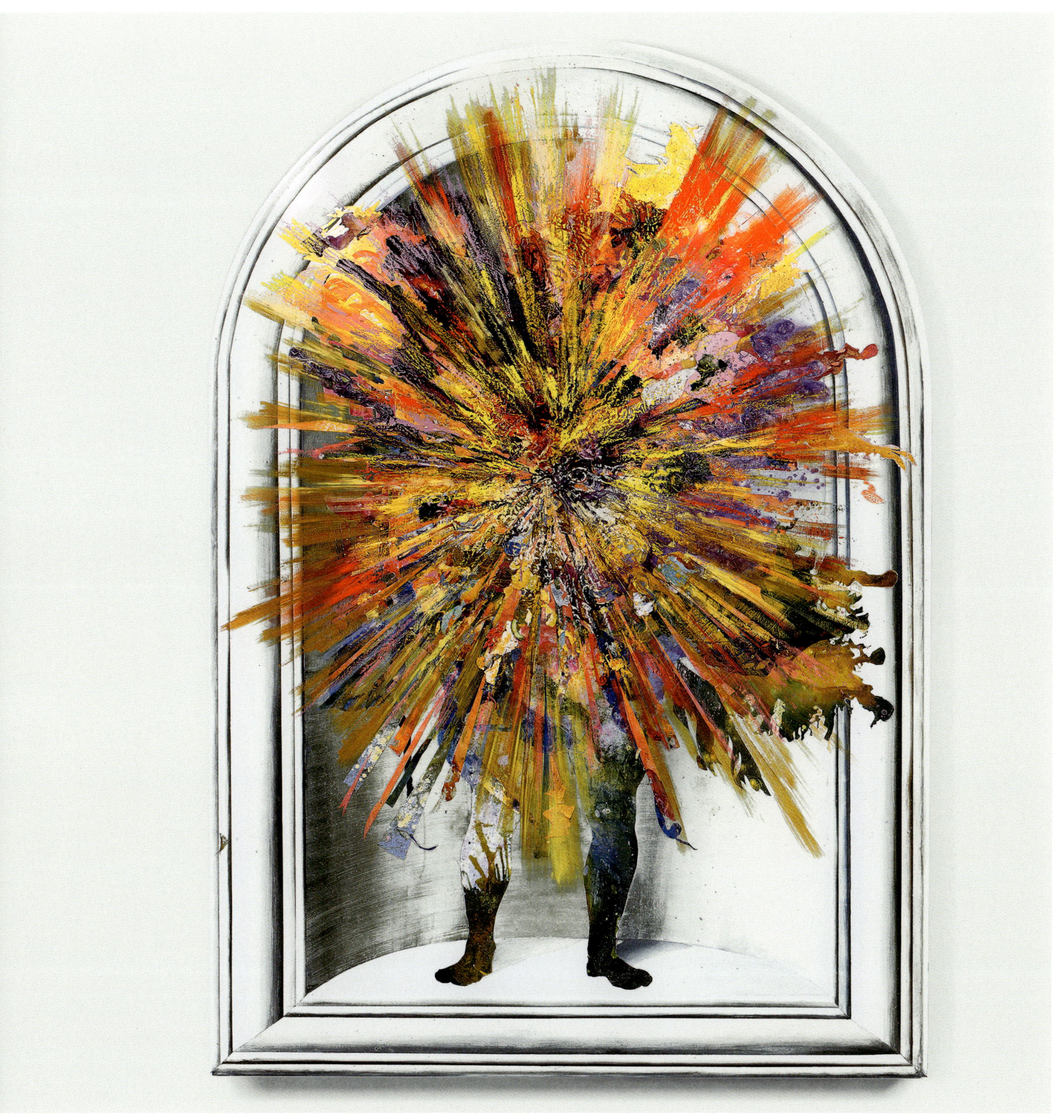

Firelei Báez, *Adjusting the Moon (The right to non-imperative clarities): Waning,* 2019–2020

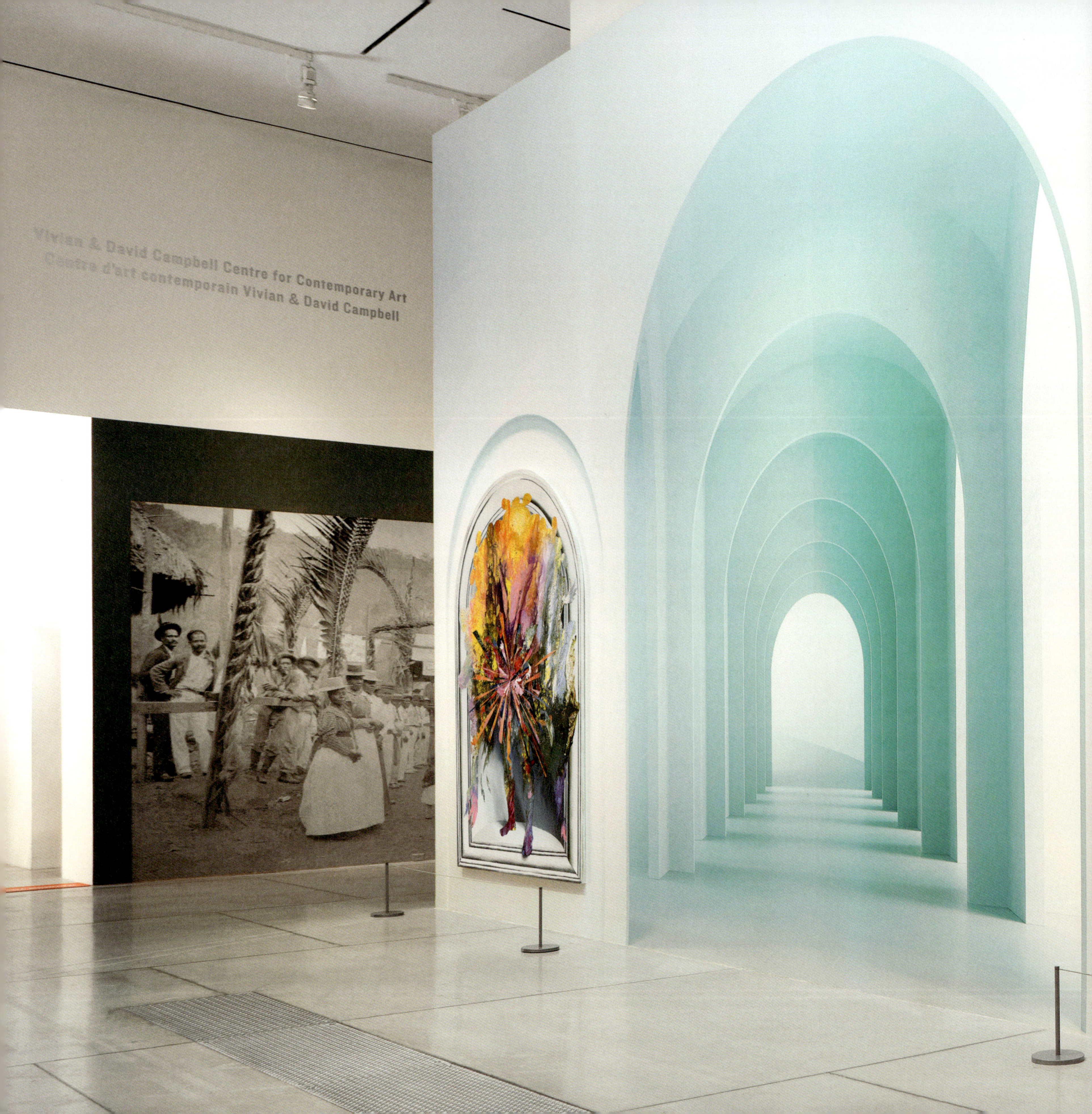

Vivian & David Campbell Centre for Contemporary Art
Centre d'art contemporain Vivian & David Campbell

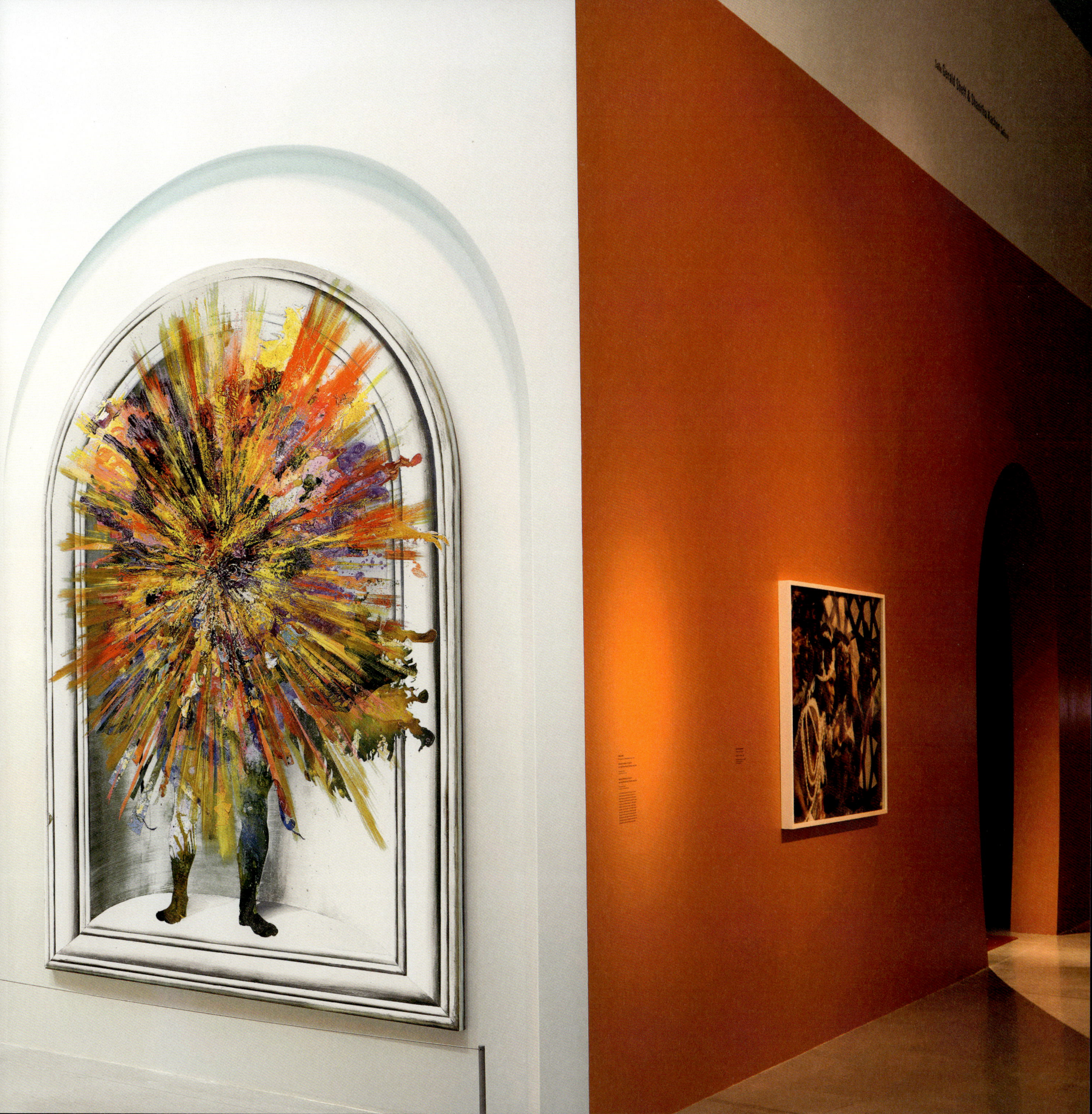

The Unity of Worlds

Kaie Kellough

billions of slow forest eyes follow me, curved and pointed at their edges

the leaves blink, the slick leaves turn and read me as i pass, a glowing amber figure, an interloper with a strange culture of concrete and wires colonizing my grey matter, the dangling vines are letters my language can't decipher, the jungle floor is fallen leaves, decomposing maps, fermenting directions, lives steaming as they sink into the earth   is fired fronds in overlapping patterns above the sun-hammered black copper floor, veined glyphs that branch and re-branch into each other, is an inchoate language simmering down into the cosmic crucible, is leaves flattened and sinking into the earth's molten core without a whisper, is the echo of the canopy's nocturnal chatter, is an infinite archive of carbon-based letterforms, is a gibberish rustle in the underbrush, is the eyelid's crocodile skin, its reptilian braille thinking, is an imprint more ancient than paper, is decomposing into the bitter, gleaming sap of a literature, is a wink in the gloaming of homo sapiens, is an organic desire to continue without hubris, heaving and exhaling a fermenting mist that drifts up between the branches, that settles into moss in the grooves of rippled trunks, that sails up into the solid beams of light rotating down through breaks in the green, up into the insectile parliament in the canopy, and up again, the earth's exhale hangs above rot and ripening alike, the forest's   jaw groans the dials of a half-million radios are tuned to the ocean, roaring white noise in the conch of georgetown jet engines launch our cellular clamor

across the magnetic equator's clouded curve, fuselage streaks down toward cheddi jagan international, suitcases straining in the cargo hold, zippers aching to burst foliage slithers out, t-shirts crinkle into petals, pant-legs cinch into vines shoes split into networks of roots, roots identical to the brown rivers' jagged graphs that pierce the terrain

books hang open paginated, lolling fronds denim seams arise green antennae receiving relative's voices cracking in through the distortion of empire's metropoles breakers surf spiralling ashore the palms transmit and receive voices of coromantee women ringing out and feeding back akan, twi, fante, bono, wasa, nzema, baule, anyi languages ground into silt word-fragments and flung by the trade winds across the entire caribbean, their phonemes salted by the sea-spray sound cured by the air the ear, this entire country an ear facing upward and listening, listening, receiving signals from the world, receiving these weeping crystals of world-stories sprinkled over its narrative canal and landing on its quivering drum

i too am nothing, *rien q'un pacquet d'eau sonore* water darker than gold, darker than what the liquid pupil can pierce, i too circulate in my charged course, am rushing, am a sonic eddy in which human voices from everywhere and every age at once dissolve standing on the bank of the potato, the verge of nihility water and earth vibrating up through rubber and marrow brown river bending along its neural course, trees' light-dappled leaves turning, conversing over either shore, spider foliage dangling

an idea forming hushed, knuckled roots clutching at soil

roots come unfastened, plunging their digits into the sepia current

a notion of home eroding where the water, where the body abrades the bank leaf-scales rippling along the potato's surface, lumbar shape-shifter, giant boa constrictor river moving under the blinking shadows, uncoiling into a numinous clearing, light slowing to signal against shadow along its surface

asemic coils unspelling over the rock drop

taut with awe, the falls' thunder bears down on being   liquid hammers
          we resonate, percussed numb   mud-gold water   charges toward the slick rocks   the body's every locked   blue atom strains   toward the current that is thoughts   we too are water, we too are ire, we too lean toward release bones and their tethering desires could liquefy and ease over   the teeth of the continent open, and we stand in the infinite library of its

rumination, pages decompose, histories compose into linked genetic alphabets, mists form, white hanging in the air, a smoke that falls upward as the water tumbles in its zigzag static   into whose charge mine would dissolve, whose power exceeds, *moi qui n'est rien qu'un pacquet d'eau sonore,* and as it rotates down toward the river's basin below, its helices carry the reptile and the howler monkey, prism of the dew, blinking, reluctant leopard of the slow eyes, marabunta poised to sting, extinction in slow electric strophes cascading   into the smoking basin into the yawning green

the force that drives the drone in our ears
in its fixed jungle course tugging at the roots, tearing at the soil
pooling in our skin, pulling our sentences into babble, sucking at our organs, our atoms
the arguments of cities in our ears
parrot's green screech and awesome question mark of the scorpion
frond's curve tonguing air, insects' hive and chatter buzzing over the roar
the falls rumble down down, all time ticks down
columbus in the slow fall entire amazonian races extinguished in a foaming
bead flying upward in a second finally released from the clock's gravita-
tion empires razed in the water's blink and the tiny golden frog, sharp as an
arrowhead watches watches

Further Reading

Archer, Melanie, and Mariel Brown, eds. *See Me Here: Contemporary Self-Portraits from the Caribbean.* Port of Spain: Robert & Christopher Publishers, 2014.

Archer-Shaw, Petrine, and Kim Robinson. *Jamaican Art: Then and Now.* Kingston, Jamaica: LMH Publishing, 2011.

Ayre, Michael. *The Caribbean in Sepia: A History in Photographs, 1840–1900.* Kingston, Jamaica: Ian Randle Publishers, Inc., 2013.

Bahadur, Gaiutra. *Coolie Woman: The Odyssey of Indenture*. Chicago: University of Chicago Press, 2013.

Bailey, David A., Alissandra Cummins, Axel Lapp, and Allison Thompson, eds. *Curating in the Caribbean.* Berlin: The Green Box, 2012.

Beckford, Sharon Morgan. *Naturally Woman: The Search for Self in Black Canadian Women's Literature*. Toronto: Inanna Publications and Education, 2012.

Boxer, David, and Veerle Poupeye. *Modern Jamaican Art.* Kingston, Jamaica: Ian Randle Publishers, 1998.

Boxer, David, and Edward Lucie-Smith. *Jamaica in Black and White: Photography in Jamaica, c.1845–c.1920; The David Boxer Collection.* London: Macmillan Caribbean, 2013.

Boyce Davies. *Caribbean Spaces: Escapes from Twilight Zones; Reflective Essays. Champaign:* University of Illinois Press, 2013.

Brand, Dionne. "'We Weren't Allowed to Go into Factory Work until Hitler Started the War': The 1920s to the 1940s." In *We're Rooted Here and They Can't Pull Us Up: Essays in African Canadian Women's History*, edited by Peggy I. Bristow, 171–191. Toronto: University of Toronto Press, 1994.
———. *Bread Out of Stone.* Toronto: Vintage Canada, 1998 [1994].

Brown, Vincent. *The Reaper's Garden: Death and Power in the World of Atlantic Slavery.* Cambridge, MA: Harvard University Press, 2008.

Browne, Kevin Adonis. High Mas: Carnival and the Poetics of Caribbean Culture. Jackson: University Press of Mississippi, 2018.

Buckridge, Steeve O. *The Language of Dress: Resistance and Accommodation in Jamaica, 1760–1890.* Kingston, Jamaica: University of the West Indies Press, 2004.

Burman, Jenny. "'Danger to the Public': Targeting and Deporting Jamaican-Born Torontonians." In *Transnational Yearnings: Tourism, Migration, and the Diasporic City*, 111–128. Vancouver: UBC Press, 2010.

Césaire, Aimé. *The Tragedy of King Christophe: A Play*. Translated by Ralph Manheim. New York: Grove Press, 1969.

Clarke, Austin. *The Meeting Point: The Toronto Trilogy.* Toronto: Vintage Canada, 2012.
———. *'Membering*. Toronto: Dundurn Press, 2015.

Cooper, Frederick, Thomas C. Holt, and Rebecca J. Scott. *Beyond Slavery: Explorations of Race, Labor, and Citizenship in Postemancipation Societies.* Chapel Hill and London: University of North Carolina Press, 2000.

Cozier, Christopher, and Tatiana Flores. *Wrestling with the Image: Caribbean Interventions.* Washington, DC: World Bank, 2011.

Cullen, Deborah, and Elvis Fuentes, eds. *Caribbean Art at the Crossroads of the World.* New York: El Museo del Barrio and New Haven: Yale University Press, 2012.

De Barros, Juanita. *Reproducing the British Caribbean: Sex, Gender, and Population Politics after Slavery*. Chapel Hill: University of North Carolina Press, 2014.

Fanon, Frantz. *Black Skin, White Masks*. New York: Grove Press, 1952.

Flores, Tatiana, and Michelle Ann Stephens, eds. *Relational Undercurrents: Contemporary Art of the Caribbean Archipelago.* Durham, NC: Duke University Press, 2017.

Flynn, Karen. *Moving Beyond Borders: A History of Black Canadian and Caribbean Women in the Diaspora.* Toronto: University of Toronto Press, 2011.

Forsythe, Dennis George. *Let the Niggers Burn!... The Sir George Williams University Affair and Its Caribbean Aftermath.* Montreal: Our Generation Press, 1971.

Foster, Cecil. *A Place Called Heaven: The Meaning of Being Black in Canada.* Toronto: HarperCollins, 2002.
———. *Where Race Does Not Matter: The New Spirit of Modernity*. Toronto: Penguin Canada, 2005.

Fuentes, Marisa J. *Dispossessed Lives: Enslaved Women, Violence, and the Archive.* Philadelphia: University of Pennsylvania Press, 2016.

Gilroy, Paul. *The Black Atlantic: Modernity and Double Consciousness.* London: Verso, 1993.

Hartman, Saidiya V. *Scenes of Subjection: Terror, Slavery and Self-Making in Nineteenth-Century America.* New York and Oxford: Oxford University Press, 1997.
———. *Lose Your Mother: A Journey Along the Atlantic Slave Route.* New York: Farrar, Straus and Giroux, 2008.

Hight, Eleanor M., and Gary D. Sampson. *Colonialist Photography: Imag(in)ing Race and Place.* New York: Routledge, 2002.

Holt, Thomas C. *The Problem of Freedom: Race, Labor, and Politics in Jamaica and Britain, 1838–1938.* Baltimore: Johns Hopkins University Press, 1992.

Kale, Madhavi. *Fragments of Empire: Capital, Slavery, and Indian Indentured Labor*

Migration in the British Caribbean. Philadelphia: University of Pennsylvania Press, 1997.

Keegan, William F., and Corinne L. Hofman. *The Caribbean before Columbus*. New York: Oxford University Press, 2017.

McKittrick, Katherine. *Demonic Grounds: Black Women and the Cartographies of Struggle*. Minneapolis: University of Minnesota Press, 2006.

Mohammed, Patricia. *Imagining the Caribbean: Culture and Visual Translation.* Basingstoke, UK: Palgrave Macmillan, 2010.

Mosaka, Tumelo, ed. *Infinite Island: Contemporary Caribbean Art*. New York: Brooklyn Museum of Art, 2007.

Newton, Melanie J. *The Children of Africa in the Colonies: Free People of Color in Barbados in the Age of Emancipation.* Baton Rouge: Louisiana State University Press, 2008.

O'Malley, Gregory E. *Final Passages: The Intercolonial Slave Trade of British America, 1619–1807*. Chapel Hill: University of North Carolina Press, 2014.

Philip, M. NourbeSe. *She Tries Her Tongue—Her Silence Softly Breaks*. Charlottetown, CA: Ragweed Press, 1989.

Poupeye, Veerle. *Caribbean Art.* London: Thames and Hudson, 1998.

Sealy, Mark. *Decolonising the Camera: Photography in Racial Time*. London, UK: Lawrence & Wishart In association with Autograph ABP, 2019.

Sheller, Mimi. *Consuming the Caribbean: From Arawaks to Zombies*. New York: Routledge, 2003.
———. *Citizenship from Below: Erotic Agency and Caribbean Freedom.* Durham, NC: Duke University Press, 2012.

Silvera, Makeda. *Piece of My Heart: A Lesbian of Colour Anthology*. Toronto: Sister Vision Press, 1991.

Smith, Cassander L., Nicholas R. Jones, and Miles P. Grier, eds. *Early Modern Black Diaspora Studies: A Critical Anthology*. London: Palgrave Macmillan, 2018.

Smith, Faith L., ed. *Sex and the Citizen: Interrogating the Caribbean.* Charlottesville and London: University of Virginia Press, 2011.

Tancons, Claire, and Krista Thompson. *En Mas': Carnival and Performance Art of the Caribbean.* New York: Independent Curators International; New Orleans: Contemporary Arts Center, 2015.

Thompson, Krista A. *An Eye for the Tropics: Tourism, Photography, and Framing the Caribbean Picturesque.* Durham, NC and London: Duke University Press, 2006.

Trexler, Richard C. *Sex and Conquest: Gendered Violence, Political Order, and the European Conquest of the Americas*. Ithaca, NY: Cornell University Press, 1999.

Trouillot, Michel-Rolph. *Silencing the Past: Power and the Production of History*. Boston, 1995.

Turner, Sasha. *Contested Bodies: Pregnancy, Childrearing, and Slavery in Jamaica.* Philadelphia: University of Pennsylvania Press, 2017.

Walcott, Rinaldo. *Black Like Who? Writing Black Canada.* Toronto: Insomniac Press, 2003.

Williams, Eric. *Capitalism and Slavery*. Chapel Hill, NC: University of North Carolina Press, 1944.

Periodicals

Anthurium: A Caribbean Studies Journal (University of Miami)

Caribbean Quarterly Journal (University of the West Indies)

Caribbean Review of Gender Studies (The University of the West Indies)

Caribbean Studies (Institute of Caribbean Studies)

Interviewing the Caribbean (University of the West Indies Press)

Journal of Caribbean History (University of the West Indies Press)

Journal of the Barbados Museum and Historical Society (Barbados Museum and Historical Society)
New West Indian Guide / Nieuwe West-Indische Gids (Brill)

Small Axe: A Journal of Criticism (smallaxe.net)

List of Works

NOTE: Objects identified with an asterisk include text with language that is outdated, reflecting the racist and colonialist attitudes of the period in which the work was produced and circulated. The titles published alongside image plates and in the List of Works have been altered to redact this language; however, visual reproductions of some historical works in this publication may include such outdated language as it exists on the objects themselves.

Objects identified with a † belong to the Art Gallery of Ontario, Montgomery Collection of Caribbean Photographs. Purchase, with funds from Dr. Liza & Dr. Frederick Murrell, Bruce Croxon & Debra Thier, Wes Hall & Kingsdale Advisors, Cindy & Shon Barnett, Donette Chin-Loy Chang, Kamala-Jean Gopie, Phil Lind & Ellen Roland, Martin Doc McKinney, Francilla Charles, Ray & Georgina Williams, Thaine & Bianca Carter, Charmaine Crooks, Nathaniel Crooks, Andrew Garrett & Dr. Belinda Longe, Neil L. Le Grand, Michael Lewis, Dr. Kenneth Montague & Sarah Aranha, Lenny & Julia Mortimore, and The Ferrotype Collective, 2019.

Objects identified with a †† belong to the Art Gallery of Ontario, Montgomery Collection of Caribbean Photographs. Gift of Patrick Montgomery, through the American Friends of the Art Gallery of Ontario Inc., 2019.

Listed dimensions of the Montgomery Collection reflect the object's overall dimensions, not necessarily the print size.

George Adhar
Active San Fernando, Trinidad and Tobago

Three Chinese Girls in Trinidad
c. 1900
Cabinet card: gelatin silver print mounted on cardstock
16.0 × 10.5 cm
Collection of Helen and Keith Atteck
Photo: Keith Atteck
Page 194

Hurvin Anderson
Born Birmingham, England, 1965

Rose Avenue (Drawing)
2006
Acrylic on paper in three parts
21 × 30 cm (each)
Private collection
© Hurvin Anderson
Image courtesy the artist and Thomas Dane Gallery; photo: Matthew Hollow
Pages 84–85

Sybil Atteck
Born Rio Claro, Trinidad and Tobago, 1911; died Port of Spain, Trinidad and Tobago, 1975

Self-Portrait
1973
Acrylic on board
59.69 × 44.45 cm; framed: 71.12 × 55.88 × 2.54 cm
Collection of Helen and Keith Atteck
© Sybil Atteck Estate
Photo: Keith Atteck
Page 195

Belkis Ayón
Born and died Havana, Cuba, 1967–1999

Untitled (Sikán with staff) [Sin Título (Sikan con baston)]
1991
Serigraph
47.5 × 64 cm
Alex Jackson Collection, 91.12
Copyright © Belkis Ayón Estate, Havana, Cuba.
Photo: Art Gallery of Ontario
Page 112

Untitled [Sin Título]
c. 1998
Collagraph
75.5 × 56.5 cm
Armand-Paul Family Collection, 98.11
Copyright © Belkis Ayón Estate, Havana, Cuba.
Photo: Art Gallery of Ontario
Page 113

Firelei Báez
Born Santiago de los Caballeros, Dominican Republic, 1981

Adjusting the Moon (The right to non-imperative clarities): Waxing
2019–2020
Oil and acrylic on panel
289.6 × 198.1 × 3.8 cm
Private collection, Toronto, Canada
© Firelei Báez
Image courtesy of the artist and James Cohan, New York
Page 246

Adjusting the Moon (The right to non-imperative clarities): Waning
2019–2020
Oil and acrylic on panel
289.6 × 198.1 × 3.8 cm
The Komal Shah & Gaurav Garg Collection
© Firelei Báez
Image courtesy of the artist and James Cohan, New York
Page 247

Sir Frank Bowling
Born Bartica, Guyana, 1934

Middle Passage
1970
Acrylic paint and oil-based ink on canvas
319.9 × 280.3 cm
National Gallery of Canada, Ottawa, promised gift of Michael Nesbitt, Winnipeg
SLB-2021.0008.1
© Frank Bowling / SOCAN (2021)
Photo: NGC
Page 57

Mother's House and Night Storm
1967
Acrylic on canvas
148.6 × 117.5 cm
Sheldon Inwentash and Lynn Factor, Toronto
© Frank Bowling / SOCAN (2021)
Image courtesy Hales, London and New York; photo by JSP Art Photography, Stan Narten
Page 6

Sandra Brewster
Born Toronto, Canada, 1973

Feeding Trafalgar Square
2021
Gel medium photo transfer, charcoal, and acrylic on wood
3 panels: 304.8 × 66 cm; 304.8 × 142.2 cm; 304.8 × 121.9 cm
Art Gallery of Ontario, commission, with funds from the Women's Art Initiative, 2021
2021/71
© Sandra Brewster
Photo: Art Gallery of Ontario
Page 211

Vanley Burke
Born St. Andrew, Jamaica, 1951

Boy with flag, Winford in Handsworth Park
1970
Archival pigment print
41.28 × 27.94 cm
Courtesy of artist Vanley Burke and BAND Gallery
© Vanley Burke
Page 157

Protesting against racism and police brutality
1972
Archival pigment print
66.04 × 66.04 cm
Courtesy of the artist
© Vanley Burke
Page 156

Young men on a see-saw in Handsworth Park
1984
Archival pigment print
27.94 × 41.28 cm
Courtesy of artist Vanley Burke and BAND Gallery
© Vanley Burke
Page 156

Charles Campbell
Born Kingston, Jamaica, 1970

Maroonscape 1: Cockpit Archipelago
2019
Mat board and wood
Dimensions variable
Collection of the Vancouver Art Gallery, Audain BC Art Acquisition Fund
VAG 2021.2.1
© Charles Campbell
Image courtesy of Wil Aballe Art Projects / WAAP and the artist; photo: Michael Love
Page 153
Photo: Art Gallery of Ontario
Page 152

Maroonscape 2: Yet Every Child
2020
Audio soundscape
Collection of the Vancouver Art Gallery, gift of the artist
VAG 2021.5.1
© Charles Campbell
** not illustrated

Robert Charlotte
Born Shœlcher, Martinique, 1966

Farmer with Dog
2014
From *Garifuna Indigenous*
Archival pigment print; printed 2021
150 × 100 cm
Courtesy of the artist
© Robert Charlotte
Page 185

Luci Collins and Son
2014
From *Garifuna Indigenous*
Archival pigment print; printed 2021
100 × 150 cm
Courtesy of the artist
© Robert Charlotte
Page 184

Andrea Chung
Born Newark, New Jersey, United States, 1978

A Litany for Survival
2019
Cyanotype and sugar
170.2 × 228.6 cm
Courtesy of the artist and Tyler Park Presents, Los Angeles
© Andrea Chung
Image courtesy of the artist, Klowden Mann, and Tyler Park Presents, Los Angeles; photo: Michael Underwood
Pages 70–71

June Clark
Born New York City, New York, United States, 1941

Untitled
1972
Gelatin silver print
45.7 × 25.4 cm
Courtesy of the artist and Daniel Faria Gallery, Toronto
© June Clark
Page 218

Untitled
1972
Gelatin silver print
45.7 cm x 25.4 cm
Courtesy of the artist and Daniel Faria Gallery, Toronto
© June Clark
Page 219

John William Cleary
Active Kingston, Jamaica, c. 1880–c. 1920

A Family, Jamaica †
c. 1890
Albumen print
18.5 × 21.8 cm
2019/789
Photo: Art Gallery of Ontario
Page 175

Coconut Palms, Kingston Harbour, Jamaica ††
c. 1895
Gelatin silver print
17.6 × 23.1 cm
2019/3069
Photo: Art Gallery of Ontario
Page 114

Christopher Cozier
Born Port of Spain, Trinidad and Tobago, 1959
NOW SHOWING 12:30
2010–2012
Mixed media on paper
149.9 × 152.4 cm; framed: 171.45 × 171.45 × 6.35 cm
Collection of Dr. Carlyle Farrell
© Christopher Cozier
Image courtesy of the artist
Page 236

John J. Donnatien
Born England, 1872, active Trinidad and Tobago; death date and location unknown

Melanie Longchallon and Elizabeth George
c. 1899
Cabinet card: gelatin silver print mounted on cardstock
16.4 × 11.0 cm
Collection of Helen and Keith Atteck
** not illustrated

A. Duperly & Sons
Active Kingston, Jamaica, c. 1843–c. 1950

Blue Hole, Portland, Jamaica †
c. 1900
Gelatin silver print
17.8 × 23.2 cm
2019/681
Photo: Art Gallery of Ontario
Page 115

Jeannette Ehlers
Born Copenhagen, Denmark, 1973

Black Bullets
2012
Single-channel video (black-and-white, sound, 4 min. 33 sec.)
Courtesy of the artist
© Jeannette Ehlers
Pages 176–177

Gaston Fabre
Born French Guiana or Saint-Pierre, Martinique, 1827; died Kingston, Jamaica, c. 1899

Woman, Martinique †
c. 1890s
Albumen print
26.1 × 19.4 cm
2019/367

Photo: Art Gallery of Ontario
Page 42

Foto Apolo
Nationality and dates unknown

Woman with Two Young Girls
c. 1905
Postcard: gelatin silver print
14.0 × 8.9 cm
Armand-Paul Family Collection
Photo: Art Gallery of Ontario
Page 192

Roy Francis
Born Kingston, Jamaica, 1933; died Waterloo, Ontario, Canada, 2018

Caribana
1982
Super 8mm film converted to digital video (colour, sound, 6 min. 5 sec.)
Filmed by Roy Francis, courtesy of Aaron T. Francis / Vintage Black Canada
** not illustrated

W.H. Freeman

Church of St. Matthias, Barbados
1853
Daguerreotype
11 × 14 cm
Private collection
Image courtesy of Archive of Modern Conflict, Toronto
Page 59

H.M.S. Dauntless in Quarantine for Yellow Fever Outbreak
1853
Daguerreotype
7 × 9 cm
Private collection
Image courtesy of Archive of Modern Conflict, Toronto
Page 58

Gomo George
Born London, England, 1957

Women's Carnival Group
1996
Watercolour on rag paper
Image: 55.25 × 74.93 cm; paper: 55.88 × 76.20 cm
Courtesy of the artist
© Gomo George
Image courtesy of the artist
Page 221

Abigail Hadeed
Born Trinidad and Tobago, 1963

The Dying Swan — Ras Nijinsky in Drag as Pavlova
2016
Archival pigment ink print; printed in 2021
Image: 20.32 × 30.48 cm; paper: 25.40 × 35.56 cm
Courtesy of the artist
© 2021 Abigail Hadeed
Page 220

Nadia Huggins
Born Port of Spain, Trinidad and Tobago, 1984

Circa no future
2016–2019
Single-channel video (colour, sound, 3 min.)
Courtesy of the artist, 2021
© Nadia Huggins
Pages 144–145

Transformations No. 1
2015
Digital photographs printed on ChromaLuxe; printed 2021
76.2 × 118.1 cm (both panels + 3.8 cm separation)
Courtesy of the artist, 2021
© Nadia Huggins
Page 209

Leasho Johnson
Born Montego Bay, Jamaica, 1984

Jaw bone (man looking back at the cane fields)
2019
Charcoal, watercolour, distemper, acrylic, oil stick, and oil paint on canvas
76.2 × 60.96 × 2.54 cm
Art Gallery of Ontario, purchase, with funds from Friends of Global Africa and the Diaspora, 2021
2021/30
© Leasho Johnson
Photo: Art Gallery of Ontario
Page 237

Sweet Sugarcane (Female Figure)
2014
Oil on canvas
63.5 × 50.8 cm; framed: 72.39 × 59.69 cm
Collection of Dr. Carlyle Farrell
© Leasho Johnson
Photo: Art Gallery of Ontario
Page 130

Sweet Sugarcane (Male Figure)
2014
Oil on canvas
63.5 × 50.8 cm; framed: 72.39 × 59.69 cm
Collection of Dr. Carlyle Farrell
© Leasho Johnson
Photo: Art Gallery of Ontario
Page 131

Reverend Dr. James Johnston
Born Scotland, 1851; died Saint D'Acre, Jamaica, 1921

Domestics with Yams and Cocoanuts †
c. 1895
Albumen print mounted on cardstock
18.3 × 22.7 cm
2019/812
Photo: Art Gallery of Ontario
Page 43

Pineapple Field †
c. 1890
Albumen print
19.0 × 24.3 cm
2019/819
Photo: Art Gallery of Ontario
Page 60

Roshini Kempadoo
Born Crawley, England, 1959

Ghosting
2004
Set of four archival pigment prints; printed 2021
77.47 × 127 cm
Courtesy of the artist
© Roshini Kempadoo
Pages 82–83

Wifredo Lam
Born Sagua la Grande, Cuba, 1902; died Paris, France, 1982

Mayombè
1962
Oil and charcoal on canvas
127.4 × 110.6 cm
The Montreal Museum of Fine Arts, on loan from a private collection
449.2018
© ADAGP, Paris / SOCAN, Montreal (2021)
Photo: The Montreal Museum of Fine Arts, Christine Guest
Page 111

Diane Liverpool
Born Montreal, Quebec, Canada, 1958

"Face of the Panther Mas" — Caribana parade on University Avenue
1981
Resin coated gelatin silver print
31 × 25.2 cm
Art Gallery of Ontario
Purchase, with funds

from Lorne Gertner, 2021
2021/48
© Diane Liverpool
Photo: Art Gallery of Ontario
Page 223

"He came out to play Mas" — Caribana parade on University Avenue
1981
Resin coated gelatin silver print
25.3 × 20.3 cm
Art Gallery of Ontario
Purchase, with funds from Lorne Gertner, 2021
2021/47
© Diane Liverpool
Photo: Art Gallery of Ontario
Page 222

Suchitra Mattai
Born Georgetown, Guyana, 1973

Demerara Dreams
2019
Artist's mother's sari, gouache, acrylic, faux flower, and oil on printed fabric
167.64 × 132.08 cm
Courtesy of Paul and Heather Wilkinson
© Suchitra Mattai
Photo: Wes Magyar
Page 197

Manuel Matthieu
Born Port-au-Prince, Haiti, 1986

Lye
2018
Acrylic, oil stick, charcoal, spray paint, tape, and chalk on canvas
190.5 × 203.2 cm
Hydro-Québec Collection
© Manuel Mathieu
Photo: Guy L'Heureux
Page 210

Felix Morin
French, active Trinidad and Tobago, Martinique, and Venezuela, c. 1869–c. 1896

Bananas, Trinidad †
c. 1890
Albumen print
22.2 × 16.7 cm
2019/2225
Photo: Art Gallery of Ontario
Page 96

Soursop Fruit (Anonna Muricata or Corossol) †
c. 1890
Albumen print
24.5 × 19.8 cm
2019/389
Photo: Art Gallery of Ontario
Page 96

Woman, Trinidad †
c. 1890
Albumen print
21.3 × 14.9 cm
2019/2209
Photo: Art Gallery of Ontario
Page 81

Woman with Clay Vessel, Trinidad †
c. 1895
Albumen print mounted on cardstock
23.0 × 17.0 cm
2019/414
Photo: Art Gallery of Ontario
Page 121

Dennis Morris
Born Jamaica, 1960

The Brothers at the Black House
1972
Giclée print
85.41 × 57.47 cm; framed: 109.22 × 83.82 cm
Dr. Kenneth Montague / The Wedge Collection, Toronto
© Dennis Morris
Image courtesy of the artist and Dr. Kenneth Montague / The Wedge Collection, Toronto
Page 171

MC & Selector — Count Shelly Sound System
1972
Giclée print
57.47 × 85.41 cm; framed: 83.82 × 109.22 cm
Dr. Kenneth Montague / The Wedge Collection, Toronto
© Dennis Morris
Image courtesy of the artist and Dr. Kenneth Montague / The Wedge Collection, Toronto
Page 170

Wendy Nanan
Born Port of Spain, Trinidad and Tobago, 1955

Nelson Island
2012
Papier-mâché and acrylic
30.48 × 53.34 × 106.68 cm
Courtesy of the artist
© Wendy Nanan; Nelson Island, 2012
Photo: Art Gallery of Ontario
Page 123

J. Nunez
Active Havana, Cuba, dates unknown

Woman with a Hat and a Bouquet
c. 1919
Postcard: gelatin silver print
14.0 × 8.9 cm
Armand-Paul Family Collection
Photo: Art Gallery of Ontario
** not illustrated

Zak Ové
Born London, England, 1966

Moko Jumbie
2021
Steel scaffold pipe, bamboo, auto body filler, aluminum, aluminum pipe, fibreglass, nylon fishing line, brass water jugs, brass chain mail, burlap, Nike Air Jordans, cotton doilies, and glass beads
Dimensions variable
Art Gallery of Ontario, commission, with funds from David W. Binet and Ray & Georgina Williams, 2021
2021/70
© Zak Ové
Photo: Art Gallery of Ontario
Page 12

Ebony G. Patterson
Born Kingston, Jamaica, 1981

...three kings weep...
2018
Three-channel video (colour, sound, 8 min. 34 sec.)
Art Gallery of Ontario, purchase, with funds from the Photography Curatorial Committee, 2020
2019/2469
© Ebony G. Patterson
Photo: Art Gallery of Ontario
Page 241

Publishers Photo Service
American, active c. 1910s–c. 1930s

Wood Collectors, Kingston, Jamaica †
c. 1920
Gelatin silver print
18.7 × 25.2 cm
2019/233
Photo: Art Gallery of Ontario
Page 109

Peter Dean Rickards / The Afflicted Yard
Born Kingston, Jamaica, 1969; died Brampton, Ontario, Canada, 2014

Proverbs 24:10
2008
Video (black-and-white,

sound, 2 min. 35 sec.)
Courtesy of The Estate of Peter Dean Rickards — Diana and Peter Rickards Trustees
© The Estate of Peter Dean Rickards / The Afflicted Yard
Pages 132–133

Sellier's Studio
Active Port of Spain, Trinidad and Tobago, 1881 to c. 1936

Fanny McLean (née Atteck), Oliver and Amy
c. 1894
Cabinet card: gelatin silver print mounted on cardstock
10 × 6.5 cm
Collection of Helen and Keith Atteck
** not illustrated

George Peter McLean Family
1890
Cabinet card: gelatin silver print mounted on cardstock
16.0 × 10.5 cm
Collection of Helen and Keith Atteck
Photo: Keith Atteck
Page 194

Margaret Jonah-Young and Son
c. 1920
Cabinet card: gelatin silver print mounted on cardstock
16.5 × 11.0 cm
Collection of Helen and Keith Atteck
** not illustrated

Kelly Sinnapah Mary
Born Les Abymes, Guadeloupe, 1981

Notebook of No Return
2017
Acrylic on paper
43.2 × 50.8 cm
Private collection
© Kelly Sinnapah Mary
Photo: Art Gallery of Ontario
Page 80

Paul Anthony Smith
Born St. Ann's Bay, Jamaica, 1988

Midnight Blue
2020
Unique picotage on inkjet print with oil stick and spray paint, mounted on museum board and Sintra
243.84 × 173.67 cm; framed: 247.65 × 177.48 × 7.30 cm
Courtesy of the artist and Jack Shainman Gallery, New York
© Paul Anthony Smith
Image courtesy of the artist and Jack Shainman Gallery, New York
Page 225

Untitled, 7 Women
2019
Unique picotage on inkjet print, coloured pencil, and spray paint on museum board
101.6 × 127 cm; framed: 104.14 × 129.54 × 4.45 cm
The Hott Collection, New York
© Paul Anthony Smith
Image courtesy of the artist and Jack Shainman Gallery, New York
Page 224

Unknown photographer

Aunt Doris
c. 1940
Postcard: gelatin silver print
15.2 × 10.2 cm
Courtesy Aaron T. Francis / Vintage Black Canada
Photo: Art Gallery of Ontario
Page 193

Boiler House at Spring Hall, St. Lucy, Barbados †
c. 1900
Gelatin silver print
14.8 × 20.2 cm
2019/294
Photo: Art Gallery of Ontario
Page 52

Boys Diving for Coins, St. Lucia †
c. 1887
Albumen print
17.5 × 22.5 cm
2019/609
Photo: Art Gallery of Ontario
Page 143

Boy with optical device at market †
Location unknown, c. 1915
Gelatin silver print
In *West Indies (Cuba, Puerto Rico, Jamaica, Panama)*, c. 1915
Album: 29 pages with gelatin silver prints
27.9 × 20.3 cm
2019/2188
Photo: Art Gallery of Ontario
Page 32

Coaling The Albatross, St. Lucia †
after 1882
Albumen print
18.2 × 23.0 cm
2019/606
Photo: Art Gallery of Ontario
Page 55

Coffee Plantation, Port of Spain, Trinidad †
c. 1890
Gelatin silver print
17.4 × 23.0 cm
2019/2236
Photo: Art Gallery of Ontario
Page 54

Drying Cacao, Trinidad ††
1910
Gelatin silver print mounted on cardstock
24.5 × 30.3 cm
Published by The Philadelphia Museums
2019/9402
Photo: Art Gallery of Ontario
Page 86

Emancipation Day, Jamaica, August 1 ††
c. 1895
Album page: gelatin silver print mounted on cardstock
10.7 × 15 cm (print); 29.3 x 23.9 cm (cardstock)
2019/2704
Photo: Art Gallery of Ontario
Pages 28–29

Group Portrait, Jamaica †† *Emancipation Day, Jamaica, August 1*
c. 1895
Album page: two gelatin silver prints mounted on cardstock
2019/2704
** not illustrated

Family at Home, Blue Mountains, Jamaica *††
c. 1890
Album page: albumen print mounted on cardstock
24.8 × 34.7 cm
2019/3075
Photo: Art Gallery of Ontario
Page 174

Family in Garden, Jamaica ††
c. 1890
Gelatin silver print
15.5 × 20.8 cm
2019/9840
Photo: Art Gallery of Ontario
Page 173

Family Picnic, Bermuda †
1887
Albumen print mounted on cardstock
39.3 × 27.9 cm
2019/2137
Photo: Art Gallery of Ontario
Page 172

Festival, Trinidad †
c. 1890
Platinum print mounted on cardstock
21.8 × 26.2 cm
2019/411
Photo: Art Gallery of Ontario
Page 44

Grand Tour through the United Kingdom ††
1906
Postcard: halftone print
8.7 × 13.8 cm
2019/9732
Photo: Art Gallery of Ontario
Page 191

Harriette Thomas Weekes, nurse with her infant charge
c. 1858
Ambrotype
10.7 × 8.3 cm; framed:
12 × 9.5 cm
From the collection of the Barbados Museum and Historical Society
Acc No. 957.62
Page 63

Jamaican Women †
c. 1900
Gelatin silver print
17.5 × 23.5 cm
2019/2210
Photo: Art Gallery of Ontario
Page 97

Market, Fort de France, Martinique ††
c. 1905
Gelatin silver print mounted on cardstock
16.7 × 23.8 cm
2019/2860
Photo: Art Gallery of Ontario
Page 87

Officer, Haiti †
c. 1880
Albumen print
29.8 × 21.9 cm
2019/672
Photo: Art Gallery of Ontario
Page 120

Old Man, Trinidad ††
c. 1900
Gelatin silver print
16.0 × 11.2 cm
2019/2773
Photo: Art Gallery of Ontario
Page 199

Portrait of a Lady
1850s–1860s
Ambrotype
7.8 × 6.7 cm; framed:
10.4 × 8.6 cm
From the collection of the Barbados Museum and Historical Society
Acc No. 970.11
Page 62

Seated Woman
c. 1936
Postcard: gelatin silver print
14.0 × 8.9 cm
Armand-Paul Family Collection
** not illustrated

Sisters
c. 1940
Postcard: gelatin silver print
15.2 × 10.2 cm
Courtesy Aaron T. Francis / Vintage Black Canada
Photo: Art Gallery of Ontario
Page 193

Snake Charmer, Martinique ††
c. 1880
Albumen print mounted on cardstock
14.8 × 12.3 cm
2019/2879
Photo: Art Gallery of Ontario
Page 108

Sugar Cane Workers, Barbados †
c. 1890
Gelatin silver print
20.0 × 24.5 cm
2019/329
Photo: Art Gallery of Ontario
Page 53

Sybil Atteck Going to a Wedding
April 22, 1937
Postcard: gelatin silver print
13.7 × 8.7 cm
Collection of Helen and Keith Atteck
Photo: Keith Atteck
Page 194

The Choir from Jamaica *†
c. 1905
Postcard: halftone print
8.7 × 13.8 cm
2019/1202
Photo: Art Gallery of Ontario
Page 190

White River, Jamaica †
c. 1915
Gelatin silver print
20.7 × 25.4 cm
2019/266
Photo: Art Gallery of Ontario
Page 45

Woman, Trinidad ††
c. 1890
Albumen print
15.0 × 10.2 cm
2019/2769
Photo: Art Gallery of Ontario
Page 198

Woman with Basket on Head ††
c. 1895
Cyanotype
9.9 × 12.5 cm
2019/9349
Photo: Art Gallery of Ontario
Page 68

Woman with Roses
c. 1919
Postcard: gelatin silver print
14.0 × 8.9 cm
Armand-Paul Family Collection
** not illustrated

Unknown photographer(s)

Passport photographs of Haitian immigrant workers in Cuba
1957–1960
5 gelatin silver prints (sizes vary from 4.1 × 3.3 cm to 5.7 × 6.3 cm)
Courtesy of Centre International de Documentation et d'Information Haïtienne, Caribéenne et Afro-canadienne (CIDHICA)
Photo: Art Gallery of Ontario
Pages 200–201

Unknown photographer for *White Star Line*

Diving for Coins, Barbados †
c. 1890
Gelatin silver print
20.5 × 25.5 cm
2019/342
Photo: Art Gallery of Ontario
Page 142

J. Valentine & Sons
Scottish, active 1851–1994

A Bit in Kingston Harbor ††
1891
Albumen print mounted on cardstock
21.9 × 25.5 cm
2019/3070
Photo: Art Gallery of Ontario
Page 69

Crossing a River ††
1891
Albumen print mounted on cardstock
24.3 × 34.1 cm
2019/1976
Photo: Art Gallery of Ontario
Page 61

The Mountains from Castleton Road, Jamaica †
1891
Albumen print
24.6 × 30.0 cm
2019/831
Photo: Art Gallery of Ontario
Page 151

Various unknown makers

Excerpts from vintage travel films
1920s to 1970s
16mm film converted to digital video (black and white/colour, silent, 6 min. 47 sec.)

Patrick Montgomery /
The Travel Film Archive
** not illustrated

Frank Walter
Born Horsford Hill, Antigua and Barbuda, 1926; died St. John's, Antigua and Barbuda, 2009

Complex of Life
1960
Oil on Masonite
25.5 × 50.5 cm; framed: 33 × 58.5 cm
Private collection
© Courtesy Sir Selvyn and Kathleen, Lady Walter
Photo: Kenneth M. Milton Fine Arts
Page 98

Plantation Fields and Workers
c. 1968–c. 1974
Oil on cardboard
31.8 × 45 cm; framed: 46 × 57 cm
Private collection
© Courtesy Sir Selvyn and Kathleen, Lady Walter
Photo: Kenneth M. Milton Fine Arts
Page 99

Rodell Warner
Born Port of Spain, Trinidad and Tobago, 1986

Augmented Archive 011 (colourized)
2020
Single-channel video with sound
Dimensions variable
Courtesy of the artist
© Rodell Warner
Page 239

Augmented Archive 015 (colourized)
2020
Single-channel video with sound
Dimensions variable
Courtesy of the artist
© Rodell Warner
Page 239

Augmented Archive 020 (colourized)
2021
Single-channel video with sound
Dimensions variable
Courtesy of the artist
© Rodell Warner
Page 239

Augmented Archive 021 (colourized)
2021
Single-channel video with sound
Dimensions variable
Courtesy of the artist
© Rodell Warner
Page 238

Dorothy Henriques Wells
Born Kingston, Jamaica, 1926; died Miami, Florida, United States, 2018

The Blue Mountains
1996–1997
Watercolour
56 × 76 cm
Courtesy of Dorothy Henriques Wells Private Collection
© Dorothy Henriques Wells Estate
Page 124

Wild Banana
1990
Watercolour
56 × 76 cm
Courtesy of Kirk Davis, Bahamas
© Dorothy Henriques Wells Estate
Page 125

Alberta Whittle
Born Bridgetown, Barbados, 1980

business as usual: hostile environment
2020
Single-channel video (colour, sound, 16 min.)
Courtesy of the artist and Copperfield London
© Alberta Whittle
Pages 154–55

Aubrey Williams
Born Georgetown, Guyana, 1926; died London, England, 1990

Carib Form
1962
Mixed media on paper
35.56 × 43.18 cm; framed: 64.77 × 72.39 × 6.35 cm
Collection of Dr. Carlyle Farrell
© Aubrey Williams Estate
Photo: Art Gallery of Ontario
Page 116

Solar Rad 1
1988
Oil on canvas
Collection of Dr. Carlyle Farrell
© Aubrey Williams Estate
Photo: Art Gallery of Ontario
Page 117

Natalie Wood
Born Port of Spain, Trinidad and Tobago, 1965

Mazalee (crossed)
2012
Gesso and deconstructed cardboard
60.96 × 45.72 cm
Dr. Kenneth Montague / The Wedge Collection, Toronto
© Natalie Wood
Image courtesy of Paul Petro Contemporary Art, Toronto; photo: Toni Hafkenscheid
Page 147

Land Acknowledgement

The Art Gallery of Ontario operates on land that is the territory of the Anishinaabe (Mississauga) nation and is also the territory of the Wendat and Haudenosaunee. The Dish with One Spoon Wampum Belt Covenant is an agreement between the Haudenosaunee Confederacy and the Anishinaabe Three Fires Confederacy to peaceably share and care for the resources around the Great Lakes. Toronto is also governed by a treaty between the federal government of Canada and the Mississaugas of the New Credit (Anishinaabe nation). Toronto has always been a trading centre for First Nations.

Credits

Thank You

Lead Sponsor

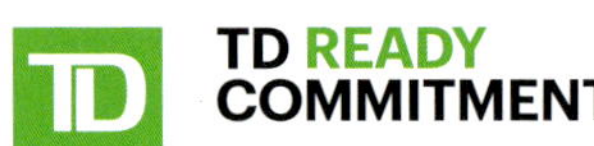

Supporting Sponsor

Panasonic

Contributing Sponsor

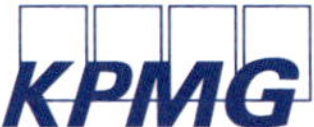

Generous Support

Phil Lind & Ellen Roland
Volunteers of the AGO
Women's Art Initiative

Generous Assistance

Cindy & Shon Barnett
David W. Binet
Dr. Carlyle Farrell
Friends of Global Africa & the Diaspora
The Michael Young Family Foundation

The Art Gallery of Ontario is partially funded by the Ontario Ministry of Culture. Additional operating support is received from the City of Toronto and the Department of Canadian Heritage. This publication is supported by the Sorel Etrog Publication Fund.

Contemporary programming at the Art Gallery of Ontario is supported by

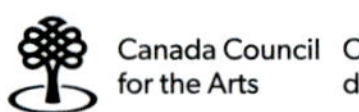

Library and Archives Canada Cataloguing in Publication

Title: *Fragments of epic memory.*
Names: Crooks, Julie, 1962- organizer. | Art Gallery of Ontario, publisher, host institution.
Description: Curated by Julie Crooks. | Catalogue of an exhibition held at the Art Gallery of Ontario from September 1, 2021 to February 21, 2022.
Identifiers: Canadiana 20210340304 | ISBN 9781636810126 (hardcover)
Subjects: LCSH: Art, Caribbean—21st century—Exhibitions. | LCSH: Artists—Caribbean Area—Exhibitions. | LCSH: African diaspora in art—Exhibitions. | LCSH: History in art—Exhibitions. | LCSH: Collective memory in art—Exhibitions. | LCSH: Caribbean Area—Pictorial works—Exhibitions. | LCGFT: Exhibition catalogs.
Classification: LCC N6591. F73 2021 | DDC 709.729074/713541—dc23

This book was published on the occasion of the exhibition *Fragments of Epic Memory,* organized by the Art Gallery of Ontario from September 1, 2021, to February 21, 2022.

Published in 2021 by the Art Gallery of Ontario and DelMonico Books • D.A.P.

Art Gallery of Ontario
317 Dundas Street West
Toronto, Ontario M5T 1G4
Canada
www.ago.ca

DelMonico Books
available through
ARTBOOK | D.A.P.
75 Broad Street, Suite 630
New York, NY 10004
artbook.com
delmonicobooks.com

Printed and bound in Belgium

ISBN: 978-1-63681-012-6

10 9 8 7 6 5 4 3 2 1

Front Cover Images

Nadia Huggins, *Circa no future,* 2016–2019. Still from single-channel video (colour, sound, 3 min.). Courtesy of the artist, 2021. © Nadia Huggins. Photo: Nadia Huggins.

Unknown photographer, *Boys Diving for Coins, St. Lucia,* c. 1887. Albumen print, 17.5 × 22.5 cm. Art Gallery of Ontario, Montgomery Collection of Caribbean Photographs. Purchase, with funds from Dr. Liza & Dr. Frederick Murrell, Bruce Croxon & Debra Thier, Wes Hall & Kingsdale Advisors, Cindy & Shon Barnett, Donette Chin-Loy Chang, Kamala-Jean Gopie, Phil Lind & Ellen Roland, Martin Doc McKinney, Francilla Charles, Ray & Georgina Williams, Thaine & Bianca Carter, Charmaine Crooks, Nathaniel Crooks, Andrew Garrett & Dr. Belinda Longe, Neil L. Le Grand, Michael Lewis, Dr. Kenneth Montague & Sarah Aranha, Lenny & Julia Mortimore, and The Ferrotype Collective, 2019. Photo: Art Gallery of Ontario. 2019/609.

Felix Morin, *Woman, Trinidad,* c. 1890. Albumen print, 21.3 × 14.9 cm. Art Gallery of Ontario, Montgomery Collection of Caribbean Photographs. Purchase, with funds from Dr. Liza & Dr. Frederick Murrell, Bruce Croxon & Debra Thier, Wes Hall & Kingsdale Advisors, Cindy & Shon Barnett, Donette Chin-Loy Chang, Kamala-Jean Gopie, Phil Lind & Ellen Roland, Martin Doc McKinney, Francilla Charles, Ray & Georgina Williams, Thaine & Bianca Carter, Charmaine Crooks, Nathaniel Crooks, Andrew Garrett & Dr. Belinda Longe, Neil L. Le Grand, Michael Lewis, Dr. Kenneth Montague & Sarah Aranha, Lenny & Julia Mortimore, and The Ferrotype Collective, 2019. Photo: Art Gallery of Ontario. 2019/2209.

Kelly Sinnapah Mary, *Notebook of No Return,* 2017. Acrylic on paper, 43.2 × 50.8 cm. Private collection. © Kelly Sinnapah Mary. Photo: Art Gallery of Ontario.

Back Cover Images

Sandra Brewster, *Feeding Trafalgar Square,* 2021. Gel medium photo transfer, charcoal, and acrylic on wood, 3 panels: 304.8 × 66 cm; 304.8 × 142.2 cm; 304.8 x 121.9 cm. Art Gallery of Ontario, commission, with funds from the Women's Art Initiative, 2021. 2021/71. © Sandra Brewster. Photo: Art Gallery of Ontario.

Sir Frank Bowling, *Mother's House and Night Storm,* 1967. Acrylic on canvas, 148.6 × 117.5 cm. Sheldon Inwentash and Lynn Factor, Toronto. © Frank Bowling / SOCAN (2021). Image courtesy Hales, London and New York; photo by JSP Art Photography, Stan Narten.

Page 2

Andrea Chung, *A Litany for Survival* (detail), 2019. Cyanotype and sugar, 170.2 x 228.6 cm. Courtesy of the artist and Tyler Park Presents, Los Angeles. © Andrea Chung. Image courtesy of courtesy of the artist, Klowden Mann, and Tyler Park Presents, Los Angeles; photo: Michael Underwood.

Publication

Editor: Julie Crooks

Managing Editor:
Jim Shedden

Production and
Copy Editors:
Gina Badger, Nives Hajdin,
Sarah Liss

Publishing Coordinator:
Kathryn Yuen

Proofreader: Judy Phillips

Designers:
Pentagram, New York
Eddie Opara, Brankica Harvey,
Lili Phillips

Photographers:
Craig Boyko, Sean Weaver

Pre-Press and Printing:
Type A Print Inc.

Exhibition

Deputy Director and Chief
Curator: Julian Cox

Curator: Julie Crooks

Project Manager:
Melissa Ramage

Curatorial Coordinators:
Alexandra Gooding,
Jill Offenbeck

Editorial Consultant:
Carlie Manners

Editors: Nives Hajdin,
Sarah Liss

Design Consultant:
Tara Keens-Douglas

Exhibition Design:
Theodora Doulamis
Graphic Design:
Evelina Petrauskas

Production:
Malene Hjørngaard,
Evelyn Quinn

Exhibitions and Collections

Chief, Exhibitions,
Collections, & Conservation:
Jessica Bright

Associate Director,
Exhibitions:
Laura Comerford

Registration: Alison Beckett,
Cindy Brouse, Jerry
Drozdowsky, Joel Herman,
Dale Mahar, Sabine Schaefer,
Curtis Strilchuk

Collection Information:
Alexandra Cousins, Tracy
Mallon-Jensen, Liana
Radvak, Joe Venturella,
Olga Zotova

Conservators:
Maureen del Degan,
Shu-Wen Lin, Meaghan
Monaghan, Sherry Phillips,
Brent Roe, Maria Sullivan,
Sjoukje van der Laan,
Joan Weir, Katharine
Whitman, John Williams

Logistics and Art Services

Gregory Baszun, Michael
Beynon, Andrew Bugden,
Scott Cameron, Colin
Campbell, Marco Cheuk,
Brian Davis, Randal Fedje,
Tina Giovinazzo, Brian
Groombridge, Roland Hardy,
Iain Hoadley, Matthew
Janisse, Ruth Jones, Jason
Laudadio, Alison Lindsay,
Paul Mathiesen, Benjamin
Oakley, Jacques Oulé, Angelo
Pedari, Damian Seguin,
Manny Trinh, Craig
Whiteside, Darin Yorston,
Tanya Zhilinsky

Education and Programming

Richard & Elizabeth
Currie Chief, Education &
Programming:
Audrey Hudson

Director, Engagement &
Learning: Paola Poletto

Education & Programming:
Danah Abusido, Lesley
Ashton, Madelyne Beckles,
Samantha Benjamin, Erica
Chan, Maureen DaSilva,
Sarah Febbraro, Nathan
Huisman, Idalette Martins,
Kathleen McLean, Deborah
Nolan, Zavette Quadros-
Evangelista, Annie Roper,
Melissa Smith

Media Production

Matthew Scott